Both Gains and Gaps:

Feminist Perspectives on Women's Leisure

Karla A. Henderson
University of North Carolina—Chapel Hill

M. Deborah Bialeschki
University of North Carolina—Chapel Hill

Susan M. Shaw
University of Waterloo

Valeria J. Freysinger
Miami University

Both Gains and Gaps:

Feminist Perspectives on Women's Leisure

Karla A. Henderson
University of North Carolina—Chapel Hill

M. Deborah Bialeschki
University of North Carolina—Chapel Hill

Susan M. Shaw
University of Waterloo

Valeria J. Freysinger
Miami University

Venture Publishing, Inc.
1999 Cato Avenue, State College, PA 16801

Production Supervisor: Richard Yocum
Manuscript Editing: Michele L. Barbin and Diane K. Bierly
Cover Designed and Illustrated by Sandra Sikorski, Sikorski Design

Library of Congress Catalogue Card Number 95-61907
ISBN 0-910251-79-7

Dedicated to all who seek the empowerment of girls and women in and through leisure

Table of Contents

Chapter Three

Feminisms: Fact and Fiction   *71*

Chapter Four

Elusive, Yet Real:

Chapter Five

Chapter Six

When I Get Old…:
Leisure Across the Course of Adulthood

Chapter Seven

"Just Do It" Is Not So Easy:
Participation, Constraints, and Possibilities

Chapter Eight

Making Women's Leisure Visible:
"Sniffing Around" and Doing Feminist Research   *213*

Chapter Nine

"She Who Continues:"
Changing/Enhancing Women's Leisure   *237*

Chapter Ten

Women and Leisure: The Future Journey   *261*

Preface

Both Gains and Gaps: Feminist Perspectives on Women's Leisure is a "book-in-progress" that elaborates on issues about women, gender, and leisure. This book is an update of *A Leisure of One's Own: A Feminist Perspective on Women's Leisure* (Henderson, Bialeschki, Shaw, & Freysinger, 1989). Although many gains have been made in understanding women's leisure, much remains to be learned. This book provides further information about women and the issues that surround both the gains and gaps associated with a construct commonly called leisure.

The analysis that we offer is primarily social psychological, but we have incorporated broader sociological and cultural analyses at times. The book is also written from feminist perspectives. It is introductory in nature, although we have attempted to provide the most current research as the basis for this foundation text. No prior knowledge in women's studies or leisure studies is assumed, and the book is designed to complement these courses.

Our efforts in writing this book are no longer termed pioneering since much has been written about women's leisure and gender issues in the past ten years. We have tried to build upon a framework that will enable further research concerning the gains and gaps related to women's personal leisure as well as social change. Many questions remain unanswered, as you will see.

The book is organized in a way that allows a reader to view women's leisure from several approaches. By identifying a number of feminist perspectives, we have attempted to show how feminism relates to leisure. The introductory chapter provides a basis for studying women and leisure by addressing the frameworks of leisure, social psychology, and feminism. Historical perspectives on women and leisure that depart from a typical chronological historical approach are addressed in chapter two. Feminisms and their theoretical assumptions applied to women's leisure are presented in chapter three. Issues of meaning for women and the leisure "containers" that exist for them are explored in chapter four. The implications of gender and age as well as life span and life course perspectives are linked to leisure and discussed in chapters five and six. Participation and constraints as evidence of both gains and gaps for girls and women are described in chapter seven. "Ways of knowing" about women's leisure and the value of feminist research are described in the eighth chapter. Pragmatic issues relative to changing women's leisure are discussed from personal and social angles in chapter nine. The final chapter provides a summary of what might be envisioned for women and leisure in the future. Several scenarios provide a framework for analyzing the future that would be likely or preferable for women.

Several cautions are offered to the reader of *Both Gains and Gaps*. We acknowledge that describing women in a "generic" sense is impossible. All women are not the same and a diversity of lifestyles is evident among them. We try to identify some of the differences among women and the great variations that exist. Much of the research about women has used white, middle-class, married Western women as samples, and we acknowledge that limitation in this book. Aspects of women's identities and lives including the impact of race, income, sexual orientation, disability, and employment are still largely unexplored areas in leisure research. Where possible, we try to bring perspectives from and about marginalized groups of women in society, but this task has been difficult. In addition, the perspectives presented are largely North American, although we attempted to use some global examples. Although gains and gaps share some commonalities across the continents, women also vary because of their cultural situations.

The thesis of this book is that women's lives need to be made more visible through opportunities for choice within leisure. Eliminating gender-imposed roles and empowering individuals to work for personal and social change will do much to enhance the leisure lives of women. Females are making gains in claiming leisure, but many gaps remain. These gaps represent gaps between men and women, gaps among groups of women based on lifestyle and demographic characteristics, gaps in the balance between work and leisure in women's lives, and gaps between research and practice.

The book is a work in progress because of the growing questions about women, gender, and leisure. More information about gains and gaps, more scholarly theoretical analyses, and ways to implement these ideas in practice are being developed each day. We invite all readers to be involved in this ongoing work.

Clearly many people are responsible for this book—colleagues, mentors, friends, and family. Many people have been helpful to us whom we have not met, but whose spoken and written words have had a profound effect. We also appreciate the interests of our professional colleagues who have provided data, insights, and encouragement about this topic. Our colleagues at our respective universities need particular thank yous: University of North Carolina—Chapel Hill (particularly Doug Sessoms), University of Waterloo, and Miami University. One of us would particularly like to acknowledge the counsel and support given by Sharon Meginnis. We are also indebted to students who continually challenge us and who have come to us with pressing questions about research on women and leisure. Lastly, we would each like to thank our "family" members who have patiently supported us through this effort: Arend, Joyce, and Leandra. Because of all who have cared, encouraged, and supported us, we had an opportunity to explore the gains and gaps in women's leisure.

Our associations with one another have been most exciting, and we have learned and grown through the support we have given one another. We are committed individually and collectively to the empowerment of women in and through leisure. Join us in celebrating the gains made in women's leisure and continuing the work needed to eliminate the gaps.

Chapter One

Women and Leisure: The Journey of 1,000 Miles Begins with a Single Step

Feminism asks the world to recognize at long last that women aren't decorative ornaments, worthy vessels, members of a 'special interest group.' They are half (in fact, now more than half) of the national population, and just as deserving of rights and opportunities, just as capable of participating in the world's events, as the other half. Feminism's agenda is basic: It asks that women not be forced to 'choose' between public justice and private happiness. It asks that women be free to define themselves—instead of having their identity defined for them, time and again, by their culture and their men.

— *Faludi, 1991, p. xxiii*

This book is about leisure and women. Both gains and gaps are addressed on this journey toward understanding. Many gains have been made in the past few years. Countries have passed laws to make discrimination against women in various aspects of society illegal. The women's movement is occurring worldwide and has helped to make women's lives visible and improve their status in many, but not all, countries. Individual women have sought to find leisure in their lives and the participation of women in various leisure pursuits seems to be increasing universally. We have cause to celebrate the gains made, but we also must be aware of the gaps that come in many forms.

Arlie Hochschild (1989) in *The Second Shift* coined the term "leisure gap" with the rationalization that "just as there is a wage gap between men and women in the workplace, there is a general 'leisure' gap between them at home" (p. 4). This gap, however, is only one example. Not only do some differences exist between males and females in the amount of time available for leisure as Hochschild suggests, but gaps also exist among groups of women. Women who are poor, for example, may face different leisure gaps than women gainfully employed in professional jobs.

Despite the gains made regarding women's rights, many women personally feel leisure gaps exist in their lives due to a lack of balance and because gender profoundly affects what people do in all spheres of life. Many men also feel these leisure gaps exist, although as research is beginning to show us, not always in the same way or to the same degree of intensity. Gender roles and relationships affect what women do. A leisure gap exists when women feel they must "juggle" all the expectations of their lives. Leisure gaps do not exist for all females, but some or all of them are a reality for many women. The lives of all men and women are gendered, and thus we find commonalities among many women and some differences between men and women. All individuals, however, want to define and find meaning and quality in their lives. Most people want to surmount any gaps that retard life's meaningfulness.

A gap also exists between research and practice; little is known about leisure and some groups of women. Although more research exists today than ever before about women's leisure, huge gaps prevail particularly in information about women of color and women in low socioeconomic situations. Further, a gap exists between the research being conducted and its translation into public policy and personal action that affects women's lives. The research that does exist is just now beginning to impact public policy and how recreation and leisure might better be facilitated for girls and women.

Leisure is important; many women, as well as men, struggle with how to have meaningful and balanced activities in their lives. Leisure often is not equally accessible or available to all people. Meaning and balance are affected by gender, gender relations in the broader society, and the ways women and men think about themselves, their perceptions, and their experiences with expected social roles. For example, Hochschild found that to deal with the problems of too much work and too little time, women "cut back on their personal needs, give up reading, hobbies, television, visiting with friends, exercise, time alone" (p. 199).

The purpose of this book is to examine leisure in women's lives through personal and social perspectives. By examining both the gaps and the gains, a sense of entitlement and opportunity to find balance in one's life and to have a preferred quality of life may be fostered. This introductory chapter sets the stage for subsequent chapters by discussing the underlying reasons for studying women's leisure. The foundation includes the basic assumptions of the book, the need to study women, the meaning of gender in society, the importance of a feminist analysis, why leisure is necessary, and social psychological and sociological perspectives on women and leisure.

A Bit of Background for the Journey

The emergence of the contemporary women's movement of the late 1960s did not result in increased visibility for women's leisure until the late 1980s. Leisure was often considered less consequential than other important women's issues related to work and family. Assumptions that women's leisure was family leisure, or that the work of a full-time homemaker was total leisure, were faulty. During the contemporary women's movement, assumptions were made that if women gained equal rights in areas such as the workplace, their leisure automatically would be equal also. As some women have gained empowerment in their lives, they also have gained a sense of entitlement to leisure and found balance in their quality of life. As Hochschild suggested and many women tell us, however, leisure gaps continue to exist in terms of time and meaning for many women.

This book uses feminist analyses of women's leisure; we focus on equity, empowerment, and social change for girls and women. Because we live in a gendered society, however, changes affecting women will also affect men. Therefore, this feminist analysis is about the meanings of leisure and how gender contributes to our understanding of leisure. No one feminist perspective reflects the diverse philosophy, politics, or pragmatic assumptions and changes about women's leisure. Although as authors, we wrote this book primarily from a North American perspective, we tried to include a global tie and attempted to move beyond the traditional white, middle-class, motherhood, heterosexual, able-bodied experience that has been commonly discussed. We hope this book will move us a step further in understanding women's leisure and help to find better ways to research leisure. Ultimately, gains in the leisure lives of women may mean that leisure gaps no longer exist for either sex.

As much as we want to believe that the plight of women globally is improving, the facts indicate that we have a long way to go. Some people believe little need exists for special articles or books related to women and leisure. Some people are tired of hearing about women's oppression as we approach the twenty-first century. They believe that women no longer face discrimination and have made gains to establish their rightful place in world cultures. This sense of "false consciousness" suggests that we no longer need to be concerned about the status of women. For example, although some countries clearly offer more positive environments for women, few countries have legislation that protects specific job and marriage rights for women. Nowhere do women have full rights with men (Seager & Olson, 1986). We must be careful not to confuse legal rights that may exist in countries such as the United States and Canada, with women's status and role in these and other gendered societies. For example, regardless of legal rights, most women are still vulnerable to violence and many lack maternity and reproductive choice.

Yet, according to Seager and Olson women are biologically stronger, live longer than men, and naturally outnumber them. Where they do not, it is only because women have suffered severe and systematic discrimination. Harrison, Chin, and Ficarrotto (1995) have argued that women outnumber men because the male role is hazardous to men's health. Thus, the study of gender, and specifically women and leisure, has implications for the understanding of culture and power related to political and personal issues. The literature is only beginning to uncover how a feminist analysis may assist in restructuring an understanding of leisure and the other two major life domains of work and family.

During the past decade many gains have been made in learning more about women and the meanings of leisure; the more we learn, however, the more we know there is to learn. Views about women's leisure are likely to continue to change as the social world changes and as we learn more about the meanings of leisure for both women and men. This book is one way of "knowing" about women and leisure. The goal is to improve clarity in thinking about both the gains and gaps surrounding women, gender, and leisure. The leisure literature about women generally has focused on identifying the problems that exist. By examining both the successes and the problems, we can embark on the next step of identifying ways to create positive personal and social change for women.

Basic Assumptions About Women

As you read a book, you can probably draw some conclusions about the perspectives of the authors. We want to put our perspectives up front so they can be examined in light of the information we present. Beyond the thesis that both gains and gaps define women's leisure today, several basic assumptions were used in the development of this text. You may not agree with these assumptions, but they provide the foundation for our analyses. Thus, to help you understand our beliefs, we state them in the beginning:

1. Largely because we live in a gendered society, differences exist between males and females. The differences are not inherently good nor bad, but simply different. (Note: A gendered society

is one in which roles for women and men are socially constructed.)

2. In gendered societies women are oppressed, or at least disadvantaged, in most aspects of their lives, including leisure.

3. Diversity exists in the lifestyles of women creating variations,
as well as commonalities, in women's leisure experiences.

Differences

Differences are of concern in the study of leisure gains and gaps. Differences
can take many forms. The key is in determining if and how these dissimilari-
ties are problematic. Regardless, difference does not necessarily imply
hierarchy and should not be associated with deficiency. Of most concern to
us is how women's leisure is affected by a gendered society and how leisure
is viewed by males and females. Due to a number of other factors related to
aspects of diversity, differences between women and men may not be as
dramatic as differences among women. For example, a working-class, single
mother may experience leisure differently than a professional woman in a
"dink" (dual income, no kids) situation. The male and female members of a
heterosexual couple in a "dink" situation may find their access and opportunity
for leisure to be similar.

A number of problems occur when we begin to identify what constitutes
"differentness." For example, how much difference makes a difference?
Different from what? Who determines what different means? How much is
difference a function of culture, not chromosomes? Clearly some biological
differences exist between women and men. The cultural and historical nature
of women's lives, however, indicate that differences are created, not discovered, and that gender-specific behavior is learned.

Leisure research about gender differences has shown how some men and
women have different participation patterns, access to leisure, and constraints
to leisure. This research determining that differences exist, however, is just
the initial step to make leisure visible for women. The reasons for the
differences need to be explored.

Recognizing the diversity among women and how social roles and
gender relations affect all women and men, but not always in the same way,
is the challenge in researching and understanding differences that result in
gender gaps. For example, comparing time and activity between women and
men may be a problem because of different realities and lifestyles of women
and men, and because specific measures of time or activity may be biased,

generally toward men as the dominant gender. As in other facets of life, women may have a different reality (Schaef, 1981) or a different voice (Gilligan, 1982a) than men in their perceptions of leisure. Where differences exist, they need to be examined, but not judged as better or worse based upon sex. Leisure gains and gaps offer a stepping off point for comparisons, but they alone are not the conclusion. Differences provide a context for further analyzing what leisure means in people's lives.

Oppression

Women as a group have been oppressed, disadvantaged, and devalued throughout history and in all societies globally. Women in some countries may be less oppressed today than in the past, but they are still not guaranteed the same respect and rights as men. Some people may think this term "oppression" is too strong, yet we do not have a better term that denotes the powerlessness that many women feel and that is imposed upon them by social structures. Saying that women are disadvantaged is true, but does not carry the same urgency or clout as the notion of oppression.

The oppression of women has been both explicit and implicit and has included economic, social, political, and sexual subjugation. Laws that reduce or regulate explicit oppression have been instituted in many countries in the world; however, implicit devaluation continues even within the most "developed" countries. For example, even though women have gained more opportunities in the work world, they generally have not been freed from the primary role as caregiver and homemaker at home (Hochschild, 1989). Examples abound in history where women received legal rights and opportunities, but continued to be disenfranchised by societal expectations. In the United States, after women received the right to vote in 1920 and were given many opportunities for recreation and leisure, a backlash followed where social control relegated women back to the home (Henderson, 1993). In the United States, Canada, and United Kingdom, women joined the workforce in droves during World War II but were implored to return to the ideology of the family so paid jobs could be given to males after the war. Women's progress toward equality continues to be met with a backlash even as the twentieth century draws to a close (Faludi, 1991).

Seager and Olson (1986) described the plight of women with complete statistics for each country in *Women in the World: An International Atlas.* Even in the latter years of the twentieth century, women still experience a number of constraints to full participation in society which also restricts their leisure. Seager and Olson, for example, found:

- Domestic violence stems from the fact that in most countries women are considered to be men's property, and girls are less valued than boys.

- Divorce is increasing worldwide. Women who don't marry or become widowed or divorced are often viewed as failures. Divorce often leaves women and children in financial disaster. On the other hand, divorce may also increase women's options and allow them an escape from unhappy and even abusive relationships.

- Motherhood is one of the true universals in women's lives, but it is not always a choice for women. The conditions of pregnancy and motherhood, however, vary greatly due to different population policies, varying standards of health and wealth, and the degree of autonomy of women and girls.

- Childcare accounts for the largest share of women's household labor and limits their ability to take paid work outside the home. Only a few countries offer affordable, quality, alternative childcare facilities.

- Women generally work longer hours than men do. Women everywhere get little financial or social recognition for working more, resting less, and doing a greater variety of work than men. Their work is often statistically invisible; it is estimated that the official enumerators count only about two-thirds of women's work.

- Women represent about one-third of the paid labor force worldwide. The share is growing slowly with the largest increases occurring in industrialized countries. The range of jobs that women fill in the workforce is much narrower than for men. In every country in every region of the world, some jobs are specifically defined as "women's work." Although varied, jobs generally defined as women's work carry low pay, low status, and little security. In a two-income family, women's earnings are often viewed as "supplemental" income. Women's continued underpayment in work is a major factor for the growing feminization of poverty worldwide. Poverty is disproportionately borne by women, especially those with children and by older women.

- Education is one of the greatest forces for change. A female who can read, write, and do arithmetic has a much better chance in life. Strides have been made in elementary school education for both boys and girls, but girls are still systematically denied the opportunity to attend secondary or higher education in favor of boys in many countries.

- Women everywhere live under the threat of rape, especially in their own homes. Rape is likely the most underreported and least convicted crime in the world. Rape has long been considered a crime against a man's property (i.e., his woman). Today it is finally being recognized in many countries as a crime of violence and power and a violation of women's civil rights.

The reality today is that women almost always function in a world that is governed and controlled by men. Males are responsible for most major political and economic decisions. Women generally are socialized to accept social roles that are subordinate to men, even though acceptance may result in their own oppression. Although overt sexist oppression today may not be as prevalent in industrialized countries or for women in upper classes, it still exists. Women's unequal access to and participation in leisure are closely linked to other more frequently analyzed areas of women's oppression such as domestic labor, reproductive roles, marriage, and waged work (Deem, 1982). Further, although women of white heritage have made important gains, many women of color have not had the same privilege.

The intent in this book is not to elaborate further on women's oppression. Most of us know about it. We want to show how women's leisure is often a reflection of their oppression in patriarchy (i.e., the social and cultural rules that privilege men over women). Moreover, leisure can contribute to the development of identities that can help women resist oppression in all aspects of their lives. Women do not need to be victims of their oppression but can be catalysts for change. Through leisure and by addressing leisure gaps, women may be able to become empowered to negate some of the oppression in their personal leisure. Addressing leisure can lead to broader social change.

Diversity

Generalizations about women can create myths and stereotypes. We believe that variability exists in the way that women throughout the world view and experience leisure. For example, in industrialized countries such as the United States, leisure is seen as something for the self that results in autonomy and independence while in some Latin American countries, the emphasis on self is culturally not as prevalent (Fox & Trillo, 1994).

Although extremely difficult, we attempt to avoid generalizations about women and leisure that add to existing ageist, racist, classist, and homophobic attitudes. Feminist perspectives must be tempered by the recognition that select characteristics cannot and should not be generalized to all women. For example, lifestyles, life situations, and developmental stages affect what women do with their time and energies. Although lifestyle and life course development research describes the common issues, roles, and concerns faced by women in particular stages of life, the research also reveals the uniqueness of individual women's lives. Gains and gaps do not occur equally for women. By understanding the experiences of women who live in gendered societies and the variations on their experiences, a phenomenon like leisure can be better understood. By addressing more social questions like "What is the experience of this group of women?" we can ask personal questions like "Is this true for me?" or "Is this true for the women whom I know?"

Although an integrated understanding of women's leisure seems desirable, it is not realistic since many perspectives exist and great diversity prevails in the situations of different women. Studying women as an oppressed group, however, may well sensitize us to understanding other marginalized or disadvantaged groups outside the dominant culture. All of us, for example, if we live long enough will eventually be marginalized by the dominant society since ageism is a common form of discrimination.

Researchers in leisure studies, and even those who have studied women's leisure, generally have not been sensitive to issues of multiculturalism. Since the study of leisure for women in general is relatively new, the acknowledgment of the real diversity that exists among women just now is emerging. Although the field of leisure studies is still lacking in multicultural dimensions, as authors, we try not to universalize the experience of women. We suggest ways that leisure may be more or less experienced by women in a variety of life experiences. We also focus on how change might occur in the leisure lives of different groups of women.

Changing Women's Leisure

Change is an inevitable aspect of life. In many societies, women's status and their leisure opportunities have changed in recent years, although this change has been evolving for some time. How we view the nature of change affects why we study women and leisure. Further, a theme of this book is that women's leisure ought to be examined from the perspective of change as it occurs personally and socially in women's lives.

Mandle (1979) summarized change into three sets of strategies: rapid change versus evolutionary stability, idealism versus materialism, and societal (macro) versus individual (micro). These three frameworks provide a context for viewing the changing roles of women in society. Stability suggests that evolutionary factors bring about small incremental changes that continue to maintain a cohesion in society. An opposing view of change suggests that upheaval is necessary and that change occurs because of revolutionary forces.

Change can occur from an idealistic perspective because ideas and attitudes change the ways people perceive themselves and their world. Other promoters of change suggest it occurs because we can point to tangible material changes in behavior, as well as institutional and organizational structures. The debate is unresolved about whether change at the attitudinal level (e.g., a belief in gender equality) or at the behavioral level (e.g., actual equal treatment in the workplace) should come first. Studies show, for example, that many young people believe in equal sharing of tasks and chores in a marriage and may intend to have an equitable marriage. In practice, the traditional division of labor with the woman bearing the bulk of the household chores usually develops (Koopman-Boyden & Abbott, 1985). Others have argued that we should require behavior changes (e.g., provide equal opportunity for girls and women in sports) and that attitudinal change (e.g., females will be accepted into sports) will follow. Regardless of which way social change occurs, the implications are great for better understanding the impact of leisure on women's lives.

We can also debate whether strategies for change should focus on individuals or on the society. Micro change proponents believe that unless we focus on individual behavior, motivation, and personality and try to understand individual dimensions, we cannot understand the effects of social change or resistance to such change. Supporters of macro change theories believe that until society and its institutions change, individuals will be slow to change.

These three frameworks of change are interconnected in any discussion of social change. Depending on how one views change affects understanding the meanings of leisure and its enhancement in women's lives. Throughout this book we assay leisure gains and gaps by examining social change and developing strategies to maximize gains and overcome potential gaps. First, however, let's determine why women ought to be studied.

Why Study Women?

People who believe that women are not oppressed, that women are equal to men, or that women are biologically and culturally inferior to men may see no reason for women's studies. Obviously, we as authors believe differently because of the facts and assumptions made early in this chapter. We are not in a postfeminist era when all aspects of women's lives have been adequately addressed and all women have integrity and equity in their lives. Thus, we believe a need to study women continues.

Some roles of women in various cultures are changing rapidly, while other roles are changing more slowly. Many women, particularly in the industrialized world, have gained greater educational, sexual, and economic freedom than they previously had. These freedoms have given rise to new lifestyles. A relatively new field of inquiry called Women's Studies emerged over 25 years ago because of the extent and impact of the changing lives of women. Women's Studies is interdisciplinary in nature, is viewed within a feminist framework, and has been concerned with making women's experiences visible within society. Women need to be studied to correct the past distortion and invisibility of their social and economic lives.

Studying women is important because a number of ideological and material forces have been instrumental in changing the lives of women including the following: technology that can potentially free women from housework and unwanted pregnancies; liberalization of divorce and abortion laws; new views on sexual morality and an increasing emphasis on permissiveness and individualism; and the women's movement with egalitarian educational and economic goals. Although these social forces have led to many improvements in women's lives, progress has been sporadic with periodic backlashes to these changes.

Demographic and social changes in women's lives are evident and need to be more fully understood. For example, labor force participation has become an experience of a larger proportion of North American women. In the United States in 1991, over 46 percent of the workers were women (U.S. Bureau of Labor, 1991). Several reasons exist for women's increased participation in the labor force: the growth of service sector employment and the classification of these jobs as "female;" the emergence of women in nontraditional occupations; longer life spans; fewer children; financial need especially in female-headed families; increased levels of education; and the availability of childcare and other services through the public and private sectors.

Women's lives need to be studied because of the problems and struggles encountered. Employment statistics in many countries, for example, clearly show that women are clustered in traditional "women's jobs" which tend to be low-status, low-freedom, and low-salaried jobs. Although some job stereotypes are breaking down and women are entering nontraditional areas of work in increasing (albeit small) numbers, a wage gap between women and men still remains. In 1990 the average household income in the United States was $29,942. For female-headed households this figure was $18,069 compared to $31,552 for male-headed households (U.S. Bureau of Labor, 1991). Most statistics in the United States and Canada still suggest that women on average earn about $0.71 for every $1.00 earned by men. Women appear to be receiving fewer rewards from their employment (i.e., both psychological and material rewards) than men receive (Seager & Olson, 1986). Moreover, since many women retain responsibility for the family and the household even when they are employed, a major struggle for the employed woman with family responsibilities is finding time for herself and time for leisure (Hochschild, 1989).

Changes in family life, educational level, and gender expectations have implications for the study of women. For example, some women are spending a smaller proportion of their adult lives in the bearing of and caring for children. Since more women are living longer and having fewer children, they are seeking other opportunities to find meaning in their lives. More women are learning to be conscious of their own needs and to value them as strongly as they value the needs of others. Some women are also finding power and independence in their ability to be successful in work and leisure situations.

Although recent societal changes have been positive for many women, the transitions have also created struggles for some women as they seek to balance paid and unpaid work. For example, the "just a housewife" syndrome is a problem for some women and men who believe that housework is of little value because nothing directly is produced in the way of monetary exchange. Homemakers may feel they have not "earned" leisure because housework is devalued, and thus, they may feel guilty for taking time for themselves (Darlison, 1985; Henderson & Bialeschki, 1991a). In addition, many women find housework boring or unsatisfying because they are overqualified for the job. The role of housewife is poorly defined and practically invisible, and the expectations for women may be unclear, contradictory, or overwhelming (Hochschild, 1989). If a woman does not find her domestic role gratifying, she may have no other major role that she considers legitimate in society. Even if she does find the homemaking and childcare roles empowering, society in general does not value these roles.

In light of all the changes that are occurring (i.e., evolutionary and revolutionary, idealistic and materialistic, macro and micro), women's lives deserve to be studied not only in terms of gender relations but also related to the meanings of being female in today's world. Moreover, the impact of changes on women's lives points to the importance of incorporating an understanding of gender and gender relations when addressing leisure.

Feminist Approaches

To move beyond understanding the behavior of women to the promotion of social change, philosophy should be combined with social action. Feminist perspectives, based on theory and philosophy, provide frameworks to understand, interpret, and change the way societies function. Feminism is defined as philosophical and theoretical frameworks that embody aspects of equity, empowerment, and social change for women and men. Certain goals for women are inherent in these frameworks: to make visible women's power and status; to redefine existing societal structures and modes of existence; and to enable every woman to have equity, dignity and freedom of choice through the power to control her life and body, both within and outside the home (Bunch, 1985).

Feminisms encompass broad ranges of meanings. Although the various approaches to feminism are discussed in more detail in chapter three, several points need to be made at this time. Traditionally, women have been ignored or described in how they differed from men; researchers concluded that these differences were a reflection of some intrinsic diversity beyond reproductive capabilities (Freeman, 1979). This view suggested that historically women had less power, less influence, and fewer resources than men as a result of the natural order or biological differences. Feminist perspectives, on the other hand, focus on equity, empowerment, and social change. Feminists believe that the different experiences females have in realizing their potential stems from externally imposed restraints that some women internalize, from the influence of social institutions, and from values.

Not all feminists agree on the same strategies or even the root of the problem, however. For example, some feminists focus on capitalism, patriarchy, inequality, and psychologically based power relationships; other feminists place importance on critically deconstructing social structures and relationships. Regardless of the strategy, feminisms seek to give women, as well as men, the opportunity to be what they can best be. The focus of feminism is on redefining the value of women's lives by empowering individual women and by making women visible in society. Feminism is a world view that celebrates both differences and similarities regardless of gender expectations and relations.

Bunch (1985) suggested that feminism is perhaps the most important social force to address world problems. Morgan (1984) stated that the goals of feminism are not only to change drastically the powerlessness of women worldwide, but to redefine existing societal structures and to honor the integrity of women. Theoretically, a global movement of women and enlightened men could affect all aspects of life (e.g., reproduction, production, natural resources, political systems, nationalism, human sexuality and psychology, science and technology, youth and the family, economics, religion, communication, health, philosophy, leisure).

The centrality of the right to choose, whether it is when to bear a child or what to do with free time, is the basis of all feminist perspectives. Feminists see the confinement of women to prescribed roles (e.g., housekeeper, primary childcare provider, nurturer in the workplace) as a major deterrent to the realization of the goals of freedom of choice; they suggest that women must be given a choice concerning the roles they will accept for themselves. Feminists recognize that this power to choose may or may not include choices of domestic roles or prescribed activities.

Issues of feminism relate directly to power relations. The totality of human interaction cannot be understood without the concept of power. Power has traditionally referred to "power-over" or domination. French (1985) described "power-to" which refers to ability and capacity, and connotes a kind of freedom. Most feminist perspectives assert the need for both women and men to discover their own "power-to" in the world. For women, empowerment means controlling one's life and body. New understandings of power are possible through feminisms and this power enlarges the human spirit.

We cannot talk about feminism, however, without also acknowledging that it is a concept that many women do not embrace. Many women feel they have no need for feminism as they associate it with radical notions that threaten aspects of their lives. Others feel that our society is in a postfeminist age and women's issues satisfactorily have been addressed. We understand these concerns, but we also feel that feminism supplies perspectives that can help us understand more about aspects of women's lives and their leisure.

To sum up this introduction to feminism, this quote by Rebecca West (source unknown, 1913) may be useful:

> I myself have never been able to find out precisely what feminism
> is: I only know that people call me a feminist whenever I express
> sentiments that differentiate me from a doormat.

Feminist Research

Feminist research has gone through a variety of changes. The first feminist researchers saw and questioned assumptions about women's lives that had been hidden through an androcentric (male-centered) focus on male patterns of behavior and experience. Making women's lives visible was the first major hurdle that feminist researchers had to confront. A similar need became apparent in the more focused field of leisure studies. The suggestion that women's lives had not been captured in the traditional studies of leisure challenged some of the central tenets in the field, including for example, whether or not freedom was a basic component of leisure for women. By highlighting the male bias in traditional research, feminist scholars have challenged us to find more inclusive theories that better describe the principal components of women's lives and their leisure.

Research in most fields, including recreation and leisure, has been primarily a male enterprise, reflecting male perspectives and values. Until the past fifteen years, women were usually neglected in the study of leisure. For example, leisure was defined in relation to the labor market where women were not visible and thus, women were ignored (Henderson & Shaw, 1994). The assumption was that women related to leisure experiences in the same way as men. Women as researchers also had been taught to pursue research as defined by men and were rewarded for their conformity. Thus, only recently have we begun to conduct research that is about, for, and by women.

One of the purposes of a feminist analysis is to examine how the goals of feminism are addressed in research. Stanley and Wise (1983) suggested that research conducted from feminist perspectives must go beyond being descriptive or even corrective, and ought to lead to social change. Eichler (1980) stated this idea more explicitly:

> Feminist research and writings center around issues of inequality. At its best, feminist writing fulfills three functions: it is critical of existent social structures and ways to perceive them, it serves as a corrective mechanism by providing an alternative viewpoint and data to substantiate it, and it starts to lay the groundwork for a transformation of social science and society. (p. 9)

This focus on critique, correction, and transformation offers a useful framework for the analysis of research concerning women's leisure and is discussed in more detail in chapter eight.

Feminist Ethics

We have established that issues or spheres of life associated with women have often been devalued or ignored in research. Feminist ethics seeks to include additional "ways of knowing" and "ways of being." No one definition or description of feminist ethics, however, exists. Card (1991) suggested that feminist ethics is born in women's refusal to endure with grace the arrogance, indifference, hostility, and damage of oppressively sexist environments. Feminists vary greatly in their issues and the approaches they take to addressing problems, but most feminists can agree that the subordination of women is morally wrong and that the experience of women is worthy of respect. Thus, all aspects of feminist ethics seek to acknowledge, justify, and explain the experiences of women.

Several assumptions are inherent in feminist ethics. First, women and men are not situated similarly. Great strides have been made toward equality in the past thirty years, yet "gender privilege" (Jaggar, 1991) is still evident. Further, this gender privilege is different for different groups of women. White women, for example, have had more privilege than women of color in U.S. society. Women with disabilities have had less gender privilege than women without disabilities and have been considered to have a double "handicap" (Deegan & Brooks, 1985). Thus, to speak of feminist ethics is to be concerned about the meaning of gender privilege for men and also among different groups of women.

A second assumption is that complete agreement does not exist among feminists concerning the issues that ought to be addressed through ethics. Thus, feminist ethics are characterized by variety, experimentation, and disagreement. Feminist critique, therefore, is an important part of the dialogue which aims to keep people questioning issues. Feminist ethics also serve to address heretofore neglected issues, such as the relationship of women to the environment, and ultimately to transform the way ethics are defined and described.

Third, feminist ethics is not the moral grounds of women only. Jaggar (1991) suggested that dichotomized women's issues and men's issues do not exist today because the lives of most men and most women are inextricably intertwined. Men and women are affected by the moral choices made by each other in both their public and private lives. Thus, feminist ethical issues are not just about women's issues but enlarge the traditional concepts of ethics to include women. Feminist ethics are not a subset of ethics, but serve to remind ethics scholars and practitioners that women's lives are no less significant than men's. Further, feminist ethics is not superior to "regular" ethics, but offers a way to extend our thinking about the meanings of ethics for work and daily living.

A fourth assumption of feminist ethics is that no attempts are made to find a single gender-specific moral voice. Attempting to find one female voice masks the diversity of women's experiences and their complexity. Feminists must be careful not to make the same mistakes made by male scholars in universalizing the female experience. As feminist researchers generally conclude, more differences exist among a group of women than necessarily between groups of males and females. The assumption of one experience and one set of feminist ethics is impossible in today's world. The call to reflect on the numerous perspectives on women's leisure through feminist ethics is politically, professionally, and methodologically necessary.

The Meaning of Gender

The study of women and women's leisure has been grounded in discussions of gender. Initial research, focusing solely on women, had been effective in making women's lives visible and calling attention to the androcentric nature of traditional history. The concept of gender, however, allows for an understanding of both males and females within the broader context of culture. The study of gender provides an analysis of relationships based on cultural distinctions between the sexes that signify relationships of power (Scott, 1986).

Gender refers to cultural connections associated with one's biological sex. When biological sex is determined at birth as female or male, a huge number of cultural expectations are immediately associated with the child. Gender, then, refers to how society determines expectations and behavior regarding masculinity and femininity. One's biological sex leads to a lifetime of relationships and expectations based on gender. Further, gender is an ongoing process rather than an inborn biological trait. Thus, gender is a set of socially constructed, deconstructed, and reconstructed relations that are produced and reproduced through people's actions (Henderson, 1994b).

Gender relations represent the product of men's power over women, individually and collectively, in both public and home-based institutions. At the macro level, gender is evident as a set of structured power relations. At the micro level, gender relations are produced and reproduced by the everyday activities and experiences of individuals.

The need to understand and analyze the meaning of gender and gender relations for both females and males emerged as a dominant feminist model in the 1980s (Ferree, 1990). Gender scholarship addresses the complexity of expectations, roles, and behavior associated with being male, as well as being female. Further, as Deem (1992) suggested, "gender is emphatically not 'a woman's problem!'" (p. 30). Researchers may apply a gender perspective to studying only women (e.g., Wearing, 1992), only men (e.g., Lynch, 1991), or may examine both sexes together (e.g., Samdahl, 1992b; Whitson & Macintosh, 1989) from a perspective of interpreting how gender, as socially learned expectations, defines behavior.

Women-centered research has tended to focus on meanings, definitions, and experiences of leisure, while the more recent gender scholarship has been more concerned with inequalities, integrity, and power relations. Shaw (1994) has argued that the dominant feminist approach to research on women's leisure has been seeking to understand how women's leisure is constrained as a result of gender relations and gendered life experiences. She also points out some new theoretical directions that are emerging; for example, the way that leisure activities reinforce or reproduce structured gender relations and, alternatively, how leisure may sometimes be seen as a form of resistance to such power relations. The examination of gender represents the move toward broader and more inclusive theoretical frameworks and interpretations of leisure.

Gender theory appears to offer potential in the 1990s and beyond for understanding leisure from feminist perspectives. These gender theory analyses may be related to roles, gender identities, gender relations, socialization, or whatever the yardstick for measurement happens to be. The relationship of gender to leisure is mutually interactive. In other words, leisure may provide a way for women to embody or resist traditional female roles. On the other hand, gender may influence an individual's leisure when, for example, expectations of femininity and motherhood prevail.

Why Study Women and Leisure?

Historically, the position of women in any community has been suggested to be the most striking index of the level of culture attained in the community (Veblen, 1899). We believe that idea is still true today. Regardless of the life situation, women have typically and traditionally been expected to have the home as the expected stage and setting for their lives. In many cultures, women's primary roles have been those of wife and mother, not worker and citizen, although in North America, many working class and women of color have not had the same experience (Andersen, 1993). The importance of women's contributions both inside and outside the home, particularly in industrialized societies, has become apparent during the twentieth century as many women have become visible in the public sphere, including the labor force. These changing roles have raised questions about micro issues such as the sense of leisure entitlement (Deem, 1986) as well as the difficulty women have in finding the time and space to fit leisure opportunities into their everyday lives. Macro issues about the availability of opportunities and institutional constraints to leisure are also raised. Leisure may be both a significant asset and an obvious gap in women's lives.

A Definition of Leisure

Leisure researchers suggest that no aspect of human behavior holds a greater potential for self-fulfillment than does leisure (e.g., Iso-Ahola & Weissinger, 1984; Kelly, 1983a; Neulinger, 1982). Kelly (1983a) stated that leisure gets a person through the day. Leisure is a phenomenon that is not easily separable from other aspects of women's daily lives; it is closely interwoven into everyday lives (Deem, 1986). Deem (1982) also suggested that the factors contributing to women's overall subordinate position in society have a strong relationship to a lack of choices and opportunities. Leisure gaps are a problem for many women. These gaps, however, do not imply only quantity but more importantly, the quality of leisure opportunities and the attitudes associated with leisure.

Leisure studies is a contemporary area of inquiry, although the concept of leisure was addressed originally by ancient Eastern philosophers as well as early Greek philosophers. Leisure connotes a number of meanings but generally it refers to free time, recreation activity, and/or meaningful experiences.

Free time has been the traditional, industrialized society's definition of leisure. **Time** refers to discretionary periods in one's life that are available to do whatever one wishes. Leisure is the time beyond that needed to do work or daily maintenance activities. Frequently, time is modified by leisure to describe the period in which one chooses what to do.

Activity refers to recreation pursuits done during free time. In the sense of activity, recreation and leisure often have been used interchangeably. Any number of activity pursuits might be considered leisure such as sports, cultural activities, or volunteering.

The **experience** of leisure as possessing meaning has become a common way to conceptualize leisure because of the importance placed on freedom of choice as a prerequisite for leisure. The experience conceptualization suggests that what a person does or when one does it does not make any difference; what is important is how the individual feels about an experience. Experience reflects a subjective, qualitative view of leisure. The dimensions of choice and intrinsic outcomes, as reflected in attitudes toward what one does, have been considered generally the most important criteria in this conceptualization.

We believe that the definition of leisure as "an experience" that occurs within the context of time and activity is the best approach to the conceptualization of this somewhat elusive notion (Kelly, 1982; Murphy, 1974; Neulinger, 1974; Shaw, 1985b). Thinking of leisure as an experience avoids the work/nonwork time dichotomy and the problem of activity categorization. This conceptualization is the way that most individuals, both women and men, understand leisure, and is intuitively congruent with everyday life experiences.

A number of researchers have attempted to identify the components of the leisure experience (e.g., Freysinger, 1988; Gunter & Gunter, 1980; Iso-Ahola, 1979b; Kaplan, 1975; Kelly, 1983b; Kraus, 1978; Neulinger, 1982; Samdahl, 1988; Shaw, 1985b). These components include free choice or freedom from constraint, intrinsic motivation, enjoyment, relaxation, role interactions, personal involvement, and self-expression which are discussed further in chapter four. Despite the number of dimensions suggested, the idea of perceived freedom or free choice is common to, and in many cases the primary component of, proposed leisure models.

Freedom, in some form at least, is essential to the leisure experience. This notion of freedom alone, however, may not provide a complete definition of leisure or permit a clear distinction between leisure and other types of experience. Freedom includes both "free from" and "free to." Leisure is "free from" obligation so the individual can be "free to" choose what to do (Talbot, 1979); leisure allows one to realize a sense of freedom, choice, and enjoyment or pleasure whether through relaxation, contemplation, or recreation activity.

Women's Leisure

Analyzing women's lives provides a broader basis for understanding their leisure. Concomitantly, an understanding of women's leisure may provide insight into the interrelationships of all areas of women's lives. Examining leisure gains and gaps is about more than the quantity of leisure time for women, although the amount of leisure women have is a significant issue. The quality of the experience and the freedom associated with leisure are essential. As women seek to have choices in all aspects of their lives, they desire choices within leisure as well. We believe that through leisure women can learn to value themselves as individuals and challenge some of the societal restrictions and stereotypes that constrain behavior. The tenets of feminism suggest that freedom from oppression for women involves not only equity, but also the right of women to freedom of choice and the power to control their own lives (Bunch, 1985).

Some women are becoming less bound to the home in their leisure as well as in their work. They are gaining more financial control and a new balance of freedom and independence in marriage. Some research would suggest that fewer women are subordinating their individual interests to the family. Instead, they are finding a greater recognition of individuality and autonomy and discovering an identity apart from the family at various stages of their lives (Degler, 1981; Samuel, 1992).

Leisure gaps, however, continue to persist: women continue to experience constraints regarding access to leisure time and spaces, and leisure activities and opportunities for women and men continue to be unequal. For example, when women are employed outside the home, they essentially have a dual career: one in the labor market and one in the home (Hochschild, 1989). When women, particularly from lower socioeconomic backgrounds, enter the labor market, their leisure is reduced but they continue to bear the major responsibility for work at home (Brock-Ute, 1985; Shaw, 1988b). Women who stay at home often work longer than their male partners, have less leisure time available to them, no vacation, no sick leave, no pension, and no salary.

Any study of leisure must take into account the interacting influence of socialization, life changes, and lifestyles. The meanings of leisure and the presence of leisure constraints may change over the course of women's lives as roles, responsibilities, life issues, and values change (Bialeschki & Michener, 1994). The interaction between leisure and these life factors may contribute to the growth and well-being of women. As a result of studying women and leisure broadly, new social psychological concepts of leisure can be developed that take into account diverse lifestyles and the importance of women's leisure.

Since leisure can be a form of freedom and self-expression, it also has revolutionary social potential (Dawson, 1986). For example, leisure participation for women could be a means of liberation from restrictive gender roles and social scripts, and thus, a means for empowerment. Empowerment through leisure, however, does not always occur. The leisure involvement or lack of involvement could be seen as acting to reinforce or reproduce traditional gender stereotypes (Shaw, 1994). Nevertheless, the potential of leisure for social and personal change through personal freedom and empowerment is always present.

In Western societies today, recreation and leisure do not always take a consciously prominent position in either women's or men's lives. The importance of leisure needs to be reaffirmed, as well as acknowledged, for the fulfillment it can bring. For some women, leisure often has been constrained and largely peripheral (Henderson, 1991b). The performance of unpaid domestic labor, the primary childcare and eldercare role of women, the generalized oppression of women, the cultural representation of masculine and feminine images, and sexual politics including female sexuality and social control all contribute to the lack of power women have in relation to leisure. With changes in society, however, potential exists for leisure to be established as significant for both women's and men's personal identities and social inter-actions. Women and leisure share a common status, and the importance of leisure to the quality of life for girls and women is a gap in need of further study.

Social Psychological/Sociological Perspectives on Leisure

Although psychological and sociological models have provided a framework for understanding leisure behavior as experience and a social process, respec-tively, they individually do not provide the needed framework for a compre-hensive view of women and leisure. People's reality, and especially the reality of women, is not just individual experience or a social construction, but is created in the interaction of the two. Thus, a perspective which recognizes that a woman acquires a style of life and leisure through interaction with others is needed (Mandle, 1979) as well as an examination of the social institutions and institutionalized sexism that affects women's leisure.

A sociological perspective focuses on traditions and social institutions as the basis of analysis. This approach is conducive to the politics surrounding access to leisure. Sociologists ask questions related to the cultural significance of leisure and the structural constraints that limit the form and frequency of women's leisure (Green, Hebron, & Woodward, 1990). Sociologists focus on how the social and economic inferiority of women can be changed to enable them to experience leisure in more frequent and satisfying ways. From this sociological perspective, women's leisure is viewed ultimately as constrained by a society that devalues women.

Social psychology is the study of the experience and behavior of individuals in relation to other individuals, groups, and culture. The central focus is on how individual forces intersect with societal forces. Social psychology suggests that it would not be possible to understand women without understanding the sociocultural environment in which they have been nurtured. Specifically, Kelly (1983a) noted that a social psychological approach to understanding leisure incorporates both the social context of the roles that change through the life course and the development of identities (e.g., personal and social) in and through those roles. Personal identity is the definition of the self to oneself. Social identity is the identity assigned by others. Role expectations strongly influence both social and personal identity and are, in turn, affected by these identities. For example, Henderson and Allen (1991) illustrated how women are more likely than men to exhibit an "ethic of care" that orients their leisure toward relationships with others. Samdahl (1992b) showed evidence that gender socialization is more significant than biological sex in determining the contexts of leisure for women and men. Thus, leisure is constructed in the interaction between personal experiences and situational/social influences. Social psychological perspectives along with sociological perspectives, give us the most potential to understand women's leisure gains and gaps.

Women deserve respect in all aspects of their lives, and this respect must coincide with evolutionary and revolutionary social change that will result in equitable power and status for women and men. These changes will require important structural changes in society, such as transforming the labor market and the valuation of women's work. They will also require a reconstruction of gender relations as well as the dominant ideologies about masculinity and femininity. Structural changes as well as personal changes represent two important arenas for the analysis and understanding of women's leisure. Both social and personal experience can contribute to the understanding of leisure gains and gaps for women.

Concluding Perspectives

The purpose of this introductory chapter was to provide a framework for beginning the discussion of perspectives on leisure gains and gaps. We defined gains in terms of psychological, social, economic, and political dimensions. We introduced gaps as they related to gaps between men and women, gaps among groups of women based on lifestyle and demographic characteristics, gaps in the balance between work (i.e., paid and unpaid) and leisure in women's lives, and gaps between research and practice. We made several assumptions that are critical to understanding the way this book is written: a different leisure experience may exist for women in general, women have been oppressed in many aspects of their lives including leisure, and great diversity is evident in the leisure lives of women.

Leisure research has focused on the effects of roles and relationships for both women and men. The research, however, has not examined a number of critical questions that we hope to address as we move through this book. Feminists advocate freedom of choice for women (and all people) to have control over their lives. The intent of both feminism and leisure is to encourage choices, not to set limits. At the core of leisure are the elements of freedom and choice, and thus, empowerment. Leisure has the potential to facilitate self-development, liberation, and behavior change in many aspects of women's lives. At the same time, a woman's gains and increased status, power, and personal control in life can enable her to challenge the leisure gaps in her life and change society. Our hope is that we have set the stage to explore these ideas in more depth in the following chapters.

Discussion Questions

1. Why should a focus be given to women in the study and understanding of leisure?

2. Discuss the similarities and differences, as well as the perceptions and misconceptions, of the terms: work, leisure, recreation, and free time.

3. Discuss the meaning of "gender." What implications might it have for understanding leisure?

4. How might feminist perspectives aid in the exploration and understanding of women's leisure?

5. In what ways might leisure serve to empower women?

6. How might leisure reinforce traditional gender stereotypes of males and females?

7. What major factors, besides one's gender, might influence a leisure experience?

8. Do you believe a social psychological or sociological perspective adds most to your understanding of women and leisure?

9. What are the macro and the micro forces that affect women's lives? Their leisure?

10. What questions about women and leisure seem most important to address as you read this book?

Chapter Two

Many Voices: Historical Perspectives on Women's Leisure

What has more feelingly and pragmatically been said by people of color, by white women, by lesbians and gay men, by people with roots in the industrial or rural working class is that without our own history we are unable to imagine a future because we are deprived of the precious resource of knowing where we come from: the valor and the waverings, the visions and defeats of those who went before us.

— Rich, 1986a, p. 141

Just as women have always worked, women have also always had leisure. Concepts of work and leisure, however, historically have not been necessarily embodied in the same way for women as for men. When analyzing the past two hundred years of American history, the leisure of women is often misunderstood and sometimes obscured, particularly for women of color, lesbians, and other marginalized women. As societal perspectives changed, so did leisure experiences. Examples of primarily white women involved in the arts, physical activities, and hobbies are found in the history of the United States to some extent (Dulles, 1965). Other structures and frameworks for leisure that brought working-class women pleasure and choice can be found in discussions of "cheap amusements" such as dance halls, amusement parks, and movie theaters (Peiss, 1986).

Yet inaccuracies exist from a historical perspective because of the social definitions of appropriate activities for girls and women. For example, only the leisure of the most visible group (i.e., white, middle-class, heterosexual women) has been described. Activities were not necessarily considered leisure for women by individuals who typically wrote the history, thus they were ignored or overlooked. In other instances, activities often associated with women's leisure were in reality, not leisure at all.

Leisure reflects the cultural values of a society. During the Greek era and more recently in the late 1800s, leisure was thought to exist only for the upper classes who did not have to work to live. At other times, such as during the Protestant Reformation, leisure was equated with "idle time" and was condemned by various religions. These religions valorized work as the way to be recognized in the present and the hereafter. Although women were subject to such historical societal views, additional circumstances existed which influenced their leisure. For example, women generally had inferior status in the patriarchal society and had expectations and restrictions (e.g., perceptions of femininity, lack of economic independence, motherhood responsibilities) placed upon them which further and most often adversely affected their leisure.

Women's History

A recorded history of women's leisure is virtually nonexistent. With the increased interest by feminist historians in creating a more representative and inclusive history, researchers generated some information about the leisure of notable women as well as "common women." A delineation of the leisure experiences of women and men has begun to be addressed; women's leisure has received some acknowledgment of its separateness from men's experiences (Gloor, 1992; Henderson & Bialeschki, 1992; Shaw, 1991). In actuality, however, the history of leisure has been a history of men's leisure. As suggested by Lerner:

> Only a new history firmly based on the recognition (of women) and equally concerned with men, women, the establishment, and the passing away of patriarchy can lay claim to being a truly universal history. (1975, p. 13)

The traditional way in which history is written has been to address change within the political sphere, especially power and conflict among nations based upon chronological time. As women's historians have discovered, though, the history of women demands a different periodization than political history (Lerner, 1975). Women's history is not a history of wars. Rather, this perspective addresses women's influence on patriarchal society in light of their inferior status and their relegation to traditional functions based on sexuality, reproduction, and childcare. This approach is applicable to all aspects of understanding women's place within a historical perspective, including one which focuses on leisure.

Gumbo ya ya is a phrase in Creole language that means "everybody talks at once" (Teish, 1985, pp. 139-140). This term describes the process of doing women's historical work and can be likened to playing jazz (Brown, 1991). In jazz, each of the individual voices can go its own way but is held together by its relationship to others. When engaged in women's historical work, everyone "talks at once" with the effect of multiple rhythms played simultaneously. The people, their experiences, and the settings do not occur in isolation but in concert with a myriad of other events and people. The problem for historians who often study one "conversation" is how to put it back in the context of the dialogue (Brown, 1991), where larger issues such as race, class, and gender are acknowledged.

Instead of isolating the one voice, historians studying women's lives often try to move away from the silence of traditional history and find the multiple voices that deny the claim that women had no role in history or that all women had the same experience. Women's history is concerned with understanding how race, class, ethnicity, and sexuality have influenced women's and men's lives. For example, when trying to understand the leisure of women, we have to acknowledge that the leisure of women of color has been influenced by the leisure of white women AND that the leisure of white women has been influenced by women of color. We lead the lives we do precisely because of the way others have lead or currently lead their lives.

Attempts to incorporate women into history are often handled in two ways: through a discussion of "notable" women, or by looking at the contributions that women have made. The problem with focusing on notable women is that the concept of noteworthiness has been defined by patriarchal standards. To limit a historical perspective to "women worthies" does not tell us much about the activities in which most women engaged, nor the significance of women's activities to the society (Lerner, 1975). In fact, some historians suggest that these notable women were *not* representative of most women, but were the "goody-goodies" who fit within patriarchal expectations and did not threaten men by their actions (Firestone, 1971).

The use of contribution history is also inadequate. This methodology attempts to apply questions from traditional history to women and to fit women's part into the empty spaces. The problem with this approach is that women's activities are defined from a male perspective. The way in which women grew into a consciousness of their own is ignored (Lerner, 1975). For example, during World War II women were heavily involved in supporting the war effort through their work in manufacturing war materials in several countries. The capabilities of women in the labor market were largely ignored when the United States, for example, returned to a peacetime economy and women were relegated to the home. Thus, the contribution of women was defined by what the patriarchal society needed at that particular time.

An emerging way to analyze the experience of women from a historical perspective is to consider the cultural situation of the time. Culture does not refer solely to behavior but rather to those patterns and abstractions that underlie behavior or are the result of everyday experience (Luschen, 1974). When the culture surrounding groups of women is discussed, this culture consists of beliefs, norms, and signs that are held to be true or acceptable for women. For example, Peiss (1986) described the culture of white, working-class, young women in New York City by detailing the perceptions held about these women, the acceptable forms of recreation, and the way their culture influenced and was influenced by the traditional Victorian culture.

The role of culture in history is complicated by the fact that in every culture, women and men play different roles within the social organization. Socially sanctioned images of femininity and masculinity are always relative. They differ from era to era, from culture to culture, and from group to group within a given social organization (Metheny, 1973). To fully understand the influence of roles and social movements, a woman's position within the specific cultural context must be considered. This consideration is no small undertaking.

Many feminist historians have tried to approach the development of women's history from the viewpoint of understanding women's culture (Fox-Genovese, 1990). This emphasis on women's culture usually referred to the broad-based commonality of values, institutions, relationships, and methods of communication that focused on domesticity and morality particular to late eighteenth and nineteenth century women. Women's historians who operate within this concept of women's culture view women's development of group identity and psychological autonomy as a way women create themselves and actively construct social life; they are not seen as being created or responding to an existing culture (DuBois, Buhle, Kaplan, Lerner, & Smith-Rosenberg, 1980). The study of women's culture, however, is not to the exclusion of the experiences of the individual average woman, nor does it subsume the philosophical or political problems encountered by these individuals (Scott, 1988).

A new historical approach to understanding women's culture and leisure is imperative. If we are to meet the dual goals of restoring women to history and restoring our history to women (Kelly, 1984), we must explore the historical context of women's lives. We must begin to see woman as a subject—as an active agent of history. The contribution of women's history is that it takes a general concern about ordinary women in the past and focuses on their social, economic, and political relationships. Few histories have as close a connection with an agenda for change and action as women's history does (Tilly, 1989).

The remainder of this chapter uses the United States as a basis to examine women's leisure based upon issues and roles that were integral to women's lives. Evidence of gains and of gaps can be seen in examining these historical perspectives. The topics range from the personal to the institutional and from self and family to group and society. Historical categories that are more appropriate to the roles and issues of the "common" woman's leisure are explored. These categories include the influences of the Victorian ideal of woman, the family, women's work, women's involvement in social reforms and voluntary organizations, the early feminist movement, women's involvement in recreation, homophobia, and the influence of the contemporary women's movement on women's leisure. We try to examine the leisure of women of color as well as white women and also women who represent a variety of life situations. The history written about women's leisure to this point has not been as inclusive as we hope someday it will become.

The Victorian Ideal

Throughout many historical periods, women have been perceived as the weaker sex. Often this perception was based on biological structural observations which showed that women in general had narrower and smaller shoulders and broader pelvic girdles than men. This perception was believed to make "running, throwing, striking, and climbing activities more difficult for her than the typical man" (Bowers, 1934). These supposed physical differences between the sexes resulted in many ideas to help explain the perceived differences. These explanations were often myth-based and attributed to Mother Nature or to mystery. Perhaps the most pervasive myth to evolve was that of "female goodness" (Williams, 1977).

The myth of female goodness created an image of the ideal woman, assumed to be of white heritage, as an ethereal person. She was put on a pedestal somewhere above the realities of life (Gerber, Felshin, Berline, & Wyrick, 1974). This ideal was praised in endless writings and from pulpits, bringing extreme pressure to bear on women to behave according to this image. To defy it was to be unwomanly.

A comparison of the Victorian ideal and the behaviors exhibited in leisure reveal that they were often antithetical to each other. For example, some leisure experiences, especially those involving physical exertion, did not allow gentility. Physical activities connoted vigor while the ideal woman was supposed to be delicate. Leisure that occurred outside the home and allowed for expression of emotions also conflicted with the ideal woman's propriety, modesty, and circumspectness. The traits of passiveness, obedience to husband, circumspectness of behavior, and most of all, attractiveness, were deemed necessary to maintain the Victorian image of womanhood. By avoiding exercise and cultivating a pale face and an incapacity to do work, a woman gave the appearance of gentility (e.g., to have facial color and muscular strength was a sign of having to work for a living) (Gerber et al., 1974).

The concept of the Victorian woman was not necessarily reserved just for upper-class white women; even working-class women who had to work hard each day were still expected to maintain a mythical gentility. In discussions of the Victorian ideal, women of color were largely ignored reflecting their invisibility due not only to gender, but also to race. Several examples (e.g., Peterson-Lewis, 1993), however, can be found that suggest women of color were influenced to some extent by the Victorian ideal. Women of color were sensitive to the desirable "pale skin" promoted by the ideal to the extent that lighter skinned women of color were perceived as smarter, more refined, and more desirable as houseworkers. The traditional African aesthetics around hair were also altered because of these ideals. For example, elaborate hair styles symbolic of particular African heritages were abandoned in the United States. In fact, African-American women often had to wear scarves to cover their hair and later on, women of color tried to straighten their hair to fit the idealized expectations for white women.

Dress and physical characteristics also reflected the desired ideal. Veblen (1899) believed that a woman's delicate and diminutive hands and feet and slender waist, as well as the other related perceived "faults of structure" that commonly went with them, were proof that the woman was incapable of useful effort and must be supported in idleness by her "owner" as valuable evidence of his pecuniary strength. Veblen's view of the ideal woman reflected his criticism of the capitalist society. In the following quote, Veblen symbolized women's position in the capitalist society by describing their attire:

> The high heel, the skirt, the impracticable bonnet, the corset, and the general disregard of the wearer's comfort which is an obvious feature of all civilized women's apparel are so many items of evidence to the effect that in the modern civilized scheme of life the woman is still, in theory, the economic dependent of the man—she is still the man's chattel. (Veblen, 1899, p. 222)

The dress of women, which was held as an important visible indication of womanliness, was much lamented by women who wanted to engage in more physical leisure activities. Women were held back more than anything else by their own image of themselves and the well-learned precept that they should always consider how their bodies looked rather than how they felt (Kaplan, 1979). Fashion not only hindered exercise, but contributed to the preservation of the weaker sex concept. For example, medical research conducted by Dickinson (1887) showed that the corset exerted pressure between 30–80 pounds which weakened the abdominal wall and damaged the liver.

Yet, some women defied the restrictions of dress and risked being perceived as less than womanly to pursue their leisure interests. Eleonora Sears, a Boston Brahmin and descendant of Thomas Jefferson, made a name for herself at the turn of the twentieth century in men's sports such as polo and shooting as well as tennis, squash, and equestrian events; in fact she was one of the first well-known women to publicly appear in pants and short hair, riding astride her polo pony (Cahn, 1994). Mary Schaffer, one of the explorers of the Canadian Rockies in the early 1900s, commented:

> Why must they settle so absolutely upon the fact, that the lover of the hills and the wilderness drops the dainty ways and habits with the conventional garments and becomes something of coarser mould? Can the free air sully, can the birds teach us words we should not hear, can it be possible to see in such a summer's outing, one sight as painful as the daily ones of poverty, degradation, and depravity of a great city? (Schaffer, 1911, p. 14)

Medical concerns also influenced the concept of the Victorian woman and had a relationship to leisure. Social practices of the late 1800s and early 1900s set the stage for the popular view among physicians and other experts that women were physically and biologically incapable of participating in physical activity and sport (Cahn, 1994). The four social practices that reinforced the perceptions of women's weakness were: (a) girls were usually confined to the house and not allowed to run, jump, and play actively; (b) tight lacing of corsets caused biological ailments; (c) few acceptable forms of birth control were available other than being "sick," and that sickness method further contributed to the public image of women's general weakness and frailty; and (d) the unhealthy conditions of the times (e.g., polluted air, poor diet, crowded and unsanitary conditions in the cities) caused general medical problems for everyone (Gerber et al., 1974).

The major medical concerns focused on the detrimental effects of physical leisure activities on girls and women. In particular, widespread concern was evident over the increased incidence of "pelvic disturbances" as a result of "over-activity." Many people were convinced that falls were inherently more dangerous for females because they might affect menstruation. Physical activity was viewed negatively; it ultimately was perceived as having a harmful effect on the all important role of motherhood. *The Journal of the American Medical Association* promoted this idea in 1925 when an article implied that young girls in this "age of feminine freedom" were overdoing athletics (Gerber et al., 1974).

The other major health concern had to do with psychological effects of physical activity. Many people felt that the emotional strain of physical leisure experiences would be injurious to the mental well-being of women. For example, Bax (1913) believed that women should not pursue leisure experiences that were physical because women were physiologically less well-organized and less well-developed than men and were mentally inferior. Bax further added that men refused to admit that a woman was entitled to enjoy all the achievements of civilization, to lighten her burdens, to improve her condition, and to develop all her physical and mental qualities. Even many women who believed that physical leisure experiences should be an option, believed that special care needed to be taken to avoid strains which could undermine either their physical or emotional stability (Bowers, 1934).

Not all people accepted these medical myths. Dissenting voices could be found, before the Victorian era, as early as 1831. For example, an article, "Calisthenics" (1831) argued that women's inactivity was dangerous and unhealthy:

> The consequences are, a greater tendency to stoop and acquire false and injurious attitudes—deformity of the spine and the like; together with an acquired nervousness of temperament, which makes them, in after years, a prey to dyspeptical and hysterical disorders, and an inequality of spirits distressing to themselves, and often exceedingly annoying to friends...nor are the monstrous absurdities of their dress, at all calculated to diminish these evils. For fear inaction of the muscles of their chest and back should not be sufficiently enfeebling, tight dresses, under various names, compress those parts and almost paralyze their actions. (p. 191)

Gradually this nineteenth century Victorian ideology surrounding women's place and the definition of femininity began to be less restrictive. Many of these changes grew from other social issues such as women's involvement in the paid labor force, the feminist movement, changing marital relationships, and a redefinition of family (Mandle, 1979; Peiss, 1986). These changes, in turn, affected other aspects of women's lives, including their leisure.

Family and Women's Leisure

In every society people have specific roles that they are expected to fulfill based on the expectations and values of the society. For all women, this social indoctrination has imposed upon them a value system which in most, if not all, cases has restricted their range of choices to a greater degree than for men. Further, some women have been restricted more than other women. Women have been trained to fit into institutions that have been shaped, determined, and ruled by primarily white men; women's own definitions of selfhood and fulfillment have remained subordinate to patriarchal concepts (Lerner, 1977).

Historically, girls and boys have been trained to fill different social roles. For most girls, the world was to be the family and the field of action was to be the domestic circle. Society has ascribed to women the functions of childrearing and family nurturing. Women's capacity for reproduction was, and still is, sacred because to survive, society needs women to bear children. In the past, women were legitimately visible in only three ways: they married, they gave birth, they died (Ulrich, 1979). Much of the meaning for women's lives became tied to the family, yet that socially constructed institution has experienced great changes during the past century.

Historical Perceptions About the American Family

When we talk of the family, two senses for the word must be understood: family as a social and economic institution and family as an ideology. Since the mid-1800s, families as a social and economic institution have been assumed to be organized around households on the basis of close kinship relations that reflected a division of labor between the male (i.e., breadwinner) and the female (i.e., childrearer). When the family is viewed as a social ideology, we find these perceptions often stronger than the reality of the institution (Barrett & McIntosh, 1991). For example, the ideological model of a traditional nuclear family life has been pervasive to such an extent that it seems to have become the familial character of the society.

In the United States and Canada, the socially constructed institution of the family has gone through significant changes during the past 100 years. Many people today lament the breakdown of the family and express a desire to return to the traditional family of bygone days. In reality, the "traditional family" is an ahistorical amalgam of structures, values, and behaviors that never coexisted in the same place and time (Coontz, 1992). The myths of the traditional family have emphasized the "desired" social organization of sexuality, intimacy, reproduction, motherhood, the sexual division of labor, and the division of gender itself (Thorne, 1992).

During the mid-1800s the concept of the ideal family was focused on the Victorian white family where household production had given way to wage work and professional occupations outside the home. Women's roles became redefined around domesticity rather than production, men moved to the public sphere of paid employment, and children were thought to need an extended period for childhood in which they could play and thrive on the gentle maternal guidance rather than the patriarchal authoritarianism of the past (Coontz, 1988, 1992). While this perception was the social ideology of the family, the reality for most families was much different. Many women and children worked in factories or on farms, and white women needed to hire household help, usually provided by women of color, to accomplish the domestic tasks and still fulfill the expanded responsibilities around childrearing.

By the end of the 1800s, reformers were advocating the return of the "true American" family that was a restricted, exclusive nuclear unit in which women and children were divorced from the world of work. During the 1920s, however, social theorists were worried about the apparent rootlessness of nuclear families and the breakdown of older solidarities where kinship and community networks were destroyed. Although the Great Depression of the 1930s placed tremendous financial hardships on many people, the importance of kin and family ties with recreational interaction centered on the kinship network was actually revived (Coontz, 1992).

After the Depression and World War II, a new kind of family evolved that today serves as one of the most powerful visions of the traditional family. This model, however, was available primarily to people of white heritage and middle or upper classes. The extended families of the past several decades gave way to a new resurgence of the ideal of the nuclear family that encouraged newly married couples to strike out on their own, establish single family dwellings, and move to the suburbs where they could escape the watchful eye of the elder generation (Coontz, 1992). The values of the 1950s family were not rooted in the past, but rather emphasized producing a world of satisfaction, amusement, and creativity *within* the nuclear family. It was the first attempt to meet all of the family members' personal needs through an energized and expressive personal life within the family (May, 1988). Beneath a superficial revival of domesticity and gender distinctions, women experienced an expansion of personal service to the point where childcare absorbed more than twice the amount of time as in the 1920s and the time spent in housework actually increased despite the availability of labor-saving devices. Men were encouraged for the first time to root their identity and self-image in familial and parental roles (Coontz, 1992).

The 1950s family, however, was an anomaly that resulted from a unique and temporary set of events based on economic, social, and political factors that took advantage of America's tremendous competitive advantage at the end of World War II. The government was generous with educational benefits, housing loans, highway construction, and job training that set the stage for family values and strategies that assumed cheap energy, low interest loans, educational and occupational opportunities, and steady employment. These opportunities resulted in early marriages and childbearing, consumer debt, and extended residential patterns.

One must remember, however, that this "ideal family" did not exist for everyone; many families were poor and the cultural diversity of families was completely ignored. For various racial and ethnic groups, this development of family is not reflective of how family was constructed either ideologically or institutionally. For example, the family life of African Americans would have been perceived differently. Until the mid-1860s, many African Americans were slaves. The concept of family held by the white owners was almost nonexistent and allowed for the continual breaking up of family units when members were sold to another owner. After emancipation was declared, these black families paralleled experiences of other poor, working-class families, but with the additional burden of unrelenting racial discrimination. The Victorian ideals of family generally were not available to African Americans but they were held to this standard and labeled dysfunctional when they did not conform.

The family of the 1950s gave way to the new realities arising from more changes in the social, economic, and political world. Today, the family has once again been reconstructed and reflects the desire and need for women to be engaged in paid employment. The "crisis" in the American family may be inseparable from the establishment of the family as the preeminent site for satisfaction of the emotional needs of men, women, and children. As stated by Coontz (1988):

> Changes in families have resolved some tensions only to create new ones. Old patterns of equality and inequality have given way to new patterns of autonomy and control. Losses for some family members have been gains for others, while gains for some family units have been losses for others.... The 'crisis of the family' is part of the historical predicament facing modern society: it revolves around the question of which decisions should or can be private, and which can and should be social. It raises the issue of what kinds of dependence and independence we can tolerate, and what social obligations we should strive to forge. We have to deal on a daily

basis with this predicament in our own families, but we have to
solve it in society as a whole. (p. 264)

What has resulted from these shifts away from the old idea of family
uniformity has been contemporary realities of new and diverse family forms,
multicultural diversity, and increasingly diverse physical and social environments (Baber & Allen, 1992; Germain, 1994). For example, we have lesbian/
gay families with and without children, single-parent families, families
headed by grandparents or aunts and uncles, and single people with family
networks of friends. We have families living in rural, suburban, and urban
areas. Some families live in extravagant homes, others in apartments, others
on the streets. Many of these families are actively involved in developing or
maintaining their own cultural ties.

Socialized Family Roles

The primary function of women related to the family has been reinforced
institutionally in subtle ways. Women have been socialized to put family
needs first and to feel that the role of wife and mother is the highest recognition
and expression of their femininity. Until the latter half of the 1900s, formal
education was not seen as necessary for girls to fulfill their life roles, and often
education was perceived as competition with traditional roles. Women's
education was typically sporadic, if at all, and often interrupted. Scheduling
of education, job training, and work developed to fit the male life cycle
(Lerner, 1977). Leisure could also be added to that list. Women's time was
perceived as time that could be interrupted for whatever needs or crises arose,
particularly those needs related to the family; the time of men generally has
been respected as private.

Sex-role indoctrination, training, and practical experience encouraged
most women to accept and to internalize the beliefs that would keep them
adjusted to living in subordinate status in a patriarchal world. Lerner stated,
"The final brick in the wall enclosing woman within the garden of domesticity
was her horror and fear of deviance" (1977, p. xxxv). The threat of deviance
was so powerful that it kept many women in line ideologically, emotionally,
and hindered them psychologically. The ways in which societal expectations
of women's role in the family have changed and some of the differences in the
functions assigned to women and men have fluctuated, but sex-role indoctrination as related to the family has remained constant over time.

Throughout history, however, some women have defied traditional roles.
For example, some white women and many women of color explicitly stepped
outside tradition when they worked outside the home even though they had

young children. Other women involved themselves as volunteers in social reforms such as women's suffrage and the temperance movement, but carried out these activities within the context of their family responsibilities. In these examples, women defied the tradition of women's sole commitment to family.

Before the twentieth century, most women fully internalized the wife/mother role. The isolation of women within their homes was not necessarily caused by environmental and economic necessities, but by societal strictures which had a decisive and often negative effect on the status and self-perceptions of women (Lerner, 1977). Women often perceived themselves as "helpless." Society had not yet developed an ideology that would proclaim the social value of motherhood (Norton, 1979). Married women were taught to feel little responsibility for the engrossing duties of the outside world, because they were to be absorbed in maternal functions (Blackwell, 1875).

In the late 1870s, however, women were starting to question more openly their complete relegation to the home. In a paper read at the Third Women's Congress of the Association for the Advancement of Women in 1875, Antoinette Blackwell stated:

> The temptation to absorb all of one's powers in home affairs is specially strong with mothers. It is they who most need warning against this influence. When they believe that duty calls them to this, they, their families, and the world will suffer together in consequence....[W]omen have no right to crystallize their whole versatile natures into any one set of functions, however central and important these may be. This would be destruction to men; it has brought destruction and desolation to women. (Blackwell, 1875)

She continued in her speech to encourage women not to claim maternity as a barrier to their own self-achievement. Blackwell (1875) contended that the time had come to repudiate the idea that marriage and a practical worklife were incompatible. Other women were also addressing the ever-increasing problems associated with traditional family roles of women. They saw the conflict arising from women becoming more individualized, yet, still suffering from the primitive and undifferentiated conditions of family life (Gilman, 1972). Of course, for working-class white women and many women of color, the combination of marriage and paid work had always been a reality.

The intersection of these socialized family roles for women and their leisure is an interesting aspect for understanding the reality of women's lives. The leisure experiences of many women have been unstructured, self-initiated, and generally connected with home and family duties. Women's leisure experience was incorporated into their daily tasks or was viewed as an extension of their mandated sex-roles. For example, as the roles of homemakers and mothers were fulfilled, white women in particular, often had fewer opportunities for social cooperation and team work. Thus, they differed in interests and tastes from men who generally experienced competition and cooperative activities in the hunt, in tribal life, in war, and in the industrialized system (Bowers, 1934). Historically, almost all women have had to make leisure secondary in importance to the needs of the family. Family was an important component, both positive and negative, for women's leisure and continues today to exert great influence on women's lives, regardless of social class, race, or other life conditions.

Work in Relation to Women's Leisure

Historically, many white women were relegated to the private sphere of the home, although at various times, such as during World War II, they were allowed access to the public sphere. The inferior status of women in industrial societies may be a result of the separation of the domestic, private sphere of women from the economic, public sphere of men (Lenz & Myerhoff, 1985; Rosaldo, 1974). Women's work was usually privatized within the household; therefore, many women were not involved in visible labor market activity or their involvement was tangential. Thus, women's general status was lower than men's and their access to valued resources was reduced (Shaw, 1985a). According to Shaw, leisure and leisure time were not as available for women as they were for men because of this lower status.

Prior to the industrial society, the family functioned as an economic unit. For example, in the agrarian setting everyone in the family contributed to the production of food. With the industrial revolution, however, men went to the public sphere of the marketplace while middle-class and upper-class women continued to work at home. As a consequence, women became separated from the activities most valued by a society that measured value in monetary terms. This change had dramatic repercussions for women. Work in the home was not valued because it was not paid for in cash; in turn, because of their continued association with and confinement to the domestic sphere, women were devalued. This condition was a double jeopardy for many women of color who had no choice but to work. Many of these women found that domestic jobs were available, but were extremely low-paying because of the low status associated with this type of work, as well as because of racial discrimination.

This shift in the value of women's and men's roles (i.e., being female or male) was evident in the United States as well as other parts of the newly industrialized western world. For example, in colonial society marriage and motherhood were the expected life pattern for women, and marriage and fatherhood were expected of men. In industrial society, a decisive shift occurred. Fatherhood became connected with a man's successful performance in labor and business as a way of showing that he could provide for his family. Marriage and motherhood remained the societally approved "career" for most woman. Thus, the world of men, work, and business became physically separated from the domestic sphere, and motherhood and the "work" associated with that role remained the world of women (Lerner, 1977) regardless of class or race.

The changes that occurred because of industrialization also sharpened class distinctions among women. Many middle-class women began to enjoy the benefits of fathers' and husbands' increasing wealth. They had more relief from household drudgery and greater educational opportunities. They became "ladies of leisure" and epitomized the ideal toward which all women were supposed to aspire (Lerner, 1977). Such a woman was the social ornament that proved a man's success; her idleness, her delicacy, her childlike ignorance of reality gave a man "class" that money alone could not provide (Ehrenreich & English, 1973). Those working-class women unable to reach the ideal of becoming "ladies" had to be satisfied with a lesser status by accepting their "proper place" in the home as mothers and caretakers (Lerner, 1979).

Barrett (1980) suggested that the family-household system that developed also could be viewed as a key to understanding women's oppression. The prescribed social structure of the household and the given ideology of the family were connected, but not parallel. The contention was that this family-household system was historically constructed to represent class relations. The structure of wage-earning husband and stay-at-home mother was not inevitable, but emerged through a historical process in which women's connection to domesticity was incorporated into capitalist relations of production (Brenner & Ramas, 1984). Domesticity, or the "bonds of womanhood," became associated with middle-class women. For working-class women, middle-class domesticity looked more like class intervention in the lives of women who were neither feminine versions of working-class men nor working versions of middle-class women. To have participated in the "bonds of womanhood" would have meant to accept the dictates of middle-class women who viewed working-class women as passive victims rescued only by the virtues of class-specific domesticity (Fox-Genovese, 1990). Oppressive conditions resulted from the focus on domesticity that had implications for women's work and leisure opportunities.

Throughout the industrial revolution, the labor of lower-class women was required. Unlike men, however, entry into paid work did not mean improvement of women's status. For employed women, industrialization meant a day of double burdens. Outside work was added on to home and childcare responsibilities. Since most women were socialized to believe that their domestic responsibilities were God-given and natural, women often felt guilty for working outside the home and rationalized that the work was only temporary (Lerner, 1977). This cultural rationalization provided an excuse for employers to pay women less than men; as temporary help, these women only required "pin money." Thus, work designated as "women's work" became characterized by poor pay, low status, and no security. As a result, industrialization and its ideology lowered women's status and diminished their opportunities for paid employment (Lerner, 1977).

According to Lerner (1977), industrialization yielded one positive outcome for women. Because of the demands and needs of industrial society, some women were able to overcome the educational discrimination that had kept them subordinate. When they faced obstacles to entering into professions, these women organized separate female institutions such as women's colleges, seminaries, and medical training schools. In the process, a "new woman" evolved who became economically independent; she was a well-educated professional whose feminist consciousness found expression in the demands for rights and the organization of female pressure groups.

As industry became more mechanized, sex differences in physical strength should have become increasingly irrelevant to occupational qualifications and perceptions of work as appropriate for women, but this assumption was generally not the case. Examples of how perceptions of differences in physical strength were irrelevant occurred during wars. For many women, the U.S. Civil War transformed their lives and proved the arbitrariness of assigned roles related to work. Some women moved for the first time from the confines of their homes. These women showed others, and revealed to themselves, that they were capable of performing demanding, previously male-defined work tasks such as managing farms and plantations, as well as providing crucial services by assuming roles once assigned to men (Welch & Lerch, 1981). During the years of World War II, women in many of the Allied nations filled jobs formerly held by men such as munitions workers, welders, and builders. Yet, after each of these wars was over, traditional patriarchal policies and values came back into effect. These values included: female passivity, expected dependence, nurturing, submissiveness, and subordination. Work and leisure activities that were incompatible with this image were, not surprisingly, seen as a threat to power relations between the sexes predicated at the most basic level on male strength and female weakness (Lenskyj, 1986).

The implications of unpaid and paid labor as it evolved over time for women's leisure are many. First, the popular definition of leisure centered around the idea that leisure was a needed opportunity to recuperate from time spent at work. Leisure gave the paid worker free time and a chance to relax and recuperate so that the individual could return to work refreshed and ready to be productive. This definition of leisure was particularly problematic for women who remained in the home as unpaid workers. Their free time from paid work was filled with unpaid household and childcare work. They experienced, as many women do today, a leisure gap. These homemakers were often perceived as not earning the right to leisure because they were not making valued financial contributions to the family. Therefore, leisure was an experience seen as existing outside the realm of their rights or needs.

Many women believed they did not deserve leisure. For example, housewives often felt guilty for wanting to take time for themselves. Since they were not paid workers who contributed to the economic welfare of the family, their need or desire for leisure as needed recuperation was not easily justified. Certainly any leisure experiences that required money were difficult for most homemakers; they were economically dependent upon a male family member and did not have responsibility for controlling money that they had not earned.

Another common misperception of women who did unpaid full-time work in the home was that *all* of their time was leisure. Again, the work they were doing was not valued by society because it was not linked to a cash product, and it happened within the private sphere of home. Many people saw a homemaker's time as basically free time to be filled with prescribed role activities, such as childcare, cooking, and cleaning. These activities were to be done "at her leisure" or perhaps more accurately, "as her leisure." The assumption that women who remained at home did nothing or only those pleasurable activities of their choosing was inaccurate for most classes of women.

Some women, however, who worked exclusively within their homes did find opportunities for leisure, or at least made their daily obligatory activities as leisure-like as possible. To adhere to the strong work ethic, women often used household obligations as a way to fulfill leisure needs. For example, cornhusking, maple syrup gathering, harvesting, quilting parties, and other sewing tasks provided women with practical forms of recreation. Although unpaid work, these activities were also seen as recreation because they gave women an opportunity to socialize with other women and get out of the isolation of their own homes. At the same time, these activities allowed women to get their work done in a more pleasant and enjoyable way.

This strong need for socializing and bonding with women through a work/leisure situation was apparent even in the immediate family situation. For example, Charlotte Perkins Gilman in 1898 pointed out the values of such experiences for mothers and daughters:

> For the daughters to sew while the mother read aloud to them was esteemed right...in the period of common sewing and reading the women so assembled were closely allied in industrial and intellectual development as well as in family friendship...hence the ease with which this group of women entered upon their common work and common pleasure. (Gilman in Cott (Ed.), 1972, p. 368)

For women who were employed outside the home, leisure experiences were still primarily home-based and home-centered. By the end of the nineteenth century, however, the strict work ethic had led to a concern for the quality of life, at least for men. Some companies started employee recreation programs in which some women participated. Formal employee services programs were the result of changing social forces, increased education, and an acceptance of leisure. Industries supported employee recreation in the early 1900s to promote loyalty, fellowship, high morale, and physical and mental health among their employees (Tober, 1988). Although women workers were still under severe restrictions because of gender-role expectations, they were able to be involved in some programs, although many of these programs were also race segregated. The 1916 Goodyear Tire and Rubber Company's women's field hockey team is one example of such participation (Tober, 1988).

A good example of the relationship between gender, paid employment, and leisure can be found in the literature from the turn of the century on young working girls employed in the mills and factories in the large cities. A brief look into the social practices of these young women open a door into the expression and legitimacy of sexuality, courtship, male power, female dependency, and autonomy (Peiss, 1986). As stated by Peiss (1986):

> Leisure activities may affirm the cultural patterns embedded in other institutions but they may also offer an arena for the articulation of different values and behaviors. The working-class construction of gender was influenced by the changing organization and meaning of leisure itself, particularly the effects of ongoing capitalist development on the organization of work and time, and

the intensive commercialization of leisure in the late nineteenth
and early twentieth centuries. (p. 4)

Yet, for these young, wage-earning women who were usually white,
single, and sent into the labor market to make money for their working-class
families, leisure as a separate sphere of autonomy was problematic. The
cultural ideologies about women's roles did not support this conception of
leisure, yet the dynamics of their working lives encouraged this orientation to
leisure. Their pursuit of leisure lead them to the newly emerging forms of
commercial recreation such as the dance halls, the amusement parks, and
movie theaters. These "cheap amusements" became the place where a
working-class variant of the New Woman emerged that linked the heterosocial
culture to a sense of modernity, individuality, and personal style (Peiss, 1986).
The leisure pursuits of single, working-class women, however, usually ceased
with marriage and motherhood.

In general, the norm for working women was similar to women working
within the home in that their leisure experiences were scarce and often tied to
their socioeconomic class. The leisure that did occur in these women's lives
was often linked to other life aspects such as work and family responsibilities,
social obligations, and economic considerations. Regardless of whether
women worked for pay because of choice or necessity, or whether they worked
without pay in the home, leisure as defined by the patriarchy was not seen as
the right of most women. Thus, many women sought ways to create social
change and legitimize their free time.

The Interaction of Women's Leisure and Social Reform Movements

The emergence of social movements all over the world, such as the woman's
rights movement, was frequently dependent on a class of educated women
with free time and leisure (Lerner, 1979). These educated "leisured" women
were shapers of history not only through their economic lives, but through
community building and politics. Women built community life as members
of families, as carriers of cultural and religious values, and as founders and
supporters of organizations and institutions (Lerner, 1977). Much of this
community building appeared to be a leisure experience for the women
involved.

In the United States, the late 1800s and early 1900s were years filled with
social reforms; women were instrumental to the success of many of these

movements. These movements were often based on compassion, spirituality, and concern for improving the quality of family life (i.e., characteristics of a proper lady). For many women the transition from the private sphere of the home to the public sphere of political action was tenuous, yet justifiable when viewed as an extension of the prescribed roles of women related to caregiving. Women who benefited most from the new found freedoms in an urbanized society, the advances in industrialization and technology, and leisure activities were educated white, middle-class wives.

To advance their rights, socially active women have always needed the time to work for social change; movements have needed the commitment of these women (Lerner, 1975). As Blackwell stated in 1875:

> Today, it is not simply exceptional women who feel impelled to put their woman's shoulders to some of the lagging wheels of social revolution…women belong to humanity; they must work, then for the human weal. (Blackwell, 1875, p. 352)

Women of various movements called upon the "leisured class of women" to take upon themselves in earnestness and singleness of purpose the world's highest work. They called upon the rich, married women, the childless wives, and the "old wives" (i.e., classes in the earlier days despised and set aside) to become the standard-bearers of a higher culture (Blackwell, 1972). Blackwell challenged these women:

> Will the matrons who have leisure, or can make leisure for themselves, consent to go on aimlessly frittering away their best energies? We have seen that they are not content.…They who have leisure are fast learning how to utilize it in line with the inquiring spirit of the times.…The time has come for women of leisure, for all they who need neither toil continuously for the bread they eat, nor spin a thread of raiment which they wear; it is for all women to begin fairly to test themselves and their capabilities. (Blackwell, 1875, p. 355)

The impulse for organizing arose whenever an urgent social need was perceived and remained unmet. Social issues and movements, such as the Women's Christian Temperance Union, anti-slavery, settlement houses, birth control, the American Equal Rights Association, and the National Woman Suffrage Association, were the types of "righteous" concerns that women felt were within their realm of action. The growth in women's clubs and especially women's involvement in the abolition movement were central to the emergence of the first American feminist movement. Through such activities, many women gained autonomy, yet generally were not perceived as being deviant from prescribed gender-roles.

A common setting for many of these social reform activities was the church. For many women, the private sphere of the home was their only domain of influence; yet, as the ones charged with being the "moral guardians of society," many women found the more public sphere of the church a comfortable setting in which to conduct their social work. The church became a place for self-help, leadership roles, and social welfare efforts (Higginbotham, 1993). Nowhere were these efforts more apparent than in the black Baptist churches at the turn of the century. These churches came to signify public space that was denied to African Americans in the rest of the community; they contained schools, libraries, restaurants, concert halls, insurance companies, vocational training, and athletic clubs that catered to a membership much broader than the individual churches. The church connected black women's spirituality with their social activism. The decades of activism with the church set the stage for the secular club movement at the turn of the twentieth century. Fannie Barrier Williams, a founding member of the National Association of Colored Women, stated in 1900:

> The training which first enabled colored women to organize and successfully carry on club work was originally obtained in church work. These churches have been and still are the great preparatory schools in which the lessons of social order, mutual trustfulness and united effort have been taught....The meaning of unity of effort for the common good, the development of social sympathies grew into woman's consciousness through the privileges of church work. (p. 383)

Another interesting aspect of women's involvement in church work can be found in the unlikely sisterhood that developed between northern white church women and southern black women. For example, during this time of Jim Crow (i.e., the racial discrimination to separate blacks from whites), northern Baptist women articulated a set of values that were counter to the trends of the 1890s and were the foundation for the belief that women were spiritually responsible for the advancement of race and gender interests (Higginbotham, 1993). This common cause prompted interracial interaction between the women as they developed projects that encompassed schools, churches, homes, and other organizational settings as they worked to transcend oppression.

The establishment and growth of women's clubs was a social movement that had ties to leisure for many women in the United States. These clubs often had a focused purpose such as literary clubs, garden clubs, or homemaker clubs. The programs were often much broader, however, and at times operated from the activist perspective of "woman's work for women" (Higginbotham, 1993).

African-American women working together was an example of how the African-American community traditions resulted in social reform. The virtual absence of social welfare institutions in many southern United States communities and the frequent exclusion of blacks from those that existed, prompted black women to organize clubs to found orphanages, old folks' homes, daycare centers, nursery schools, and other educational institutions. These black education institutions often became the centers for community organizations, women's activities, and a network of supporting institutions. The black community turned to their voluntary associations to resolve their own internal problems, not as a way to imitate white society (Shaw, 1991).

Recreation was, at times, the starting point for some of these women's clubs and organizations which eventually broadened their focus toward other social concerns. These ventures brought the women closer together, gave them confidence in their own abilities, and inspired them to look for other community problems to solve. From this original recreation need, the focus expanded to include children's clubs for recreation, education, and daycare. Clubs also attracted children's mothers to other activities (Lerner, 1979). Similarly, in large cities we have numerous examples of women's involvement in the Settlement House movement (Henderson, 1982).

The social movements that occurred were largely a result of women using their free time to create positive social change. The outcomes of these movements in providing meaningful leisure, as well as a better quality of life, were beneficial to racial groups, all socioeconomic groups, and to both women and men. Although many social movements were influential, one of the most important social movements for women was the women's movement.

The Influence of the Early Women's Movement on Leisure

The early women's movement of the nineteenth century occurred in various parts of the world. This social movement of the largest disenfranchised group in the world was instrumental in extending women's rights to include the right to leisure experiences. As can be seen from the previous discussion about women's involvement in church activities, clubs, and other voluntary organizations, the quest for gender equity and the rights of women was the focus of many women during the nineteenth century.

The first women's movement of the nineteenth century and early twentieth century in the United States was the result of many social factors and concerns converging. For example, in America: (a) during the Civil War, many women succeeded in positions formerly occupied by men; (b) many women from all racial and ethnic groups began to get involved in the public sphere through social reform movements; (c) women were beginning to be allowed further educational opportunities; (d) women began to question the contradictions between the "ideal woman" and her supposed capabilities, and the realities of women's lives; and (e) a "class" of women with the inclination and time to organize existed with strong motivation to extend rights for all women. To reach a consciousness that questioned "the ideal woman" took a long time, but the groundwork was set for historic change in women's lives throughout the world.

Dramatic differences prevailed in the philosophy and goals of some of the initial women's organizations. Basically two divisions emerged from the early organizing years: a suffrage focus and a feminist focus. The single-issue suffrage groups were primarily concerned with getting the right to vote extended to women. The feminist group was broader in its goals and approaches. This group also was concerned with women being allowed to vote. Voting, however, was only one of many critical issues that feminists believed all women faced. They believed that rights, such as reproductive rights, equal opportunity in work, and educational rights, were denied to many women because of the patriarchy. As a consequence, women's autonomy often was sacrificed. These feminists formed formal organization, such as the American Equal Rights Association, as well as informal feminist groups, such as the Heterodoxy luncheon group in New York City in 1912 (Schwartz, 1982).

At times, members from these two major divisions worked together, but at other times, the more conservative suffrage groups did not become involved with, and often did not even support, the issues of the feminist movement. For some women, the feminist movement was too radical. Feminists were suggesting changes that brought into question some of the most basic underpinnings of societal institutions such as the church, the family, and the law. At times, the ideological differences were so great that some suffragists retarded the movements by isolating activists, leaving them open to charges of deviancy, and discouraging women from getting involved. Some of these same divisions are problematic today.

The radical feminist movement was built by women who had few rights. The demands for equality and for freedom from oppression came from the women themselves and not through the government, the educational system, religious institutions, or professional groups (Williams, 1977). Even though the feminist movement lost prominence after suffrage was granted to women, it continued to spread and legitimize a new image of women, family, and marriage, and developed an alternative set of ideals and values. The emancipation of women came about through women finding heroines within themselves which enabled them to overcome obstacles in their path to autonomy (de Castillejo, 1973). For example, women like Amelia Earhart pursued their dreams by resisting stereotypes and believing in themselves (Backus, 1982). She pursued her dream of flying even though flying was perceived as a male pursuit. She developed a sense of self-determination, independence, and mental strength that served to empower her to achieve her goals.

These early suffrage and feminist movements did much to promote and advance opportunities for women's leisure. Most women were aware that they had virtually no rights that extended beyond the care of their homes and families. Women found that although they had few legal rights, they certainly had fewer leisure rights.

Even though leisure rights were not a primary focus of the major women's organizations, most of the groups did give some attention to the leisure needs of women, particularly for physical activity. For example, Stanton criticized the traditional clothing of women as a detriment to physical activity and, therefore, the health of women:

> How can you…ever compete with man for equal place and pay with garments of such frail fabrics and so curiously fashioned, and how can you ever hope to enjoy the same health and vigor with men, so long as the waist is pressed into the smallest compass, pounds of clothing hung on the hips, the limbs cramped with skirts, and with high heels the whole woman is thrown out of her true equilibrium. (Stanton, Anthony, & Gage in Welch & Lerch (Eds.), 1981, p. 469-470)

Other organizations of the women's movement also assigned increasing importance to women's recreation. At the National Woman Suffrage Association Convention in 1893, Haven (Anthony & Harper, 1981) gave a speech on "The Girl of the Future" and predicted that women would have some "leisure for recreation." In the fall of 1920, representatives of the National Woman Suffrage Association, the National Women's Trade Union, the Young Women's Christian Association, the National Women's Christian Temperance Union, and the General Federation of Women's Clubs agreed to promote physical health among women. They also recommended use of recreation centers for educating women about the importance of emotional, as well as physical, health (Goodsell, 1923).

From these women's movements came some major societal changes. Women were granted the right to vote and increased freedoms such as less restrictive clothing and greater sport opportunities. The notion of the "ideal woman" also began to wane. Although an era of conservatism returned in the United States in the 1930s, women's strides were never lost. Feminist issues continued to exist and were supported by various organizations, albeit more quietly, until the years of the Depression, World War II, and the 1960s when they once again began to gain new visibility. These war years were times when society could not ignore the talents of half its population. From the time of that first feminist movement until present day, many gains were made by women in opportunities for leisure, particularly in the area of physical activities and sport.

Recreation Activity and Leisure Experiences of Women

Throughout history, the actual experiences in which women found leisure have been as varied as the women themselves. As previously discussed, leisure was often an outgrowth of a household task, a part of social encounters, a function of family interactions, part of a broader social movement, or a concept of time attached to class status. Regardless of the type of experience, the concepts of time and activity, as well as the way in which the experience was perceived psychologically, were critical factors that interfaced with the social conditions of women.

Historically, leisure has often been defined as any activity related to recreation. For example, if a woman was attending a party, she was assumed to be experiencing leisure. As one analyzes women's leisure more critically, activities traditionally defined as leisure were not necessarily found to be leisure experiences for all women. For example, many women who went on camping trips with their families during the mid-1900s often had sole responsibility for packing, for gathering together the necessary provisions, for carrying out "female work" at the site (e.g., preparing the food, taking care of the children, cleaning up) and upon returning home, for unpacking the gear, and heating up water to wash the clothes, children, and equipment. Whether or not camping was a leisure experience for some women is questionable. Much of the existing historical literature addresses the leisure activities of women without looking at how women perceived those activities. In this section, the growth of women's involvement in various recreation activities, particularly sport, is addressed. Although not all traditional recreation activities were actually experienced as leisure by all women, these activities and women's participation in them have had an influence on women's lives.

Spectating

One of the first shifts in women's transition from home-based leisure was through spectating. Although most women were not actively involved in the activity while spectating, they were given a connection to and made familiar with many activities. One of the earliest spectating activities was ice-skating (Gerber et al., 1974). Women in the audience were thought to make a sport more respectable. Thus, "ladies' stands" were erected for horse racing, baseball, and other male athletic meets.

This early solicitation of women as spectators was supported by society at large. Such involvement was praised because it got some women outdoors and provided women with needed social contact. Although spectating got women out of the home and in contact with sport, it nonetheless helped to teach them that their chief role in sports was to provide applause (Gerber et al., 1974). Women were filling the role of supporter for males and found themselves as the "givers."

Taking Up Activity

From spectating, a few white women began to challenge the passivity of females and began to take up physical activities and sports. An article in *The Journal of Health* in 1831 encouraged women to engage in restricted calisthenics such as making circles with their arms, jumping rope, and playing badminton (Calisthenics, 1831). At this same time, frontier women, particularly the elderly and the young unmarried women, began to demonstrate outstanding riding skills (sidesaddle, of course) and attended shooting matches where the women also sewed and exchanged stories (Welch & Lerch, 1981).

A primary purpose of early physical recreation for women was to provide the opportunity for a respectable social encounter between men and women. In an age of Puritanical sexual morality for women, recreation provided a common ground for mixed-sex activities. Thus, most early physical activity, including competitive sport, was conducted in a mixed setting (Gerber et al., 1974). For example, croquet was one of the first social sports adopted by American white women and was firmly established by the time the Civil War ended in the late 1860s (Welch & Lerch, 1981).

Although sports gained in popularity after the turn of the century, they were essentially activities of the upper class. Most female participants were white women who had the leisure time and the finances to belong to clubs with appropriate facilities. These upper-class women entered into a culture of conspicuous leisure that also included dining, bathing, and drinking at the nation's most exclusive resorts and clubs (Cahn, 1994). For many of these women, sport became a liberating and adventuresome pastime that allowed them to display their wealth and strengthen elite social ties. For example, tennis was one activity that became popular through tennis clubs. The women who first played tennis during the late 1800s, however, had to be wealthy enough to join the clubs as well as have access to the needed equipment.

The upshot of these activities being connected to the wealthy was that they became socially acceptable pastimes consistent with the refinement expected of "proper ladies." The notion that refined women played refined games protected elite sportswomen from violating the boundary between proper womanhood and "vulgar" women of other classes (Cahn, 1994). Thus, individual sports such as tennis and golf became associated with the upper class and were acceptable competitive activities for young women while team activities, such as basketball and softball, were associated with men from lower classes and were viewed less favorably for women.

Many of the early recreation activities for women in the late nineteenth and early twentieth century were outdoor-oriented. Indoor recreation facilities had not yet been constructed on any large scale. Also, being outside was considered healthy for women. Some of the popular outdoor activities were horseback riding, swimming-bathing, ice-skating and roller-skating, biking, and sleigh/carriage riding (Gerber et al., 1974). During this time of initial growth in women's outdoor recreation, most of the accepted activities were still those endeavors that did not interfere too drastically with the perception of the "ideal woman." Any activity that emphasized beauty and aesthetic appeal was most in keeping with the transcendent female image and was more acceptable from the viewpoint of society. This attitude affected not only the choice of outdoor activities, but the style in which they were played:

> Essentially, sport for the 19th century American woman was initially in a few acceptable activities. Croquet, archery, bowling, tennis, and golf were the primary sports, though a few women played baseball, rowed, and participated in track and field competitively....Sports were chosen which could be performed without acquiring an indelicate sweat. (Gerber et al., 1974, p. 4)

Perhaps one of the single most important outdoor activities that encouraged the growth of women sport enthusiasts was the popularity of bicycle riding. Where roads and nerve permitted, the old, high bicycle gained its advocates. With the velocipede and tricycle even more women were able to bike. In 1887, with the advent of the safety bicycle (chain driven with wheels of equal size) and with pneumatic rubber tires that were soon devised, new worlds were opened to women (Paxson, 1974). To accommodate the ladies' need for modesty, a drop frame was designed. Women could also purchase a folded screen that attached to the front of the bicycle to keep the feet and ankles from view when mounting or riding the bicycle (Welch & Lerch, 1981).

By 1898 the League of American Wheelmen had over 100,000 female and male dues paying members and it seemed that white women, in particular, had taken a great step toward equal treatment by freely participating with the men. In fact, many women like Margaret LeLong of Chicago pushed at the imposed boundaries of women's behavior through their cycling pursuits; in 1896 she set off for San Francisco on her two-wheeler with only a change of underwear and a pistol. Arriving safely two months later, she said "no one bothered her in the least" (Stephens, 1992, p. 51). Frances Willard, the leader of the Woman's Christian Temperance Union who took up bike riding in the 1890s, said that this activity would lay to rest the "old fables, myths, and follies associated with the idea of woman's incompetence" and augment "good fellowship and mutual understanding between men and women who take the road together...rejoicing in the poetry of motion" (Willard, 1979, p. 105, 110).

Recreation Clubs

Clubs were often formed during this early period of recreation growth so white women would have the opportunity to participate. These clubs offered facilities as well as organized competitions. One of the first clubs in North America was the Ladies' Club of the Staten Island Cricket and Baseball Club. It was started in 1877 and the chief activity for women was tennis. Another well-known club was the Ladies' Berkeley Athletic Club in New York. This club was known as "that temple of feminine sport and gymnastics" (Gerber et al., 1974, p. 29). Bowling became an upper-class activity for both women and men, with many clubs for women in New York City and other large cities (Welch & Lerch, 1981). Prominent society women formed the Chicago Women's Athletic Club in 1903 as a lavish setting for exercise and leisure with a gymnasium, a swimming pool, bowling alleys, fencing rooms, a Turkish bath, and various sitting and dining rooms (Knobe, 1905).

Some recreation opportunities were also available to young, working women. For example, the YWCA ran a summer camp program in 1874 at Asbury Park, New Jersey, that provided working women with "pleasant respite from their jobs" (Welch & Lerch, 1981, p. 226). The YWCA encouraged improved physical health to enable young women to withstand the rigors of factory and shop work. By 1916 thousands of women were enrolled in gymnasium classes and swim programs (Welch & Lerch, 1981). It should be noted however, that these programs were often segregated due to the legislation that existed until the Civil Rights Movement of the 1960s. For other working women in large cities, dancing at the dance halls, visiting amusement parks, and going to movies became the "cheap amusements" offered through commercial recreation (Peiss, 1986) and these cheap amusements were most often racially segregated.

Social Control of Leisure

The male members of the recreation and sport clubs, however, almost always exerted control over what was acceptable in the way of women's participation. For example, in February of 1889, Madison Square Garden hosted its first women's "go as you please" bicycle competition. The field consisted of one Irish, one English, and ten American women competitors. Hopeful contestants biked a track inside Madison Square Garden over a six-day period ranging from Monday to Saturday. An American, Miss Stanley, earned first place honors (and $1,634) by pedaling 624 miles and two laps ("Women on Bicycles," 1889). Women's racing was brought to an end, however, as a result of social pressure and by the efforts of the influential American Wheelmen's Bicycling Club who did not approve of contests among females. In another example of male control of women's involvement in sport, the New Orleans promoter, Harry H. Freeman, put together a touring women's baseball team which folded under rumors of illicit sexual activities (Guttmann, 1991).

Women continued to demand and take their place in the world of physical activity at the end of the nineteenth century and took a big step toward their personal and collective freedom. This advancement was summarized in the following quote:

> And who shall say that when our women took up tennis and the bicycle they did not as well make the great stride towards real emancipation, or that the quickened pulse, the healthy glow, the self-respect of honest sport have not served in part to steady and inspire a new Americanism for a new century? (Paxson, 1974, p. 96)

Up until the twentieth century, most recreational activities for women were not team sports. Change began to occur when colleges developed programs of physical activities for women that included some team sports.

College clubs had competitions for females only, however, and even male spectators were not welcome. For example, the first intercollegiate women's basketball game was between Berkeley and Stanford on April 4, 1896. Only women were allowed to observe the game because it was not considered proper for men to see women sweating from vigorous effort. As documented in the newspaper the following day:

> A man looked in at one of the windows. Instantly the spectators broke forth in hisses so loud and vehement that he fled in terror. The hissing of an assemblage of women [was] a formidable affair. ("Waterloo for Berkeley Girls," in Welch & Lerch (Eds.), 1981, p. 11)

In the early decades of the twentieth century, it was more important for women to look well than to win. People, especially men, wanted women first and foremost to have a neat, attractive appearance. Disagreeable expression, uncouth language, yelling, screaming, or any form of "masculine" behavior were thought to detract from the aesthetic feature of the game. For example, in 1906, it was a rule at one college "that form was one of the requirements for making the university class teams and that no girl who persisted in careless dress and playing could play in any match game" (Gerber et al., 1974, p. 13).

Even though the aesthetic received the most attention, many white women continued to increase their participation in physical pursuits. The belief that girls and women had the right to participate in sports in and out of school and that school sports should not be limited to just boys' programs continued to grow (Cozens & Stumpf, 1974). A 1901 issue of *Cosmopolitan* indicated that open-air athletics for girls were very popular the entire year. Among the sports mentioned were skating, tobogganing, rowing, tennis, golf, lacrosse, swimming, riding, cycling, and certain track-and-field events (Cozens & Stumpf, 1974). The following year *The Delineator*, a popular women's magazine, ran a series of nine articles on the appropriate attire, the proper execution of skills, and the benefits of participating in fencing, basketball, swimming, bowling, rowing, golf, tennis, track and field, and horseback riding (Welch & Lerch, 1981).

During the 1920s, recreational activities also gained a place of prominence for women in the African-American community. Track and field, basketball, baseball, and tennis gained a foothold as acceptable sports for girls and women and helped to develop a cohesiveness in the community. Athletic events became community social events that enhanced racial pride and neighborhood identity as the women played to packed audiences in churches, recreation centers, or gymnasiums that seated more than three thousand fans

(Cahn, 1994). Attitudes toward the body and concepts of femininity developed in these communities that allowed and accepted women to be strong and athletic (Welsh-Asante, 1993, 1994). Beauty, personality, and athleticism were not considered to be mutually exclusive qualities in African-American women (Gissendanner, 1994).

As in other areas of women's lives, progress was frequently followed by periods of backlash and retrenchment. By the end of the 1920s a wariness and suppressed hostility in gender relations was being felt in women's sports. No doubt existed that assertive female athletes posed a challenge to men and masculinity. As more women moved into community-based recreation programs, they invaded the previously exclusive domain by claiming "masculine" strength, speed, and power as a right of womanhood (Cahn, 1994). The media persisted in making the leap from athletic competition among women to an antagonistic battle between the sexes that threatened men's rule over sport.

Criticisms of female sporting activities were made because women's sport participation represented a threat to traditional gender roles and to the patriarchy in general. Sporting ability was hardly compatible with women's traditional subordinate role; in fact, sport had the potential to equalize relations between the sexes. By minimizing socially constructed differences that had only tenuous biological bases, sport posed a serious threat to the myth of female frailty (Lenskyj, 1986). Time after time, the desire to engage in physical recreation activities led to the belief that participation in such activities brought out unladylike behavior and masculine appearance, particularly in white women. Since women were believed to be unable to bear prolonged mental and physical strain, games and sports were modified for women and women were encouraged to cultivate good form rather than establish records (Welch & Lerch, 1981). A statement by Sargent represented this opinion:

> [Women should] know enough about sports to be sympathetic admirers of men and boys....This kind of devotion has made heroes of men in the past, and it will continue to make heroes of them in the future. (1909, p. 171)

Many women were also trying to overcome restrictions based on gender in less widely accepted leisure pursuits than sports, where elements of life-threatening dangers were ever present. Women had always been portrayed as needing protection, and yet, by participating in certain activities, some women were demanding that this perception be changed. The adventures of women explorers document clearly the fact that in some cases women were successful in overcoming the stereotypes and the view that their actions were aberrations from the norm (Olds, 1986). For example, Mary Schaffer and Mary Adams explored many areas in the Canadian Rockies at the beginning of the twentieth century, including many places in the Banff-Jasper area. The following passage, taken from Schaffer's diary, illustrates the frustration and yet the determination of wanting to explore even though they were women:

> From the States came Allen and Wilcox, men of course, to tell again to our eager-listening ears of the vast, glorious, unexplored country beyond...came Fay, Thompson, and Coleman—all men! There are few women who do not know their privileges and how to use them, yet there are times when the horizon seems restricted and we seemed to have reached that horizon, and the limit of all endurance—to sit with folded hands and listen calmly to the stories of the hills we so longed to see, the hills which have lured and beckoned us for years before this long list of men ever set foot in the country....We looked into each other's eyes and said: 'Why not? We can starve as well as they, the muskeg will be no softer for us than for them; the ground will be no harder to sleep upon, the waters no deeper to swim, nor the bath colder if we fall in'— so we planned a trip. (Schaffer, 1911, p. 4-5)

After the liberal decade of the 1920s came several decades of conservatism concerning women's recreation involvement. The vote had been won, but many women's rights issues were still unsolved. Male supremacist values tended to be fostered by the post World War I economic depression, the growing influence of antifeminist Freudians, the "Red Scare" (which swept the United States and Canada after World War I and targeted such women as Jane Addams, Carrie Chapman and organizations such as the Women's Christian Temperance Union and the Young Women's Christian Association), and the growth of the authoritarianism in governments.

Addressing Girls' and Women's Needs

Conservative attitudes influenced women's leisure and sport experiences. For example, many of the women who were teaching physical education or planning organized recreation programs for girls and women accepted the philosophy that the problem with physical activities for women was that they should *not* follow the male model. For girls and women, according to this philosophy, the emphasis was supposed to be on the joy of playing rather than on winning championships. Unlike the men's programs, women leaders did not want to neglect the "many" in order to train the elite. They did not want sport and recreation activities professionalized. They wanted to avoid excessive publicity about women athletes and the sporting events in which they engaged. Female physical educators and recreation programmers did not want to see women exploited in the ways that men had been (Bowers, 1934).

An alternate approach for girls and women who wanted to participate in physical activity grew. On one hand, the approach was conservative, because protection of girls continued to be the focus; on the other hand, the approach was radical because it was antithetical to the traditional sporting values of competition, elitism, and winning at all costs. Some physical education teachers and recreation leaders also promoted leadership by women. They felt that women were more experienced, sympathetic, tactful, and capable of meeting the individual needs and interests of girls and women (Bowers, 1934).

Most physical educators and recreation programmers during the 1930s emphasized that recreation and leisure could be a means for emphasizing altruism, a characteristic attributed to girls and women. Physical recreation with a de-emphasis on competition provided an outlet for the perceived "natural urge" for females to care for and help somebody or something; caring for others developed social understanding, broadened outlooks, and helped girls and women find joy in altruistic service. By focusing on group welfare, girls and women could participate in sports and avoid developing into self-centered women who were unhappy and unpopular (Bowers, 1934). Once again, the image of the "ideal" woman emerged, even though it was slightly less restrictive than previously.

During the 1930s many communities started Girls Recreation Councils that were organized to promote more and better recreation for girls and women. These councils were organized by physical education and recreation professionals from organizations such as Girl Scouts, Campfire, Girl Reserves, city recreation departments, YWCAs, YWHAs, settlement houses, Girls' Friendly, and industrial plants. Often the councils worked with the Mothers' Clubs of the town. Mothers' Clubs helped by: purchasing and developing play areas; employing women leaders on all playgrounds; and helping pass laws, ordinances, and bonds to further recreational development (Bowers, 1934). The councils had ambitious objectives to accomplish as detailed in the following quote:

> The objectives were to strengthen and broaden recreation programs; to provide more leisure time activities for all girls; to educate girls for wise use of future leisure time; to protect and aid girls in health, morals, character, and social growth by providing proper environment, leaders, and programs....
> (Bowers, 1934, p. 261)

Addressing girls and women's needs set the stage for contradictions, particularly related to sport. On one hand, women and girls were allowed freedom, expression of self, and pleasure in bodily strength and skill. On the other hand, the acceptability of these expressions often came with parameters that did not allow women to step outside certain gender expectations. Some of the gap occurred because of the homophobia connected with women who participated in physical activity, particularly sport.

Homophobia and Women's Leisure

As women's culture moved from the homosocial world of intense women's friendships of the nineteenth century to the heterosocial world of the early decades of the twentieth century, the public nervously struggled with the lack of clarity around masculinity and femininity in physical recreation activities. The strong link between sport and masculinity made the arena of physical recreation ripe for the accusations of lesbianism for women who chose to engage in such activities, particularly in team sports. Some sports advocates tried to assert that athleticism could be feminine (e.g., gymnastics) and proof of heterosexuality, but this strategy did little to diminish the lesbian stigma of sport. Thus, the traditional view of what was feminine had a powerful, often discouraging, influence on women's participation. To step beyond these ascribed gender roles often resulted in a woman being labeled as masculine, therefore a lesbian and deviant. This accusation was threatening to many women who did not want the stigma to interfere with the rest of their lives. Thus, homophobic attitudes and the fear of being accused of being masculine deterred some girls and women from active pursuits, especially sports.

Leaders of women's sports unwittingly contributed to the homophobic climate when they oriented their programs toward the new feminine, heterosexual ideal athlete (Cahn, 1994). For example, when girls began to play in the All-American Girls Baseball League (the league made famous by the movie, *A League of Their Own*), they wore skirts while playing and took part in charm classes to ensure that their femininity on and off the field was not questioned. These practices, however, only resulted in instilling society's fear and loathing of lesbians into the practice and imagery of sport. As suggested by Cahn (1994): "Intentionally or not, policies designed to mollify a homophobic public merely added to the institutional bulwark that privileged heterosexuality and condemned lesbianism" (p. 184). Thus, the lesbian athlete became the negative symbol of female social and sexual independence; she became the mark of unacceptable womanhood. She came to represent the line not to be crossed or risk falling into the despised category of mannish (i.e., not-woman) women.

From the ensuing conflict between the stereotypic views of femininity and a woman's desire to pursue "nontraditional" leisure interests arose the "female apologetic." These "apologetic" women, both heterosexual and homosexual, often tried to avoid being labeled as deviant by assuming the seemingly insurmountable task of trying to remain feminine and yet excel in nontraditional leisure pursuits such as sports and outdoor activities. The apologetic was seen when women attributed their success to luck and not skill, when they dressed and presented themselves in an overtly "feminine" way, and when they treated their achievements as trivial.

The conflict between women's involvement in physical recreation and conventional notions of femininity continues today. Although the "apologetic" worked in some subtle situations, more blatant attempts have been made to reassure the public that women in sports, particularly exceptional athletes, were "normal" women. The possibility of a rejection of conventional femininity as defined through heterosexuality was too great a transgression of gender lines and the social order. For example, the Ladies Professional Golf Association (LPGA) struggled with a lesbian image, so it launched a sexy marketing strategy campaign in 1989 to restore heterosexual credibility to women golfers. The golfers modeled bikinis and exotic swimwear on Hawaiian beaches as a way to squelch the lesbian "whisper campaign" (Cahn, 1994, p. 266).

The fact is, however, that physical recreation activities did create a space for some women to explore unconventional gender and sexual identities (Peper, 1994). Athletically inclined lesbians did find possibilities for self-expression and a social life through sport. Even though public condemnation was an ever present reality, most lesbians constructed an alternative set of affirmative meanings and experiences from within the culture of sport. Many lesbians in the mid-twentieth century found the athletic life to be compatible with coming to terms with homosexual desires as well as providing a collective process through which to forge community ties with other lesbians. Given the danger of open declarations, however, lesbians in sport communicated their presence primarily through action, style, and unspoken understandings; they often followed a code of "play it, don't say it" in a way that ensured their survival in a hostile culture, yet preserved one of the few social spaces that offered a degree of comfort and freedom (Cahn, 1994).

This strategy of concealment and secrecy provided a degree of protection but also kept lesbianism underground. It allowed the rumor of a gay sport culture, but one that was never revealed. The silence around lesbianism never permitted lesbian athletes to speak to the wider public. Instead, the "open secret" of the lesbian sport culture operated on, but did not challenge, the fine line between public acknowledgment and practiced ignorance (Sedgwick, 1990). For example, not until Martina Navratilova "came out" as a lesbian did the public acknowledge a lesbian presence within tennis. Although the rumors were present, the reality was ignored. Thus, the silence, innuendo, rumor, and outright discrimination perpetuated fear and ignorance (Griffin, 1993; Peper, 1994) and the old fears between masculinity and sport linger on as do the cultural fears about physically strong, sexually independent women. As stated by Nelson in her book, *The Stronger Women Get, the More Men Love Football: Sexism and the American Culture of Sports:*

> Female athletes have a long tradition of dissociating themselves from feminism. Their desire to be accepted or to acquire or keep a boyfriend or a job has often equaled their passion for sports. Thus athletes have taken great pains—and it can hurt—to send reassuring signals to those who would oppose their play: 'Don't worry, we're not feminist. We're not dykes, we're not aggressive, we're not muscular, we're not a threat to you. We just want to play ball.' It has been a survival strategy. It's time to tell the truth. We are feminists. Some of us are dykes. Some of us are aggressive, some of us are muscular. All of us, collectively, are a threat—not to men exactly, but to male privilege and to masculinity as defined through manly sports. (Nelson, 1995, p. 30)

Influence of the Contemporary Women's Movement

From the decades of the 1930s-1950s, women continued to make small gains in their "public leisure activities." Much of women's leisure was still centered within the home and was a function of family and role expectations. Not until the social tumult of the 1960s-1970s was recreation and leisure for women perceived as an issue of freedom and equality.

Gains in recreation activity for women in North America were reflective of societal changes in attitudes wrought by continued social reforms based on the revived feminist and equal rights' movement, the civil rights movement of the 1960s, and the increased social awareness and commitment to change of the 1970s. These movements demonstrated a renewed sensitivity to fairness and discrimination. Particularly in the women's movement, an awakening occurred that resulted in a raised consciousness, an identification of oppressions experienced by women, and a strength in sisterhood in recognizing the personal and political connection (Bailey, 1993).

Sport was a most visible example of how the contemporary women's movement related directly to girls' and women's leisure. For women in sport, emerging societal attitudes toward justice meant that they could approach athletic resources and opportunities from a political perspective and were aided by organized feminism (Cahn, 1994). Women were encouraged to take up sport and fitness activities as pleasurable recreation in response to the increased positive perceptions about physical freedom, bodily pleasure, and leisure.

Title IX

One of the most significant legislative advances for women in the United States was the passage of Title IX of the Education Amendments of 1972. This act required that schools provide equal opportunity for both sexes to participate in intramural, interscholastic, intercollegiate, or club athletic programs. Title IX legislation was in direct response to unequal treatment received by women athletes. For example, in one midwestern Big Ten university, men's athletics received $1,300 for every $1 spent on the women's program. In another example, Washington State University appropriated less than one percent of the two million dollar athletic budget for the women's sports program (Cahn, 1994, p. 250). This legislation was to guarantee that women and girls in public institutions and programs would have the same opportunities as their male counterparts (viz., as participants, coaches, and administrators). The full reality of this legislation, however, has yet to be realized.

As was true back in the late 1920s and 1930s, women's increased visibility and strides toward sport equality were met with mixed responses. For many people, women's advances in sport represented both the personal and collective empowerment of women. Confident and strong in their individual bodies, women as a group were mounting an effective challenge to men's athletic monopoly and privileged status in society (Cahn, 1994, p. 253-254). For other people, the personal and collective empowerment of women was perceived as threatening. For example, the National Collegiate Athletic Association (NCAA) organized a campaign to reverse Title IX; in fact the NCAA Executive Director, Walter Byers, denounced the legislation and said it would spell the "possible doom of intercollegiate sports" (Carpenter, 1985). In other instances, officials and administrators in charge of implementing or enforcing Title IX mandates often were caught dragging their heels.

Another parallel can be found between the 1970s and the 1920s in leadership and control over women's sports. Women in the 1970s believed that they should maintain control over the wildly expanding arena of women's organized sports, especially at the collegiate level. The Association for Intercollegiate Athletics for Women (AIAW) was the main governing body for women's sports. Fearing a loss of female autonomy and power, they struggled with issues in the 1980s similar to those from the 1920s; they felt steamrolled by a powerful male organization and faced with the possibilities of women's sport succumbing to the crass commercialism, corruption, and win-at-all costs attitudes in men's sports (Cahn, 1994). AIAW's efforts to maintain control, however, failed largely because the NCAA offered something to schools that the AIAW could not: money and TV exposure. The NCAA took over women's sports, forced the AIAW to close operations in 1982, and shut the organization down for good when the AIAW lost its antitrust suit against the NCAA.

As feared, the take-over of women's intercollegiate sports by the NCAA, plus the ramifications of Title IX, changed the complexion of the administration and control of women's sports. For example, the loss of female coaches for women's teams with no gains made in women coaching men's teams is often a point of contention. Although Title IX guaranteed equality in pay for coaches, women actually lost ground in the leadership opportunities within women's sports.

Another potential setback related to Title IX occurred in 1984 when the Supreme Court issued its ruling in the Grove City College vs. Bell case that completely reversed the existing interpretation of the law. In the case, the Court ruled that Title IX could be applied only to those programs that received direct federal funds and had no bearing on nonfederal funded programs, even if the sponsoring school received federal support. The passage of the Civil Rights Restoration Act in 1988 by the U.S. Congress, however, restored the original interpretation of Title IX and again mandated that schools eliminate gender discrimination in all programs, including athletics (Cahn, 1994).

Although the passage of Title IX only addresses leisure as it pertains to physical activity, the implications are far-reaching. The message communicated is that females have the same right to sports opportunities as males. Having the choice and the "right" to involvement sets the stage for choices and rights in other areas of women's lives.

Leisure Today

Assessing how far women have come in their ability to pursue physical recreation activities is a difficult task. The attitudes of the public seem to have broadened concerning what is acceptable behavior for women. The notion that recreation is important in building character in girls and women seems to be a key change that is exerting influence on the socialization of girls. Seldom has recreation and sport been viewed as a way to "build" women since "real women" were not supposed to be independent, assertive, competitive, or oriented toward mastering their physical environment. Although not all leisure is manifested as action and not all girls and women are challenge seeking, leisure does have the potential to be growth producing as a means to develop identity. Structured activities such as sports can contribute in developmentally formative ways (Kleiber, Caldwell, & Shaw, 1993; Kleiber, Larson, & Csikszentmihalyi, 1986; Larson & Kleiber, 1993) as discussed in chapter five.

Present day girls and women often describe their leisure as enhancing self-confidence and feelings of self-empowerment made possible by defying rigid gender role norms (Freysinger, 1988). Many girls today take for granted the rights that they now have and often feel talk of discrimination, inequality, and male dominance in sport is foreign and oddly irrelevant to them (Cahn, 1994).

Yet, beneath the surface, an undercurrent of resistance and backlash is present. Sport and many other forms of recreation still manage to be maintained as bulwarks of male privilege and as subtle forms of male domination. Feminist activists continue to weather the new antifeminist backlash waged by conservatives of the New Right, supported by conservative political administrators who dig in their heels to preserve sport as the dominion of men and for men, especially if they are white and heterosexual. Gains in sport and leisure by women sometimes are interpreted as a loss for men and a threat to their masculinity. Possibly one of the best examples occurred in the 1992 Winter Olympics when women made up only 34 percent of the total U.S. squad but earned 82 percent of the honors, including nine of the eleven medals won by Americans and all five gold medals. The press explicitly linked the results to a crisis in masculine identity ("An identity crisis of ice and snow," 1992).

Today, women involved in physical recreation activities are facing the barriers to their involvement with a greater sense of entitlement supported by the inroads of feminism and feminist activists. They are energized by personal power and enjoyment attained through their own participation. This sense of entitlement and determination stamps the recent period of history and provides hope for a future in which adequate leisure, athletic pleasures, and physical power are available to all women. As suggested by Cahn (1994):

> Women's athletic freedom requires that certain attributes long defined as masculine—skill, strength, speed, physical dominance, uninhibited use of space and motion—become human qualities and not those of a particular gender....Ultimately women's efforts to attain meaningful leisure, unrestricted access to sport and athletic self-determination will be part and parcel of transforming the broader social relations of gender within which sporting life takes place. (p. 279)

Learning About the Past Helps Us Understand the Present

The private sphere of nineteenth century women developed in relation to the emergent market economy and industrialization that heightened the sexual division of labor. The Victorian ideology of true womanhood that focused on domesticity, moral guardianship, and sexual purity made a moral and social duty out of traditional household and childcare tasks (Peiss, 1986). This ideology both enforced women's subordination as well as offered opportunities to assert female influence in and out of the home. It generally encouraged a rich female-centered reality that encompassed passionate same-sex friendships, female self-awareness, and activism. The result was a concern on the part of middle-class women to pass on this homosocial world with its defined status and ideals, particularly domesticity, to the working-class women.

By the end of the nineteenth century, this dominant cultural construct was under severe stress due to the changing realities of women's lives. Opportunities for many women to move into employment, education, and political activism expanded women's place and challenged the division of power. The emergent New Woman gave women in the public domain a new sense of female self who was independent, athletic, sexual, and modern (Peiss, 1986). With an increased interest in the emotional and sexual bonds between women and men, the move to heterosociality was pervasive, particularly in commercial recreation. Women's self-definition became bound to heterosexuality and marriage while the homosocial world of close friendships and intimacy between women became labeled as deviant. This move into individualism and heterosocial companionship did not encourage a feminist consciousness, however, because a lack of substantive changes in the allocation of power, work, and resources by gender did not accompany these new social realities (Peiss, 1986).

As illustrated throughout this chapter, the leisure of women has been heavily influenced by patriarchal structures that dictated gender roles, family structures, work, and appropriate characteristics for women. At times these structures have been overly repressive and oppressive of women in all aspects of their lives; at other times, when demanded by women or needed by the society, these strict expectations have eased and have sometimes been transformed. Women, then, were allowed more freedom in which to grow personally and collectively and develop their own leisure apart from the patriarchal definition. The advancements were sometimes slow, yet, the striving for rights in all aspects of women's lives, including leisure, continued to progress. When Gertrude Ederle swam the English Channel in 1926, Carrie Chapman Catt, a leading suffragette, said,

> It is a far cry from swimming the Channel to the days to which my
> memory goes back, when it was thought that women could not
> throw a ball or even walk very far down the street without feeling
> faint ("How a Girl...," 1926, p. 56).

In addition to being a personal experience, leisure participation can be seen as a social institution. A parallel has existed between the changing social roles of women and emerging opportunities for recreation and leisure. The leisure of women has been broader than that portrayed through the historical leisure literature that described traditional recreation activities based on what men were doing. Throughout this chapter, the institutionalization of the contexts, roles, expectations, and attitudes of society have been explored to provide a framework from which to view participation, perceptions, and meanings of leisure for women coming from a variety of life situations.

Concluding Perspectives

As illustrated in this chapter, women's socially constructed roles have remained focused on the family and definitions of appropriate femininity as set by standards of the time. Yet, many women are struggling to find ways to acknowledge a heightened awareness of self and autonomy. We have illustrated areas where gains have been made in women's leisure, yet have acknowledged that large gaps remain. As evidenced by the historical leisure research currently available, one of the most noticeable gaps is the lack of information on women who are not white, middle class, and heterosexual. History is needed that includes information on women of color, working-class women, lesbians, older women, women with disabilities, and other overlooked women who have voices that need to be heard. Only then will we begin to understand the historical realities of all women and the effects on the ways that leisure is experienced.

During the past century, opportunities have expanded for women and some barriers have been overcome. Although most of the examples in this chapter have focused on changes in the United States, similar changes have often occurred around the world. Women have shown their strength and power to overcome social and leisure obstacles. Greater challenges remain. Women must not be content to remain below their capabilities in any area of their lives, including leisure, but must continue to strive to reach their ultimate potential, as their foremothers have done before them.

Discussion Questions

1. What are the feminist concerns with the way that traditional history has been written?

2. Discuss how the concept of "the ideal woman" has influenced the leisure pursuits of women of white heritage? Women of color? Women who have disabilities? Lesbian and bisexual women?

3. What have been the positive and negative aspects of linking women to the "private sphere" of the home? How has this influenced their leisure?

4. Describe the relationship which evolved between women's leisure and social movements? How did this fit with the concept of the "ideal woman?"

5. What parallels can be found between the early feminist movement and women's involvement in active leisure activities?

6. What is the "female apologetic" and how has it affected women's leisure?

7. What has been the value of "women-only" groups such as women's clubs and universities for women?

8. If you were to write a history of women in leisure twenty years from now, what might you identify as the "historical events" affecting women's leisure during the present time?

9. What contributed to the emergence of the twentieth century New Woman from the Victorian ideal of the nineteenth century?

10. How has the link between lesbianism and sport affected women's involvement in physical recreation activities?

11. In your opinion, has Title IX advanced the cause of women in sport? Do you think women's sports would have been different if the control had remained with AIAW?

12. What role has legislation such as Title IX or any kind of civil rights laws had in changing women's opportunities for leisure?

13. What gaps continue to exist in the leisure that women have?

14. What is the image of the ideal woman today? The ideal man? How are these images reproduced and promoted?

Chapter Three

Feminisms: Fact and Fiction

"I'm not a feminist, but I think women and men should be treated equally."

"No, I'm not a feminist—some of my best friends are men. I like men and I'm sure not a lesbian."

"I think I'm a feminist, because I believe that women can be strong, independent, and do whatever we dream about."

"Sure, I believe in feminism, but I'm not a feminist. I don't go out and carry banners and signs and stuff like that."

"I'm proud to call myself a feminist. Women are oppressed and feminism is a way of claiming our power as women."

"I don't like labeling myself a feminist. I think it is a negative term, even though I think deep down I might be one."

—Typical comments from undergraduate women students when asked if they were feminists

When the subject of feminism enters a conversation, comments such as the preceding quotes are often heard. People often support the rights of women, and yet, are not willing to claim the label of feminist. Many people hesitate to be associated with feminism for fear of the repercussions that could arise from some of the negative stereotypes about feminists. Other people proudly acknowledge their feminist views and find ways of working toward feminist goals. They see feminism as an empowering strategy that will allow them to address the oppression and discrimination faced by women at a personal, as well as societal level.

In this chapter, we will explore our collective thinking about the broad meanings and connotations associated with feminism as well as the implicit and explicit connections to leisure. Many meanings arise when the words "feminism" and "women" are used as generic phrases. Exceptions and disparate views are always present. The purpose of this chapter is to explore the relationship that exists between feminisms, women's lives, and leisure. We describe different perceptions of feminism and their influence on social change that has helped women make gains in their leisure as well as confront the gaps. As we will see, feminism and leisure can be inextricably linked by the shared components of choice, freedom, and autonomy.

A Feminist View of the World

During the past three decades, attention has been directed toward the concept of feminism and its importance in women's lives. The term is generally identified with controversial political stances taken by women and men concerned about the plight of women. To some people, feminism symbolizes the struggle of women for recognition, acceptance, and equity; to other individuals, feminism is a negative epithet that brings to mind angry women who do not like men and are not supportive of family.

As mentioned in chapter two on history, the feminist movement of the past 25 years is rooted in a philosophy developed over 125 years ago. The current feminist movement, however, has a broader approach than any of the previous movements. Today, feminism is viewed as a global, political movement organized around women's oppression that addresses more than purely economic issues. The ultimate goal of the present movement is to change the powerlessness of women worldwide and to redefine existing societal structures to honor the integrity of women. As a philosophy, feminism challenges the typical views about everyday reality. Feminism is both personal and political. The personal emphasizes the validity of women's experience, and the political focuses on women understanding and seeking to change their own lives when juxtaposed to their oppression and subordination in society.

Lerner (1986) suggested that evidence of women's subordination can be found in the earliest recorded history and institutionalized in the earliest law codes enforced by the full power of the state. She also asserted, however, that female subordination was not universal. Morgan (1984) suggested that an indigenous feminism has been present in every culture in the world and every period of history since the subordination of women began. The concept of feminism is neither geographically narrow nor a recent event. Feminist activity and thought are recognized as a transformational global movement occurring within all classes and ethnic groups. The global perspective has been useful to feminists and has reinforced the need to understand the diversity of women's lives. We also need to remember that women constitute a political minority, even though they are a numerical majority of almost all national populations and of the entire human race.

Defining feminism can be a complex task. To define the word, however is to get at the heart of feminism's nature. Feminism has a dual character that involves both theory and practice; it is a way of thinking about the world and acting in it (Sapiro 1994). The meaning of feminism comes not just from academic books, but from experiences and actions of generations of women around the world. Therefore, disagreements in definition are actually disagreements about how people should act and interact.

As stated in chapter one, feminism is a philosophical perspective and practice that embodies equity, empowerment, and social change for women and men and seeks to eliminate the invisibility and distortion of women's experiences. Feminism is not only a set of beliefs but also a set of theoretical constructs about the nature of women's oppression and the part that oppression plays within social reality (Stanley & Wise, 1983). Feminism is the belief that all people should be treated as human beings independent of categorical judgments based on such aspects as sex and gender roles, race, class, and sexual orientation.

Bunch (1985) described feminism as a political perspective on all issues of human life. She stated that freedom from oppression for women involves not only equity, but also the right of women to freedom of choice and the power to control their own lives. To follow feminism is not to be antimale; rather, it becomes an alternative to the traditional distinctively patriarchal way of approaching the world (Eisenstein, 1981; hooks, 1984, 1989). Most feminists try to bring women and men together in a collective resistance to gender-based oppression (Warhol, 1995).

Feminism is also a practice and a social movement. As such, feminism is a collective effort by a large group of people to solve a set of shared problems (Mandle, 1979; Taylor & Whittier, 1993). Usually social movements like feminism do not have the political power to achieve change through the regular governmental channels, so people band together for collective action (Sapiro, 1994). This process occurs when a group sees a new perception of its problem, can critique the problem, and sees possibilities for change. The special awareness or new consciousness serves as the focal point for the movement and the mobilization of support.

Goals of Feminism

Three major goals of feminism seem to be foundational to most feminist perspectives. The first goal is the correction of both the invisibility and distortion of female experience in ways relevant to social change. For example, women's roles in history have been largely overlooked. As historians develop a more complete picture that includes the diverse lives of women, these new insights may lead to social change in areas such as education. A second goal of feminism is the right of every woman to equity, dignity, and freedom of choice through the power to control her own life and body within and outside the home. The most prominent example of this goal can be found in the global work surrounding women's reproductive rights. Another example would be women who choose to pursue leisure experiences such as body building, rock climbing, and rugby playing without having to confront the traditional expectations around femininity or gender identity. A third goal is the removal of all forms of inequality and oppression in society. An example of this goal is the quest for equal opportunities not only for women but also for people of color and varied ethnicities, people who are gay and lesbian, and people with disabilities. In many ways, feminism is a revolutionary idea and yet, as illustrated by the goals, a philosophy that epitomizes basic human rights with women at the center of the analysis.

These goals demonstrate the encompassing nature of feminism as a philosophy and social movement (i.e., both theory and practice) that can benefit both women and men. Feminism is a perspective that arose from oppressive patriarchal conditions encountered by women, but any man concerned with fundamental change can and should explore what feminism means for men as well as for women. Examples can be found where profeminist men have become allies with feminists. These men are supportive of feminist efforts even though they acknowledge they can never experience the oppression and discrimination that women have endured. Profeminist men can be helpful in addressing feminist goals. The philosophy of freedom and equity for everyone serves as the base of support for anyone concerned with principles of equality, integrity, and freedom from restrictive gender expectations and responsibilities.

The Holograph of Feminism

Morgan (1982) described feminism as a holograph. In other words, one cannot examine feminism by focusing on one dimension, but must view it from a variety of perspectives. When this shift in perspective occurs, multiple feminisms seem to emerge that point to distinct as well as intersecting explanations for women's personal, professional, and political conditions (Tuana & Tong, 1995). Gender, race, class, sexual orientation, global politics, family structures, economics, and leisure are all important to the understanding of feminism as we view the holograph from changing perspectives. The result is a multiplicity of feminisms that provide a variety of differing recommendations for improving and transforming the conditions of women's lives.

Feminism is not a single body of work, and one cannot make any general statements or review it comprehensively (Donovan, 1993; Kramarae & Spender, 1992; Stanley & Wise, 1983; Stimpson, 1988; Tong, 1989; Tuana & Tong, 1995). Rather, feminism is an overarching framework that has application to numerous facets of society, yet may be reflective of each individual's life experiences and values. These different perspectives mean that not all feminists agree on the same issues or strategies. For example, they may disagree on which aspects of women's lives (e.g., work, sexual relations, family) best explain women's oppression, repression, and suppression under patriarchy; they often disagree on which legal remedies, job opportunities, reproductive technologies, and language revisions are most likely to liberate women; and they sometimes disagree about the forms of oppression (i.e., racism, classism, homophobia, ageism) they need to address (Tuana & Tong, 1995).

Feminisms

The concept of feminism encompasses a myriad of interpretations and perspectives. These different views come about as women examine and apply feminist perspectives to other familiar frameworks. Varied feminist perspectives accentuate the fact that not all feminists experience or interpret happenings in the same way. No monolithic, female "groupthink" exists because each individual woman's race, class, ethnicity, sexual orientation, age, education, and physical and mental ability mediate her thoughts and feelings (Tuana & Tong, 1995). Thus, talking about feminism as "political correctness" or a single movement that allows only one way of thinking about social problems does not make sense. Most feminists advocate ongoing and lively debates about research and social action directed toward the goals of feminism.

The following sections briefly describe selected feminist perspectives. New perspectives are constantly emerging while the more common views also continue to evolve. Further, many feminist scholars do not fit neatly into one or the other of these perspectives.

Liberal Feminism

Liberal feminism is one of the oldest forms of feminist thought. Examples of liberal feminist thought can be found in the eighteenth and nineteenth century writings of people such as Mary Wollstonecraft (1759-1797), John Stuart Mills (1806-1873) and Elizabeth Cady Stanton (1815-1902) (Tuana & Tong, 1995). The core belief for liberalism is the importance and autonomy of the individual and the natural equality and freedom of all human beings.

Contemporary liberal feminists focus on gender justice by working to eradicate oppressive gender roles and, through changed socialization practices, to eliminate restrictive legislation and social conventions that limit women's and men's professional opportunities. Much of this social effort was begun in the early 1960s as the second wave of feminism was underway, lead by such women in the United States as Bella Abzug, Betty Friedan, Eleanor Smeal, and Pat Schroeder in organizations such as the National Organization for Women (NOW).

Liberal feminism parallels theories of individual rights (Donovan, 1993; Tong, 1989). Theorists concerned with individual rights argue that rights and opportunities should be equally available for women and men. This idea is evident in the causes they have championed such as voting rights, women's right to own property, equal educational access, freedom of expression, and equal employment opportunities.

As liberal feminists began to remove legal and educational barriers to gender justice (i.e., Title IX and Family Leave Act in the U.S.), they discovered the complexities of the impediments to social change such as comparable worth, poor childcare facilities, and the double workday for many women (Tuana & Tong, 1995). These experiences have forced liberal feminists to recognize that their goals may be difficult to realize unless there is a more radical transformation in society than they had originally believed necessary.

Liberal feminists have been criticized by other feminists on several points. First, by placing the emphasis on rights, a dichotomy is established between autonomy and nurturing, between individual freedom and relations with others, and between independence and community (Benhabib, 1987; Tuana & Tong, 1995). The worry is that an emphasis on rights will result in a devaluation of nurturing and caring. These characteristics as well as others associated with females could be perceived as less viable and less worthy with only male characteristics perceived as important. Gilligan's work (1982a), however, suggested that an ethic of care held by many women is preferable to an ethic of rights, because some women often seek ways to comprehend the needs, desires, and motivations of others, so the moral concepts of rights and duties are replaced with responsibility, bonding, and sharing (Warren, 1995).

Related to this criticism is a spin-off that suggests that liberal feminists are too quick to adopt male values and standards (Jaggar, 1983). The outcome of this emphasis is that "male" becomes "human." The logical conclusion to this line of thought is that women can become like men if they set their minds to it, that women want to become like men, and that women should want to aspire to masculine values. For example, if a woman wants to compete for the highest level of administrative leadership, she may have to adopt male leadership characteristics (e.g., aggressive, competitive, autocratic) rather than use female leadership traits (i.e., cooperation, consensus, and caring) to be perceived as capable and competent. For many liberal feminists, these requirements are unsettling.

Lastly, a criticism exists about the way in which liberal feminists hope to bring about change. Many liberal feminists believe changing the patterns of socialization or changing attitudes will overcome patriarchy. Legislation and education are tools frequently used by liberal feminists. Other feminists would argue that those strategies alone are not enough to bring about the large scale social changes needed to achieve the goals of feminism.

Eisenstein (1995) suggests that liberal feminists may adopt a more radical approach in the future, particularly as women who must work inside and outside the home struggle with the inequities of the workplace where they are excluded from economic rights simply because they are women. She suggests, however, that the emphasis on liberal demands for equality, autonomy, and freedom of choice has been and is a strategic benefit to all feminists. Liberal feminists have pointed out the social inequalities faced by women and have directed the public's consciousness toward a critique of capitalist patriarchy.

The outlook for liberal feminism is unclear. Although this perspective has been attractive to many people because of its unarguable focus on equality and rights, the real life experiences of women are problematic for liberal feminists to address. Can the liberal notion of autonomous and self-interested individuals be replaced with the individual in relation to others? What would this transformed liberal political theory look like? How can we reconcile the fact that the "man" with whom liberal feminists have sought equality is in fact "white man?" How do liberal feminists deal with the fact that women are not even equal to each other, and that individuals may not want to "become white" to attain social and economic power? In the present form, liberal feminism is much more a perspective suited to white women than women of color (hooks, 1989, 1994b).

A leisure example of the application of liberal feminism can be found in the following true situation. A 29-year-old female college student and amateur body-builder was arrested for trespassing after she refused to leave the men's weight room in a city-owned gym in Boston (Webster, 1995). She explained that the weights in the women's gym were not heavy enough, so she had to use the weights available only to the men. In this case, a liberal feminist perspective would be that the woman should have equal access to the equipment and that her individual rights are violated if she is denied that opportunity. Her demands for equality, autonomy, and freedom of choice should not be threatened based upon the fact that she is female.

Marxist Feminism

Marxist feminists believe women's oppression began with the institution of private property (viz., property primarily or exclusively held/owned by males) that led to a class system whose contemporary outcomes are capitalism and imperialism (Lerner, 1986; Tuana & Tong, 1995). This view holds that capitalism, not patriarchy, is the fundamental cause of women's oppression. Therefore, women's oppression is seen as not so much the result of intentional actions of individuals, but the product of political, social, and economic structures associated with capitalism (Tong, 1989).

Marxist feminism represents an advance over traditional Marxist theory because it illustrates the interrelatedness of gender and class struggles. These feminists are also critical of standard Marxist theory, particularly around traditional sociological and anthropological conceptualizations. They extend Marxism and use Marxist methodology as a way to understand gender oppression as well as class issues. For example, Hartsock (1995) suggested the insights Marx gained by looking at issues from the proletariat's (i.e., the worker's) eyes parallel the work of Marxist feminists who wish to go beneath patriarchal ideology by examining the issues from the eyes of women who are subjected to the oppressive patriarchal system. Marxist feminists also build and support the praxis aspects of Marxism. This perspective advocates for strong ties between theory and practice. In other words, the theory has to work in terms of practice, or reality.

Marxist feminists often focus on the conflict experienced by women around paid and unpaid work. Although differences among women are readily acknowledged, Marxist feminists point to the commonality of "women's work" regardless of age, race, class or religion. Therefore, women's work that includes not only the production of goods but also the production and reproduction of human beings within the family, becomes the standpoint from which all women could interpret reality. Hartsock (1995) suggested women need to understand both the exploitive and liberatory dimensions of their work. Only when women begin this process will there be enough revolutionary momentum to overcome the destructive tendencies of the patriarchal system that trivializes women's work, yet could not exist without it. Thus, by Marxist feminists insisting that women's reproductive work is also "real work," they elevate the gender struggle between men and women to an equally crucial human struggle on par with class struggles. In the past men have tried to control reproduction by initiating it (i.e., with or without consent) and/or claiming the child as their private property. With reproductive technologies, however, women have a means for resisting men's control over their bodies. The gender struggle in the future between women and men over reproductive issues is likely to be as intense as the struggle between capitalists and workers over productive issues (O'Brien, 1995).

Problems can also be found with this Marxist feminist perspective. One of the major issues is that Marxist feminists tend to overlook the oppression that arises from other life aspects, particularly race and sexual orientation. These issues get largely ignored because they lie outside the traditional parameters of focus. Marxist feminists are also criticized for simplistic conceptions of family and the dismantling of the family as an economic unit that bolsters capitalism (Tong, 1989). For example, some Marxist feminists have suggested that the family is a creation of capitalism, manufactured to reproduce labor power at women's expense, with housework and childcare economically devalued to keep women in subservient, economically disadvantaged positions. Some Marxist feminists ignore the opportunity to see the family as a socializing mechanism outside of the control of the state; therefore, they miss the role the family can play in preserving social diversity. The criticism of family is made even more difficult when the family is a lesbian or gay family that does not seem to fit the Marxist feminist concerns. Moreover, Marxist feminists have also been criticized for their preoccupation with the nature and function of women's work as the only means for understanding and ending women's oppression.

In a western culture such as in the United States or Canada, Marxist feminism may be difficult to comprehend. Understanding the implications of capitalism is difficult when other structures such as socialism, are unfamiliar and the capitalist system is unquestionably accepted. The Marxist critique of family and its effect on women may be misunderstood especially when the liberation of women is equated with the transformation of family that will result in a different private structure. The present family structure with woman as reproducer and man as producer is seen as a capitalist construction that must be transformed. As suggested by Tong (1989):

> The private sphere, so near and dear to the liberal feminist's heart, is a veritable prison to the Marxist feminist. It subordinates woman by permanently excluding her from the public, productive world and leaving her with a life comprising little more than the emotional support of man who engages in 'real' human activity. (p. 67)

Marxist feminism can be found in a critique of leisure as "re-creation" of work to benefit capitalists. An example might be the commercialization of leisure as seen in theme parks like Disney World. Marxist feminists would critique the idea of family leisure if it means reproducing capitalism and bringing profits to a large corporation, all under the pretense of choice and fun.

Radical Feminism

Firestone (1971) first articulated one of the most central tenets of radical feminism: man's domination of woman is the most fundamental form of oppression and is so intricately woven into virtually all facets of our lives, that it pervades our sense of what it is to be woman or man. Radical feminists claim women were historically the first oppressed group and that the oppression of women provides a conceptual model for understanding all other forms of oppression (Tong, 1989).

Radical feminists suggest gender has been socially constructed as a way to keep women subordinate. Women's oppression will not be overcome by simply reforming political and educational institutions because the whole gender system must be transformed. Daly (1978) admonished that women not only recognize the destructive patriarchal images of women that permeate our sense of self, but that a world other than patriarchy must be created.

Radical feminists analyze and critique the social constructions that serve to ensure male domination such as medicine, religion, ecology, and racism, but particularly focus on reproduction and mothering as well as sexuality and gender. Radical feminists were the first feminists to bring visibility to the controlling of women's sexuality by men when they provided analyses on sexual harassment, rape, pornography, abortion, contraception, and compulsory heterosexuality (Tuana & Tong, 1995). MacKinnon (1995) suggested that male domination of women originates in heterosexuality and that the power of men over women arises from the pervasiveness of male sexual violence against women to the point where male domination and female submissiveness have become eroticized.

Radical feminists (e.g., Frye, 1995; Hoagland, 1988; Rich, 1986b) do not claim that heterosexuality necessitates male domination, but that human sexuality has been constructed to ensure that women's sexuality is for men. They demand a moral revolution that would call for a "movement of women" who withdraw from the construction of "femininity" and redefine reality to reconstruct the concept of "woman" and female sexuality (Tuana & Tong, 1995).

The critique of radical feminism has centered primarily on the more extreme perspective of radical feminism that advocates a separation and isolation from male culture and institutions (Sapiro, 1994) and the misperception felt by some people that radical feminism is equated with lesbianism. Although many people agree that women need to work together to rediscover or re-create a "woman culture" based on females' valuation of the virtues of nurturing, sharing, and intuition, disagreement comes when women try to create their own alternative organizations and communities (Sapiro, 1994). The linkage between radical feminism and lesbianism seems to rise from the analyses of heterosexuality by radical feminists. These analyses suggest heterosexuality is the cornerstone of male supremacy and in large part, is responsible for women's oppression (Rich, 1986b).

Radical feminists are also criticized for their lack of interest in developing strategies to influence law and policy since they see those institutions as patriarchal and beyond influence. In fact, some radical feminists would say they are not interested in making patriarchy "friendlier" to women. Rather they want to dismantle patriarchy and its institutions. They often choose a more "witness-oriented politics" where the personal life is the arena for creating change; other feminists think that this idea is not sufficient for bringing about needed societal changes because it ignores the focus on other diversity issues such as race, class, and age. As with other feminist perspectives, a continuum exists within radical feminism. In other words, not all radical feminists are lesbians, not all lesbians are radical feminists, and not all radical feminists are separatists and isolationists.

A good example of a radical feminist perception about a leisure experience can be found in women-only wilderness trips. Some of these trips could be viewed within a radical feminist perspective, because they are designed to focus on women's needs for skill development, usually encourage cooperation and caring friendships among trip members, and build a sense of autonomy and self-esteem. These women-only trips also provide an opportunity to disregard oppressive gender role expectations and operate in nonpatriarchal structures. While lesbians would be welcome on such trips, women-only experiences are not exclusively for them and are often chosen by heterosexual women because of the positive aspects previously described.

Socialist Feminism

Socialist feminism arose in the 1970s in Europe and North America in response to Marxist and radical feminist perspectives. Socialist feminists are similar to Marxists because they believe in the importance of class analysis of power, but they also acknowledge the radical feminists' belief that patriarchy is a critical contributor to women's oppression (Cole, 1994). Socialist feminists argue that capitalism is not solely responsible for women's oppression, but rather that power, and thus oppression, arises from issues related to gender, race, and class. For socialist feminists, the key to addressing power and oppression rests in patriarchy, racism, capitalism, and structured power relations. For example, socialist feminists would acknowledge Marxist class analysis that identifies the exploitation of women and men as wage laborers, but would point out that it fails to recognize the oppression of women due to the roles in the patriarchal sexual hierarchy such as mother, domestic laborer, and consumer. Socialist feminists would also acknowledge how racial oppression relates to class exploitation and sexual oppression (Tuana & Tong, 1995).

Socialist feminists focus on the relationship between the material conditions of societies and the social structures and ideologies that are a part of them. For example, unlike liberal feminists who emphasize individual equal rights with men and are generally uncritical of the broader societal sources of oppression and liberation, socialist feminists look more deeply at the structures and relationships within social institutions such as religion, education, the economy, and the family.

Above all, socialist feminists focus on people as social beings who exist as part of larger social institutions, not just as individuals with abstract rights. Therefore, they look at what is good for people as part of a community, not just what is good for the individual (Sapiro, 1994). Socialist feminists value equality, cooperation, sharing, political commitment, freedom from sexual stereotyping, and freedom from personal possessiveness (Jaggar, 1983). Unlike liberals, they stress the greater struggle of women of color, ethnic groups, and economic classes in gaining equal opportunity; unlike Marxists, they do not assume that a classless society will eliminate male privilege nor that economic oppression is secondary to women's oppression (Boutilier & SanGiovanni, 1994).

Socialist feminists believe that for oppression to be eliminated, human reproductive labor, as well as productive labor, will have to be reorganized. Jaggar (1995) suggested reorganization will have to address issues of reproductive freedom, childcare, adequate family support, and compulsory heterosexuality and mandatory motherhood as promoted by male-dominated systems. Ehrenreich (1995), however, cautioned socialist feminists against commodifying and depersonalizing women by always asking questions in terms of male perspectives; values should be shifted so socialist feminists ask, "How can we account for what men do outside the home in feminist terms, in women's terms?" (p. 270). She also warned socialist feminists to be respectful of the sense of autonomy and human subjectivity of women who choose to raise children and perform domestic labor.

The greatest concern with socialist feminism is that the differences among women will become erased or eroded (Tong, 1989). For example, if socialist feminists try to develop a unitary standpoint, they may fail to consider the consequences of racial, ethnic, and other individual differences while extolling the valor and essentialness of women's similarities. Since the socialist perspective is a combination of several major feminist perspectives, socialist feminism ultimately has the potential for resolving the differences among the varied feminisms. Any unified theory, however, runs the risk of achieving unity at the expense of diversity.

A leisure example of a socialist feminist perspective is a women-only "open" basketball league. A time was established by the women and the local recreation center administrator when the gym was available for them to play. A minimal fee was assessed to the "league" to cover the cost of having the gym open. Any woman was welcome to play whenever she could make it, even if she couldn't afford to pay, thus the "teams" were flexible and not limited. No hierarchical win/loss structure was present, no championships with league winners existed, no uniforms were required, and no paid officials were scheduled. The women basically ran the basketball league themselves. The games were competitive, but had a more cooperative, social atmosphere than traditional leagues. The women viewed the time as their "work-out time," as an opportunity to learn a sport that they had not been able to play when younger, as time purely for social interaction, or as time away from their daily demands. For women with children, childcare was available at no cost and operated by their partners who used the time to interact with all the children. For lesbian families, this arrangement allowed the partners to both play basketball and occasionally take a turn caring for the children.

Additional Feminisms

The preceding discussion of liberal, Marxist, radical, and socialist feminisms should not be viewed as all encompassing. As mentioned earlier, many perspectives of feminism continue to emerge and evolve. Addressing all of the emerging perspectives in detail is not possible in this book. Several additional feminist perspectives, however, need to be mentioned. More information about these additional feminisms can be found in other sources.

Cultural feminism (Donovan, 1993) evolved in opposition to liberal feminism. Cultural feminism is the ideology of a female nature or female essence reappropriated by feminists in an effort to revalidate undervalued female attributes (Alcoff, 1995). Therefore, cultural feminist politics center on the creation and maintenance of a healthy environment for the female that is free of masculinist values. Instead of focusing on political change, cultural feminists advocate broader cultural transformation. They recognize the importance of critical thinking and self-development but also stress the role of the intuitive, collective side of life that females tend to possess. Cultural feminists stress the differences between women and men and affirm the personal strength and pride that arise from unique feminine qualities such as an emphasis on relational connections. Underlying cultural feminism is the belief in a matriarchal framework for society where strong women provide leadership guided essentially by female concerns and values. An application of this perspective to leisure services might be the selection of female leaders in recreation programs because of the presumption that the feminine qualities will be more appropriate for the group work that needs to be done. Cultural feminists would emphasize uniquely female attributes rather than seek to copy a male model such as advocating that women's football be just like men's.

Another relevant form of feminism is *ecofeminism*. Ecofeminists suggest that no other feminist perspective recognizes the importance of healing nature/culture divisions, and that this concern for the relationship between human and nonhuman nature is critical to addressing male dominance (King, 1995; Russell, 1990). Ecofeminism describes "how an understanding of human liberation (feminism) and a concern for interdependence and relationships between humans and nonhumans (ecology) can provide a personal philosophy for both males and females" (Henderson & Bialeschki, 1990-91, p. 1). Fox (1994), and Fox and McAvoy (1991) suggested any outdoor ethic that does not address the domination of nature and women is inadequate. Ecofeminists embody this commitment by developing management and programming practices aimed at ending the exploitation of women and of nature in any situation, including leisure pursuits and recreation activities.

Postmodern feminism is another relatively new perspective on feminism that was originally referred to as "French feminism" (Tong, 1989). This perspective has roots in critical theory and cultural studies. Postmodernists reject epistemological assumptions (i.e., how knowledge is constructed), refute positivist methodological traditions, and believe that no one truth exists (Rosenau, 1992). Postmodernists recognize no one central voice of authority and no central source of power that designates some people to be part of a dominant culture and everyone else to be "other" in relation to that dominant culture. Some postmodern feminists view difference (i.e., marginalized, rejected, neglected, excluded) as a positive state that permits women as outsiders to criticize norms, values, and practices established and applied to everyone by patriarchy. They believe that other feminists have fallen for "male-thinking" that insists on telling only one true story about reality. Their approach is to deconstruct (i.e., reinterpret, reread) cultural trends and images (Bordo, 1995), especially as a way to illuminate power structures that perpetuate oppression. Postmodern feminists are sometimes disregarded by feminists working for political change because the language used is often inaccessible and their deconstructions offer no solutions to problems that will result in policy (Fraser & Nicholson, 1990; Tong, 1989). As much as people enjoy the postmodern feminists attacks on unitary answers, the fear is that postmodern feminism will lead to confusion and lack any ability to create a sense of community. The total multiplicity and diversity could ultimately lead to complete disintegration of society. In planning recreation programs for women or in doing research, a postmodern feminism might mean that women are given many options for participation (e.g., Henderson & Bialeschki, 1995a). For example, recreation programs might be planned anew each year through a decentralized cooperative process that incorporates information from an ad hoc women's advisory group.

Poststructuralism is another perspective that has gained in popularity. Poststructuralism is often considered synonymous with postmodernism. Although they have areas of overlap, they are not identical. The major difference, as described by Rosenau (1992), is one of emphasis more than substance. For example, postmodernists are more oriented toward cultural critique while poststructuralists emphasize method and epistemological matters. Thus, a poststructuralist would concentrate on deconstructing text (viz., language, discourse, meaning, and symbols) while postmodernists would be broader and include aspects of daily living. Individuals embracing both perspectives, however, are interested in deconstructing and critiquing positivist science where most leisure research has its roots, and in repudiating the status quo and effecting change. Deconstruction strips away "categories" that implies an objective truth and then reconstructs alternative meanings. An example of a poststructuralist analysis could be a feminist critique of leisure as time. This concept of leisure is not relevant to women who do not delineate their day into work and nonwork. Thus, leisure can be redefined by women in a way that is more appropriate to their lives (Kivel, Pearce, & Lyons, 1995).

The variety of feminist perspectives described in this section will serve as a starting point for understanding, appreciating, and respecting the wide variety of feminist thought. These perspectives hopefully can serve as reference points for interpreting and analyzing the gains and gaps in women's leisure. Depending upon the perspective taken, one might see more gains or more gaps than when viewed from another perspective.

Feminist Consciousness

Feminist researchers (e.g., Collins, 1993; hooks, 1989; Sapiro, 1994; Stanley & Wise, 1983) have identified three commonly accepted beliefs about women that seem to be reflected in most feminist perspectives: (a) women are oppressed and share a common set of oppressions, (b) the personal is political in that the personal experience is affected by the "social system" in everyday life, and (c) a feminist consciousness and the understanding of what it means to be female can be developed. Examples of the oppression of women were given in chapter one and we make numerous references to the need for personal and political change as they are related throughout this book. The third belief about understanding how a feminist consciousness is established may be useful to grasp in examining the significance of feminism.

To become a feminist is to develop an altered consciousness of oneself, of others, and of a "social reality" that is often apart from traditional patriarchal views of women's roles (La Fountaine, 1982). In her books focused on the creation of feminist consciousness, Lerner (1986; 1993) described five steps in developing a feminist consciousness:

1. An awareness that women belong to a subordinate group and that as members of this group, they have suffered wrongs;

2. The recognition that their condition of subordination is not natural, but socially determined;

3. The development of a sense of sisterhood;

4. The autonomous definition by women of their goals and strategies for changing their condition; and

5. The development of alternative visions of the future.

Women athletes' struggle to gain access to varsity competition in the United States is an example of the development of a feminist consciousness. Women who wanted to compete at the varsity level in sports were aware that they were not afforded the same athletic opportunities as their male counterparts. They were not given the same access to money, coaching, or competitive structures, so were denied equal participation. The reason they were denied participation was socially determined because of the way in which sport has been socially constructed as a male arena. As women athletes and their supporters recognized this wrong, they banded together in solidarity at first informally; as interest grew, they formed more organized protests. These groups of women athletes and their proponents began to articulate goals and develop strategies that would allow them to challenge the sporting traditions and create social change that would provide them access to competitive sports. As they developed this alternative sporting future, legislation was developed that helped them attain their goals. Thus, the passage of Title IX guaranteed women athletes equal sporting opportunities in programs that received federal funding. Many women in sports now have a vision that someday they will receive extensive media coverage and receive the same status as male athletes.

As can be seen in this example, not everyone has to directly experience the wrong before they can identify with those who do. Supporters of women athletes could recognize inequalities, feel the solidarity with the women directly affected, and work to create the social change even though they, themselves, had never personally experienced the oppression in sports. As the consciousness developed, the people involved were able to adopt a feminist perspective that permitted them to critique the existing social structures in ways that allowed for a transformation to occur.

Stanley and Wise (1983) also indicated three stages of feminist consciousness: false consciousness, consciousness raising, and true consciousness. No beginnings or ends exist for these three stages; feminist consciousness is a spiraling type of realization that exists as a state and a process. A false consciousness is the beginning stage where the individual goes from not seeing and understanding women's oppression to sensing that something is wrong, or understanding that a wrong once existed but that everything is now "fixed." Consciousness raising involves a woman's understanding of her life being transformed so that she feels and understands in a new and different way, but at the same time has the perspective available from her old ways of thinking or behaving. True feminist consciousness implies the daily "doing of feminism" in ways that focus on the power within each woman. As suggested by Romo-Carmona in her introduction to *Companeras: Latina Lesbians*:

> The stages of increasing awareness become clear when we recount the story of our lives to someone else, someone who has experienced the same changes. When we write or speak about these changes, we establish our experiences as valid and real, we begin to analyze, and that analysis gives us the necessary perspective to place our lives in a context where we know what to do next. (cited in hooks, 1989, p. 13)

If feminisms are to provide an alternative view on women's lives, the acknowledgment and development of a feminist consciousness is imperative. For feminisms to be truly liberatory practices (hooks, 1994a, 1994b), the theory and practice must stay on the cutting edge of real social change that makes a difference in women's lives. Creating the consciousness and practicing the theory are the challenges, and in their production lies the hope of equity, dignity, and integrity.

The Value of Feminist Theory

Feminist theory and/or philosophy can guide one's understanding of social change. A philosophy is a basic world view, love or pursuit of wisdom, and a search for underlying causes and principles. As applied here, a theory is a belief, principle, policy or procedure proposed or followed as a basis of action (hooks, 1984). Theory provides the generalizations and principles that are used within a practice or a field.

One of the most important potentials of feminisms is the development and use of theory applied to an understanding of women's leisure. Theory has two primary purposes: it helps develop a body of knowledge about women's leisure and it provides a framework for informing a better understanding of leisure in the lives of both women and men. Theoretical frameworks are necessary to understand the workings of society and the meanings of leisure so a basis for ideological, institutional, organizational, and subjective knowledge can be built.

Different theories of gender relate to different feminisms in that theories may fit into one or more of the broad feminist perspectives. For example, some theories put greater emphasis on equal opportunity through socialization and education (e.g., liberal feminism). Other perspectives emphasize the importance of social class, race, poverty, and relation to the labor market (e.g., radical feminism, socialist feminism).

Gender theory has great potential for contributing to the feminist body of knowledge about women's leisure. Ferree (1990) suggested that a gender analysis may underlie any aspect of behavior or attitudes and leisure seems to be an area that lends itself to the impact of gender. If we accept the proposition that gender is an axis around which all social life revolves, then a gender analysis ought to underlie all research done on leisure behavior. Gender theory analyses may be related to gender roles, gender identities, gender relations, or whatever measurement happens to be used. The theory must, however, be developed in a way that will make it accessible and applicable to practice.

The use of gender theory applied to leisure research is just beginning (Henderson, 1994b). The sociology, psychology, and sports literature has provided the best examples of theoretical frameworks that may help understand gender and leisure. Leisure and sports are not synonymous, but physical activities are a major symbol of leisure in many societies and act as an indicator of attitudes toward leisure (Leaman & Carrington, 1985).

Several examples exist regarding how theory helps us understand women's leisure gains and gaps. Within the leisure literature, for example, Bella's (1989) radical feminist perspective has alluded to the theory of patriarchy as a means for explaining the subordination of women in her analysis of androcentrism and leisure. Glancy (1991) used Jungian psychoanalytic theory to analyze archetypes of women in relation to leisure. Gender intensification, the liberal feminist hypothesis that after adolescence females follow a more rigid set of gender roles than before puberty, was used by Archer and McDonald (1990) in their studies of adolescent girls and sports. Models of gender stereotyping and the perception that particular activities are more appropriate based on gender have been used by Archer and McDonald (1990) and by Kane (1990). Another potentially useful way of understanding gender is liberal gender equity theory that suggests gender is a hierarchical structure of opportunity and oppression as well as an affective structure of identification and cohesion. Henderson and Bialeschki (1995b) and Frisby and Brown (1991) used this theory in their research on women in the leisure services profession.

The theory of domination is closely aligned with Marxist, socialist, or radical feminism because it suggests social structures are constituted and reconstituted through gendered power relationships. Gender relations represent the product of men's power over women, individually and collectively, in both public and home-based institutions. Gender dominance theory can help explain why women have had fewer opportunities for leisure because of how women subordinate their needs for others and defer to the wishes of men. In theories of power relations, the analyses of women generally have focused on dominance or resistance. Issues of domination also are central to gender relations theories. Whitson and Macintosh (1989) and Bryson (1987) used the theory of gender domination to describe, respectively, women's involvement (or lack of involvement) in sports organizations and women's involvement in sports. Deem (1986), Woodward and Green (1988), and Wearing and Wearing (1988) framed their analyses of women's lack of leisure based on their relationships with men in their own homes. New understandings of power and domination may help to present a framework that transcends the dualism of gender differences and presents a range of the complexity of sources of power which women and other "disenleisured" groups confront in their daily lives. Several researchers also are beginning to analyze power by addressing issues of resistance to domination (cf., Wearing, 1990; Freysinger & Flannery, 1992; Shaw, 1994).

Socialization theory, as a liberal feminist perspective, has been used in interpreting gender differences for some time, but new thinking is emerging about gender role expectations and relationships. Role theory grew from a traditional functionalism view suggesting roles are taught, and learned, so societies and subsystems can function efficiently. In the past, gender/sex role theory has suggested that differences between masculine and feminine roles were complementary and "natural." Gender role is theoretically self-contradictory, however, for there is no distinct and dichotomous "role" that uniquely embodies the variety of gender norms and meanings (Ferree, 1990). The emerging agency theories of socialization suggest that roles are constructed, modified, and adapted based on changes in society. Socialization theory, although a descriptive way of explaining the influence of leisure on the lives of girls and women and boys and men, often does not take into account other influences pertaining to power relationships (e.g., the popular culture as represented through the media) that result in keeping people in roles that are difficult to change.

As defined in chapter one, gender identity is the fundamental sense of one's maleness or femaleness, an acceptance of one's gender as a social psychological construction that parallel's one's biological sex (Deaux & Major, 1990). The sense of gender identity is acquired early in life and is one of the most central identities. Identity, however, can change over the lifetime and among individuals because most people are engaged in a process of negotiating and recreating their identities. Wearing (1991) offered an example of how men differ from women based on identity: male identity is generally linked to physical strength, women are excluded from male activities like sporting activities that require physical strength, females are supposed to support males, and females may resist these traditional identities and develop alternative identification.

These examples of gender theories may set the stage for future interpretations concerning women's and men's leisure (Henderson, 1994b). Further, these gender theories can impact our understanding of leisure in contradictory and complementary ways. Gender is reflected in the cultural norms and societal structures that may lead to immediate circumstances such as participation, perceived benefits, or constraints to leisure. In considering gender theory, interpretations need to show how some women's experiences and/or men's experiences lead individuals to make choices contingent on contexts and relationships, not just because they are biologically female or male.

Understanding women's leisure is most useful when gender is a departure point for further discussion and sex differences are not just the conclusion. For example, to say that women are more constrained in their leisure than men does nothing to help us understand the meanings of those constraints. By developing and incorporating gender theory into descriptions of differences, the differences and similarities can be better understood in a way that will illuminate an understanding of women's leisure. Further, rather than insisting on the dichotomous use of gender as either promoting solidarity or oppression, gender models suggest gender may be altruistic and self-seeking, supportive and oppressive, all at the same time. It may not be dualisms, but pluralisms (Gagnier, 1990) when gender is taken into account that can best help to explain leisure behavior. In other words, no one is purely feminine or purely masculine but each of us has many dimensions. Thus, the context of gender becomes important as a tool in understanding leisure experiences and gaps if we examine the range of possibilities that it offers.

The Backlash to Feminism

In 1991 Susan Faludi wrote a bestseller entitled *Backlash: The Undeclared War Against American Women*. In this book she detailed the vehement backlash that developed in the 1980s in response to the gains made from the women's movement. Not only has this backlash questioned and placed in jeopardy the advancements made by women, but it has sought to restore women to a more subordinate, traditional place. As stated by Faludi (1991):

> The backlash has succeeded in framing virtually the whole issue of women's rights in its own language. Just as Reagan has shifted the political discourse far to the right and demonized liberalism, so the backlash convinced the public that women's 'liberation' was the true contemporary American scourge—the source of an endless laundry list of personal, social, and economic problems. (p. xviii)

Some people have suggested that the backlash is actually just a continuation of American society's long-standing resistance to women's rights and independence. Historically, one can find that these backlashes seem to coincide with women's progress toward improving their status (e.g., Henderson, 1993). When this occurs, men feel a threat to their economic and social well-being, and hence, their masculinity. As suggested by Faludi (1991), the antifeminist backlash was set off not by women's achievement of full equality, but by the increased possibility that they might win it. A tactic of backlash has been to divide-and-conquer; that is, to pit single women against married women, employed women against homemakers, women of color against women of white heritage, lesbians against heterosexual women, and middle-class women against working-class women. Rewards and punishments are handed out in a way that elevates women who follow the rules, and punishes and isolates those women who believe feminisms are still needed.

Numerous reasons have been suggested for why the backlash has occurred (cf., Faludi, 1991; hooks, 1994a; Paglia, 1990; Sapiro, 1994; Tuana & Tong, 1995; Wolf, 1994). One of the arguments is that if women are given equal treatment and opportunities in society, they will lose protection offered by traditional patriarchal structures (i.e., breadwinning husbands) and become overburdened. The suggestion is that equality will result in injustice for women.

Another point of opposition has risen from some religious groups and their leaders. They believe that feminists attack what they view as the moral order of female and male difference and worry that changes in the familial, sexual, and reproductive mores will occur.

Some opposition arises from economic concerns over equality issues. For example, insurance businesses opposed feminist causes in the 1970s for fear of the money they would lose if they had to treat women and men as equals. In Canada, in particular, this point has been a major concern for opposition to employment equity legislation. Further, legislation directed towards changing women's rights often requires government involvement and monetary support.

For some individuals, the backlash reflects "society's" desire to maintain the status quo. They believe that society has been well structured in the past and seems to work just fine, so they see no need to tamper (i.e., "if it ain't broke, don't fix it"). These opponents see concern over gender equity as an attack on the merit system and argue that women are underrepresented or receive less reward because they have not wanted it or are not good enough to do better.

Many of the opponents to feminism are from the most conservative sectors of societies. These individuals often perceive feminists as extremists (i.e., socialists or communists) because they support social programs and governmental regulations that benefit women. These opponents are fearful that feminism will lead to the break-up of the family and doom society.

Widespread homophobia seems to be another area of backlash for feminists. Feminism has often become linked to lesbian and gay issues. The resulting accusation that to be feminist is to be lesbian is a powerful threat to many women's sense of identity and safety (Andersen, 1993).

The arguments between feminist and antifeminist supporters often seem to be led by feminist groups of women on the one side against antifeminist men who represent business, government, and religious organizations on the other side. In the early 1990s, however, a more organized and focused antifeminist movement was mobilized. For example, groups such as the Moral Majority, Women Who Want to be Women, Real Women, Promise Keepers, and other groups in the United States have focused on prolife, profamily, and traditional Christian moral values in response to the feminist successes in reproductive, family, and antidiscrimination policies (Sapiro, 1994). Moreover, antifeminist women are often used as the representatives of these groups; leaders believe the visible presence of women in these movements will bolster public support.

The emergence of the "new feminists" such as Paglia (1990) and Wolf (1994) has been disturbing to many feminists because upon closer scrutiny, they do not appear to be feminist at all. Defining who is a feminist and who is not, however, is problematic. The "new feminists" have charged that the "old feminists:" (1) have stifled the views of dissenting women; (2) are paranoid whiners who like to imagine all women as helpless victims; and (3) spread falsehoods and myths about women's condition (Faludi, 1995). Hooks (1994a) suggested that in fact, most of Paglia's primary ideas are "rooted in conservative, white supremacist, capitalist, patriarchal thought" (p. 90) while Wolf's readers, who are charmed with her enthusiasm, "overlook the frightening dismissal and belittling of feminist politics at the core..." (p. 97). Hooks admonishes feminists, however, that they must strive individually and collectively to make their voices heard to a larger audience; if women do not enter the popular culture, they will be complicit in the backlash that is at the heart of the media's support of antifeminist women who claim to speak on behalf of feminism (hooks, 1994a). Clearly the backlash is an issue that not only manipulates the public but also further divides women who call themselves feminists.

Perspectives on Feminism and Leisure

Views on feminism and women's reality have particular implications for examining and understanding the leisure of women. In general, feminism provides a means for addressing social change that may result in greater opportunities for women to experience leisure. Traditionally, recreation programming (Darlison, 1984) and leisure research (Henderson, 1990a) have been conservative with little linking of feminism and leisure.

Several parallels exist between feminism and leisure as defined in Western cultures:

1. At the core of leisure are the elements of freedom and choice (Carpenter, 1985; Henderson, 1986); freedom and integrity are the core of feminism. Thus, freedom is central to both concepts.

2. The goal of both feminism and leisure is to encourage choices, not to set limits. Women have not had the same opportunities for leisure because of the oppression they have faced (Henderson, 1986, 1994b; Shaw, 1994). For example, when the average American woman makes about $0.71 for every dollar the average American man earns, the discretionary income available for her to use is limited, and thus, recreation choices may be limited.

3. Leisure has been largely an androcentric concept just as society has been largely patriarchal. Both feminism and leisure focus on a revolt against domination. Both are devalued by people in power. Both offer a transformational perspective with new goals for social change.

4. Leisure and feminism are both engaged in acts of resistance that lead to greater empowerment. The social change that happens around leisure and feminist activities can contribute

to cultural transformation that addresses the issue of gender and the oppression of women.

The goals of the feminist movement can be applied directly to women's leisure (Henderson, Bialeschki, Shaw, & Freysinger, 1989) by connecting the invisibility of women and by striving for the inclusion of women as a central focus for understanding the world. As leisure researchers address the specific experiences of women and build theory upon this information, a comprehensive understanding of leisure behavior will be formed. Through leisure, a woman has the opportunity to take responsibility for herself and her time and to control her own life and body.

The varied feminist perspectives offer ways to understand leisure and social change. The perspectives present frameworks for viewing leisure as a universal right of women as well as of men. In the past leisure has been grounded in androcentrism and masculine subjectivity. With increased interest in feminist theory and research as related to women's leisure, women's interests and experiences are described in the leisure literature and are becoming a part of leisure theory. Although greater attention has been focused on women's leisure during the past ten years, women's oppression and subordination are still of concern. Considerations such as race, class, sexual orientation, and ability/disability must be addressed in the research and taken from the descriptive phase of study into more in-depth analyses and interpretations.

Proponents of a liberal view of feminism suggest that equality in leisure means that women have equal opportunity for participation in activities of their choice. Liberal feminists would interpret the facts about discrimination and sex bias found in leisure participation and prescribe the need for equity through increased education and awareness. They would seek modifications to make participation possible on an equal basis.

Marxist feminists view women's lack of leisure as one example of a repressive society. In specifying the causes of women's subordinate position in leisure, they would focus on the relationship between leisure and capitalist societal structures. Marxist feminists would say that the content and the process of leisure reinforces roles of dominance and submission. They would also argue for the need to recognize class differences as they influence leisure. Some Marxist feminists, however, tend to have a narrow view of leisure as re-creation of the labor force (i.e., making people ready for involvement in productive labor).

An important strength of a radical feminist perspective for leisure is in its call for an end to the dichotimization of world views and gender roles. The focus of radical feminists is on the centrality of women. They argue that women must not be set aside, addressed in relation to others, or "added in." All leisure experiences of women must be considered valid in their own right. Radical feminists not only challenge leisure's androcentric orientation, but consider women's experiences worthy of study. They would like to dramatically alter perceptions of leisure for women and create new alternatives for the conceptualization and embodiment of leisure that would result in a greater sense of autonomy.

Socialist feminists would suggest that capitalism and patriarchy combine to exert pressure on women's leisure. They would be concerned about the social relations that could be enhanced through leisure and the ways in which leisure could contribute to a sense of community for all people regardless of race, class, or gender. Socialist feminists would also be concerned about the sexual division of labor. For example, the ways that children and home responsibilities influence women's ability to experience leisure would be a major concern to socialist feminists.

The contemporary feminist movement has been concerned with increasing the choice, visibility, and entitlement of women. This entitlement seeks to provide women with the opportunity to make choices about what they will do and what activities they will pursue for their self-expression and identity. The attainment of the goals of equality, liberation, and integrity through the power to control one's self may increase the visibility of women's experiences in leisure. The feminist struggles to remove the inequality and oppression in society cannot help but advance the potential of leisure for women.

Concluding Perspectives

The discussion of feminism described in this chapter offers frameworks for exploring and understanding leisure in a more inclusive way. The variety of feminist perspectives should help individuals understand the ways that feminists approach and solve problems faced by women in a patriarchal society. For example, when women say "I'm not a feminist but...," it may be important to understand their points of view. Although the strategies may differ, the goals of bringing visibility to the female experience, the right of women to equity and choice through the control of their lives, and the removal of oppression and inequality in society remain consistent for feminists. Ironically, the threat of feminism is once again being used to silence women and to make their lives invisible.

Feminist perspectives are, however, a challenging and an applicable way to study women's leisure. As described in this chapter, many parallels and similarities between the concepts of feminism and leisure can be found. Both are concerned with freedom of choice, self-definition, autonomy, and elimination of constraints. Feminist perspectives offer ways of thinking about the world and the interactions that occur. The degree to which an individual wants to apply feminist concepts to understanding leisure may be more a matter of degree than philosophy. For example, most individuals would not argue against equality of the sexes and freedom from constraints based upon gender roles. The conscious actions of the leisure researcher or leisure provider, however, will determine the extent to which feminist concepts are applied to leisure behavior.

The challenge of understanding leisure within feminism lies in getting beyond the stereotypic images and terms to the symbolic meanings of leisure for women and the social issues surrounding leisure. The focus on women and leisure goes beyond simple equality. The focus of feminism is not just a matter of assimilating women into already established notions about leisure lifestyles. The main issues are the recognition that women, like men, have a right to freedom of choice within leisure and the right to define and construct leisure that fits an individual woman's life. Given the gendered structure of society, this freedom of choice and right to define are not always available.

Discussion Questions

1. Describe the commonalties between feminism and leisure. Why do they exist?

2. Discuss examples of how the three goals of feminism could be applied to women's leisure.

3. How have you noted the backlash to feminism in your life or among the people with whom you associate?

4. Why do you think you are/are not a feminist?

5. Describe the possible feminist perspectives, and how leisure would be perceived within each.

6. How might leisure service professionals implement a feminist perspective in recreation programming?

7. What types of sexism can you identify that you have experienced in your leisure?

8. Should leisure researchers and recreation providers be concerned with issues of social change? Why or why not?

9. To what extent does leisure serve to oppress women, people of color, economically disadvantaged people, people with disabilities, and other groups such as these?

10. Can men be feminists?

Chapter Four

Elusive, Yet Real: The Meanings of Leisure in Women's Everyday Life

I was thinking in terms of leisure, what I do with leisure time. Gee, when I'm not too exhausted to do anything else, I lay down and read mystery books. It's not like I set aside time for recreation...it's not a segment of my life. I mean, it's part of life, but it's not something I set aside and say, oh, I'm going to do this for recreation now....I probably do things for more than one reason. I need to be outside and if I'm troubled in my soul and my body, I go for a long walk. I'm getting exercise and I'm doing something for my soul. Recreation is like that...it's feeding my soul....

—Transcript of an interview with a thirty-something-year-old woman with post-polio syndrome

The question of what exactly is meant by the term leisure, and how it should be defined, has been widely discussed in the leisure literature. Understanding the meanings of leisure may be particularly important, and especially difficult when we think about women's leisure. For many women, their everyday lives tend to be holistic; work and leisure may coexist and be difficult to distinguish. This difficulty with definition, however, does not mean that leisure does not exist for women, as some scholars have suggested (e.g., Bella, 1989).

On the contrary, considerable evidence suggests that most women do experience leisure, that it is a meaningful concept in their lives, and that leisure makes a significant contribution to their overall life quality. The difficulty of defining leisure for many women lies in the fact that leisure may not occur in clearly demarcated blocks of time, in particular settings, or during particular activities. For many women leisure may be glimpsed in brief fleeting moments or may be associated with social interactions in different settings. Some activities are not always experienced as leisure by women because of the responsibility for others (e.g., children, family members, friends) in traditionally defined recreational activities (e.g., sports, fitness, watching TV).

Despite the complexity in understanding the meaning of women's leisure, a knowledge gap exists in understanding the ways most women define and experience leisure. Such knowledge not only validates women's life experiences, but also means that ways can be found to make leisure more accessible for women. In this chapter, the nature of these elusive, but significant, leisure experiences is explored. The discussion includes how leisure is defined, the social psychological parameters that make up "the leisure experience," and when and under what circumstances leisure typically occurs for women. This chapter also examines the potential impact of leisure on women's lives. Questions include: How important is leisure for most women? What are the benefits that women can gain from leisure experiences and leisure participation? Is the outcome of leisure always beneficial?

As we have stressed throughout this book, important differences exist among women in terms of leisure experiences, accessibility, and outcomes. Although women share some commonalties simply because they are women in a patriarchal society, we cannot conclude that women's leisure experiences are necessarily similar. Social class, marital and familial situation, employment status and type of occupation, and individual factors affect the availability of leisure, the manner and circumstances in which leisure is experienced, and the benefits that accrue from leisure involvement.

The Leisure Experience

Thinking of leisure as an experience seems to be the most appropriate way to define this concept. The notion of leisure as an experience, rather than as a particular activity or period of time, is congruent with the way people think about their own leisure in everyday life. When asked about our own leisure, most of us think about everyday experiences and occurrences (Samdahl, 1992a). The quality of a particular experience and the nature of that experience are important to people and result in their perceptions of leisure meanings.

During the latter half of the twentieth century, leisure theorists advocated for the need to describe leisure as an experience. The "classical" theorists, such as de Grazia (1964) and Pieper (1952) viewed leisure as a "state of mind" or "state of being." For example, Pieper described leisure as both "an attitude or contemplative celebration" (1952, p. 42) and as "an attitude of nonactivity, or inward calm, or silence" (1952, p. 41). The roots of these classical conceptualizations of leisure can be traced to the Greek philosophers, especially to the ideas of Aristotle and Plato.

Psychological theories also have implications for leisure as an experience. Maslow's (1954) concept of "self-actualization" (i.e., a peak state reached only after other basic human needs have been met) has been equated with leisure by some writers like Farina (1973). Other leisure theorists think that Csikszentmihalyi's (1975) notion of "flow" (i.e., an optimal experience where skills and challenges are ideally matched) might be a useful way to conceptualize leisure.

Regardless of the terminology used (e.g., flow, self actualization, state of mind), most leisure theorists subscribe to the notion of leisure as a subjective experience. This conceptualization should not suggest that participation in recreational or leisure activities is irrelevant or that the study of activities is unnecessary. Rather, the type of activity in which one participates, the physical setting or environment, and the social context combine to form the "container" within which the individual defines the situation as a leisure experience (Shaw, 1985b).

The idea of a leisure container is important. Although leisure can occur in almost any kind of container (i.e., during different kinds of activities, in a variety of physical and social settings), some containers are conducive to leisure experiences while others constrain leisure. Moreover, the concept of a container for leisure provides a link between social psychological approaches that emphasize individual meanings and sociological factors. An individual's situation with respect to such factors as class, race, age, or gender influences her family, work and social settings, and thus, affects the containers that are available for leisure. Positive leisure containers are not equally available to everyone in North American or other societies.

Defining the Social Psychological Dimensions of Leisure

Various attempts have been made by researchers to empirically describe and define the leisure experience. These descriptions have meant, in most cases, trying to determine the most significant dimensions or parameters of leisure. Neulinger (1974, 1981) suggested two basic dimensions that combine to create the leisure experience. These dimensions are perceived freedom and intrinsic motivation. In Neulinger's model, the primary dimension that distinguishes leisure from nonleisure is the perceived freedom–perceived constraint continuum. At the perceived freedom end of the continuum, a leisure state of mind will be experienced; increased constraint as perceived by the participant leads to a nonleisure state of mind. The motivation dimension qualifies the leisure and nonleisure states. In this model, perceived freedom and intrinsic motivation lead to "pure leisure" and the presence of extrinsic motivation leads to "leisure-work" or "leisure-job." Iso-Ahola (1979a) empirically tested Neulinger's model of leisure and found that perceived freedom was the critical regulator used by people to distinguish between the subjective states of leisure and nonleisure. He also found that motivation had some effect, though weaker and less consistent, on leisure definitions.

Another study by Mannell and Bradley (1986) attempted to create the leisure experience in a laboratory setting. The theoretical base for this experiment was Csikszentmihalyi's concept of flow. Although this research used a different technique and theoretical framework from Iso-Ahola's study, Mannell and Bradley also found that perceived freedom was a significant factor affecting the leisure experience.

Other empirical research studies on the meaning or definition of leisure have used qualitative and grounded theory approaches. In these studies, respondents were allowed and encouraged to describe leisure and leisure activities in their own words rather than respond to a predetermined set of questions. Interview studies by Shaw (1985b), Bialeschki and Henderson (1986), Freysinger (1988), and Samdahl (1988) explored the meanings of leisure experiences in everyday life and the subjective factors that affected people's perceptions about a particular situation as leisure. Gunter and Gunter (1980) applied a grounded approach to explain the dimensions of leisure by using self-report essays that focused on memorable leisure experiences.

All of these studies found freedom of choice to be a crucial element to the experience of leisure. They also uncovered other important factors or dimensions of leisure as well. These factors included: enjoyment (all five studies), relaxation (Freysinger, 1988; Shaw, 1985b), intrinsic motivation and lack of evaluation (Shaw, 1985b), a sense of involvement (Gunter & Gunter, 1980), self-expression (Freysinger 1988; Samdahl, 1988), and a desire to separate or escape from the everyday routine world (Freysinger, 1988; Gunter & Gunter, 1980).

Based on these and other studies, freedom of choice and lack of constraint appear to be a central and essential aspect of leisure experiences. Free choice, though, cannot be equated with leisure. Perceived freedom appears to be a necessary, but not sole, condition of leisure. In other words, leisure would imply an active positive dimension as well as simply the absence of constraint.

This active dimension can be seen as enjoyment (i.e., positive affect), affiliation (i.e., positive relationships with others) or autonomous action (i.e., positive self-determination), and goes beyond a simple lack of constraints to embrace active decision making in the construction of leisure experiences.

Thus, the positive dimension of leisure may well include actively seeking enjoyable and intrinsically motivating activities as well as emotional involvement in activities that express, construct, and reconstruct the individual's sense of self. "Self" includes presenting and thinking of oneself in a positive way because of a particular leisure involvement and feeling good about that self-presentation.

Leisure Experiences as Shared Meanings, But...

Relatively little attention has been given to differences in leisure meanings among people despite the substantial body of research and scholarship concerned with defining and understanding leisure from the participant's perspective. Few researchers have addressed the question of whether class, race, age, gender, or other differences affect the dimensions which comprise leisure experiences. A general assumption seems to exist that leisure meanings are universal or are consensually shared among individuals and among different social groups.

Some empirical evidence, in fact, suggests that the important dimensions that make up the leisure experience are similar for women and men, at least in the European–North American culture. Studies by Iso-Ahola (1979b), Shaw (1984) and Freysinger (1988) systematically examined gender differences in leisure definitions and found few differences. More recent studies including other population groups, however, challenge this universality of meaning. For example, a study of women who had emigrated to Canada from India (Tirone & Shaw, 1995) showed that the idea of individual choice and freedom was not considered important or valued by these women. Rather, relationship to family was central to their sense of personal identity and satisfaction with life. Leisure, for these women, could not be separated from family interactions and family activities. Similarly Fox (1993) and Fox and Trillo's (1994) work on women immigrants from Central America showed that the European–North American research describing the personal value of leisure may not necessarily be applicable in other cultures.

Clearly more research needs to be done that recognizes the diversity across cultures as well as within countries. In the United States, for example, leisure meanings may not be as consensually shared as once believed. A study of aging black women in the U.S. suggested that these women may have additional mitigating perspectives on leisure (e.g., racism, church affiliation) (Allen & Chin-Sang, 1990).

Even when the basic dimension of leisure (e.g., freedom of choice and autonomy of action) are commonly agreed upon, the accessibility of leisure activities and the social and physical settings (i.e., the containers) for such experiences may vary considerably. Some women, for example, may associate leisure with different activities and settings than typically associated with men's leisure (e.g., socializing as opposed to watching sports). Women also may have less access to leisure and fewer leisure spaces or containers conducive to freedom and autonomous action because of their greater responsibilities for home, children, and other family members. Differences in opportunities for freedom of choice and self-determination also exist among women based on their background and life situation such as educational level and financial independence.

Freedom and Constraint

Although many researchers have supported the contention that freedom or free choice is central to understanding leisure, this concept is not as obvious or straightforward as it may appear. Social psychologists of leisure have been careful to distinguish between absolute freedom and perceived freedom (Neulinger, 1981; Iso-Ahola, 1980a, 1980b). They suggest that knowing the individual's perception of freedom is more important than whether freedom exists in any absolute sense.

This distinction between absolute and perceived freedom makes sense from a social psychological perspective but has potential dangers. One danger is assuming that perceived constraints are only in the mind and are not "real," or thinking that the solution lies only in an individual having a simple change of perception or change of attitude. For example, if some women feel constrained by the responsibilities of caring for children or other family members, the suggestion might be that they should change their attitude to give themselves relief from feeling their responsibilities. This attitude change, however, ignores the profound socialization into such responsibilities and the value women place on caring activities and concern for others' well-being. A change of attitude in this case may be neither easily accomplished nor necessarily desirable from the woman's point of view.

Related to this issue of perceived or real freedom of choice is the broader question of ideology. Societies consist not only of social and cultural systems (e.g., educational systems, political and economic systems, justice systems, cultural systems), but also of ideological systems comprised of commonly accepted ideas, values, and beliefs. The ideological system suggests that the economic, legal, and other transactions that take place in society are fair and just, and indeed "natural" or inevitable. When ideological beliefs remain unquestioned, however, real inequities and injustices for certain groups may be masked. For example, the ideology of the family in our society suggests that the traditional family (i.e., the biological mother and father with the mother's primary responsibility focused on the care and upbringing of the children) is "natural" and fair, and thus serves the best interests of the children. As discussed in chapter two, this ideology gained a strong foothold in North American society in the 1950s but is increasingly coming under challenge today. Recent custody cases involving adoptive parents, employed mothers, and lesbian mothers have challenged the often taken-for-granted belief that children are always better off with their biological parents.

Ideologies can also be seen to apply to leisure situations and leisure choices. For example, aerobics is often considered a leisure activity of choice for all ages of women. This belief is considered self-evident because of the large numbers of women who sign up for aerobics classes. Researchers have suggested that women may be "constrained into" aerobics because of a strongly felt need to lose weight or to remain slim that arises from cultural beliefs about the ideal female body image (Frederick & Shaw, 1995). Thus, what seems on the surface to be an individually chosen leisure activity may not be experienced as leisure at all for some participants. Similar examples also can be made about women's fashions, including leisure fashions. Does the range and availability of women's fashion stores mean that women have a high level of choice and freedom with respect to fashion? Should the women's fashion industry be seen as a constraint on women's freedom (i.e., constraining them to continually conform to the industry's view of appropriate female appearance)? The ideologically related question can be raised of whether shopping for clothes should be seen as a leisure activity or an obligation driven by ideological beliefs about the need for women "to look good."

Clearly, freedom of choice is a complex question. Thinking of any particular situation as representing either freedom or constraint is too simplistic. Accepting that choice exists along a continuum from freedom to constraint may be helpful. Even so, "real" freedom versus perceived freedom and lack of freedom due to internalized responsibilities and ideological beliefs about appropriate behaviors are difficult to incorporate into the continuum.

The issue of freedom and constraint continuum is further complicated by the notion of "anomic leisure" (Gunter & Gunter, 1980; Samdahl, 1988). This term is used to describe a situation of negative freedom or freedom that lacks a positive dimension. From a social psychological perspective where the meaning system of the participant is deemed to be paramount, the term anomic leisure is problematic. Situations exist in which people report free choice, or freedom from constraint, but the conditions are not pleasurable. An example of this situation is people with "time on their hands," or who are simply "passing time." Their experience may be predominantly one of boredom, even depression, and they would be unlikely to define such a situation as "leisure." This condition is one reason why the situation of people who are unemployed or retired cannot be seen simply as one of "leisure."

Anomic leisure, then, is a researcher-imposed concept used to categorize a particular type of experience. From the point of view of women and men in their everyday lives, it would appear that only situations perceived as positive freedom or freedom *and* active enjoyment or autonomy are experienced as leisure. That is, a difference exists between "freedom from" where a lack of obligation exists and "freedom to" where individuals are able to take advantage of the lack of obligation to actively choose an enjoyable and rewarding activity (Gunter & Gunter, 1980; Talbot, 1979).

Despite the problems with the concept of free choice or perceived freedom, some attempts have been made to measure perceived freedom in everyday life situations. In a time budget study of 88 employed and nonemployed women and men, Shaw (1987) asked respondents to rate all recorded diary activities in terms of the degree of freedom of choice. Overall, the women perceived less free choice in their daily lives than did the men. Gender differences were particularly large with respect to childcare activities which were seen as more constraining by the women compared to the men. Women also reported less freedom than did the men in both household labor activities and family activities. In other words, when the men did housework they reported that they did such activities out of choice, while the women reported that they felt they had to do household chores (i.e., it was their responsibility).

Various reasons exist to explain why women may experience less freedom, or a "freedom gap" that may result in a "leisure gap" in their daily lives compared to men. The most obvious reason includes role-related constraints particularly associated with family responsibilities. The ideology associated with the traditional family, or "familism," includes a belief that the obligation for running the household and care of children is primarily women's responsibility. If women and men accept these ideological beliefs, a particular constraint is placed on women and their freedom of choice is reduced.

Similarly, because of societal beliefs about women's roles, employment opportunities for women have been historically limited to occupations that have been "appropriate" for women. Jobs such as nursing, teaching, cleaning, and clerical work are thought to complement or reflect women's family roles. Traditional women's jobs, however, tend to be low paid, low status, and provide only low levels of individual freedom, autonomy, and control in the workplace.

Women's relative lack of freedom in their everyday lives reflects the overall structure of our patriarchal society. Thus, although European–North American women and men may define the experience of leisure in similar ways, that does not necessarily mean that they have equal access to leisure, or that gaps do not occur. Many women face particular problems with respect to freedom of choice, and these problems are associated with societal values about the family and women's roles. This relative lack of freedom of choice in everyday life activities also means that women may have fewer opportunities to pursue positive leisure experiences.

Leisure as Positive Experience: Time for Self, Connections, and Autonomous Action

The positive component of leisure can be conceptualized simply as enjoyment. Indeed, this concept is the way many women verbalize the meaning of leisure and explain the difference between leisure and nonleisure in their daily lives (Bialeschki & Henderson, 1986; Henderson & Bialeschki, 1991a; Shaw, 1985b). The enjoyable activities that women report can be blocks of time linked to activities or social or physical settings (e.g., watching movies, having family birthday parties, being at the beach), or they may be more fleeting intermittent moments such as brief interactions with others or moments of reflection or humor. Although enjoyment is clearly central to the leisure experience, the term enjoyment covers a range of different types of situations that have different meanings and varied sources of pleasure. Three important aspects of the positive leisure experience are: leisure as time for self; as affiliation or connection with others; and as self-determination or autonomy.

Self

Many women report enjoyment in "doing nothing," relaxing, or simply taking time for themselves (Freysinger, 1988; Henderson & Bialeschki, 1991a; Shaw, 1985b). Women who are mothers of young children or who care for children with disabilities, aging parents, or dependent spouses are "on call" 24 hours a day, seven days a week; they often need a break from responsibilities and time for themselves.

Women with dual responsibilities of work and home have a need for relaxation. The majority of mothers, in both two-parent and one-parent families are now in the labor force in the U.S., Canada, Australia, New Zealand, and in many western European countries. These women clearly experience the burden of the double day (Hochschild, 1989). Even married women without children at home often face the dual responsibility of paid work and housework, since household chores continue to be unevenly distributed between women and men (e.g., Blair & Lichter, 1991; Sanchez, 1994). According to Schor (1991), North American society has experienced a decline in leisure and an increase in work and work-related stress; working hours have increased and the numbers of employed women have escalated. Much of the stress falls on the shoulders of employed women, so it is not surprising that they seek quiet times for relaxation, or times when they can "do nothing." They define such situations of taking time for themselves as enjoyable leisure.

Connections (Affiliative Leisure)

Another source of enjoyable leisure for women is affiliation or relationality. For women who are mothers, leisure activities with family are highly valued, and family interactions can be important sources of enjoyment and satisfaction (Kelly & Kelly, 1994; Freysinger, 1994). In the 1970s Kelly developed a model of leisure in which he distinguished between intrinsic leisure (i.e., activities are done for their own sake) and social leisure (i.e., activities are done primarily for social reasons). In his model, "relational leisure" consists of social activities that are freely chosen and provide positive interaction experiences, whereas "role-determined leisure" is also social in nature and purpose but is constrained or perceived to be obligatory (Kelly, 1983a). Both types of leisure are evident in women's lives, and relational leisure clearly brings women considerable leisure enjoyment and satisfaction.

Research has consistently shown that family activities are highly valued by women (e.g., Kelly & Kelly, 1994; Freysinger & Flannery, 1992; Horna, 1989b). Women often seek out situations that they believe will provide positive leisure experiences for their children (Horna, 1989b), and they seek to strengthen family relationships and family togetherness through such joint activities (Freysinger & Flannery, 1992). A study by Bialeschki, Pearce, and Elliot (1994), for example, showed the use of leisure to strengthen the sense of family was particularly important for lesbian mothers whose families did not always receive recognition by society.

Leisure as affiliation, though, is not limited to interactions with family members. Connections and interactions with friends, work colleagues, and neighbors are also central to the leisure lives of many women. These interactions can include reunions with long time friends, going on trips with friends and family members, attending community and church activities, and developing new acquaintances and friendships. In these situations, the relationship and interactions with others often is central to the leisure experience and deemed to be more important than the activities themselves.

Although leisure as affiliation has many positive aspects, affiliation has some drawbacks as we discuss in detail in chapter seven. Many women put a considerable amount of effort into ensuring that leisure interactions go well, and that the situation is enjoyable for everyone concerned. Caring for others takes up energy and can make the potentially enjoyable experience feel more like work than leisure. This situation may be particularly true for activities with children where a family leisure situation can quickly turn into a caregiving or work situation if children are uncooperative or not enjoying the activity. Thus, to use Kelly's terminology, relational leisure can easily become role-determined or obligatory in these circumstances, thereby decreasing the quality of the leisure experience.

Leisure as affiliation is closely linked to the "ethic of care" (Gilligan, 1982a) which women often learn and internalize at an early age as discussed in chapters five and six. Although the ethic of care can lead to positive relational leisure, some women may find themselves caring about the needs of others more than their own. Thus, caring activities, found in affiliative leisure, can prevent women from thinking about their own leisure needs and actually act as a constraint to their own leisure experience (Harrington, Dawson & Bolla, 1992).

Autonomy (Self-Determined Leisure)

Researchers have stressed the need to distinguish between affiliative leisure and self-determined, or autonomous, leisure for women (Freysinger & Flannery, 1992; Samuel, 1992). The idea of autonomy is similar to self-determination in that it means being independent of others and making one's own decisions according to one's own wishes (Samuel, 1992). Self-determined leisure, also called agentic leisure (Freysinger, 1995), can be seen as activities over which the individual has control and feels freedom to do whatever she wishes. Autonomous leisure may include an expression of self and a determination to do something for oneself that reflects personal interests rather than concern for others.

Both self-determination and autonomy can be seen as freedom from societally imposed roles such as mother or wife. Thus, in Samuel's (1992) research, autonomy for mothers meant finding leisure activities and experiences that were apart from family commitments and family interaction. Autonomy can also mean playing team sports that may not necessarily be thought of as appropriate for girls.

Autonomous and self-determined leisure may be particularly important for women who have learned to put the needs of others before their own needs. Even in adolescence, many young women in North American society seem to learn an ethic of care. Their moral decision making, unlike that of adolescent males, is often focused on concern for others' well-being rather than concern for individual rights and freedoms (Gilligan, 1982a). Researchers have shown, for example, that adolescent girls are more likely than boys of the same age to participate in leisure to please other people such as girlfriends, boyfriends or parents (Shaw, Caldwell, & Kleiber, 1992). Thus, for women who have learned to put the needs of others before their own needs, autonomous, self-determined leisure can be an important source of empowerment that can lead to resisting restrictive gender roles and embracing new ways of thinking about self and relationships to others.

Leisure involvement and serious leisure are other concepts that may be related to autonomous, self-determined leisure. Leisure involvement refers to the emotional attachment or the psychological state of motivation, arousal, or interest that individuals may have for particular leisure activities (Havitz & Dimanche, 1990). The concept emerged from consumer behavior literature and the study of people's attachment to particular consumer products. The idea may be useful for understanding leisure as well. According to researchers, leisure involvement incorporates a number of dimensions or components including an importance-pleasure and a centrality dimension. For example, a woman who is highly involved in downhill skiing would be someone who not only enjoys skiing a lot but who values skiing as a centrally important part of her life. Highly involving leisure, according to these dimensions, is different psychologically from casual involvement in activities or participating for the sake of others.

The concept of serious leisure is an idea that has emerged out of the work of Stebbins (1982, 1992) who studied amateurs, hobbyists, and volunteers. Stebbins examined a variety of forms of serious leisure including amateur musicians, athletes, and liberal arts enthusiasts (1992, 1994). He found that when people are involved in "serious leisure," their involvement is central to their lives. They become committed to the activity as a "career" involving special skills, knowledge, and experience.

To date, few researchers have examined the influence of gender or gender relations on leisure involvement or serious leisure, but gender may prove to be a significant factor. When activities require a considerable commitment of time and/or money, such as the activities of amateur musicians, marathon runners, or mountain climbers, they are often male-dominated activities. Many women may feel they do not have the resources, either temporally or financially, to commit themselves to such activities. Instead, these women would seek less involving activities which "fit" better with their home and interpersonal responsibilities. When women do become highly involved in specific activities, however, they may be experiencing self-determined or autonomous leisure. High levels of involvement in such activities may be linked not only with individual empowerment but also with self-expression, self-efficacy, and self-esteem.

Women's Leisure Containers

As indicated earlier, the term *leisure container* refers to the activity, social settings, and physical locations within which leisure may be experienced. The discussion of leisure meanings has made reference to some of the activities that are associated with leisure for women, but social and physical locations for leisure have received less attention by researchers.

One way to explore leisure containers in women's lives is to look at the distribution of self-defined leisure across different daily activities and settings. A Canadian time budget study gathered data on the daily activities of 60 married women and their husbands over a 48-hour period (Shaw, 1985b; 1988b). The frequency with which different daily activities were defined by the participants as leisure experiences was examined and the "containers" for these experiences were analyzed. The data showed, as expected, that free-time activities were more likely to be experienced as leisure than obligatory activities such as paid work, housework, or childcare. Some free-time activities such as reading, social events, and media activities were particularly likely to be experienced as leisure. Among obligatory activities, personal care activities were more likely to be experienced as leisure compared to paid work or housework. The women in this study, including half employed in the labor force, recorded more household labor activities than any other category of activity. Household labor was the main at-home activity and was the least likely of all daily activities to be experienced as leisure.

Since the diaries also recorded the location and social settings for all daily activities, analysis of these container components was possible. Social setting seemed to have a clear effect on the definition of the situation as leisure. The highest leisure ratings were in settings where friends and family members were present or when a woman was alone with her spouse. Lower leisure ratings were found for settings in which the woman was alone, with work colleagues, or with children. Of course, these ratings were not due entirely to the social setting, but also reflect the fact that time with colleagues is usually work time, and that time alone and time with children is very often time devoted to household labor activities for married women (Shaw, 1985b, 1988b).

These data do serve to illustrate, however, that although family may be an important source of leisure gratification and satisfaction for many women with children, most of the time they spend with their children is actually experienced as work rather than leisure (Shaw, 1992a). Analysis of the physical location for leisure showed that place of employment had the lowest leisure ratings followed by home location. Activities away from both home and place of work were the most likely to be experienced as leisure.

This conclusion reflects the debate in the literature about the home as the center of leisure for women. Gregory (1982) has argued that women who work in the home (i.e., both paid work and housework) have a distinct advantage because of the potential for the integration of work and play. More recently, work sociologists have suggested that modern technology and the availability of home computers and Internet facilities will allow women and men the luxury of working at home. Other researchers have argued, however, that the home does not represent a place of relaxation and leisure for women, as it does more often for men, but rather that women experience home as a place for work and never-ending household chores (Lenskyj, 1988). Deem (1986), for example, concluded that many British women have difficulty finding leisure "spaces" (i.e., both temporal and physical opportunities for leisure) while in their own homes. When women are at home, they typically seem to find chores to do such as cleaning, tidying, or organizing.

The idea of leisure containers not only helps in understanding the factors that influence leisure meanings and leisure experiences but also serves to show how gaps in leisure exist, and how they are unevenly distributed between men and women, and among women. Some women have more opportunities for activities outside the home, and some women have more access to leisure spaces within their own homes. Factors such as age, marital and family situation, class, and race may combine to determine opportunities for leisure, including whether leisure is affiliative or self-determined.

Leisure Meanings and Life Situations

Focusing on the meanings of leisure for women as a group and on the leisure containers for women can help illuminate the differences that exist among women. Although commonalties such as societally-based gender role expectations, ideologies about the family, and notions of femininity exist among most women, women's leisure containers and contexts vary considerably according to their life situations.

Women's opportunities for leisure as well as other resources such as income and education are structured by societal relations of class, race, and ethnicity. Health status and the presence of disabilities also impact on leisure because of the energy required just to get through the day (Henderson, Bedini, Hecht, & Shuler, 1995). Thus, life situations determine the everyday settings available for leisure and the degree to which women have control over such settings. For example, many upper and upper middle-class women can hire other women to help with household chores and childcare responsibilities. Their access to income allows them to select times and settings for activities at home and with their families which are conducive to leisure experiences. Women without such resources, however, may find themselves in settings less conducive to leisure and with little control over daily life events.

Another major factor affecting women's leisure is whether or not they are employed in the labor market. Although employment increases the number of work roles and obligatory activities, it may also lead to more leisure opportunities and options. Employed women often seem more able to compartmentalize their work and free time and thus, to set time aside for their own leisure (Deem, 1986). That is, they think of themselves as "working women," feel that many household chores are "work," and make sure that they have leisure activities at home as well as household work activities. On the other hand, as Hochschild (1989) found, women working for pay who are also in heterosexual family situations may be faced with a "double shift" regarding work. Accordingly, employment for women represents a trade-off between a greater sense of entitlement to opportunities for leisure and less time to enjoy such leisure (Shaw, 1988b). This conflict between entitlement and time may be why some women opt for part-time work if their economic condition makes this situation feasible (Harrington & Dawson, 1995).

Apart from employment status, type of occupation may affect the availability and meaning of leisure for women. A study by Allison and Duncan (1987) compared the leisure experiences of professional and blue-collar women. The study focused on women's "flow" experience (Csikszentmihalyi,

1975), and on "anti-flow" (e.g., boredom, frustration, anxiety). Professional women were found to experience flow both in work (i.e., employment) settings and in nonwork spheres. Clearly the professional women were benefiting not only from greater economic reward and financial independence, but also from the quality of work life where flow and presumably leisure experiences were a possibility. For both groups of women, flow in nonwork experiences revolved around free-time activities, especially in the interpersonal domain of the family. Moreover, anti-flow in nonwork settings was typically associated with doing household chores (Allison & Duncan, 1987).

Age, marital status, living arrangement, and the number and ages of dependent children may affect women's everyday lives and the meanings of leisure. Each life course transition affects not only the distribution and allocation of time, but also the type and quality of that time as you will see in chapter six. Of all the life course transitions affecting women, having the first child probably has the most dramatic effect on leisure. These effects include the availability of leisure in general and the type of situations where leisure is possible. We are not saying that motherhood is all work and no leisure, but leisure opportunities, meanings, and values are usually different after becoming a parent.

Leisure Enablers

Another way to think about the diverse life situations of women is to conceptualize them as potential leisure enablers. A leisure enabler is the opposite of a constraint and functions to allow and facilitate leisure experiences. Thinking back to the section in this chapter on leisure meanings, we could argue that leisure enablers are likely to function in different ways. First, they might provide opportunities for relaxation; second, they might provide opportunities for leisure affiliation; and third, they might facilitate self-determined or autonomous leisure. For relaxing leisure to occur, women need to be able to take a break from their ongoing work and family responsibilities.

For women with children, the need for leisure as relaxation is particularly crucial and often particularly difficult to attain. In two-parent families a break for leisure can be accomplished if childcare and housework are shared. Single mothers, however, often have great difficulty finding time and space for relaxation (Streather, 1989). Single parent mothers often have financial hardships as well as full-time responsibilities for children; finding time alone becomes all the more difficult. Both full-time, stay-at-home mothers/homemakers and married employed mothers need time for relaxation away from their responsibilities. Employed mothers in dual career marriages, however, are more likely to have the financial resources and independence to arrange help with childcare and/or household chores.

On the other hand, many women who have children or are in secure relationships have an advantage over most single women in terms of access to leisure as affiliation. The situation may be particularly difficult for women who are widowed or divorced, since during their marriage they may have relied on their partner for companionship during leisure. For married women with children, the immediate family (i.e., husband/partner and children) provides the easiest and most accessible group for positive relational leisure.

Moreover, family activities are often structured around particular religious, family, or national celebrations (e.g., Christmas, birthdays, Passover, Independence Day celebrations), making affiliative leisure at least a possibility at these times. Although these occasions are not without drawbacks (e.g., the work women put into making the occasions positive experiences for everyone), these situations can also provide women with satisfying and meaningful leisure experiences.

For single women, a more concerted effort is sometimes necessary to arrange situations for affiliative leisure. Making such arrangements is easier for some single women than others, depending on such factors as their work situation (e.g., whether they have friends at work), their community situation (e.g., whether community integration and interaction occurs), and their connection to the local community.

Factors that enable women to enjoy autonomous and self-determined leisure are somewhat more difficult to determine. Little research has been done on this question. A few indicators of leisure enablers, however, are available. One of the foundations for a leisure enabler is the issue of entitlement to leisure (Henderson & Bialeschki, 1991a). Entitlement can be defined as the individual's belief that she has a right to leisure for herself and should take advantage of leisure opportunities. Women who have learned to always put others' leisure needs first, such as the needs of their husband and children, may not feel that they are entitled to, or deserve, leisure for themselves. Thus, a sense of entitlement is a leisure enabler for women.

Some research has shown that education, employment and the financial independence that comes with employment may be enablers that lead to a greater sense of entitlement, and thus greater access to self-determined leisure (Harrington & Dawson, 1995). In a comparison of employed and nonemployed married women, for example, Shaw (1988b) found that employed women had more positive leisure experiences and more opportunities for leisure for themselves, even though they were more time constrained than women doing full-time, unpaid work in the home. Education and paid employment also can provide women with confidence to pursue their own interests. Education and paid work connote a feeling of worthiness for leisure. The enduring work ethic in Western societies pointed out in chapter two still influences many people to think that leisure is a "reward" for hard work. Thus, women who are homemakers sometimes feel less worthy of leisure themselves because, although they work as hard as people in paid employment, their work in the home is often less visible in and devalued by society.

This brief discussion indicates that different types of leisure enablers work for different categories of leisure. Moreover, varied life situations and backgrounds affect the availability of leisure and women's opportunities for "true" leisure experiences in different ways.

Benefits of Leisure for Women

The benefits of leisure for women and men sometimes go unnoticed. Society tends to devalue leisure and think of it as a "frill," a reward for hard work, or even a waste of time. Therefore, people sometimes pay little attention to the need for leisure and the many benefits derived from involvement. Nevertheless, leisure activities can have important and positive effects on women's lives in a number of different ways including health, relational, personal, and societal benefits.

Health Benefits

The physical benefits of participation in leisure are fairly obvious. Physically active recreation helps prevent cardiovascular disease (Froelicher & Froelicher, 1991) as well as many other physical health problems such as certain forms of cancer, and respiratory and circulatory disorders (Paffenbarger, Hyde, & Dow, 1991). Physical activity helps maintain physical strength and flexibility, particularly for older women, who want to keep active and independent longer.

Leisure involvement, including both active and passive forms of leisure, also contributes to mental and emotional health. This benefit is important for women because they tend to have higher reported rates of mental health disorders compared to men. Some research has shown that physical activity participation reduces stress and stress-related problems (Ulrich, Dimberg, & Driver, 1991). Leisure research also has demonstrated the benefits of other forms of recreation. For example, higher levels of participation in a range of leisure activities are thought to be associated with stress reduction and general health and well-being (Caldwell & Smith, 1988; Coleman & Iso-Ahola, 1993). Why the relationship between leisure and well-being exists is not entirely clear. The social component of leisure and the perceptions of freedom, control, intrinsic motivation, and self-determination through leisure may carry over into other aspects of life and result in overall well-being (Coleman & Iso-Ahola, 1993).

Relational Benefits

The relational benefits of leisure have typically been discussed in terms of marriage and the family. A consistent finding in the research literature is that wives and husbands who spend time together in joint leisure activities are more satisfied with their marriages than couples who do not (Orthner & Mancini, 1991). On the other hand, the high levels of participation in independent, individual activities is negatively associated with marital satisfaction. This negative assessment of individual activities seems to be particularly true for women who tend to place higher value than men do on leisure as a means of communication, connectedness, and bonding among family members (Orthner & Mancini, 1991). The crucial variable, however, may be quality of interaction that occurs during leisure, not the amount of time itself.

The research on leisure benefits for the family has been done primarily in the United States but with significant contributions from England, Australia, and other countries. For example, one study of Korean wives found that the relationship between leisure and marital satisfaction was evident among younger, better educated women but was not as strong for other Korean wives (Ahn, cited in Orthner & Mancini, 1991). Similarly, a study carried out in China found that the family was not the preferred context for leisure in that culture, but rather that leisure was pursued alone or with friends (Freysinger & Chen, 1993). Thus the role of leisure in marriage relationships may vary in different cultures, perhaps particularly between western and eastern cultures.

The benefits of joint leisure in an intimate relationship may not mean that the ideal partnership is one in which all leisure activities are shared. Research by Bialeschki, Pearce, and Elliot (1994) indicated how lesbian mothers value family leisure, time with each other, and time with their children. They also recognized the need for women to have some independence in their leisure and some time for themselves as well. The challenge may be for women and men to find the ideal balance in their own lives and relationships regarding shared leisure with its affiliative benefits and independent, autonomous leisure that has other positive outcomes.

The interaction benefits of leisure, of course, are not limited to marriage, family, or intimate relationships. During adolescence leisure activities are primarily social in nature and leisure settings provide the main context in which friendships are built and maintained (Kleiber, Caldwell, & Shaw, 1993). The social benefits of leisure are also true at other stages of the life span, and leisure interactions may be particularly important in helping individuals deal with major life transitions such as starting a new school or job, moving to a new geographic location, and/or dealing with a relationship breakdown, a divorce, or the death of a spouse (Kelly, 1983b). Leisure participation can also provide benefits for community integration (Allen, 1991). Further, the importance of community participation in diverse, geographically mobile and sometimes socially isolating modern culture, is being increasingly recognized (Pedlar, 1995).

Personal Benefits

Although physical and relational benefits of leisure are important for women, personal benefits may deserve even greater emphasis. In a society where women's work, both paid and unpaid, is often devalued (i.e., the low status sometimes experienced by homemakers and the low pay of women in "pink collar" occupations), leisure can provide women with rewards not available to them in other aspects of their lives. Leisure activities can provide girls and women with a sense of personal identity (Haggard & Williams, 1991); that is, an individual can gain self-confidence and self-esteem by identifying herself as a basketball player, an outdoor adventurer, an artist, a baseball fan, a gourmet cook, or a jazz enthusiast.

The notion of individual benefits implies that individuals can grow and develop in positive ways and make beneficial changes in their lives. Since leisure activities are characterized by freedom of choice, changes can probably be accomplished most easily in this sphere of life compared to other spheres such as work or family. Despite the fact that women face constraints in their access to leisure as you will see in chapter seven, taking up a new leisure activity can provide most women with tremendous satisfaction and enjoyment and, perhaps most importantly, a sense of control over at least that one aspect of their lives. Through autonomous and self-determined leisure, whether that means learning to windsurf, mastering the Internet, or deciding "it's OK" to take time out from other responsibilities to read a novel, women can experience a feeling of independence, autonomy, and empowerment (Freysinger & Flannery, 1992).

Societal Benefits

Another benefit of leisure that can be seen as both a personal and societal benefit is the role that leisure can play in changing gender roles and improving the status of women in society in general. Leisure participation can affect the ways in which gender roles are societally constructed in a number of different ways. First, individual women sometimes use leisure activities to resist or challenge traditional roles. When a woman takes up a "nontraditional" activity (e.g., playing rugby, playing a tuba) and presents herself as strong, independent, or athletic, her actions challenge the traditional view of femininity whether she deliberately seeks to make such a challenge or not. Wearing's (1992) study of identity in late adolescence, for example, described ways in which young women resisted gendered stereotypes through participation in athletic activities.

A second way that individuals challenge traditional gender constructions is by asserting their right to leisure and claiming time for themselves. For example, mothers of young children may seek independent and autonomous leisure (Wearing, 1990; Samuel, 1992). By taking personal time, they are, de facto, challenging the idea of motherhood as total devotion to family, even if they do not verbalize their actions in this way.

A third way in which societal change can be accomplished through leisure behavior is when leisure leads to personal empowerment and that sense of empowerment spills over into other aspects of women's lives. That is, self-determination in leisure can encourage women to challenge forms of inequity or discrimination that they might face at work or at school.

This discussion indicates that leisure can provide a range of different benefits. Typically researchers have focused on the individual or family interaction benefits of leisure, and on ways in which leisure can improve the quality of individuals' lives. Community and societal benefits are also important but sometimes overlooked. In fact, the ways in which personal benefits can spill over and become social benefits serves to reinforce the well-know feminist slogan that "the personal is political."

Concluding Perspectives

This chapter has suggested that thinking of leisure as a positive experience is the best way to understand the meanings of leisure in women's lives. Exactly what that leisure experience is, and what it means to different women are difficult to define. Freedom of choice and freedom from constraint are important components of leisure; the lack of freedom and choice that some women face in their everyday lives means that the leisure experience often is difficult for them to attain. Other important aspects of the leisure experience include affiliation and social connectedness with others, opportunities for independent and autonomous action, and time for self away from family and other responsibilities. Women's leisure does not exist in a social vacuum, but the social and physical contexts for leisure can be seen as leisure containers. These contexts vary for different women and show how life situations, including such factors as age, race, class, sexual orientation, physical ability, marital, maternal, and occupational status, affect leisure experiences. Although some life situations facilitate containers for relaxing leisure, other situations facilitate affiliative leisure or self-determined leisure. Understanding the meanings and experiences of leisure leads to a better understanding of the range of benefits that women can derive from leisure participation. These benefits include not only health, relational, and personal benefits, but the potential to facilitate positive social change through leisure.

Discussion Questions

1. How important is leisure for most women?

2. What are the benefits that women can gain from leisure experiences and leisure participation?

3. Are the outcomes of leisure always beneficial? If not, is it leisure?

4. Develop a definition of leisure for yourself and describe the elements that make up a leisure experience for you.

5. How might gender expectations and responsibilities influence the meanings of leisure?

6. For 24 hours keep an activity time budget. Every half hour list the activity, the degree of choice and enjoyment you felt during the activity, and whether you thought the activity was leisure for you.

7. How does leisure entitlement relate to leisure experiences?

8. What life situations influence your leisure experiences (e.g., being a student, having little money, being away from your family)?

9. How will your definition of leisure change as you get older and your life situation changes?

10. How might the meanings of leisure differ for people from different ethnic or cultural backgrounds?

Chapter Five

The "Gender Journey:"
Child and Adolescent Development

*Without a strong sense of self, girls will enter adulthood at a
deficit....To raise healthier girls, we must look carefully at
what we tell them, often unconsciously, often subtly, about
their worth relative to boys'. We must look at what girls value
about themselves—'the areas of importance' by which they
measure their self-esteem—as well as the potential sources of
strength and competence that, too often, they learn to devalue.
It's time for the gender journey.*

—Orenstein, 1994, p. xxviii-xxix

To talk about girls' and women's leisure in relationship to age includes
discussion about the dialectic of self and social structure—the micro and macro.
Just as leisure is defined and experienced, and continually redefined and
experienced anew, so is development (i.e., the process of age-related change)
as the individual interacts with her culture, society, and historical moment.
What is known about the relationship between age and leisure or how and why
age is important to understanding girls' and women's leisure, therefore, varies
according to what age is believed to signify or mean, and subsequently, how
it has been understood.

In this chapter and the next, we present what is known about leisure in
childhood, adolescence, and young, middle, and later adulthood. Continuity
and change in leisure with age is also discussed although no consensus exists
about this topic. Even though much leisure research has focused on the
influence of maturation (i.e., biological and psychological changes experienced by the individual), other research has emphasized socialization and the
importance to leisure of sociocultural forces, institutions, relationships and
roles which individuals encounter across the life span.

Recently, traditional psychological, social psychological, and sociological explanations of both leisure and aging have been questioned (e.g., Freysinger, 1990; Maddox, 1987; Thompson, 1994) because of the gaps in understanding that are being uncovered. Although empirical research has yet to fully incorporate these challenges and criticisms and we do not have perfect answers about how girls and boys mature into and through adulthood, suggestions are made for how critical perspectives might inform future research and thinking about the relationships among leisure, age, and gender.

Perspectives on Age and Development

Chronological age is important to understanding girls' and women's leisure for a number of reasons. First, age is often believed to be indicative of physical, cognitive, emotional, or social aptitudes, skills, and capabilities of the individual. For example, because a child is eight years of age, we assume she will be able to walk, run, skip and jump. Further, certain interests and motivations are attributed to age. Not only do we expect an eight-year-old girl to be physically capable of walking, running, skipping, and jumping, in North America we might also expect that she will be interested in a game like hopscotch or Double Dutch that requires such skills because children at that age "have a lot of energy" and "like to be active." In contrast, in North America we might not expect an 80-year-old woman to participate in Double Dutch because we believe that at age 80, she will not only lack the motor control, strength, and agility such activity requires but also the motivation or interest. Why motivation or interest is lacking may be attributed to the simplicity of the task, to the social acceptability of such activity, or to lack of knowledge about the game. In other words, age has personal, social, cultural, and historical meanings.

Further, age-related meanings often are gendered. To take the previous example, while in North America we might expect an eight-year-old child to have the physical, cognitive, and social skills required for hopscotch and Double Dutch, we are unlikely to expect that an eight-year-old boy would be interested in such physical activity. In fact, in North America an eight-year-old boy likely would be teased by friends and discouraged by parents and teachers from participating in hopscotch even though it may be a "developmentally appropriate" activity. In other words, when talking about age and development, separating them from other dimensions of individual identity (i.e., not only gender but race/ethnicity, social class, physical ability/disability, and sexual orientation) is impossible. Yet little effort has been made in leisure research to address the complexity of leisure, age, and gender.

In addition, the research on development across the life span (i.e., maturation and socialization) has been dominated by two opposing schools of thought: the organismic and the mechanistic. Thinking about the differences between these two perspectives simply, we can say that theories of development based in the organismic model focus on change as a process internal to the individual. Mechanistic theories, on the other hand, focus on individual change as a consequence of external forces. These two perspectives, however, are more complex than this basic difference.

Organismic and Biological Growth Models

The organismic perspective emerged from biological growth models of development and is represented by Loevinger's (1976) work on ego development and Kohlberg's (1976) work on moral development. Development, from the organismic perspective is age-related change that occurs in a sequence of stages or phases that are essentially predetermined in the genetic make-up or internal structure of the human being. An end point or optimal stage of development is thought to exist. Movement from one stage to the next is primarily dependent on internal readiness or maturation. Although interactions with the environment are acknowledged as an influence on individual change, the locus of change is believed to reside within the individual. In this sense, the individual is seen as "active" in her development.

Development is also believed to bring about qualitative change; that is, change involving "structural transformation" and elaboration. For example, stage theories of development, such as Kohlberg's (1976) theory of moral development, maintain that once the transition to a "higher" or more advanced stage of moral reasoning occurs, the individual cannot retreat or go back to a previous stage. Retreat is not possible because in reaching the new or more advanced level, the internal structure of reasoning or thinking has been transformed. In other words, change is progressive and hierarchical.

To understand the concept of structural transformation, think of how flowers grow. If you wanted to have flowers on your windowsill you would buy flower seeds, plant them, place them in a sunny spot, and water them. If you have a "green thumb" (a big "if!"), the seeds will eventually become shoots, stems, leaves, and flowers. All along the way, at each stage of growth, what was initially a flower seed, has a different structure. At no stage can the plant return to an earlier stage. The flowers cannot go back to being seeds. In fact, at some point growth will end or full maturation will be reached. According to stage theories, individuals develop personality, cognition, and moral reasoning in a similar fashion and at some stage full maturation is achieved.

Developmental theories emanating from the organismic model basically ignored adulthood. Research on older adults in the 1950s and 1960s, however, indicated that change does not end in adolescence. As a consequence, a life span perspective evolved in North American developmental psychology. The life span perspective emphasizes that development occurs from birth to death. Further, although people adhering to a life span perspective still focus on development as a process primarily internal to the individual, the sociocultural and historical contexts of individual lives are also seen as central to development (e.g., Haan, 1977).

Mechanistic and External Process Model

In contrast to the organismic model, the mechanistic perspective on development maintains that development is not an internal process and is not necessarily age-related. Rather, development depends upon stimuli from the external environment and could occur or not occur at various ages. The locus of change is external, the individual passive, and development occurs as the individual responds to external stimuli. If the correct stimulus (e.g., punishment or reward) is applied, the correct response will result in change or development. For example, a child will be able to throw a ball when she is given the appropriate training or stimulus. The work of Skinner (1971) is representative of this school of thought.

As suggested, developmental change from the mechanistic perspective is quantitative or additive and involves no transformation of the "inner structure" of the individual. In addition, development has no end point. In other words, from the mechanistic perspective it is possible to "regress" to an earlier or lower level of functioning (e.g., not being able to throw a ball). At the same time, functioning or performance can be improved if appropriate stimuli are applied.

Another way to think about the tenets of the mechanistic perspective is to think about building blocks. Blocks can be combined with other blocks to make new forms. Even after being put together into a new form (e.g., a tower), however, each block is still essentially a block. The blocks can be broken back down into single blocks. In this sense, no structural transformation occurs. The blocks have not lost their essential quality or structure. At the same time, blocks can continually be added to the tower, with no limit to the new form's shape or size.

Although not sharing the same disciplinary base, traces of the mechanistic perspective can be seen in socialization theories and the life course perspective on development which emphasize the social environment and the influence of societal roles and institutions. Similar to developmental psychologists, North American sociologists in the mid-twentieth century also felt existing theories of individual change to be inadequate. Traditional socialization theory suggests that humans learn and change up through adolescence, at which point they are either prepared to enter adulthood or not. After adolescence, according to the theory, they continue on the same path through adulthood with no additional substantial learning or change occurring.

The increasing proportion of older adults in North American societies in the mid-1900s and the availability of longitudinal studies have indicated the traditional theory of socialization often is inadequate. Thus, a life course perspective that acknowledges lifelong change and the interaction of the individual and her social and historical contexts has emerged (Riley, Johnson, & Foner, 1972).

Recognizing the Limitations

Most of the existing research on leisure, age, gender, and development has emanated from organismic and mechanistic conceptual and theoretical contexts. Hence, leisure research focused on age and development shares both the strengths and the limitations of developmental perspectives. The organismic and mechanistic models provide insight into the nature and importance of internal and external factors to development. The life span and life course perspectives require us to recognize the interaction of internal and external factors, as well as the centrality of time (e.g., chronological age, history) in understanding human practices.

A problem with the research informed by the life span or life course perspective is that it has barely begun to address how the processes and experiences of aging or development may be viewed for girls and women from different or similar life situations or backgrounds. First, developmental and socialization theory and life span and life course perspectives generally have not originated from research on diverse peoples. Research that focuses on the development and leisure of women of color, single or never married women, socioeconomic disadvantaged women, or single mothers is still rare in North America.

Second, whether or not study participants are diverse, the majority of life span, life course, and associated leisure research is not situate in the gendered, racialized, classified reality of individuals' lives. Hence, how relationships of power and privilege shape individuals' experiences of age, development, and leisure have not been addressed. In addition, developmental and leisure researchers have not examined the meanings individuals make of their development and leisure practices.

Finally, the historical embeddedness of theories of development is problematic and has led some to question whether patterns of age-related change can even be identified (Riegel, 1976). Regardless of whether or not existing theory or knowledge is representative of the diversity of human lives, the reality is that such theory and knowledge set the standards or norms to which all children, youth, and adults are compared and evaluated. Hence what we "know" about leisure and girls' and women's development must be read with the limitations of existing research in mind. Further, the need to learn from previously unacknowledged diverse voices through research is blatantly clear.

Childhood and Adolescence: Play, Recreation, and Leisure

According to Kleiber and Kelly (1980), leisure both influences and is influenced by development. From the perspective of developmental psychology, a child's physical maturation, intellectual or cognitive abilities, and stage of moral reasoning influences the play in which she or he engages because of the skills that the play requires. For example, spontaneous play and the informal games of children require what Finnan (1982) calls "cultural knowledge" or knowledge of the norms, values, and beliefs of the culture.

Play with others, whether as spontaneous, informal, or formal games, also requires a certain level of cognitive and social development (Piaget, 1954). For example, a child cannot play interactively with other children unless she has a rudimentary sense that she exists as an entity separate from others. Further, a girl will have a difficult time participating in formal or rule-bound games, such as sports, unless she has an understanding of the necessity of rules and the need for reciprocity. Without these understandings on the part of those involved, the game cannot be played.

At the same time, children's play has also been found to influence their development. For example, research on the relationship between participation in organized sport and moral reasoning suggests that sport may serve to keep adolescents at what Kohlberg (1976) termed, the preconventional and conventional stages of moral reasoning (Loy & Ingham, 1973; Weiss & Bredemeier, 1990). To put it simply, at the preconventional stage of moral reasoning individuals comply or obey to avoid punishment or gain rewards; at the conventional stage, they comply or obey to emulate or gain the respect of important others. At these stages, the welfare of others and society as a whole is not of concern to the individual. Rather, personal well-being is paramount and seen as separate from or in opposition to the well-being of others. This assertion is supported by the research of Duret (1994) in France who found that eight- to twelve-year-olds involved in club sports perceived sport as opposition, not cooperation, and that this perception increased with age. In other words, the perception that sport requires cooperation and the well-being of others for the competition that is central for sport to exist was not recognized by children.

A relationship exists between play and the development of girls and boys. Coakley (1980) suggested that although spontaneous play and informal games "contribute to the development of an ability to create, organize, and change," children's involvement in adult organized sport contributes to "the development of obedience, conformity to authority, and an ability to meet expectations in highly structured settings" (p. 444). Holmes (1994) found four essential elements in the play of three- and nine-year-old children: authentic engagement, emotion, contextual influences, and possibility. The play of three-year-olds was characterized by emotion, authentic engagement, and a possibility for action and thought. The play of the nine-year-olds, on the other hand, was shaped more by contextual influences (e.g., perceptions of others, other children's and adults' notions of appropriate behavior).

Other individuals, and parents in particular, have a strong influence on children's play and recreation both directly through the provision of resources and opportunities (Howard & Madrigal, 1990), and indirectly through the role models provided and the socialization of attitudes and motivations (Barnett & Chick, 1986; Robertson, 1994). At the same time, children are not passive receptacles for others' attributions and expectations. Research has shown that children also influence parental leisure practices and satisfactions. For example, Unkel (1981) reported that adults who were parents of school-age children had higher levels of physical activity participation than nonparents because of children's involvement in physical activity. Wearing & McArthur (1988), in a study of married couples with young children, found that mothers' and fathers' leisure satisfaction was adversely affected by the demands and obligations of parenting, though fathers reported significantly greater negative reactions than mothers.

Social processes, structures, and institutions and cultural norms, values, and beliefs that exist at a given time in history also shape the relationships among age, development, and leisure. The contexts of girls' lives shape the meanings and expectations attached to and the opportunities and support provided for their development, play, recreation, and leisure. Development and leisure are not processes or experiences that solely reside within the individual but are constructed by individuals in relationship to others (i.e., in terms such as gender, race/ethnicity, age, social class, and sexual orientation).

For example, as discussed in chapter two, at one time girls and women were excluded from sport and physical activity because such activities were seen as antithetical to being female and feminine. Notions of gender and opportunities for sport and physical activity evolved gradually as women and men gained a different sense of themselves through the interaction of economic, social, and political changes across time. Because the majority of psychological, social psychological, and sociological research on leisure across the course of life does not situate itself socioculturally, historically, or politically, it must be interpreted with these contexts in mind.

The Play and Recreation of Girls in Childhood

According to Erikson (1950), as children develop from infancy through early and middle childhood, three levels or stages of play exist: the *autocosmic*, the *microcosmic*, and the *macrocosmic*. Autocosmic play consists of self and self-and-significant-other play. Examples of autocosmic play include the infant's fascination with her waving hands and feet and her consternation and joy over peek-a-boo with mom or dad. Erikson maintained that this type of play helps the young child gain a sense of herself, trust, and security in the persistence or continuity of self.

With the development of rudimentary motor skills, children move into microcosmic or "small world" play. Play with toys and dolls often serves as a surrogate for human companionship (e.g., Linus's blanket) and provides children with initial role rehearsal vehicles.

As a child's social world widens and motor skills increase, she moves into "large world" or macrocosmic play. At this stage the child is aware of separate others, has the ability to communicate with others verbally, and has acquired some mastery of the "tool world" (e.g., scissors, crayons, a computer mouse). Erikson identified three purposes of macrocosmic play: anticipatory socialization, fantastic socialization, and practice in impression management. Anticipatory socialization means practicing and learning the skills and attitudes required to perform future adult roles (e.g., that of doctor, teacher, mother). Fantastic socialization is playing with roles we are unlikely to ever perform (e.g., Catwoman, a princess). According to Erikson (1950), play involving fantastic socialization (or make-believe) helps keep alive the myths and legends of a culture. Finally, in play children also learn the rudimentary skills of impression management or how to present oneself in a desired way.

The role of these types of play in the development of gender identity in childhood has received research attention. Studies have shown that girls' play is likely to occur in small groups or dyads, is more cooperative than competitive, tends not to be rule-bound but is orderly, and is likely not to involve aggressive physical contact or domination but is focused on caregiving and nurturing.

According to Lever (1976) and others (e.g., Metheny, 1970; Sage, 1990; Shapiro, 1990) such play reinforces traditional views of femininity and masculinity in western cultures. Lever further contended that the play of girls puts them at a disadvantage later in life as they are not prepared for economic (i.e., paid work) roles that are valued and necessary for survival in capitalistic societies. In other words, the play of girls often reproduces their lack of power relative to that given to boys. On the other hand, the play of girls may be seen as promoting the resolution of conflict through talking and negotiation, emotional expression, and sharing and intimacy rather than violence (Miedzian, 1991).

These findings on gender differences in play may be related to research on the moral development of children; girls tend to stay with moral dilemmas or conflicts with friends until they are resolved while boys are more likely to walk away from such conflicts (Bardige, Ward, Gilligan, Taylor, & Cohen, 1988). The relational, cooperative play that is encouraged for girls may also be related to what Belenky and her colleagues (Belenky, Clinchy, Goldberger, & Tarule, 1986) have called "connected knowing," a type of intellectual reasoning that incorporates the perspectives of other people.

Based on her studies of children's free and spontaneous play on playgrounds, Finnan (1982) concluded that white girls are less satisfied with their play and their sex roles than are white boys. According to Finnan, girls are limited to "immature" games or games that do not have "meaning beyond the moment." In general, the types of play encouraged for girls cannot be parlayed into adult roles that are valued in the United States. For example, hopscotch and jump rope do not develop skills that are useful in roles later in life. On the other hand, the types of play in which boys are encouraged to participate (e.g., sport) allow them to develop and practice skills that can be carried into later life (e.g., ability for lifetime sports and fitness; competition; subjugation to authority) and meaningful roles in youth and adulthood (i.e., the athlete).

The findings of an interpretive study on the meaning of "fun" to Caucasian-American children aged 8 to 10 years involved in organized youth sport supported this notion of play reinforcing gendered adult roles (Harris, 1994). Harris found that boys connected their current sport involvement and their fun in it with a future (e.g., becoming an athlete) and with existing adult role models (i.e., professional athletes). Girls on the other hand, even though their current sport participation was important to them, were unlikely to talk about a connection between their play and the future or to talk about role models in sport. This research is consistent with research that has indicated that children are not naive about or unaware of who has power and status (Loy

& Ingham, 1973). They know whose play has status on the playground, and in the larger world, by adult reactions and role models seen, or not seen, in the media. "Girls' play" obviously does not have status.

In observations of playground practices, Finnan (1982) found that the play of girls was restricted physically and spatially, unless girls could get boys involved. When girls could get boys involved in their play, it lost the order of "girls' play;" freedom to act with physical aggressiveness was gained. With such freedom comes increased expression of all aspects of self (viz., physical, emotional, and social) and increased challenge and excitement. Although we might presume that playground practices have changed since the late 1970s, more recent research suggests that girls continue to be restricted in the use of their bodies and expression of physical self. For example, Shapiro (1990) and Wearing (1994) have discussed gendered play and the limits put on girls' and women's expression of excitement in leisure.

African-American girls may not be as dissatisfied with and may value their play more than European-American girls (Finnan, 1982). Further, several recent studies have indicated that African-American girls do not show the same decline in self-esteem and self-confidence between childhood and adolescence that European-American girls do (American Association of University Women, 1991; Orenstein, 1994; Winkler, 1990). Ward (1990) suggested that African-American parents are likely to emphasize racial pride in the upbringing of their daughters because of the realities of racism and sexism in the United States. Ward's research, however, was based on interviews with a group of relatively privileged African-American girls (i.e., they were students in a private all-girl boarding school). Further, studies of self-concept typically have not examined self-concept as a multidimensional construct. Whether racial differences in girls' experiences of play exist and if and why the play of girls of different races is related to various aspects of their development and well-being are topics in need of further study.

Researchers have found that being physically playful or active has positive developmental consequences for girls even though girls may be restricted in the physical boisterousness and aggressiveness of their play. Barnett and Kleiber (1982) studied playfulness, intelligence, and creativity in Caucasian children aged three to six years and found that physically active girls measured higher on creativity (i.e., divergent thinking) than physically passive girls. This relationship held true even after controlling for IQ. For boys, the relationship between physical playfulness and creativity disappeared when IQ was controlled, thus suggesting that this type of play was more important and had more far reaching consequences for girls than for boys.

Other researchers have also found a positive correlation between girls' sport and physical activity involvement and their ego strength, internal locus of control, and self-confidence. Kleiber and Kane (1984) hypothesized that acting with physical aggressiveness or competitiveness holds developmental potential for girls because such practices require girls to create their own stages on which to play. Recent studies have supported their expectations. For example, a positive relationship between involvement in informal leisure activities and identity development in both girls and boys was reported by Shaw and Smale (1994) and Shaw, Kleiber, and Caldwell (1995). For boys, on the other hand, involvement in physical activity holds no special developmental outcome because in so acting, boys are just doing what is expected of them (i.e., playing on the stages created for them by society).

In other words, when children step outside of the expected (e.g., gender) norms, the developmental potential or opportunity for personal growth is greatest. As Kleiber and Kane (1984) acknowledged, however, to step outside social expectations is not without punishments and may require a strong sense of self, at least initially. Yet their suggestion is consistent with recent work on leisure as a site of resistance to prevailing notions of gender and feelings of empowerment that accrue from such resistance (Freysinger & Flannery, 1992; Wearing, 1990). This potential for resistance also appears to be salient for girls and offers developmental potential.

In sum, the research on the play and recreation of girls suggests gendered practices. Girls' are encouraged, discouraged, and sometimes prevented from participating in different realms of play and games because of their sex. These practices have consequences for girls' sense of self—their sense of their abilities, their aspirations, and their attitudes. At the same time, play may be a context within which girls reshape others' expectations and the opportunities provided for them.

The Recreation and Leisure of Adolescent Girls

Adolescence is relatively recent social construction in North America. Adolescence is not an inevitable and universal biological and psychological stage of life. Coleman (1961) contended that the notion of adolescence as a distinct stage of life is a twentieth-century creation and became widespread in the 1950s. Pervasive ideologies as represented in the popular media, tend to characterize the adolescent years as ones of conflict, turmoil, and unrest subversive to the order and stability of society (Davis, 1990). Certainly images of youth as troubled (viz., by drugs, violence, gangs, and unwanted pregnancy) permeate the popular media as we approach the twenty-first century. In the United States, low-income youth and/or youth of color tend to dominate such images, but affluent and/or suburban youth are not immune from such portrayals (e.g., Gaines, 1990).

Nevertheless, research suggests that youth are instrumental in maintaining the basic values and institutions in society. According to Coleman (1961) negative depictions of adolescents may serve to justify adult power and control over youth (Hendry, Shucksmith, Love, & Glendinning, 1993) and are related to what is commonly seen as the developmental task of adolescence: to establish a sense of autonomy and independence from adult authority including parents, teachers, or other adults.

Identity Development, Recreation and Leisure

The recreation and leisure interests and motivations of adolescent girls are influenced by the developmental tasks and changes they are experiencing. According to Erikson (1968), identity formation, defined as a psychosocial process of individuation and identification, is the primary task of adolescence. Individuation means gaining a sense of self separate from others. Individuation is accomplished through asserting oneself and becoming autonomous or independent in action, thinking, and feeling. Adolescents need not only become autonomous; they also need to identify with or relate to future roles and possibilities whether through adult role models encountered in "real life" or media images.

In western culture, however, the dominant image of the "perfect girl" (viz., cooperative, quiet, not bossy, putting others first, dependent) runs counter to the individuation component of identity formation. Adolescent girls often are faced with reconciling contradictory messages. For example, they are told to be independent and assertive but also dependent and to put others first (Winkler, 1990). In fact, the research of Gilligan and her colleagues (Gilligan, Lyons, & Hanmer, 1990) indicated that for some girls, adolescence means "losing voice" or "going underground" because of the contradictory messages received.

Adults, as well as adolescents themselves, contribute to the creation of contradictory expectations. For example, the research of Stanworth (1981) and others (American Association of University Women, 1991; Orenstein, 1994) has revealed that youths' experience of schooling varies considerably by sex. Specifically, boys receive more attention from teachers than girls in classrooms, teachers are less likely to know girls' names than boys' names, and teachers have lower expectations of girls than boys. Further, boys are allowed by teachers and their peers to dominate classroom discussions.

Stanworth (1981) found that girls were caught in a double bind: girls who were assertive and spoke up in class were unpopular with other girls, while girls who were silent (i.e., the "invisible ones") in class were disliked by the boys. These mixed messages undermine girls' self-confidence and positive sense of self and they are likely to have implications for girls' participation in recreation and leisure.

Research on the process of identity development among African-American adolescent girls, however, reveals a somewhat different picture. Based on her interpretive study with girls attending a private school in the northeastern United States, Ward (1990) concluded that identity development for African-American teens involves not only the development of a personal identity, but also the development of a racial identity which is central to personal identity. The process of racial identity development involves a negation of the demeaning images of African Americans the teen encounters on a daily basis in a racist society without a negation of being African American. In Ward's terms, positive negotiation of identity development requires teens to say, "I am African American, but I am not what you think it means to be African American." Ward found that positive resolution of the identity crisis was facilitated by opportunities for interaction with and leadership roles among same-race peers and by parents providing interpretation of race-related incidents and the skills needed for surviving as a black woman in a racist and sexist society.

The gendered and racialized process of identity development may help explain the greater decline in self-esteem that has been found among European-American girls as opposed to boys and African-American girls as they enter the adolescent years. This decline among white girls, however, varies depending upon what aspect of self-esteem is measured. Neither pubertal development nor moving into a larger, more impersonal school environment has much of an impact on the self-esteem of girls or boys (Blyth, Simmons, & Carlton-Ford, 1983; Offer, Rostov, & Howard, 1984; Simmons, Blyth, Vancleave, & Bush, 1979). Adjustment to gender roles, however, seems to be the primary challenge to the self-concept of girls (Douvan, 1979).

According to Hendry, Shucksmith, Love, and Glendinning (1993) and others (e.g., Gilligan, Lyons, & Hanmer, 1990; Montemayor & Eisen, 1977), girls confront "two watersheds" in the adolescent years that challenge a positive sense of self: (a) during their transition into adolescence when they are confronted by the disadvantages of their gender and experience the resultant lack of confidence and confused sense of self and (b) in the school to work transition when they realize how limited their occupational prospects are compared to boys' and have to make difficult choices about career and personal life. If racial pride is emphasized among African-American girls (Bowman & Howard, 1985) and they are socialized by families to be assertive and self-confident as required to survive both racism and sexism (Ward, 1990), the difference in self-esteem that has been recently reported may be explained. Racial minority girls' negotiation of gender and race in the process of development has been rarely studied, however, so whether or not such an explanation is valid awaits examination and confirmation.

Recent research offers some interesting insights into the role of leisure in identity development during the adolescent years. Leisure, because of its relative freedom from role constraints and freedom for self-expression (Kleiber, Caldwell, & Shaw, 1993; Samdahl, 1988), is viewed by many researchers as a context in which adolescents may develop a positive self-concept and personal and social identities (Haggard & Williams, 1992; Hendry, Shucksmith, Love, & Glendinning, 1993; Iso-Ahola, 1980b; Kelly, 1990; Kleiber, 1980; Kleiber & Rickards, 1985; Samdahl & Kleiber, 1989; Shaw & Smale, 1994). The most that can be said about the validity of this hopeful contention is that the results of research have been mixed, particularly in relation to girls' participation in physical activity and organized sport. For example, Shaw and Smale (1994), found that level of participation in informal physical activities (e.g., jogging, bicycling, ice-skating) was positively associated with identity development, self-esteem, and body image for females only. Further, participation in team and individual sports were positively related to body image for girls only, but not significantly related to identity development or self-esteem for either girls or boys. Similarly, the study by Shaw, Kleiber, and Caldwell (1995) showed the developmental benefits of sports participation to be evident for girls but not for boys.

How British youth go about making decisions to participate in organized sport and informal physical activity was studied by Coakley and White (1992). They found that girls' participation in sport was highly influenced, and most often negatively, by their experiences in school physical education classes. For young women, physical education was often associated with embarrassment and discomfort because of arrangements around gym wear, the changing and showering routine, and body image. These findings were both consistent and inconsistent with an earlier study by U.S. researchers Smith and Caldwell (1994) who found that becoming a high school athlete did not significantly affect female adolescents' feelings of attractiveness, perceptions of self as an adult, or self-esteem.

Other research has indicated that girls' participation in high school athletics has a direct and positive impact on female athletes' perceptions of their popularity (Melnick, Vanfossen, & Sabo, 1988) and involvement in physical activity is positively related to self-image and coping skills (Covey & Feltz, 1991). If adolescent girls, however, are involved in activities that are seen as sex-neutral or masculine, they are perceived by others as less attractive (Kane, 1987). In other words, although girls' participation in sport and physical activity has increased tremendously in the last two decades in North America (Sabo, 1988), no consensus exists on girls' experiences of and the benefits gained from their participation in terms of self-esteem and positive identity development.

We might conclude that leisure is not *necessarily* a context for positive or healthy development (Carnegie Council on Adolescent Development, 1992; Kleiber, Larson, & Csikszentmihalyi, 1986). For example, in a study of high school students' experiences of their activities, Kleiber, Larson, and Csikszentmihalyi (1986) identified two types of leisure. One group of leisure activities were experienced as intrinsically motivating, freely chosen, and challenging in a way that required effort and concentration. Activities included in this category were organized sport and games, arts, and hobbies. The other group of leisure activities (i.e., socializing, TV watching) were also perceived as freely chosen and intrinsically motivating, but were low on challenge and concentration. Because the demands or tasks of adulthood require effort and concentration, leisure that incorporates these elements (i.e., what the authors termed "transitional leisure") served a developmental function, bridging the childhood world of play and the adult world of work. A conclusion might be that if girls can learn to find pleasure in demanding tasks requiring effort and concentration, then they are likely to be happier, more satisfied adults. On the other hand, although diversionary, time-filling activities that present little challenge to and require little effort from adolescents might restore girls' energy and spirit, in and of themselves they are not a "step toward adulthood."

Leisure for teens generally means relaxation, free choice, and enjoyment and often is not experienced in or associated with challenge (Kleiber, Caldwell, & Shaw, 1993). Particularly for the females in this study, leisure was associated with "a condition of relaxed, easy enjoyment, with little emphasis on action and challenge-seeking." Csikszentmihalyi and colleagues (Csikszentmihalyi, Rathunde, & Whalen, 1993; Csikszentmihalyi & Larson, 1978, 1984), suggested that without challenge, little engagement (i.e., high boredom) may exist; without engagement, a sense of mastery, intrinsic motivation or meaning may be missing; and without meaning, destructive behavior that is directed towards either self or others may result (Carnegie Council on Adolescent Development, 1992; Iso-Ahola & Crowley, 1991; Iso-Ahola & Weissinger, 1990; Smith, Caldwell, Shaw, & Kleiber, 1994; Weissinger & Iso-Ahola, 1984).

In summary, identity development is the task of the adolescent years because of the interaction of "personal" changes and social forces. The process of identity development, however, is not universal. It varies by factors such as gender and race. Identity development influences participation in recreation and leisure because it influences interests, motivations and opportunities. Participation in recreation and leisure may also have a positive or negative impact on identity development and the future adult roles for which a girl is prepared.

Physical Development, Recreation and Leisure

In western societies adolescence is typically marked by the development of secondary sex characteristics. Sexual maturation is a "mixed bag" for girls. Although a girl may gain status among her peers by looking older, if such maturity occurs "early," adults often react with concern and negativity. Parents and other adults may feel justified in their concerns because it is the girl who "pays" the consequences of sexual behavior. Some scholars (Steiner-Adair, 1990; Sugar, 1979) suggest, however, that this concern reflects not only a sexual double-standard but also the devaluing and fear of female sexuality and maturity.

Cultural devaluation of female maturity may be manifested in eating disorders. Eating disorders among teenage girls reflect the fashion, advertising, and media industries, all of which promote thinness (viz., small breasts and narrow hips) in girls and women. Such a physique suggests immaturity and "child-likeness," and hence justifies girls' and women's lack of access to power (Steiner-Adair, 1990). Historically the body was, and currently is, used as a political statement and as a means of oppression, incorporation, or resistance (Ehrenreich & English, 1973). Based on her research, Steiner-Adair (1990) concluded that:

> Girls with eating disorders have a heightened, albeit confused, grasp of the dangerous imbalance of the culture's values, which they cannot articulate in the face of the culture's abject denial of their adolescent, intuit truth. So they tell their story with their bodies. Perhaps, on a *cultural* level, theirs is a story about the enormous difficulties of growing up female in a culture that does not value the feminine 'voice,' which speaks about relationships and the importance of interdependence. The girls will not break their fast until they are sure they can gain adulthood without the loss of their relational values. (p. 176)

Societal ambivalence about girls' "growing up" and becoming independent, deemphasis on the importance of relationships with others, the contradictory cultural degradation of femininity and female maturity, and the cultural norms that assume all females should be "feminine" shape what opportunities society provides for girls and have ramifications for female adolescents' interest and involvement in recreation and leisure. For example, researchers consistently show that girls' participation in physical activity and sport, specifically sports requiring physical contact and strength, reflect a marked decrease as girls enter the middle adolescent years (Anderson, Lorenz & Pease, 1986; Butcher, 1985; Melnick, Vanfossen, & Sabo, 1988; Smale & Shaw, 1994).

Coakley and White (1992) found that the decisions young (13 to 23 years of age) British working class women and men made about sport participation reflected five aspects: (a) a consideration of the future, especially the transition to adulthood; (b) a desire to display and extend personal competence and autonomy; (c) constraints related to money, parents, and opposite-sex friends; (d) support and encouragement from parents, relatives, and/or peers; and (e) past experiences in school sports and physical education. Neither the females nor males wanted to be involved in playing sports in any setting that could not somehow be linked to adulthood or that allowed others to perceive them as childish. Young women were more likely to see that sport had little or nothing to do with adulthood. Because young men were able to see sport as an affirmation of masculinity, they were more likely to see sport participation as consistent with the transition to adulthood even though it had no connection to work.

Some females in Coakley and White's (1992) study took exception to this perspective. They saw sport as an avenue to prove competence to themselves and to males. The issue of competence was important for these adolescents although the young women were less likely to consider themselves "sportpersons" than the young men, even when regularly involved in physical activity. This perception seemed to be due to dominant images of sport as competitive, organized, team-based and thus, male. School experiences with inadequate facilities and inconvenient times for women's athletics also conveyed the message that sports really were for males, not females.

The gendered nature of young women's experiences of sport and physical activity also emerged in several other ways (Coakley & White, 1992). Young women faced pervasive parental constraints to their leisure activity participation. For example, their schedules were closely monitored and where, when, and with whom they were doing things were controlled. Girls were expected to give an accurate accounting of their activities; activities were seen as more legitimate if they were with a close friend. The girls in this British study seemed to accept such parental supervision as natural. The reality was parental cooperation was needed to initiate and maintain participation, because girls were not allowed to be out after dark alone and not expected to go places on their own. If the girls had boyfriends, the boys' interests also took precedence. Girls were also more influenced in their leisure by same-sex friends than were the boys. Girls, therefore, seemed to be more careful in selecting and becoming committed to leisure activities than the boys. Although their study of youth was not designed to highlight the effects of gender, Coakley and White concluded that gender emerged as an important factor.

These findings may help explain the results of research on constraints to leisure experienced by teens in North America. For example, girls generally perceive more constraints to leisure than boys. Wrong time of day, not offered for girls, and location of the activity were constraints more likely to be reported by girls (Hultsman, 1991). Hultsman (1993) also found for fifth to eighth graders, that parental influence was greatest in adolescents' decision not to *start* an activity; significant other adults (e.g., coach, activity leader) were most influential in their decision to *cease* participation. The influence of adults varied by type of activity and gender, age, and race of the youth (Hultsman, 1993; Jackson & Rucks, 1995). In general girls were less likely to report parents as a constraint to starting an activity than boys. This finding might be interpreted as meaning that parents allowed daughters more freedom than sons. More likely, however, is the conclusion that young adolescent boys had greater expectations for autonomy from parents than girls and thus, parental influence was more of an issue for them. On the other hand, young adolescent girls may be less likely to report parents as an influence on recreation decision making because they accept parental monitoring as the norm (Coakley & White, 1992; Noe & Elifson, 1976) and thus, are less likely consciously to experience or report parental influence as a constraint.

Constraints, however, are not simply passively accepted by youth (Jackson & Rucks, 1995). Some teens are able to negotiate through constraints to participate. Why and how they are able to negotiate is yet to be examined. For a variety of reasons (e.g., employment opportunities, income, ability to transport self), age of the teen is a factor (Hultsman, 1993). Social class, race and ethnicity, and physical ability also would likely impose different challenges and personal and social opportunities. For example, Raymore, Godbey, and Crawford (1994) found that white, American, twelfth graders having lower levels of self-esteem perceived more constraints in their recreation activities. Females were found to have significantly lower self-esteem and more intrapersonal constraints (e.g., too shy to start a new activity and unlikely to do a new leisure activity that makes one feel uncomfortable) as well as total constraints than males. Youth of lower socioeconomic status were also more likely than other youth to report these kinds of personal constraints. Further discussions about constraints can be found in chapter seven.

Limited research about physical activity and sport participation of girls of racial heritages other than white is available (Birrell, 1990). An interpretive study of African-American collegiate female athletes' experience of sport by Stratta (1993) suggested that these athletes did not perceive the same conflicts between being physically skilled and feminine as white female collegiate athletes did. Race and girls' and boys' high school sport participation was the topic of a nationwide longitudinal study of African-American, Hispanic, and Caucasian youth from the sophomore year to four years beyond high school conducted by the Women's Sports Foundation (1989). The results showed that sport participation was significantly lower among African-American and Hispanic girls than white girls. At the same time, participation in high school athletics had a positive impact on the high school academic performance of Hispanic females attending rural schools as measured by standardized tests and grades, a negative relationship with high school drop-out for Hispanic girls, and a positive relationship with other extracurricular and community involvement for African-American, Hispanic and white girls and boys. Further, Hispanic female athletes were more likely to attend and stay in college than their nonathletic peers while African-American female athletes fared no better or worse in higher education than their nonathletic peers.

High school sport participation was less likely to be an avenue of upward social and academic mobility *after high school* for African-American girls in particular. Indeed, high school athletic participation was actually found to have a negative effect on the employment of urban black females who entered the labor market after high school. This finding was attributed to (a) the combined demands of sport, school, and family that are particular to young, urban, African-American women from impoverished communities that allowed them little time or energy for part-time employment during high school and (b) the "failure of urban schools to provide their female athletes with enough resources to facilitate their entrance into the work force" (Women's Sports Foundation, 1989, p. 15).

Cognitive Development, Recreation, and Leisure

Cognitive development, or how a teenage girl reasons and is capable of seeing herself and others, also influences her participation in recreation and leisure. The cognitive change during adolescence is from "concrete" to "formal operational thinking" (Piaget, 1954). It is defined by a shift from absolutist, dualistic thinking to the ability to think abstractly, take the perspective of others, and see incongruities or inconsistencies in thinking, especially that of parents or other adults. The development of formal operational thought allows the adolescent to consider not only her own thoughts, but also the thoughts of other people.

Adolescents are aware that other people can have thoughts about them just as they have thoughts about other people. In leaving the egocentrism of childhood, this awareness leads adolescents to take on a new egocentrism. Adolescents are continually anticipating the reactions of others and assume that others will be as admiring or critical of them as they are of themselves. The preoccupation with appearance, the wish for privacy, and long hours of bedroom or telephone conversation with friends are often attributed to this concern with the perceptions of "the imaginary audience" and "fear of abnormality" (Elkind, 1967; Hendry, Shucksmith, Love, & Glendinning, 1993). Concern with the perceptions of others, enhanced by sexual maturation and the press for identity development, may account for adolescents' greater interest in the social context of any given leisure activity rather than the activity itself (Kelly, 1990).

Emerging adolescent cognitions and dominant cultural messages about female attractiveness and femininity combine to create a concern with physical appearance and attractiveness for many girls. The "glamour-consumer" role for girls—a role by which status or popularity among peers may be gained and a positive self-concept maintained—is encouraged even as access to other roles is denied (Bloch, 1993). For some girls, apparel shopping and discussing clothing is a major leisure activity (Deem, 1986; Jansen-Verbeke, 1987). Attention to attractiveness through grooming, reading fashion magazines, and shopping may serve as a source of pleasure for adolescent girls as well as generate stress and feelings of inadequacy.

Self-adornment is experienced as recreation for some females. Self-adornment may provide feelings of mastery and competence, an escape through self-indulgence, a relief from boredom, and a means of self-expression (Bloch, 1993). Young women who perceive self-adornment as recreation are more likely to have higher than average interest in the mass media's representations of attractiveness and perceive themselves as attractive competent in grooming (Bloch, 1993). Marketers and retailers play a role in encouraging material consumption by youth that may be pursued and experienced as leisure (Bloch, 1993; Kelly, 1991; Roberts & Parsell, 1994). Some people have even contended that in comparison to 20 or 30 years ago, youth today are more united by commodities than values and beliefs.

To the extent that girls and women feel more powerless than boys and men, the body and its adornment and construction becomes an arena for control (Freedman, 1986). For example, the preponderance of females in exercise and aerobics classes, the lack of interest on the part of some females in participating in such activities (Dattilo, Dattilo, Samdahl, & Kleiber, 1994), as well as females' greater involvement in self-adornment and related behaviors (Bloch, 1993) express the power males and their values have over females. Of course, attention to appearance is not exclusive to women as has been revealed in the research on men involved in sport, specifically body building (Messner & Sabo, 1990).

Social comparison is a human tendency (Festinger, 1954) that requires an ability to cognitively see self as separate from others and realize that others have thoughts and perceptions of their own. This ability emerges with the cognitive development of adolescence. It is coupled with "new" bodies, emotions, and social contexts of interaction. Girls (and boys) clearly receive a message from the mass media and popular culture that a certain type of physical appearance is desirable for females and that effort should be put into acquiring it (Frederick, Havitz, & Shaw, 1994). As a consequence, more effort might be made by recreation professionals and other professionals to help girls use their developing cognitive abilities to think critically about those messages, their leisure, and the identities they want to develop.

Other Influences on Girls' Play, Recreation, and Leisure

We have shown in this chapter that gender, age, and race are central to girls' motivations for, participation in, and experiences of play, recreation, and leisure. Other aspects of identity, such as sexual orientation and social class, have begun to attract attention in relation to girls' experiences of leisure.

Estimations are that 10 percent of the 30 million adolescents between 10 and 20 years of age in the United States are homosexual (Deisher, 1989). As previously discussed, adolescence is a demanding and challenging time for many young people because of the multiple changes being experienced. Gay, lesbian and bisexual youth may be more challenged, especially when they have little support and few visible role models to call upon in negotiating and developing positive personal, sexual, and social identities. Few recreational programs exist for lesbian and gay youth (Grossman, 1992). The fear of discrimination and violence (i.e., fear for personal safety) keeps many homosexual teens away from organized recreation programs even though "coming out" allows teens to feel a greater sense of freedom and enjoyment in leisure (Kivel, 1994). Because the nonwork realms of life are extremely important during the adolescent years, these settings offer opportunities where identities can be worked out (Kelly, 1990) and because children and youth have a great deal of discretionary time (Carnegie Council on Adolescent Development, 1992), more research with and understanding about lesbian and gay youths' experiences of development and leisure are needed (Kivel, 1994). Further, awareness of how heterosexual youth and adults are privileged in their development and leisure because of their heterosexuality is required.

Social class has generally not been central to leisure research in North America. Social class is often considered as one variable among many that has little meaning beyond the categorical level. Further, in the United States in particular, research on social class is often combined with an interest in race (Birrell, 1990). Researchers in Britain, on the other hand, have situated social class along with gender at the center of analyses of youth recreation and leisure. McRobbie (1991), Griffin (1985), Griffiths (1988), and Deem (1986) examined girls' leisure as practices located in both gender and class relations. The study of physical activity participation of youth by Coakley and White (1992) found that gender and class were central to such leisure. Thus, leisure is often an expression of class identity and a context for the reproduction of class relations by youth.

Roberts and Parsell (1994), however, questioned the centrality of social class and gender to youth leisure. Based on their secondary analysis of Economic and Social Research Council's 16-19 Initiative, they concluded that:

> [Y]oung people's leisure patterns in the late-1980s continued to reflect gender and social class differences but neither set of differences was entirely of the type that previous theories had led us to expect. (p. 46)

What distinguished females from males was their lower levels of participation in sport and their high social contact scores. Most striking was that middle-class girls and working-class girls and boys were much less likely to be as heavily committed to sport, politics, pop music, and drinking (in terms of frequency, intensity and duration of involvement) as middle-class boys were. In this sense, middle-class males dominated the variety of leisure contexts in which youth participated. Thus, we might conclude that class is gendered too.

Roberts and Parsell (1994) maintained that their findings were more likely due to changes in youth culture itself over the past decade than to problems of how to measure class position. For example, Roberts and Parsell indicated that middle-class youth have "infiltrated" the pop music industry in Britain. The homogeneity of youth culture in the United States has been remarked upon as well, and leisure is central to this homogenization. The increasing number of youth with part-time employment and the availability of credit in the U.S. makes material goods widely available, if not affordable. Girls' recreation and leisure is unlikely to be immune from this homogenization. If and how adolescent girls' leisure has been shaped by class in North America needs to be examined further.

Race and ethnicity have defined youth cultures in the U.S. as much as social class but some social commentators suggest that these boundaries are also being bridged, at least in the context of popular culture, by music, movies, and sport (West, 1993). Tinning and FitzClarence (1992) maintained that for adolescents, the postmodern world of mass media dominance, global capitalism, and individualism means that they are now required to be producers of their own biographies. Unless recreation and leisure service providers have an understanding of this postmodern world with its wide diversity or experiences and individual identities, their impact upon girls' development will be limited.

Concluding Perspectives

Play, recreation and leisure both influence and are influenced by changes in girls' physical, mental, and social selves as well as their resources and opportunities for involvement. In addition, the sense of self and possibility girls have and the resources and opportunities for leisure available to them have to be examined in the larger sociocultural context of gender, age, race, and class relations. Furthermore, an understanding of play, recreation and leisure in childhood and adolescence is important for several reasons. Leisure has a relationship to the development of identities and physical, cognitive, and social abilities and skills as well as physical and mental health. Children and youth have a relatively large amount of discretionary time that can lead to both opportunities and risks. Further, leisure activity participation in childhood and youth has been found to be a predictor of adult leisure activity participation (Freysinger & Ray, 1994; Kelly, 1974; Scott & Willits, 1989). This research on childhood and youth development has pointed to some gains, but also numerous gaps that exist in the literature that make our current understanding of the gender journey incomplete.

Discussion Questions

1. Is the expression of excitement a gendered practice? Are girls socialized to limit their excitement in play? Does this limitation transfer into adult life?

2. As a child and an adolescent, how did you experience gender, race, class, age and sexual orientation shaping your play, recreation, and leisure?

3. How are girls' orientation towards relationships and cooperation an expression of oppression or resistance?

4. What could (and should) a recreation/leisure service provider do to support and enhance girls' development? Do your views reflect those of liberal, Marxist, socialist, or radical feminism?

5. How do you perceive the mass media shaped your development as a child and adolescent? Was this shaping positive?

6. What would need to change to make sports and physical activity more appealing to girls?

7. How did your participation in leisure activities during adolescence help you to develop your own personal identity? How would your development been different if you had been involved in other activities?

8. Do you think of clothes shopping as a leisure experience? Why or why not?

9. In what kinds of activities would you like your son or daughter to participate? Are these activities gender-typed?

Chapter Six

When I Get Old...: Leisure Across the Course of Adulthood

When I am an old woman, I shall wear purple
With a red hat which doesn't go, and doesn't suit me.
And I shall spend my pension on brandy and summer gloves
And satin sandals, and say we've no money for butter.
I shall sit down on the pavement when I'm tired
And gobble up samples in shops and press alarm bells
And run my stick along the public railings
And make up for the sobriety of my youth.
I shall go out in my slippers in the rain
And pick the flowers in other people's gardens
And learn to spit...

—*Joseph in Martz (Ed.), 1987, p. 1*

This chapter on women, leisure, and development focuses on women from young adulthood through older adulthood, or from the second decade of life through what is commonly called old age. Although many gains have been made in our understanding of the leisure opportunities that women have across the life course, many gaps still exist. These gains and gaps pertain to the patterns of women's development and to the continuity or discontinuity of leisure behavior, attitudes, meanings, and motivations across the course of adult life. The process and experience of development and how the significance and meaning of leisure may be different or similar for women of varied life situations or backgrounds are important to consider. Up to this point, however, the leisure literature has rarely focused on women of color, single or never married women, socially and economically disadvantaged women, or single mothers. Thus, the developmental and leisure research discussed in this chapter primarily reflects the lives of white, middle-class, married, North American women.

We will examine leisure in relation to developmental perspectives. First, the development of women across the course of life is summarized related to women's changing roles, their psychological or psychosocial development, the social construction of age and gender, and the gendered and age stratified distribution of resources and opportunities. Developmental models are presented next. Stability and change in leisure meanings and activities over the course of life are discussed as external (i.e., social) and internal (i.e., psychological) factors that define historically and culturally situated life courses of women.

Perspectives on Adult Development

As noted in chapter five, dominant notions and understandings of development changed in the mid-1900s in North America. Scholars now see development as influenced by a number of interacting forces: psychological, sociocultural, historical, and biological. Behavior is understood to be multi-dimensional and complex in its meaning and development. People act according to who they are as an integration of all that they have been and expect to be. Therefore, to add to the understanding of leisure behavior at any particular point in time, an understanding of leisure behavior across the course of life is important. Although times and strands of stability occur in our lives, change can also be expected as a function of chronological age, time or current situation, and/or cohort or generational experiences.

The separation of chronological age, time (i.e., current situation), and period (i.e., cohort or generational) effects is integral to adult developmental models. For example, researchers have noted the low level of involvement in physical activity by current cohorts of adult women, particularly by older women. Although lower levels of physical activity in participation may be partly due to the changes in physical strength, stamina, and flexibility that occur with age, different generational experiences also have an influence. As presented in chapter two, current cohorts of older women experienced fewer opportunities for and greater sanctions against their involvement in sport and physically active leisure than have younger generations of females. Thus, older women's lower levels of participation may best be explained by a combination of social, historical, biological, and psychological factors.

As noted in chapter five on "The Gender Journey," identity, physical, and cognitive development have been closely tied to age during childhood and adolescence. Starting in early adulthood, however, normative patterns of age changes are difficult to find. This lack of normative patterns has been attributed to factors including the lack of universal physical changes during adulthood, the diversity of contexts and demands experienced by adults, and the greater choices allowed adults as compared to children and youth. For example, if development occurs through the interaction of psychological and social factors, the demands faced by a single, career-oriented woman and a married, full-time homemaker who has five children would be quite different.

Concerning gender, researchers are increasingly challenging the applicability of developmental theory for adult females (i.e., Baruch, Barnett, & Rivers, 1983; Gilligan, 1982a, 1982b, 1982c; Veroff & Smith, 1985). Developmental theory has been predominantly derived from studies of male populations. Women's lives, however, are believed to be less predictable and less uniform than men's. Women's lives and development are affected by their reproductive and family roles in a way that men's are not (Barnett & Baruch, 1978). Gilligan (1982c) contended that women and men differ in their moral and psychosocial development because of differential sex role socialization and norms and because of the different roles women and men are expected to fulfill in a patriarchal society. Basically, women's lives and their development are influenced by an ethic of care which evolves from women's dominant role or function of nurturing others. Women's sense of themselves and their psychological well-being have been affected by this expected caring role (Livson, 1981).

Leisure is a developmental issue for adult women in that leisure behavior, motivations, values, and attitudes are shaped by social roles, psychosocial preoccupations, and opportunities and resources that change across the course of life (Bialeschki & Michener, 1994; Freysinger, 1988, 1995; Freysinger & Ray, 1994; Iso-Ahola, 1980b; Iso-Ahola, Jackson, & Dunne, 1994; Kleiber & Kelly, 1980; Rapoport & Rapoport, 1975). Concomitantly, leisure may stimulate development. The experience of leisure may assist individuals in coping with the changes and transitions that are a part of human growth or development. For example as indicated in the previous chapter, Csikszentmihalyi (1981) hypothesized that leisure was a crucial factor influencing adolescents' transition to young adulthood and the world of work. Kleiber, Larson, and Csikszentmihalyi (1986) further suggested that the enjoyment found in adolescent leisure may lay "a groundwork for experiencing enjoyment in more obligatory adult activities" (p. 11).

Other researchers have also shown how the experience of leisure may assist individuals in coping with change. Kelly, Steinkamp, and Kelly (1986) found that leisure was used to cope with the transitions of aging. Similar findings were reported in the research of Freysinger (1995) who found that leisure as separation from everyday demands enabled adults to adapt to the roles and responsibilities, as well as the psychosocial preoccupations of middle adulthood.

Specific to women, research indicates that leisure is a place where ideologies of age and gender can be resisted and transformed (Freysinger & Flannery, 1992; Henderson & Bialeschki, 1991a; Wearing, 1990). These findings illustrate the potential that leisure holds for individual growth and empowerment as well as social change. The focus of this chapter is on the examination of the roles and psychosocial issues that constitute women's adult lives as a way to better understand change and continuity in women's leisure.

The Roles and Psychosocial Issues that Define Women's Development

An understanding of women's development may be found in the series of life events and roles which delineate stages or transitions of female life. Some of these events or roles include chronological age, parenting status, change in work-life events or roles, hormonal changes, and the mix of activities in which one is engaged (Brooks-Gunn & Kirsch, 1984). Adjustment to changing roles and events usually depends to a large extent on their "timeliness" or to the extent to which one feels the changes are "on time" (Neugarten, 1977). This "life course" approach to the study of adult development is situated in a sociological perspective and focuses on social patterns in the timing, duration, spacing, and ordering of life events.

In contrast, those researchers exploring adult development from a life span approach are more likely to be interested in individual development and to focus on psychological qualities like ego strength, personality, or moral development. Thus, research on adult development takes account of both the psychological and social aspects and increasingly, the interaction of the two.

Roles and Events

Sociologists define adulthood in the sequence and timing of social roles. For individuals, roles define behaviors expected by others; are major sources of feelings about the self; and expose individuals to experiences that can affect subsequent attitudes, feelings, and behaviors. The major roles that most women occupy at some time during adulthood include worker, spouse or significant other, parent, and homemaker. Increasingly, the roles of retiree, student, and caregiver of aging spouse/partner or parents/in-laws are also defining the lives of many women. As noted by Sales (1977), the age at which an individual experiences life stages has wide variation. The sequence of stages, not the ages, appear to have the most general applicability.

Adaptability is a major theme in the course of women's adult lives. Across adulthood women are faced with attempting to fulfill the external expectations placed on them while building additional roles that may enrich their personal satisfaction. These additional roles may include leisure. Women's adaptability allows them to adjust more easily to changes that occur; at the same time, this adaptability impedes long-range planning. The result is that women are often deprived of the pleasure of attaining goals that require extended time commitments. An exception to this result is in women's maternal or parenting role (Sales, 1977). Many women with children see their child's progress toward maturity as a woman's most substantial contribution to the world.

Barnett and Baruch (1983) explored the relationship between the various role combinations women held in mid-life and their psychological development or well-being. They found that the major source of stress for women in the middle years of life was the parent role, rather than that of paid worker as traditionally had been cited. Women who were not employed outside the home appeared to experience a lack of structure and legitimacy in their commitments. They were often seen by themselves and others as endlessly available and thus, their lives were spent juggling the demands of others. Barnett and Baruch reported that full-time homemakers often experienced feelings of having too much to do. These women attributed such feelings to personal inadequacy rather than to the nature and structure of the homemaking role.

Research by Lopata and Barnewolt (1984) on the importance of various roles for women ages 28-55 found that:

1. The role of worker took a primary focus when the roles of wife and mother were absent from a women's current life.

2. Women tended to see their involvement in social roles in life course terms, expecting a shift from the role of mother to that of wife if they were presently involved in childrearing.

3. Women expected their involvement in roles outside the home (e.g., friend, organizational membership) to increase after age 55.

4. Women in the middle years were especially likely to ignore roles outside of home and family. Few identified the role of worker as being, having been, or going to be important at midlife.

Lopata and Barnewolt used a cross-sectional representation of women in 1956 and again in 1978 and found that both groups gave similar importance to roles. In other words, despite any social-structural changes that may have taken place during this time in terms of changing gender roles, women's perceptions of the importance of various roles did not change.

Although women's roles appear to be changing, Rossi (1980) suggested that some of the gains actually have not taken women far from where they have been in the past. In particular she noted the popular myth that couples in their forties are largely postparenting. According to Rossi, the postparenting stage is not reached until retirement age for a number of reasons:

(a) the higher unemployment rate of youth and increasing years of post secondary education have resulted in a longer economic dependency of children on their parents;

(b) first births are taking place at an older parental age and childrearing is extended to later ages; and

(c) a greater change has taken place in the status of women in the workplace than in the division of labor at home.

As the number of older people are increasing and the years of a dependent old age are extended, women of all age groups but predominantly those in the middle years, are assuming the caregiving role for older family members. Further, a growing number of women are parenting grandchildren. The notion of "retirement" in later life is also a misnomer for women who are married. Domestic work continues, especially if the woman's spouse is retired (Szinovacz, 1992; Vinick & Ekerdt, 1991). In other words, rather than being a time of increased freedom, the trend may be for middle and later adulthood to be a time of continued family obligations and responsibilities for women (Horna, 1989a; Zuzanek & Smale, 1992).

So much variation exists in the age at which roles are taken on and left that some have contended that age is less relevant in shaping adulthood (Giele, 1982). Researchers, however, have also shown that remarkable consistency in the timing of social roles continues (Atchley, 1994). This finding is not surprising since social and economic policy, as well as cultural ideologies surrounding age and gender, construct normative standards related to the appropriate sequence and timing of social roles. These normative standards are powerful influences on the course of women's lives because they inform notions of deservedness and undeservedness. Ideologies and policies facilitate, discourage, or punish change and deviation. For example, in the United States if a woman bears a child and is unmarried, she is seen as less deserving of public sympathy and support (and hence, receives fewer benefits) than a woman who is a widowed mother (Rodeheaver, 1987). Cultural ideologies and social and economic policy tend to lag behind the way individuals experience life (Riley, Kahn, & Foner, 1994).

In summary, adulthood for women is characterized by changing roles and responsibilities. Most research has found that family roles are central in defining women's lives (Baber & Monaghan, 1988; Roberts & Newton, 1987). These roles influence a woman's perceptions of personal adequacy and identity, as well as her leisure opportunities and resources. Little comparative research, however, exists on the central life interests of women with various lifestyle patterns such as women who are not and/or do not intend to be wives and/or mothers, women who have established careers before starting a family, women who are parenting grandchildren, or single mothers. Further, our understanding of women, family, development, and leisure is limited because white and heterosexual families have been the foci of most of the leisure research (Bialeschki, Pearce, & Elliot, 1994; Stoller & Gibson, 1994; Vaz, 1995).

Psychosocial Tasks and Issues

Issues or concerns typically defined as psychosocial are believed to evolve out of the interaction between the individual woman and her environment. Much of the research on women's psychosocial development tests or challenges established theories that were developed on male populations. Thus, gender differences must be noted because they reflect the research to date.

Developmental Tasks and Psychosocial Crises

Havighurst (1972) delineated developmental tasks for each stage of heterosexual life including young, middle, and older adulthood. The tasks of young adulthood include selecting a mate, learning to live with a marriage partner, starting a family, rearing children, managing a home, getting started in an occupation, taking on civic responsibility, and finding a congenial social group. Middle adulthood tasks focus on achieving adult civic and social responsibility, establishing and maintaining an economic standard of living, assisting teenage children to become responsible and happy adults, developing adult leisure-time activities, relating to one's spouse as a person, accepting and adjusting to the physiological changes of middle age, and adjusting to aging parents. In older adulthood the tasks include adjusting to decreasing physical strength and health, adjusting to retirement and a reduced income, adjusting to the death of a spouse, establishing an explicit affiliation with one's age group, meeting social and civic obligations, and establishing satisfactory physical living arrangements.

These tasks are widely accepted as reflective of the various stages of development. Developmental tasks come from physical maturation, cultural and societal expectations, and personal values and aspirations (Merriam & Mullins, 1981). According to Havighurst, through the achievement of these tasks, growth occurs and personal well-being or happiness evolves. This assertion of Havighurst assumes that the individual values and supports what culture and society expect. Further, if and how an individual is able to achieve the tasks are likely to vary by a number of factors.

Merriam and Mullins (1981) noted that Havighurst's developmental tasks are often cited by researchers discussing adult development, but they rarely have been empirically tested. Their relevance for women and men, different income groups, individuals choosing alternative lifestyles, and different age cohorts has been questioned. Merriam and Mullins (1981) found the young, middle, and older-aged adults in their study were likely to see the tasks of young and middle adulthood as equally important. In terms of gender differences, women in general saw the tasks of every stage as more important than the men. In addition, the tasks tended to be seen as more relevant by middle-class persons.

Grounded in psychoanalytic theory, Erikson (1950) defined development as the resolution of a series of psychosocial crises or conflicts. In adolescence the conflict is one of identity formation (i.e., individuation, establishing an autonomous sense of self) versus identity diffusion. For young adults the concern is with establishing an intimate relationship. The crisis of middle adulthood is generativity (i.e., the capacity to guide and nurture succeeding generations in their development) versus stagnation. Integrity (i.e., the ability to integrate the successful and disappointing experiences of one's life and find meaning) versus despair is the psychosocial issue faced by most older adults.

Gender Influences

Erikson's theory has been criticized for being androcentric and its applicability for women has been explored only recently. For example, Ryff (1985) combined and examined the major theories of adult development, including Erikson's, in an examination of gender differences in personality development. She found that women did change in the ways proposed by these developmental theories and that early adulthood was characterized by concerns with intimacy, middle adulthood with generativity, and late adulthood with ego integrity.

Since Ryff was studying adult development, however, she did not consider gender differences in the psychosocial issue of adolescent identity formation versus identity diffusion. As discussed in chapter five, adolescence is the time when females and males diverge and identity development is the issue which distinguishes subsequent development (Gilligan, 1982a, 1982c). Erikson (1950) proposed that girls and boys resolve the identity issue differently. A girl's resolution of the identity issue is held in abeyance because identity for females is found by merging with another or in intimacy. Adolescent boys, on the other hand, are encouraged to forge ahead and establish autonomous, initiating selves. According to Gilligan:

> While for men, identity precedes intimacy and generativity in the optimal cycle of human separation and attachment, for women these tasks seem instead to be fused. Intimacy goes along with identity, as the female comes to know herself as she is known, through her relationships with others. (1982c, p. 12)

The sequence of development for women is one of intimacy, individuation, and generativity, while for men, development is individuation, intimacy, and generativity (Gilligan, 1982a). Even though Erikson recognized this difference, he did not change his life cycle stages (Gilligan, 1982c).

The research of Stewart (1976), that actually preceded Gilligan, offered support for Gilligan's conclusions. Stewart explored the applicability of Levinson's (1974) theory of adult development for women. She found that for many women, the thirties were a time of transition and unease when issues of individuation and a sense of an independent, identifiable self needed to be addressed. The developmental tasks of women in their thirties varied greatly depending on whether a woman had formed a stable marriage and family life in her twenties, remained single, and/or pursued a career during this decade. Sales (1977) suggested that women who did not seek roles outside of family roles in their thirties experienced difficulty later in life. Other researchers have shown, however, that women who were exclusively family focused during early and middle adulthood scored lower on measures of well-being and were less satisfied in their later years (Barnett & Baruch, 1983; Maas & Kuypers, 1975). Multiple roles appear to serve to mitigate or buffer the stress in any one role (Henry A. Murray Research Center, 1995; Pietromonaco, Manis, & Frohardt-Lane, 1986) and may also affect the leisure that women have.

Women who are in their forties are often characterized as exhibiting a sense of increased freedom, increased time and energy, and a satisfying change in self-concept (Neugarten, 1968b). For married women with children, needs for achievement and for making an impact outside the realm of marriage and family are often felt (Baruch, 1967; Holahan, 1994; Huyck, 1994). For women with health and financial stability, the forties are often a time of increasing self-awareness, reflection, selectivity, manipulation and control of the environment, mastery, and competence. For both women and men, this stage seems to be a time of self-assessment, reevaluation, and examination of personal control and power. Depending on the roles and responsibilities a woman still has, latent talents and abilities may be put to use in new directions during middle adulthood.

The relational, affiliative character of women has been attributed not only to adult roles and socialization for these roles, but also to the different initial developmental experiences of females and males. Chodorow (1978) and others (e.g., Dinnerstein, 1977; Huyck, 1994; Hunt, 1980) have noted that because mothers are the primary caregivers, the formation of gender identity is experienced differently by female and male babies, as is individuation or separation in adolescence. Male identity is contingent on separation from the mother. For females, identity is an ongoing primary relationship with the mother that does not involve separation. As a result of this lack of separation, women often do not differentiate self from others and tend to feel a diffuse guilt for the welfare of their families and a responsibility for others. These initial differences in childrearing and development are further supported by social-ization processes which foster achievement and self-reliance in boys, and nurturing and responsibility in girls.

Although women are usually perceived as more relational and nurturing, Astin (1976) noted that we do not know if this assumption is invariably true. She noted:

> Even though the literature on adult development has described developmental differences between youth and adulthood and between adult men and women, it has not differentiated adult women by past roles and experiences. Adult women described in the literature have the primary roles of wife and mother. There is no information on the similarities and differences between women with career commitments and those primarily with family commitments. Also, do women who had careers, who were involved in scholarly, scientific, and artistic endeavors, have adult crises similar to those of men? Do adult women who have always been outwardly oriented show needs for affiliation in adulthood similar to those of men? (1976, p. 1)

Women's focus on the roles of mother and/or wife at different ages may reflect a lack of meaningful employment opportunities just as much as a relational orientation. Another unexplored issue is the ability of different women to "call forth" the repressed "masculine" sides of themselves, even though the detri-mental effect of constricted roles and traits on women's psychological health or well-being has been noted. Indeed, the development and well-being of both the individual and society are seen to lie in women's and men's acceptance and expression of both the so-called masculine and feminine in themselves (Gilligan, 1982c; Jung, 1933).

Reconstructing Gender

Feminist researchers who conceive of gender as relations of opportunity and oppression have criticized the work of Chodorow and Gilligan. In these critical analyses, the relational or affiliative orientation of women is explained as an outcome of subjugation, not gender. "That is, it behooves any subjugated group to be attuned and responsive to those who have power over them" (Turner, 1994, p. 7). Women's orientation toward affiliation/relatedness and independence/autonomy, however, changes with age.

Researchers have found that beginning in middle age, women become more responsive and less guilty about aggressive and egocentric impulses (Chiriboga, 1981; Gutmann, 1964; Huyck, 1994; Rodeheaver & Datan, 1985). Women become more expressive of all aspects of self. Cooper and Gutmann (1987) described middle age as the "addition of masculine characteristics" and a "return of traits that had been repressed." This repression has been attributed to what Gutmann (1964) called the "parental imperative." The responsibility of women for the care and nurturing of others, particularly children, is a responsibility that requires the suppression of the aggressive, competitive, independent self. When such responsibilities no longer dominate, women are free to express other aspects of themselves, including leisure (Bialeschki & Michener, 1994). Cooper and Gutmann (1987) found that postparenting women saw themselves as more "masculine" than did parental women. Postparenting women, however, still perceived themselves as nurturing.

Women vary in their experiences of this reconstruction or transformation of gender. A woman's way of negotiating shifting gendered identities is believed to be influenced by both psychodynamic processes (e.g., a woman's experience of herself in relation to other women) and sociocultural forces (e.g., media representations of femininity) (Huyck, 1994). As suggested in chapter five, recreation and leisure can play a role in this process by being a context within which women can reconstruct notions of femininity and what it means to be a female (Freysinger & Flannery, 1992; Wearing, 1990).

Other Dimensions of Women's Development

In addition to a re-emergence of the "masculine," older adulthood is a period when women report a changing time perspective, a restructuring of the social world, changing self-concepts and identities, and both role losses and role changes. The instrumental activities of family and/or paid work may no longer predominate in later life as they did in young and middle adulthood. The household or domestic work of older women who are married continues, however, and may even increase with their husband's retirement (Szinovacz, 1992; Vinick & Ekerdt, 1991). "Too many family obligations" have been found to be a barrier for some women and the stress that constrains women's leisure across the life cycle appears to be more related to family concerns than for men (Freysinger, 1995; Witt & Goodale, 1981).

Changes in physical functioning and health also characterize the later years. Physical health has a major effect on most women's involvement in leisure and their satisfaction with life (Riddick, 1993; Riddick & Daniels, 1984; Riddick & Stewart, 1994). Although older adulthood is often seen as a period of declining energies, such degenerations do not necessarily indicate declining interests as noted by Florida Scott Maxwell:

> Age puzzles me. I thought it was a quiet time. My seventies were interesting, and fairly serene, but my eighties are passionate. I grow more intense as I age. To my own surprise I burst out with hot conviction. Only a few years ago I enjoyed my tranquillity; now I am so disturbed by the outer world and by human quality in general that I want to put things right, as though I still owed a debt to life. I must calm down. I am far too frail to indulge in moral fervour. (1979, p. 11-12)

Fortunately, the onset of disabling age-related physical and mental decline is shifting upward. Such declines are increasingly confined to what are known as the "old-old" years of later life (i.e., 75 years of age and older). Further, tremendous variation is evident among individuals in physical aging. "Use it or lose it" is a maxim that has been found to hold true for both physical and mental functioning across the course of life (Iso-Ahola, Jackson, & Dunne, 1994; Schooler & Schaie, 1987).

Recently, a call has been made for a new philosophy or a redefinition of old age that takes into account the tremendous potential and individual variation that is evident in women's experiences of development (Fischer, Blazey, & Lipman, 1992; Friedan, 1993). Adult life has often been perceived as a series of psychological stages or social roles. The focus of research, however, is shifting away from universal stages and neat and orderly transitions toward explaining why changes occur when they do (Giele, 1982) and examining the impact of race, gender, and class relations on age and development (Stoller & Gibson, 1994; Thompson, 1994; Turner & Troll, 1994).

According to Giele (1982), some people experience distinct stages of development while others do not. She noted that a critical factor is the degree of social complexity on the job or in other aspects of everyday life. Giele stated:

> Those who must learn a great deal and adapt to many different roles seem to be the most concerned with trying to evolve an abstract self, conscience, or life structure that can integrate all these discrete events. By contrast, those with a simple job, limited by meager education and narrow contacts, are less apt to experience aging as a process that enhances autonomy or elaborates one's mental powers. (1982, p. 8)

Thus, developmental stages are not consistent for all people and in all social settings. Other researchers (e.g., Neugarten, 1968a; Farrell & Rosenberg, 1981) have also concluded that the timing, issues, meanings of adult age periods, and differences in perceptions of change or development may vary by social class.

The chronological boundaries and experiences of age periods are distinguished by race and ethnicity (Stoller & Gibson, 1994; Thompson, 1994). For these reasons, age should be thought of not only as an independent variable but also as a dependent variable which is mitigated by different life experiences and circumstances (Laws, 1995; Maddox, 1987). The interaction of race, ethnicity, gender, and class influence access to education, income, and occupation that shape women's health, cognitive development, leisure activity involvement, resources for coping, and work patterns. Thus, in this sense aging and leisure are political issues (Freysinger, 1993).

Other factors that influence an individual's ability to cope with the role and psychosocial changes that occur across the life span include the "timeliness" of events or transitions and the success of previous coping strategies. Those adults who are going through role transitions "on time" and who have adapted well previously are better able to cope with life's transitions.

A perception of choice or self-determination also is positively related to psychological well-being in adulthood. A sense of self-determination is particularly important to well-being in later adulthood. Ageist stereotypes and changing opportunity structures can undermine personal control and create dependence. Older women with limited economic resources and health, in particular, often are less able to shield themselves from ageist attitudes and the real-life consequences of these attitudes (e.g., lack of employment opportunities, elder abuse).

Leisure, as an expression of choice and a context for a sense of personal competence, has been proposed as a way for older adults to maintain or enhance a sense of control and independence (Iso-Ahola, Jackson, & Dunn, 1994; Mobily et al., 1993; Searle, Mahon, Iso-Ahola, Sdrolias, & van Dyck, 1995). The stress on independence in later life, however, has been questioned (Rodeheaver, 1987). Rodeheaver maintained that women's and older adults' lives are defined by interdependence. Circumstances of dependence have been created for these groups, however, by social policy. At the same time, U.S. culture denigrates dependence and values independence. Hence, the marginalization of older adults, and older women in particular, is reproduced in the formulation of social policy.

Although no agreement exists on whether there *is* a single pattern to women's development or what that pattern *should be*, an examination of women's changing roles is useful for understanding women's concerns and interests. Researchers have shown that women's lives are characterized by diversity in multiple changing roles and perceptions of self. Adaptation is a major theme of women's lives. The extent to which women are able and allowed to be adaptable, however, varies by individual (Huyck, 1994; Livson, 1981). Despite the number of unanswered questions, insights into the development of women provide a sense of the diversity of life patterns as well as the commonality and uniqueness of being female. Such insights also provide a challenging perspective from which to examine women's leisure.

Stability and Change in Leisure

Both women's roles and their psychosocial concerns influence leisure behavior in adulthood. The effects of changing adult roles and responsibilities on leisure activities and involvement have been explored by many researchers. Family and work are important dimensions of women's lives that interact with leisure in varying ways (Allison & Duncan, 1987; Bialeschki & Michener, 1994; Freysinger & Ray, 1994; Horna, 1985; Kelly & Kelly, 1994; Shaw, 1982, 1985b, 1992a; Witt & Goodale, 1981). In addition, the work of several researchers suggested that personality, when viewed as preoccupations, concerns, and psychosocial issues of stage of life, also influences leisure behavior (Freysinger, 1995; Iso-Ahola, 1980a; Kleiber, 1985; Osgood & Howe, 1984; Rapoport & Rapoport, 1975).

Overall, the psychological and sociological research has found that both continuity and change in leisure behavior exist across the life span. Research from a sociological perspective usually discusses adulthood in terms of changing roles. Thus, distinctions in women's leisure behavior are increasingly being made on the basis of marital, parental, and/or work status or roles and not on the basis of age.

Research on the relationship between the psychosocial preoccupations of various stages of adulthood and leisure behavior and meanings is limited. The possibility of purposive, patterned change in psychosocial concerns is rarely recognized. Change in leisure behavior is often examined from a static perspective and interactions of various social and psychological factors across the life span are not considered (Iso-Ahola, 1980b). Furthermore, much of the research on leisure defined as activity, time, and experience does not examine both women and men, the specific leisure activity, or how leisure is a gendered and aged practice. We do have, however, some information about how change and stability can be found in women's experiences of leisure in adulthood.

Developmental Models of Leisure

Before examining what the research has shown in regard to women's leisure activity and motivation over the course of life, three developmental models of leisure that build on life-span and life-course research are presented briefly:

(a) a family life cycle model (Rapoport & Rapoport, 1975) that focuses on the interaction between social and environmental conditions and the individual,

(b) a model of personal expressivity (Gordon, Gaitz, & Scott, 1976) that explores the relationship between leisure and mental health or inner psychological growth, and

(c) a model of continuity in aging and activity across adulthood (Atchley, 1993).

Although the research for these models did not focus specifically on women, gender differences were explored in the first two. Both of these models were based on cross-sectional studies and the findings reflect age (i.e., cohort) differences, not necessarily age changes or development. All of the models, however, provide insights into the nature of change that might be expected in women's leisure over the course of life.

A Family Life Cycle Model

Individual lives are defined by the weaving together of three strands: work, family, and leisure (Rapoport & Rapoport, 1975). The patterns of one's overall lifestyle are predominantly defined by one's "preoccupations." Preoccupations are mental absorptions or concerns which arise from psychobiological development, maturation, and aging processes as they interact with social and environmental conditions. Given preoccupations may be present all through the life cycle, and they reflect patterns of development and change over the course of the life span.

These changing preoccupations are manifested in interests that: "...arise in people's awareness as ideas and feelings about what they want or would like to have or do, about which they are curious, to which they are drawn, through which they feel they might derive satisfaction" (Rapoport & Rapoport, 1975, p. 23). Leisure activities are an expression of interests that are an outcome of the interaction between preoccupations and social environments salient for individuals at different phases of the life cycle. Interests and their meanings for individuals may change or remain constant. Any activity may have various meanings for different people in relation to their interests.

The social environments and preoccupations of young, middle, and older heterosexual adults were explored in depth by Rapoport and Rapoport (1975). They found that the most salient preoccupation of young adults was that of identification with social institutions. Rapoport and Rapoport discovered that occupational roles and interest had a strong influence on young adults' expectations and activities in the contexts of family and leisure. Gender differences were evident in the importance of occupational interests which were a more predominant focus of the males than the females. The compatibility of leisure interests and activities also were found to be an important element in the "mate selection" process. Assisting young adults in maintaining interests and activities was advocated as a base or resource for later in life. This maintenance of interests is particularly important for women who often are more constrained in their leisure by family and household responsibilities and likely to be more affected by changes in family structure and dynamics in middle adulthood. Research has suggested that women adapt or give up interests more than men do after marriage and the birth of the first child (Bernard, 1984; Bialeschki & Michener, 1994; Kelly, 1983a).

Rapoport and Rapoport (1975) referred to middle adulthood as the "establishment" phase or the phase of life investments. The preoccupation of early establishment (i.e., when preschool age children are present) is with productivity, making choices, and plans. For both women and men, this early establishment phase tends to be a home and child-centered time when self-interests (e.g., leisure) are sacrificed for the sake of establishing oneself and meeting the demands and needs of others.

The midestablishment phase (i.e., when children are of school age) is characterized by a concern with performance, sensory gratification, and competence and effectiveness at what one has chosen. The midestablishment phase is potentially a period of great enjoyment with a peak in family-centered activities, both in and outside the home. During this phase, working-class individuals were more passive and less articulate in the pursuit of leisure interests and activities than were middle-class individuals. This finding was attributed to differences in financial resources and levels of education.

During the late establishment phase (i.e., when children are out of school), adults were preoccupied with evaluation and revision concerning the meaningfulness of commitments. Adults were confronting whether to change, what to change, and how to make those changes.

Rapoport and Rapoport (1975) noted that the establishment phase was experienced differently by individuals with a complex of variables affecting the degree of turbulence and concern experienced. These variables included: personality, social class background, values and aspirations, and the specific event in context. Rapoport and Rapoport concluded that work commitment marks the establishment phase as a whole and leisure meaning and activity patterns were related to the type of job held. Involvement in family networks also had the greatest potential during this phase. Because gender was not a factor of interest in their study, the applicability of these conclusions for both women and men was assumed but not discussed.

Older adults' focal preoccupation is that of achieving a sense of social and personal integration. Rapoport and Rapoport (1975) found that:

> In the later years the 'recreative' element of 'leisure' has less relevance than in the establishment phases when, in many instances, it made sense to think of 'free time' activities in terms of their restoring the individual to productive efficiency. (1975, p. 271).

A number of factors were found to influence activity in the later years including education, income, and health. When all three of these factors were high, activity was high. Family and kin relations as well as housing and residential situations also influenced the development of lifestyles during this phase.

The validity of the Rapoports' (1975) developmental model of leisure has rarely been tested. Horna (1985) examined the concept of "preoccupations" by focusing specifically on the establishment phase and its comparison with other phases. She found family and marital relationships to be a "pervasive and ubiquitous" preoccupation at all stages. Horna (1985) and others (Kelly & Kelly, 1994; Shank, 1986) reported that work and leisure domains "did not even approach" the predominance of the family. When women in her sample engaged in leisure activities, most of them preferred activities with their spouse or other family members. Whether or not these women worked outside the home was also strongly associated with family needs. The shifts in preoccupations that were found in middle adulthood were largely manifested not as an abandonment of the preoccupation with the family, but rather as a relative de-emphasis of the family and marital relationship. Horna reported that this de-emphasis was consistently more apparent with the men than with the women in her study. This finding contrasts with developmental research cited earlier in this chapter that suggests although women turn their interests and energies to pursuits outside the home during middle to late adulthood, men often emphasize relationships and turn to the family for fulfillment. The age and family stage of Horna's sample may have influenced her findings. At the same time, research continues to show that the time that mothers devote to children and housework exceeds that of fathers (Firestone & Shelton, 1988; Freysinger, 1994; Horna, 1993; Mauldin & Meeks, 1990; Nock & Kingston, 1988; Zuzanek & Smale, 1993).

Griffin (1981) criticized the Rapoports' (1975) developmental model for the emphasis given to personal resourcefulness and the lack of attention given to the impact of social-structural factors in creating a meaningful life. According to Griffin, the model's concept of the family life cycle is present, situation-based, and divorced from the cultural and sociohistorical context of women's lives. Rapoport and Rapoport recognized social constraints as barriers to be overcome rather than:

> ...material conditions which are based on sets of power relations inherent in patriarchal society, and which, if challenged, can have equally real and problematic effects on women's lives. (1975, p. 114)

Thus, from Griffin's view, the Rapoport and Rapoport developmental model can provide only a limited descriptive account of women's leisure.

A Model of Personal Expressivity

Gordon, Gaitz, and Scott (1976) conceptualized leisure as activity which varies according to the intensity of expressive involvement. In other words, leisure activities range from low to high in personal investment. Five levels of activity exist: relaxation, diversion, developmental, creativity, and sensual transcendence. Gordon, Gaitz, and Scott coupled this concept of leisure with Gordon's (1971) life span framework to gain an understanding of changes in leisure across the life span. Eleven stages constitute Gordon's developmental framework. The stages are produced by the interaction of physical maturation, cognitive elaboration, social role acquisitions and relinquishments, and economic resources throughout the life span.

The underlying assumption of Gordon's (1971) developmental framework is that human action is oriented toward the attainment of one or more socially-defined goals or value themes. Value themes are a cluster or complex of culturally defined, idealized aspects of human life and social interaction, such as achievement, acceptance, compliance, and self-control.

To test this model of personal expressivity, Gordon, Gaitz, and Scott (1976) interviewed persons concerning their participation in different types of leisure activities (e.g., active, passive, external, internal-homebound, individual leisure), their participation in activities constituting the five different levels of the expressivity continuum, and their leisure pleasure. They found that the older the respondent, the lower the general level of leisure activity. External, high-intensity activities decreased with age. Homebound, moderate-intensity activities did not change over the life span. Relaxation and solitude (i.e., low-intensity activities), increased with age. While few gender differences existed, females were higher generally in internal, individual, low-intensity activities, and males were higher generally in external, social, high-intensity activities. Women and men scored essentially the same, however, on level of involvement in active pursuits, and males scored slightly higher on passive leisure.

Gordon, Gaitz, and Scott believed that leisure activities enhanced personal development because they performed a "bridging function, bringing together and integrating major meanings from the security and the challenge themes at any particular stage" (1976, p. 333). In addition, they concluded that the qualitative form and breadth of leisure activities may be more related to roles than is the absolute amount of pleasure derived from the activity. They found no important differences on leisure pleasure by gender at any age. In terms of age changes the researchers stated:

> Development and creativity do not vary with age, but diversion and sensual transcendence are negatively associated with position in the lifespan. The overwhelming majority of our respondents have either traded away the intense levels of potential happiness and even joy obtainable from some of these highly expressive leisure forms for a more sedate existence, or perhaps they had been socialized in a time when highly intense forms of leisure activity were not part of one's social psychological repertoire. (Gordon, Gaitz, and Scott, 1976, p. 334)

Such a conclusion seems particularly relevant to women for whom negative sanctions to intense leisure often exist (Wearing, 1994). The extent to which the decline in engagement in highly intense leisure is due to age-related psychosocial and physical changes (Iso-Ahola, 1980a; Iso-Ahola, Jackson, and Dunne, 1994; Kleiber, 1985) or cultural ideologies and social opportunity is unclear.

A Model of Leisure Continuity

Atchley's (1993) continuity theory of normal aging differs from the previous two models because it was developed to describe the process of aging, not the age-related experience of leisure, work, or family. Atchley (1994), however, recently applied this theory to leisure activity involvement in adulthood.

Continuity theory conceives of aging as a process of adaptation and adjustment to change. In making adaptive choices, middle-aged and older adults attempt to preserve and maintain existing internal and external structures. Continuity does not mean sameness or lack of change. Continuity means coherence and consistency of patterns over time. In seeking to maintain continuity across adulthood, the individual links current changes to her perceived past and expected future.

Internal and external are both dimensions of continuity. Internal or psychological continuity is a persistence over time of mental constructs about who we are, what we are capable of doing, and what is satisfying to us. The mental constructs involved are identity, self-concept, ideal self, and self-esteem. Internal continuity requires memory. Lack of internal continuity (e.g., because of Alzheimer's disease) can be stressful to the individual since a remembered structure of selfhood orients the individual to the world. A remembered self is also used to get a sense of direction, make decisions, and take action. Thus, lack of internal continuity is stressful to other people with whom the individual interacts since each of us gets a sense of our own continuity through consistency in our interactions with others. The persistence over time of a structure of relationships and overt behaviors (i.e., roles, activities, physical and social environments) is what defines external or social continuity.

According to this model, we are motivated towards continuity because continuity provides us with a sense of security and integrity. Continuity is also a basis for effective decision making and self-esteem. Further, we are motivated towards continuity by others who expect us to present ourselves in a certain (i.e., consistent) way. In addition, continuity enables us to cope with physical, social, and mental changes that may accompany aging such as widowhood, retirement, empty nest, and illness. Finally, if patterns of being and interacting have gotten us to where we are right now, they are likely to be seen as successful and are our "best bets" for the future.

Inner continuity and external continuity (i.e., continuity of activities) reinforce one another. In our activities we are motivated toward consistency in activity settings, preferences (i.e., the activities we value), and the knowledge and skills needed to engage in activities. Continuity in settings, preferences, and skills provide us with a sense of competence. According to Atchley (1993, 1994), by middle age, we have spent at least 40 years selecting, refining, and developing areas of activity competence. Hence, the reduction in range of activities that accompanies aging, is matched by increasing time spent in fewer activities. This decline is not a matter of disengagement, but a lifelong process of gradual selection that allows for efficient functioning and is a reflection of knowing oneself.

The notion of the "ageless self" which has been described by scholars of adult development supports continuity theory (Bateson, 1989; Kaufman, 1987, 1993). Research on leisure activity involvement across adulthood also reveals a pattern of continuity (Crawford, Godbey, & Crouter, 1986; Iso-Ahola, 1980a; Iso-Ahola, Jackson, and Dunne, 1994; Jackson & Witt, 1994; Kelly, Steinkamp, & Kelly 1986; Searle, Mactavish, & Brayley, 1993). Many women's lives, however, are characterized by change. In their orientation toward an "ethic of care," women are constantly adapting to the demands and expectations of other people, particularly family members. Continuity theory has not been explored in relation to women. If continuity is important to women's psychological well-being, then how women maintain a sense of continuity, what assists them in doing so, and the role of leisure in this process are questions in need of examination.

These three models provide developmental frameworks within which to study leisure behavior. Although not specific to women, they provide suggestions as to the multiple factors that may affect the leisure activity, meanings, and time of women. Some research has examined changes in leisure by age, but most researchers have "substituted" the more discriminating factor of roles associated with various stages of life. Roles related to stage in the family life cycle, however, actually explain little of the variance found in leisure behavior (Holman & Epperson, 1984; Witt & Goodale, 1981). Other factors such as personality and age, also need to be considered.

Leisure Motivation, Meanings, and Activity Across Adulthood

Many factors may affect the leisure motivations, satisfactions, and activity of women. Women's personal development, growth, and well-being may be linked to the way leisure time, activity, motivation, and meanings are perceived over the course of life.

Motivation and Meanings

Osgood and Howe (1984) noted that meanings and motivations are not always clearly distinguished in the leisure research. Motivations are the "reasons which underlie why an individual behaves as he or she does" (Osgood & Howe, 1984, p. 179). Meanings, on the other hand, refer to a phenomena's essence. According to Osgood and Howe (1984), little is actually known about the changing motivations for and meanings of leisure across the life span and the relationship to changing developmental issues. They concluded, however, that the same activities can have varied meanings for different individuals or even for the same individual at points in the life cycle. For example, a woman's place in her family career as well as her work career may have an impact on her motivations for leisure.

Havighurst (1957-58, 1961) was one of the first researchers to study changes in leisure motivations in adulthood. His exploration of leisure focused on the significance of or motivations for leisure activities as related to individuals' psychological characteristics rather than sociodemographic categories. He found that even though the significance of adults' favorite leisure activities was highly related to personality and moderately related to social class, the relationship between leisure significance and both age and gender was weak. The principle leisure motivations identified by these adults included: just for the pleasure of it, welcome change from work, new experience, chance to be creative, chance to achieve something, contact with friends, makes time pass, and service to others. In terms of gender differences:

(a) men indicated development of talent more often than women as the significance of leisure;

(b) women were more passive than men in physical energy input;

(c) for women, recreation "fits in" with their housework but was seldom seen as a relief from or contrast to work while the opposite or no relationship existed between men's work and leisure; and

(d) women clustered at the service end of the service vs. pleasure scale.

Havighurst concluded that the significance of leisure is an aspect of personality. More variability in reasons for pursuing favorite leisure activities could be found among people of a given sex, age, or social class than could be found between groups.

As discussed in chapter four, leisure can be oriented toward connections with others (i.e., affiliative, sharing) or towards autonomy (i.e., independence, agency, and self-determination). These predominant themes are not surprising given that a task of adulthood is balancing the two "drives" of affiliation and agency (Freud in Smelser, 1980). Erikson's stages of intimacy (young adulthood) and generativity (middle adulthood) reflect an orientation toward affiliation. Women report that leisure influences affirmation of family, satisfaction with family, development of children, development and mainte-nance of friendships and interactions with others. In these ways leisure is affiliation (Freysinger, 1995).

By focusing on men, Erikson's theory of psychosocial or ego develop-ment left out women's need for an independent sense of self or identity (Gilligan, 1982c). Across studies, women report a need for self-determined personal or autonomous leisure (Bialeschki & Michener, 1994; Freysinger & Flannery, 1992; Shank, 1986) as a means of recuperation and renewal. Renewal may come through relaxation and disengagement from everyday concerns and demands. Another type of renewal can emerge from autono-mous or self-determined leisure, for example through self-expression, learn-ing and development, challenge and accomplishment, and recognition and credibility (Freysinger, 1995; Freysinger & Flannery, 1992). Self-determined or agentic leisure allows women to renew and redefine themselves and provides a sense of strength, vitality, and possibility.

For many women, however, self-determined agentic leisure is difficult to realize because of the orientation toward an ethic of care (Bialeschki & Michener, 1994; Harrington, Dawson, & Bolla, 1992; Shank, 1986). Women are challenged to put themselves at the center of their attention and actions by a patriarchy which negates women's need for self-care and pleasure. As French (1985) noted:

> To act against one's impulses to pleasure is to act against one's best self, and makes all subsequent actions wretched. To deny one's own desires and needs is the first step into loss of self, into adoption of the image urged by patriarchy...nothing in patriarchy is more demoralizing in the true sense of the word than a morality that calls pleasure and selfhood *vice* and *selfishness*, and miserable submission to imposed identity and goals *duty* and *virtue*. (p. 539)

Women report that they need leisure for relaxation as well as for self—to maintain personal health and well-being. Without self-determined leisure, women's ability to care for others is undermined.

The need for a balance of affiliation and autonomy is evidenced in later life. In a study of later life leisure, Kelly, Steinkamp, and Kelly (1986) identified seven clusters of leisure motivations including: companionship in the activity, strengthening primary relationships, competence and skill-building, expres-sion and personal development, health and exercise, meeting role expecta-tions, and general enjoyment. Although meeting role expectations was seldom mentioned, enjoyment almost always was described. In examining age and gender differences, the researchers found that males ranked higher than females on health and exercise, companionship, and skill development motives. Kelly, Steinkamp, and Kelly (1986) concluded that leisure was important to later life adults as a context for expressing and maintaining primary relationships and as an opportunity to express and develop self-definitions of ability.

Leisure motivations and meanings do appear to vary somewhat over the life span as the "containers" of leisure change. The significant changes in women's leisure related to age are likely a reflection of changes in opportunities, physical capabilities, economic resources, roles and responsibilities, and preoccupations that occur over the life span. At the same time, affiliation and agency, caring for others and caring for self, are themes in women's leisure that transcend age.

Activity

The research on activity consistency across the life span provides contradictory and inconclusive findings. From a review of the research on adult development and social activities, Knox (1977) noted that except for times of major change, adult activities are characterized by a high degree of stability and are based on a characteristic structure of participation in family, occupational, political, organizational, church, educational, and leisure activities. Cheek and Burch (1976) also found that continuity across the life span was more likely in nonwork or free-time activities than in work activities.

Conversely, Kelly (1982) concluded that leisure, as relatively free activity, may be the part of life with the least continuity. A similar assertion was made by MacPherson (1984) who argued that the meaning and function of leisure activities often varied from one stage in the life cycle to the next. MacPherson attributed this variation to role transitions, age-based norms, and changing opportunities. Iso-Ahola (1980a, 1980b) contended that leisure activity patterns continuously change over the life span because of an individual's socialized need to seek novel and arousing experiences. He further suggested that leisure behavior reflects a basic human need for both stability (i.e., security) and change (i.e., variety) which is evident in patterns and total behavior but not individual activities.

The importance of childhood play or recreation as a basis for adult leisure behavior has been a research focus. Iso-Ahola (1980a) suggested that early recreation experiences provided the setting and direction for individual changes in leisure patterns during the later stages of life. Most studies on the significance of childhood recreation patterns for adult leisure behavior indicated that approximately half of all adult recreation activities are "carry-overs" from childhood (Kelly, 1974; Yoesting & Burkhead, 1973; Yoesting & Christiansen, 1978). Based on such findings, Kelly (1983b) developed the "core and balance" model of leisure activity. The "core" are those activities which are fairly stable across the individual's life, while the "balance" of activities vary according to the current life situation, roles, and preoccupations.

The influence of early adulthood (i.e., in the twenties) activity patterns on later adulthood activities was examined by Maas and Kuypers (1975) in their exploration of personality and lifestyle. They discovered that lifestyle categories differed in the degree to which they exhibited stability and change. Some lifestyles and associated recreational activity and interest patterns remained more stable than others. For example, the early adult life of "visiting" mothers (i.e., those mothers whose lives were characterized by many recreational interests) had low relevance for their later adult lifestyle. In general, Maas and Kuypers found that early adult life had more relevance for the aging lifestyles of men than women; the lifestyles of men were more stable than those of women. This finding was supported by other research that has shown women's lives characterized by flexibility and adaptability. The implications for a woman's sense of continuity and integrity, as well as for the delivery of leisure services, has yet to be explored.

In a panel study, Freysinger and Ray (1994) examined, from a gender perspective, the changes in and predictors of frequency of participation in discretionary activities of European-American individuals between young (21–24 years of age) and middle (35–38 years of age) adulthood. Categories of discretionary activity involvement were adult education, informal education, voluntary associations, and recreation. Women's involvement in adult education, informal education, and voluntary associations increased between young and middle adulthood. Although this finding is inconsistent with other research that suggests a decline in activity involvement with age, a number of the specific activities within the informal education and voluntary associations categories were family-oriented (e.g., going to the library, watching an educational television program, attend a PTA meeting).

In young adulthood, level of formal education and locus of control predicted women's activity involvement. Women with higher levels of formal education and who were internal in locus of control reported greater involvement in discretionary activity. Women with higher levels of young adult activity participation had an internal locus of control, were dissatisfied with homemaking, and had lower levels of income. They also reported greater involvement in discretionary activity in middle adulthood. Several variables, however, did not predict activity involvement: twelfth-grade club and organizational involvement, employment status, family status (i.e., a combination of marital, parental status, and presence of child in home), and job satisfaction (Freysinger & Ray, 1994).

The relationship between current activity involvement and level of formal education and previous activity involvement are consistent with other research. Somewhat surprising was the finding regarding satisfaction with homemaking. The findings were unclear about whether women who were dissatisfied with homemaking engaged in discretionary activities to compensate for their dissatisfaction or if women who were highly involved in discretionary activities were dissatisfied with homemaking because it interfered with their participation in such activities.

The type, content, and degree of involvement in leisure activity across the life span have also been studied. Findings suggest a gradual decline in activity involvement (e.g., educational, recreational, and voluntary) with age (Cookson, 1986; Cross, 1981; Gordon, Gaitz, & Scott, 1976; Havighurst, 1957-58; Johnstone & Rivera, 1965; Knox, 1977). Besides age, patterns of involvement also may vary by activity type (Knox, 1977; Smale & Dupuis, 1993), adult roles, and gender. For example, Unkel (1981) examined differences in both the intensity and variety of adults' participation in three types of physical recreation activity by age, sex, and family stage. She found a decline in both frequency of participation in and number of physical recreation activities with age. The overall decline, however, was influenced by family status. For example, participation declined significantly faster for single persons of either sex than for nonsingle persons or persons with children. Her conclusion that consideration should also be given to type of activity when studying involvement is important. Smith, Stewart, and Brown (1980) also concluded that the rapidity of decline in activity participation depended on the kind of activity being studied.

Havighurst (1957-58) found that types of leisure activity varied by age and sex. The main gender differences he found were that women were more likely to be involved in formal and informal association and reading while men were more involved in sports, fishing, and gardening. Age differences were also found in a number of categories. Participation in formal association declined with age, though not among women until they reached their sixties. Men's participation in informal groups was highest from 50 to 60 years, but women's participation in such activity was equal at all ages.

Angrist (1967) was one of the first and only researchers to examine the effects of women's multiple roles on their leisure activities at various life cycle stages. Angrist hypothesized that stage in life, involving specific sets of constellations of roles such as wife-mother or having a preschool-age child, was related to amount and type of leisure activity. The findings showed that women in the role constellations did not differ significantly in overall leisure activity scores but they did differ in terms of specific types of activities. Furthermore, those financially privileged women with regular household and childcare help were significantly more active in leisure participation in all categories than those women with little or no help. Angrist concluded that the general hypothesis cannot be either entirely accepted or rejected. Role categories were similar in leisure activity level but the differences found among women in type of activity suggested that each category may have predominant interests which can be pursued under conditions of available time. Because of the influence of domestic help, Angrist suggested that research needs to explore if highly active women seek help so they can be freer for leisure pursuits or if women with domestic help find themselves with time to fill and, therefore, seek out activities.

This research indicates that it is not enough to look at age or gender alone when examining leisure motivations and activities over the life span. Consistent with a developmental perspective, personal as well as sociocultural and historical factors also need to be taken into account.

Concluding Perspectives

Women's lives are characterized by changing roles, preoccupations, opportunities, and resources. Research suggests that the differences that have been found either between women and men or among women in leisure motivations and activities across the life span can be attributed to these changes. Yet, little is actually known about how changing role demands affect leisure over the life course. Nor has research explored if and how women in various life situations perceive change in work, leisure, and family across the life span. These gaps will need to be filled before a fuller understanding of stability and change in women's leisure can be attained.

Discussion Questions

1. How does a life span perspective provide insights into the life patterns, commonalties, and uniqueness of women and their leisure?

2. Select one model of development and describe the implications this model has for leisure in your life.

3. Women are presumed to be more relational than men. How does this influence the leisure of a female over the life span?

4. Since women's lives are characterized by flexibility and adaptability, what implications does this have for leisure service providers?

5. What effect might age, time, and cohort have on gender differences in leisure?

6. How do you see your leisure interests and motivations differing from those of your mother, your grandmother, or your younger sister? What might be the reasons for these differences?

7. Think of your favorite (or most frequently participated in) leisure activities. When did you begin them, where/from whom did you learn them, have your reasons for participating in them changed, have your satisfactions gained from them changed?

8. How do you envision your leisure activities, motivations, and interests changing in the next 10–20 years? How have they changed in the past ten years?

9. Does leisure enhance or influence your life? How or why not?

10. Do you believe highly active women seek help (e.g., from hired help, from the family) so they can be freer for leisure pursuits or do women who get help find themselves with time to fill and, therefore, seek out activities?

11. Is it "elitist" and inaccurate to say that the lives of working-class women are less complex than professional women? How would this assumption influence the questions researchers would ask about women's leisure?

Chapter Seven

"Just Do It" Is Not So Easy: Participation, Constraints, and Possibilities

From the beginning of time girls as well as boys have had their play ways, women as well as men their recreation, although the leisure-time activities for girls and women have been largely individual, self-initiated, and in the main connected with home duties. Recently, however, many radical changes in women's lives have indicated that some of their recreation needs to be organized if every girl is to have an adequate opportunity to play and every woman wholesome and satisfying ways of using her free time.

—Bowers, 1934, p. xi

The idea that women and girls have a need for recreation and leisure in their lives is not new. Some of the reasons why recreation and leisure are needed by girls and women have been discussed in the preceding chapters. Advocates of women's rights have talked about the right to leisure since the turn of the twentieth century, as can be seen from the quote above. Many early advocates talked about "wholesome" participation and emphasized the need for "appropriate" activities for women and girls. As detailed in chapter two, they often expressed concern that sports activities would be "too competitive" for women and dangerous to their physical health. They were particularly concerned that physical activities might damage women's reproductive organs and interfere with their ability to get pregnant and to give birth (Hall & Richardson, 1982). Thus, the call for the provision of leisure activities for girls and women in the early to mid-1900s was a call for activities that would not threaten traditional female gender or mothering roles but would be deemed socially appropriate (Henderson, 1993).

This idea of socially appropriate leisure for women and girls is still evident today in the activities that are offered by recreation service providers and by the activities in which parents typically enroll their daughters. Although the range of socially appropriate activities has expanded and competitive and physically active recreation is encouraged for girls, some activities such as football, hockey, baseball, and wrestling are still primarily male activities; an active debate continues about whether girls and women should be allowed or encouraged to participate in such events.

The first part of this chapter examines women's leisure participation today including the activities and experiences commonly available to women. We examine gains in leisure and the extent to which some women participate in "socially appropriate" activities while other women use leisure participation as a way to challenge and resist traditional views of female gender roles. As discussed in chapter four, women's leisure participation cannot be seen simply as freely chosen activities. Learned gender roles, gendered power relations in society, and the material condition of women's lives all affect women's level and types of participation.

In the second part of this chapter the notion of leisure constraints is introduced and the ways in which these constraints affect leisure participation for women are discussed. Constraints help explain some of the gaps in women's leisure including gaps in participation and in the quality of leisure experiences. Constraints affect women differently, and some women are more able than others to overcome or negotiate such constraints. A number of leisure constraints, however, are commonly experienced by women and these constraints reduce or affect their level of participation. At the end of the chapter, ways of dealing with leisure constraints are addressed and the possibilities that leisure might challenge, rather than reinforce, traditional restrictive gender roles are discussed.

Leisure Participation

Women's participation in leisure might seem to be a fairly simple and straightforward issue to address. Gathering reliable and valid data on participation, however, is not an easy task. Issues that researchers face in collecting participation data include: what leisure activities to examine; how to group or categorize different activities (e.g., is swimming in the ocean in the summer the same as a recreational swim in an indoor pool in the winter? and is this the same activity as participating in a competitive swim meet or training for such a meet?); whether to look only at the activity or to consider the context as well; whether to look at the leisure experience, and if so, how to do this; and whether to gather data on women's participation only or to compare these data to men's participation.

Much of the research on the leisure participation of women has been the collection of data on activities without looking at social or physical context and has reported comparisons between the participation rates of females and males. The research has used either recall survey techniques (i.e., asking people in what activities they participate, and sometimes including a question about how often they participate), or time-budget techniques (i.e., asking people to record activity participation over a set period of time). Both the survey and time budget research have shown that women participate less than men in sports and physical activities, and that these gender differences are evident from a young age (e.g., Altergott & McCreedy, 1993; Bonen & Shaw, 1995; Kinsley & Graves, 1983). The research also shows that women have somewhat higher levels of participation in social and cultural activities (e.g., going to the theater or art shows, or spending time in social gatherings with friends) (Altergott & McCreedy, 1993; Kinsley & Graves, 1983).

The data on sports and cultural activities give us an overall picture of male and female participation, but they also hide many of the complex differences that exist both between men and women and among women of different ages, ethnic backgrounds, or socioeconomic levels. For example, to examine only the gender differences in sports participation is not simply a question of males participating more. In some sports (e.g., football, hockey, wrestling, boxing, fishing, hunting), male participants greatly outnumber female participants at all levels of competition, but there are also physical activities and sports in which females predominate (e.g., dancing, gymnastics, synchronized swimming, figure skating, cheerleading, aerobics). Both males and females participate in some sports, but a gender difference is evident in terms of number of participants and numbers of highly competitive or professional athletes (e.g., basketball, soccer, volleyball).

Although some stereotypes are breaking down with respect to girls' and women's sports participation, perceptions of "female sports" and "male sports" are based on how appropriate such activities are thought to be for each gender. Recreational activities for children are often open to both girls and boys, but parents may differentially enroll their male and female children in activities and tend to select stereotyped activities that they believe are appropriate for the gender of their child. Thus, girls and boys tend to learn and enjoy different activities from an early age. A stigma still exists regarding participation in activities thought to be more appropriate for the opposite sex, and this stigma may be particularly strong for boys wishing to participate in stereotypically female activities rather than the other way around (Colley, Nash, O'Donnell & Restorick, 1987; Kane, 1988; Theberge, 1991).

A similar analysis can be done of the data that shows women tend to have higher rates of participation in social and cultural activities than men. Although the overall difference may be small, considerable gender differences in types of social cultural activities that men and women choose may be masked. Women tend to be more involved in arts and crafts activities, both as creative participants and as visitors or spectators of shows and performances. Men, on the other hand, tend to be more involved in hobbies, collections, and video and computer games.

Even in activities which seem to be fairly equally divided among men and women, such as television watching or reading, differences continue to exist in the types of programs watched and the books or magazines read. A quick look at a magazine rack in almost any store shows that magazines on display are grouped according to those appealing to a male audience and those thought to appeal to females.

Collecting leisure participation data, therefore, is a complicated process. The choice of categories of activity is important. If categories are too broad, real differences between men and women and among women may be obscured. On the other hand, if too many multiple categories of activity are used, the data are fragmented and difficult to interpret.

Shaw (1985a) suggested that the activity categories used in some participation studies have a male bias. That is, researchers may have selected those activities central in men's lives, such as sport, but that may be less central in the lives of many women. Compared to research on sports participation, few researchers have analyzed the role of informal social interactional settings (e.g., sitting in the kitchen having a cup of coffee with a friend) in people's leisure lives. These affiliation activities seem to be more common to women.

Moreover, researchers have commented on how women's lives may be more holistic and less segmented than men's lives (e.g., Glyptis & Chambers, 1982; Gregory, 1982; Shaw, 1990b). Women are more likely than men to participate in more than one activity at the same time (e.g., watching television while doing the ironing, or gardening while looking after children). The division between what is work and what is leisure is also less clear for women compared to men. This merging of work and leisure occurs because home is the main place of work for many women, and much of the time spent at home is a combination of work and leisure or as some researchers have termed it, "semi-leisure" (Horna, 1989b). Obviously, finding appropriate categories to reflect women's leisure lives is not an easy task.

The question of leisure meanings also makes participation research difficult. If the researcher defines leisure as participation in certain categories of activity (e.g., sports, television, reading, socializing), the questions of whether such activities are always experienced as leisure by the participant, or whether they might sometimes be work are ignored. Although researchers generally agree that leisure is best defined as a type of experience rather than a type of activity as we discussed in chapter four, this definition is generally not put into practice when carrying out participation research. Ignoring the participant's experience may be particularly problematic for women because they usually have greater responsibility than men for household chores and childcare. For example, going to a movie with a friend may be a different experience from taking three or four young children to a movie. For women who are mothers, family recreational activities may sometimes be experienced as work rather than leisure because of the effort and energy required to organize such activities, to ensure appropriate food and clothing is available, and to look after the children and deal with disputes and behavior problems (Hunter & Whitson, 1992; Shaw, 1992b).

Perhaps because of these difficulties in conducting participation research, the results of such studies have been inconclusive and sometimes contradictory. In a content analysis of sexism in leisure research, Henderson (1984) found that about half of the studies that examined gender differences uncovered no difference in activity involvement. Zuzanek (1978) noted that the similarities between women and men in leisure participation rates were more striking than the differences. Kelly (1983a) also contended that differences in participation in most leisure activities between men and women in the United States were negligible or nonexistent. For example, Kelly stated that the frequency of activity participation was the same for both sexes for swimming, working out, bowling, playing tennis, attending movies or concerts, gardening, giving parties, watching TV, and driving.

Other studies concluded distinct gender differences in activity participation. For example, Colley (1984) suggested that for women the chief incentive in leisure activity was social, but for men it was competitive. Colley also confirmed that sex-typing of activities existed with certain activities such as knitting and shopping being considered more suitable for women. In Shaw's (1985b) time-budget study based on activities and whether or not they were experienced as leisure, women were found to spend less time in leisure activities than men. This gender difference was particularly evident on weekends when men were relatively free of work responsibilities, but women continued to have housework and childcare responsibilities which decreased their time in leisure.

Apart from the difficulties in conducting participation research, the idea of doing gender difference research has been criticized. One reason for this criticism is that on many dimensions, that researchers might measure—such as level of participation in sports—considerable overlap exists between the sexes. Although overall male participation may seem to be higher, many men have low levels of participation, and many women have high levels. The problems with gender differences research are described in detail in chapter eight.

An alternative way to examine women's leisure participation that does not rely on establishing gender differences is to focus only on the leisure experiences and participation of women and not to make comparisons to men. When this approach has been used, researchers tend to put more emphasis on the meanings of the activities as well as the social and physical contexts. For purposes of our discussion, we will focus on both the activities and settings surrounding women's leisure participation.

Women's Leisure Activities and Settings

As we found in chapter four, activities are an important component of leisure, but the meanings of activities can vary and particular meanings depend on the containers (i.e., physical and social context of the activity). For many women, the family and home are the most available context for leisure. Other activities and settings, such as social activities with friends, television and media activities, and sports, are important, too.

Family Activities

The structure and form of families in North America have changed dramatically over the last twenty to thirty years. Only a small minority of families now fall into the "traditional" pattern of an employed father, a mother who is a homemaker, and two children. Throughout the 1980s the diversity of families became increasingly apparent. This diversity includes single-parent families, gay and lesbian families, blended families, custodial and noncustodial families, foster families, and families without children. Despite this diversity, the family, in whatever form it is experienced, remains an important center for meanings, leisure activities, and satisfaction for many people (Kelly & Kelly, 1994), especially for women.

Although reliable research on whether family activities and family leisure contribute to family stability (i.e., whether the family that plays together does actually stay together) is rare, family activities do seem to make a positive contribution to marital satisfaction (Holman & Jacquart, 1988; Orthner, 1975; Orthner & Mancini, 1978). In marriages where husband and wife share joint activities, they also have more positive patterns of interaction and happier marriages. Although the causal direction of this relationship is not clear (i.e., people in more satisfying relationships may tend to do more activities together in the first place), the research does show a connection between shared leisure and relationship satisfaction.

The effect of family activities involving children has received little attention from researchers, probably because of the difficulty of involving children in research studies. Survey research with adults indicates that parents, especially mothers, often seek recreational activities that children and parents can do together. Parents believe that shared family activities help to build and maintain good connections among family members and help to teach positive values (Horna, 1989b).

Studies have shown that the most common family activities in which parents and children participate together are television watching and other passive activities, e.g., video games and movies (Shaw, in press). The next most common category of family activity is sports and physical activities, including going for walks, cycling, swimming, skating, and other family outings (Shaw, in press).

Family activities are common in all kinds of families including prechild, postchild, and no-child families. These family activities can involve the couple only or may also involve members of the extended family. The birth of the first child is probably the most important event in a woman's life in terms of the effect on her leisure patterns (Kelly, 1983a). After the birth of the first child, leisure patterns tend to be more home-centered and child-centered for both mothers and fathers. The presence of children has a particularly strong effect on mothers' leisure (Bialeschki & Michener, 1994; Shaw, 1988b). When the children in the family are young, parents particularly from middle-class families, tend to find activities that are defined as suitable for the child or children, such as going to the park or to the zoo. As children grow older and are enrolled in more formal recreation programs, family and parent activities may decline as parents spend more of their time driving children to and from activities.

Family activities can have positive outcomes and are highly valued by parents; however, some negative aspects of family leisure also exist. According to Horna (1989b), family leisure is largely role determined, meaning that fathers and mothers typically perform traditional gender roles in the enactment of family leisure. Men not only participate less in family leisure than women, but they also do more of the "playing," especially with regard to sports activities; women do more of the planning, organizing, providing food, and childcare (Horna, 1989b; Shaw, 1992b). Thus, for women, family leisure may be experienced as "work" rather than leisure, implying that women's efforts in providing leisure for their children may sometimes be at the expense of their own personal leisure experiences.

Family leisure activities can also be conflictual. According to Orthner and Mancini (1991), approximately one-third of families experience stress from conflict over leisure activities. This conflict can range from what channel to watch on TV, what to do while on vacation, or the expected behavior and discipline of the children. In general, though, the growing body of research on family leisure activities suggests that such activities are centrally important to family members, especially mothers. They can, and often do, provide enjoyment and satisfaction, but they can be experienced as work-like and stressful as well. Fostering positive leisure activities and experiences for all family members is not always easy.

Social Activities with Friends

If the primary interaction for most women is through the family, the next most important social setting is with friends including women-only and mixed friendship groups. Bialeschki (1984) found visiting friends to be one of the most common activities in which women participated. Only sleeping, jobs, media (television/radio), eating, and meal preparation/clean-up were participated in with greater frequency. The research on friendship, particularly female friendship, is difficult in relation to leisure research because friendships are not a social role as work and family are, and they are voluntary associations which may or may not be publicly visible.

The nature of friendship patterns may differ for women and men (Tesch, 1983; Wood, 1994). Women tend to be more intimate with friends, more likely to have one-to-one relationships, and to receive understanding, support and security in their relationships. Men tend to have friendships in groups that are less relational and revolve around activities. Women's friendships can also revolve around shared interests; this shared activity, however, may take a number of forms ranging from structured sport activities to "just talking." Friendships between women may also be a way to combine work-related tasks with recreation activities. For example, a mother might meet a friend in the local park so the children can play on the playground; this experience may give her an opportunity to socialize with her friend at the same time as she is taking care of the children (Wearing, 1990).

In leisure, opportunities exist for women to be involved in women-only activities as well as mixed groups (Henderson & Bialeschki, 1987; Mitten, 1992, 1995). Women-only groups can provide a different experience because women can be themselves and are relatively free of role expectations (Sadker & Sadker, 1986). In recent years, women-only activities, such as women's camps, wilderness outings, and vacations, have become increasingly popular.

Some women prefer women-only activities and feel more comfortable in such groups, because they provide personal growth and a sense of control and empowerment (Henderson & Bialeschki, 1986, 1987). Other women may prefer co-ed groups for leisure activities. Individual differences also exist in preferences for small groups (e.g., one or two friends) versus large group settings. Even though many women like to spend time alone, the social aspect of leisure and interacting with others seems to be an important dimension of women's leisure enjoyment and satisfaction (Freysinger & Flannery, 1992).

Sexual Behavior and Intimacy

Little has been written about the relationship between sexual behavior and leisure. In particular, research about sex as leisure for women is lacking. Sexuality, however, is a significant aspect of most people's lives. Sexuality is closely related to personal and social identities, and sexually intimate relationships are highly valued (Kelly, 1982, 1983a). The quality of these relationships may be a good predictor of the overall quality of people's lives.

Sexual behavior can be defined as behavior related to arousal, eroticism, and the gratification of sexual feelings. The sexual experience may be very similar to a peak leisure experience or flow experience (Csikszentmihalyi, 1975) and can be rich, complex, and provide pleasure and gratification. Intimacy may be more broadly defined to include feelings of caring and closeness that are highly valued by women.

Comfort (1976) suggested that sex has three functions in North American society. These functions are procreational sex for parenthood, relational sex where the significant factor is the intimate relationship between two people, and recreational sex where sex is a type of physical play. Victorian morality, based upon Puritanism, maintained that the only acceptable function for sexual activity was as a duty within marriage in the service of procreation. This attitude still affects thinking today, although many cultures have become more liberal in thinking about sex outside marriage. Acceptance of the legitimacy of relational sex is increasingly widespread (Godbey, 1985), although negative attitudes towards gay and lesbian relationships and other unmarried people living together still exist in certain segments of our society. Recreational sex seems to have only limited acceptability today, and the AIDS epidemic and awareness of other sexually transmitted diseases may be making this option less exciting.

Any meaningful discussion of sexual behavior and attitudes has to take into account the different realities of women and men. All too often textbooks and articles ignore or gloss over such differences particularly as they pertain to sexuality. In the Victorian era a double standard existed; recreational sex for men was widespread and tacitly acknowledged, if not actually condoned. Women on the other hand were not expected to have sexual feelings or desires and were supposed to remain "chaste." Even today, such attitudes continue to have an effect. In many parts of the world women are still considered to be the "property" of their husbands and their sexuality is tightly controlled, although men in such societies may have much higher degrees of sexual freedom without fear of social sanction. In North America, too, a double standard is still evident in that sexually active women face greater social disapproval than do men. This double standard makes life particularly difficult for teenage girls who typically gain approval for looking "sexy" but disapproval for being sexually active.

When considering women's sexual activities, the three functions of sex as procreational, relational, or recreational are insufficient. Sexual activities are not always freely chosen, pleasurable, or experienced as leisure. Sex can also be work. This work is obvious for prostitutes who are mostly women or teenage girls and who experience sex without eroticism and receive payment for their services. Sex can also be work or a "chore" when participation is seen as a duty or simply for the purpose of procreation. This sense of duty is more likely to be the case for women than men and especially noticeable in societies where women are expected to "service" their husbands.

The association of sex with fear and violence is also a constraint on women's experiences of sexuality as leisure. Not only is sex often associated with violence in the media, but a number of women have been victims of child abuse, rape, date rape, and other forms of sexual violence. This association of sex with violence, especially violence against women, may greatly inhibit women's enjoyment of sexual and intimate activities and may limit women's leisure options.

Despite these barriers, the potential for sex as leisure for women remains high. Sex and sexual intimacy evoke powerful responses in both women and men. Sexual activities can be extremely rich and rewarding in the context of an equal, caring relationship, freedom of choice, and control over one's own sexuality and reproduction. A gap remains, however, in our understandings of women's sexuality, eroticism and intimacy, and the barriers to achieving leisure through sexual activity.

Sports, Fitness and Outdoor Activities

As stated earlier in this chapter, females generally participate less in sports and physical activities than do males. This difference is especially true regarding highly organized, competitive sports and sports that involve physical contact. Men generally watch more sports on television and attend more sporting events as spectators (Kinsley & Graves, 1983; Messner & Sabo, 1990).

Despite the male-domination of sports for many years, the participation gap between males and females may be closing. A nationwide Canadian survey of participation in sports and physical activities found that more than half of the women surveyed were active in their leisure in that they participated for three hours or more per week (Canadian Fitness Survey, 1985). Another survey done in Canada with high school students found that rates of participation for males and female adolescents were similar for informal activities (e.g., swimming, jogging, skiing) and for individual competitive sports (e.g., tennis). Only in the category of competitive team sports did males show higher levels of participation than females (Shaw & Smale, 1994). Females, however, were less satisfied than the males with their level of participation in sports and physical activities and were more likely to want to increase their rate of participation.

Other studies have shown how sports participation changes over time. For both women and men, participation levels decline with age; a steep decline is particularly obvious in late adolescence and early adulthood (Bonen & Shaw, 1995; Smale & Shaw, 1994). The decline is not due to age but because of the changes in opportunities, time, and responsibilities. In addition, Bolla and Pageot (1987) found a difference in sports participation frequency between male and female college students in their first year of study, but this gap narrowed over four years with increased education and opportunity for women. In general, the research on sports activities shows that women are interested in participating, though they may lack the skills and opportunities to learn, and may receive less encouragement from parents, friends or teachers (Henderson & Bialeschki, 1994).

The health and fitness benefits of participation in physical activities are obvious as we described in chapter four, but researchers have uncovered other benefits that may be particularly important for women. For example, sports participation has been linked to increased self-esteem and feelings of self-worth for some girls and women (Hall, Durburow, & Progen, 1986). Sports and fitness activities can also be liberating for women because they defy the cultural stereotype of women as passive and weak (Kleiber & Kane, 1984). Some activities may be more beneficial than others in negating gender stereotypes. Although sports that emphasize strength and speed may help young women to challenge restrictive gender roles (Shaw, Kleiber, & Caldwell, 1995), other activities (e.g., aerobics) that emphasize physical appearance and weight loss may reinforce rather than challenge traditional gender role prescriptions (Frederick & Shaw, 1995).

Researchers have also given consideration to outdoor recreation for women. As with other studies of gender differences in participation rates, results are inconclusive, with some studies showing men participate more (e.g., Kelly, 1987; Zuzanek, 1978), and other studies showing no difference between the sexes (Eastwood & Carter, 1981). Thus, trying to understand the experience of women in the outdoors is more fruitful.

Women may perceive and react to outdoor experiences differently than men do. According to Schaef's (1981) cultural feminist view, women unlike men, typically consider themselves to be a part of nature and not dominant over nature. Thus, they perceive the outdoors through their rhythms and styles, including the elements of nurturing, caring, community, and sustenance (Eckart & Cannon, 1981). In the outdoors, women's concern for relationship to others and with nature often is emphasized (Henderson & Bialeschki, 1986). Cultural background may also affect the value systems associated with the outdoors, and the participation patterns of women (Roberts, 1995), so it cannot be assumed that all women experience the outdoors in a similar way.

The spiritual value of the outdoors may also be evident for women, particularly in terms of solitude. The importance of spiritual concerns may well be associated with ethnicity and culture. Women are often socialized to believe that aloneness is to be feared and avoided, not sought and enjoyed. Many women, however, have learned to value solitude. An outdoor experience may lead toward wholeness, as women begin to integrate the beauty, the strength, and the power of the outdoor experience into their lives. Women may also be able to transfer this new learning about themselves into other aspects of their lives at home and gain strength and confidence in themselves (Mitten, 1992). Thus, outdoor activities as well as sports activities may benefit women in a number of different ways, both physically and psychologically.

Television and Media

Television watching is the predominant at-home leisure activity for both women and men (Kubey & Csikszentmihalyi, 1990) and the most common family leisure activity. For example, together with movies and videos, television watching occupies nearly two-thirds of all the time that Canadian parents and children spend together (Shaw, in press). Given that media activities form such a large part of women's (and men's) leisure time, it is surprising that leisure researchers have given relatively scant attention to this form of participation. Television has only became widely available since the 1950s, and in less than 50 years it has become the main leisure-time activity that greatly influences people's everyday lives and free-time use.

Some of the research on television watching has shown that, despite the prevalence of the activity, it is often not highly engaging, involving, challenging or social (Kubey & Csikszentmihalyi, 1990). In fact, high levels of television viewing have been associated with depressive symptoms among college students (Dittmar, 1994). Some media activities are enjoyable, and watching movies that have been individually selected tend to be more enjoyable than television shows, but ironically, few people rate television watching as an important or valuable aspect of their leisure lives or leisure satisfaction.

One reason for the high levels of television watching is that this type of activity is cheap, easily available, and convenient; almost everyone in North America has at least one television at home. A second reason is that television watching is relaxing, both physically and mentally, and is often used by people as a way to unwind. Third, watching television and movies is something that can be done easily with other family members (e.g., partners, children, parents). In this sense, television can be seen as a social activity, although it is typically a "parallel" rather than a "joint" activity because interaction among people who are watching is rare (Kubey & Csikszentmihalyi, 1990; Orthner, 1975). Fourth and especially relevant for many women, television watching is something that can be done at the same time as other activities, such as ironing, sewing, childcare, or letter writing. The combination of housework or childcare with television is common among women and may help to explain why television may not always be experienced as leisure. Another reason for reduced pleasure during television watching is interpersonal (i.e., typically interfamilial) conflict over what program to watch. In addition, women may be watching programs selected by their spouse or children that provide little personal interest.

Much of the research that has been done on television has analyzed the effect on people's attitudes and behaviors. A considerable body of literature on violence in movies and television programs describes the concern about the extent to which exposure to violence in the media leads to violent behavior and/or desensitization to violence (Bandura, 1973; Huesmann & Eron, 1983; Miedzian, 1991). The concern about violence is often posed as a problem associated with the viewing habits of children and youth, although the role of sexually violent material and its impact on violence towards women is also a matter of significance (Malamuth & Donnerstein, 1984). Another issue addressed by researchers has been the role of television in teaching traditional gender role attitudes and behaviors (Signorielli, 1989; Wood, 1994). Much television programming, including advertising, has been criticized for being sexist and for promoting negative and stereotypical views of women as sex objects.

In sum, although television and other media are common free-time activities for women as well as men and children and provide family-time entertainment and needed relaxation, media activities do not necessarily provide high-quality leisure experiences. Some programs and movies may reinforce traditional gender roles and violence against women. Clearly more research about television and media activities is needed, including an understanding of how television may effect other family and individual attitudes and activities. In other words, does television become a default because the individual or a family is not willing to think of other creative leisure pursuits?

Other Activities: Church, Volunteering, and Education

Women do participate in a range of other activities that are too numerous to include in this discussion. Three activities, though, may be of particular significance to women in North America. These are church activities, volunteering and community service, and education.

Participation in church activities is an important aspect of life for many women, particularly older women who are single or widowed and for women of color (Allen & Chin-Sang, 1990). The church provides a place outside the home where women can meet to socialize as well as participate in religious activities. Although church-related activities are not typically thought of as leisure, they do provide a container for leisure interactions and connections with others. In small communities the church is often the focal point for gatherings and celebrations and can be especially significant in terms of life transitions such as birth, marriage, death, and bereavement. Church women's clubs and educational opportunities for children are also a way that some women experience meaningful activity through organized religious groups.

Spirituality can also be an important force in women's lives, even among women who do not belong to or attend church functions. For women who find traditional church structures and teachings to be male-dominated, personal spirituality provides a way of maintaining a religious component in their lives (Spretnak, 1982; Starhawk, 1982). Spirituality can connect women with others and can help build connections with nature and the outdoors. Thus, spirituality can also relate to leisure and contribute to leisure experiences.

Volunteering has traditionally been an activity of women, and this type of community service has been both invisible and visible. Many of the social reforms in the United States and elsewhere can be attributed to the volunteer activities of women as was noted in chapter two. Some volunteer activities (e.g., helping in hospitals) have reinforced traditional gender roles, while other activities (e.g., political activism) have countered such roles.

Today, as in the past, women are more likely to volunteer than men. Women's motives for volunteering also seem to be somewhat different from those of men. Horna (1987) found that women tended to do voluntary activities directly related to the family (e.g., school-related, youth-oriented activities). Men, on the other hand, were more likely to serve on administrative boards. Similarly, Henderson (1983) found that female volunteers placed importance on being with their children and helping others, while men were more motivated by the recognition that volunteer work might bring.

Although volunteering can provide a social network and meet women's affiliative needs, it can also be experienced as work rather than leisure (Allen & Chin-Sang, 1990). Recent data show that volunteering and community association activity seem to be on the decline (Schor, 1995). This decline may be because of women's increased level of participation in paid-work activities and the lack of available free time. The decrease also may be due to the lack of value that has been placed on volunteering and community service, because volunteering is more often seen as the domain of women. This decline is cause for concern, not only because of the important work that is done by volunteers, but also because of the general decline in community participation which is an important aspect of quality of life.

In the 1970s and 1980s women constituted the fastest growing segment of adults participating in educational activities (Freysinger & Ray, 1987). Participation rates in adult and continuing education activities continue to be high, particularly for women who are not employed outside the home. For these women, education may offer mental stimulation and challenge that contrasts to their routine and often "mindless" household tasks. Another explanation for women's high level of participation in adult education is that such activities are a socially acceptable form of leisure activity for women (Deem, 1982), and an easy way to make friends. In addition, women may be seeking job skills so that they can enter the labor market in the future.

The motivations for participation in education relate to the way such activities are experienced. That is, education may be perceived as work (i.e., if the purpose is to gain job skills) or as leisure (i.e., if the purpose is intrinsic or social in nature). Apart from the experiential aspects of education, these activities have also been associated with self-confidence, increased self-esteem, and self-actualization. These dimensions reflect many of the characteristics of leisure described in chapter four. Adult education, especially for women, can be enjoyable, challenging, and self-rewarding (Darkenwald & Merriam, 1982) leading to personal growth and development.

This brief discussion of church, volunteer, and educational activities serves to illustrate the complexity of most women's work and leisure lives. Many of the activities in which people participate are not clearly leisure in its pure or intrinsic form. Instead, for many women, free-time activities are closely tied with their family responsibilities and their paid and unpaid work. This observation underlines not only the holistic nature of women's lives, but also that most women rarely have complete freedom to choose leisure activities for themselves. They typically have to take into account the constraints associated with their home, family, and other responsibilities.

Time for Self and Time Alone

Women's solitary activities (i.e., just being alone) may also be an important container for leisure. Research with midwestern American farm women (Henderson & Rannells, 1988) showed the importance of "minute vacations" or short periods during the day when women can take the time just to enjoy being alone. Similarly, the concept of daydreaming is an example of enjoying time for self. An appreciation of the aesthetic and beauty around oneself is another example. Moments of humor or remembering past experiences are also important solitary moments that may reflect leisure. These examples can be described as short-term "vacations" into the psyche. They are portable experiences that may occur at any time with any amount of joy or even sadness. It is the experiencing of these moments that is important for one's quality of life (Csikszentmihalyi, 1975; Kelly, 1983a; Neulinger, 1981; Pieper, 1952).

A cross-national study of family leisure has also indicated the importance to women of having the time and space for leisure of their own (Samuel, 1995). Despite the fact that women who are mothers spend much of their free time with family members, the research findings showed that many women desire and actively seek out some autonomy in leisure when leisure becomes a time they do something for themselves and a time free, if only briefly, of their responsibilities for others.

Leisure Constraints

The information on women's leisure participation shows not only a range of leisure interests, but also an indication that leisure is important in women's lives. Some gains have been made over the last few decades in terms of accessibility to what used to be "male" activities, and the recognition that women need leisure for themselves. These gains do not mean, however, that women have equal access to leisure. Research has shown women to have less leisure time than men and less resources for leisure (Shaw, 1985b). With the increase in paid work time in American and Canadian societies (e.g., Gratton & Holliday, 1995; Schor, 1991; Shaw, 1990a), an increase in time stress and stress-related diseases, a reduction in association and community activities (Schor, 1995) and a general decline in leisure (Schor, 1991) have also occurred. This lack of time for leisure is particularly acute for women who have home and family responsibilities in addition to paid-work responsibilities (Hochschild, 1989).

Lack of time, however, is not the only problem affecting women's leisure. As discussed in previous chapters, a variety of factors associated with work, family, and structured gender relations are operating in societies and function to constrain women's leisure. Thus gaps continue to exist both in terms of the gaps between women's and men's opportunities for leisure, and the gap experienced by women in their own lives. Many women experience a lack of balance in their lives due primarily to a lack of leisure. They may lack time free from obligations, space for themselves, and/or opportunities and resources needed to enjoy leisure.

Since the mid-1980s, leisure constraints research including both conceptual and empirical research studies has grown tremendously. The idea of a leisure constraint has been broadened from the original conceptualization of a barrier that prevented or stopped participation in a particular type of activity. The broader, generally accepted definition of leisure constraints includes any factor that affects leisure participation negatively, either in terms of preventing participation, reducing the frequency, intensity or duration of participation, or reducing the quality of experience or satisfaction gained from the activity (Goodale & Witt, 1989; Jackson, 1988a, 1988b).

Various models have been developed to help conceptualize and understand leisure constraints. For example, Crawford, Jackson and Godbey (1991) proposed a model that included three categories of constraints: intrapersonal constraints, interpersonal constraints, and structural constraints. Intrapersonal constraints, which are similar to the idea of antecedent constraints as discussed by Henderson, Stalnaker, and Taylor (1988), refer to factors that affect preference or lead to a lack of interest in a particular type of leisure activity. For example, family influences, the attitudes of friends, or one's own lack of self-confidence can affect individuals' preferences. Such individuals may express lack of interest in an activity disapproved of by others, whereas if they had been encouraged to participate they might have enjoyed the activity.

Interpersonal constraints, according to Crawford, Jackson and Godbey (1991) are intervening constraints associated with relationships with other people. Some aspect of an individual's interaction with others may affect the level or quality of participation in a desired activity. For example, an activity may require a partner or co-participant, or the individual may not wish to participate alone; participation may be reduced or prevented if a partner or friend who is interested in the activity is not available.

Structural constraints are intervening factors not associated with relationships with others but mitigate between the expression of interest in an activity and actual participation in that activity. For example, lack of time, lack of money, lack of transportation, and lack of facilities or programs may prevent or reduce desired leisure participation. Structural constraints also may lead to suboptimal participation in that a rushed activity or use of inferior facilities may lead to a reduced level of enjoyment or satisfaction.

Crawford, Jackson, and Godbey (1991) further suggested in their model that these leisure constraints functioned in a "hierarchical" way in that intrapersonal constraints had to be overcome first followed by interpersonal constraints, and only then would people face structural constraints to their leisure. Support for this hierarchical model of leisure constraints has been mixed. Raymore, Godbey, Crawford and von Eye (1993) used a survey instrument of reported constraints to "beginning a new leisure activity" and found some support for the idea of a hierarchy. However, Allen (1994), in an examination of constraints to participation in corporate wellness programs, found that different types of constraints (i.e., intrapersonal, interpersonal and structural) could all be experienced at the same time by the same person, and that specific constraints did not cluster together into these three categories as expected. Thus, in Allen's study, little evidence of a hierarchy existed. Henderson and Bialeschki (1993c) also found with a qualitative study that both antecedent and intervening constraints influenced one another with no evidence of a hierarchical pattern when they examined the leisure of women.

Whether the hierarchical model is shown to have empirical support or not, the conceptualization of leisure constraints into the three suggested categories may be a useful heuristic tool for understanding the gaps in women's leisure participation and experience. Although not all constraints fit neatly into one of the categories, thinking of factors that affect expressed preference separately from those that affect participation once an interest is apparent is useful. Examining how women's relationships with others might constrain their leisure, as well as how external factors related to opportunities and resources also act as constraints, makes sense.

Intrapersonal Constraints

Defining intrapersonal constraints as factors that constrain preference or interest makes these constraints difficult to measure empirically. Whether lack of expressed preference is simply disinterest (e.g., someone who is not interested and never was interested in specific activities such as hunting or needlecraft), or whether interest and enjoyment in the activity could have been possible but were somehow stifled or constrained is not always clear. Despite the difficulties in empirically determining an intrapersonal constraint, constraints obviously might occur. Knowing that an activity is considered socially inappropriate or unsuitable may mean that a girl or woman does not even consider the possibility of participation and decides that she is "not interested." For example, a teenage girl may decide she is "not interested" in car mechanics, or a retired woman may decide she is "not interested" in learning how to tap dance. Another type of example might be when a woman who is a single mother decides that she is "not interested" in marathon running or in downhill skiing. Without consciously thinking, marathon running may be out of the question because she has to be home to look after her children or because downhill skiing is too expensive. Whether she might enjoy such activities may barely cross her mind.

When attempts have been made to measure intrapersonal constraints in empirical research studies, the questions asked have included whether being shy, self-conscious, or uncomfortable led to lack of interest in participation (e.g., Raymore, Godbey, Crawford, & von Eye, 1993). These kinds of constraints may be particularly prevalent among women, especially young women who tend to be more self-conscious than young men and more concerned about how they appear to others as we discussed in chapter five. In her book, *The Beauty Myth*, Wolf (1991) described how society values "beauty" in women, and the difficulty most women have in living up to society's expectations of the "ideal body image" and ideal appearance. As a result, many women learn to dislike their own bodies, to feel that they are "overweight," whether objectively the case or not, and to worry about what to wear and look like. Thus, they are likely to be self-conscious and uncomfortable in new social settings.

This self-consciousness can be particularly problematic in leisure settings or activities where shorts, tight-fitting, or skimpy clothes are worn, such as in aerobics, swimming, dance, or a number of different sports activities (Shaw, 1989). Apart from self-consciousness and shyness, body image can be seen as a direct intrapersonal constraint on participation as well (Henderson, Stalnaker, & Taylor, 1988), although few studies have included this factor. Dattilo, Samdahl and Kleiber (1994) found that body image was reported as a constraint to leisure among low-income, "overweight" women, but body image may also constrain women who are average or below average weight. In a survey and interview study with undergraduate students, Frederick and Shaw (1995) found that body image problems negatively affected women's enjoyment of aerobics activities, even though participation was not prevented or reduced. The emphasis on appearance, clothing, and weight loss in the aerobics classes attended by the students made them all the more conscious and concerned about their appearance, regardless of their body weight.

Self-consciousness, social discomfort, and concern about body image are also associated with low self-esteem which may be another constraint that affects women. Researchers have not asked about whether self-esteem prevents interest in activities possibly because individuals are not consciously aware of this constraint. Some evidence does suggest, however, that low self-esteem is associated with low levels of participation and high reported constraints (Dattilo, Samdahl, & Kleiber, 1994). Low self-esteem suggests lack of self-confidence; these problems are particularly prevalent among white teenage girls as we saw in chapter five. The decline in confidence and esteem among girls during the adolescent years has been well-documented (e.g., Bibby & Posterski, 1992; Josephs, Markus, & Tafarodi, 1992; Orenstein, 1994) and may make it difficult for many teens to get up the courage to start new activities, resulting in an expression of a lack of interest in such activities.

Some studies have found that lack of skills can constrain leisure (e.g., Jackson & Rucks, 1995) and expressed interest in leisure activities as well. Since perceived rather than absolute lack of skills appears to constrain leisure, low self-confidence and self-esteem may be the antecedent causes of the constraints. The problem with dealing with low self-esteem and low skill level as constraints on leisure is that a circular problem is created. Both esteem and skill level are typically boosted through participation but to encourage participation in the first place is difficult if these factors act to deter or squash interest.

Another factor that can be seen as an intrapersonal constraint on women's leisure is lack of a sense of entitlement to leisure. Various studies have shown that commonly many women feel that they do not have a right to leisure for themselves. Some women feel that leisure is selfish, or that they must consider the leisure needs of others before their own (Bialeschki & Michener, 1994; Green, Hebron, & Woodward, 1990; Harrington, Dawson, & Bolla, 1992; Henderson & Allen, 1991; Shank, 1986). According to Henderson and Bialeschki (1991a) this lack of a sense of entitlement to leisure seems to be characteristic of many women. This intrapersonal constraint is not something that is easy to measure but may well affect women's expressed interest in leisure activities. Some women can list the leisure interests of all their family members (viz., their children and their husband), but they have a much more difficult time listing their own leisure interests. Clearly such women have not given much attention to their personal, self-determined leisure needs.

The lack of entitlement to leisure has been linked, both empirically and conceptually, to the ethic of care. Although an ethic of care can be a positive aspect of women's development, and caring for others is a positive attribute for all people to have. Several research studies, however, have documented how this ethic constrains women's leisure. For example, a study by Harrington, Dawson, and Bolla (1992) found that the ethic of care was the major factor constraining the leisure of married women. In another study of nurses' work, family and leisure, the ethic of care was again identified as a significant constraint on nurses' leisure lives (Lamond, 1992).

A different, though related, set of intrapersonal constraints on women are those constraints associated with female gender roles (Henderson, Bialeschki, Shaw, & Freysinger, 1989). If expectations about how females should behave are narrowly defined (i.e., women should be gentle, caring, nonaggressive, noncompetitive and passive), some women may be limited in leisure activities to be undertaken if these activities do not support their image of the "ideal woman." Although many people think that this narrow definition of the social role of women is old-fashioned and a thing of the past, some evidence exists that this thinking still influences the leisure choices that women and girls make, and affects the activities in which they express interest. For example, far fewer women than men express interest in risk activities such as rock climbing or extreme skiing. In addition, Allen's study (1994) showed that lack of approval of an activity by either family members or friends was reported to be a stronger constraint on leisure than other intrapersonal or structural constraints. Moreover, while lack of approval from specific significant others has been shown to constrain leisure, simply knowing that a society tends to disapprove of certain activities for women may constrain interest as well.

From this discussion of intrapersonal constraints, we can see that such constraints may be conscious or unconscious. Fear of disapproval of others may not be consciously recognized, but may still affect behavior. In the

Victorian era many women simply may not have contemplated riding a bicycle, or going swimming at a public beach, or playing tennis, because they had learned at an early age that such activities were not socially approved. Today, no stigma is associated with women's participation in such activities, but women still may not think of taking up an interest in motor racing or carpentry because of some latent preconceived ideas.

Understanding that these intrapersonal constraints exist does not mean easy solutions can be found. Indeed, proposed solutions may depend upon one's perspective. From a liberal feminist perspective, the solutions to intrapersonal constraints are likely to be posed in terms of changing patterns of education and socialization of girls. Knowledge of available opportunities, encouragement to participate, and educational programs geared to improving self-esteem during the adolescent years are all possible solutions.

From a radical feminist perspective, however, the argument would be that changes in educational and childrearing practices are not sufficient. More basic and radical change is needed in the gendered power relations of society, and the dissolution of patriarchy. This perspective is probably best understood when thinking of the problem of the sexual objectification of women. As long as women's bodies continue to be bartered by men, the objectification and the unhealthy emphasis on women's appearance, body weight and body image will be hard to overcome. The media, too, including television as well as the pornography industry, perpetuates the idea of women as sex objects. Addressing this intrapersonal constraint of objectification which often results in low self-esteem and potentially constrained leisure is difficult to address through education alone, although education is certainly a step in the right direction.

Interpersonal Constraints

Interpersonal constraints, such as the lack of leisure companions, can be a constraint for both men and women. In fact, given the research on gender differences in women's patterns of friendship, finding a leisure companion may be less of a problem for women than for men. The most common times when women experience these problems are likely to be after the loss of a partner or husband (e.g., through death or divorce) and after a geographic move to a new village, city, or country. In such life transitions, leisure activities may be particularly important (Kelly, 1983a), but also particularly susceptible to interpersonal constraints.

Although the idea of a leisure companion is the most common example of an interpersonal constraint in the literature (e.g., Raymore, Godbey, Crawford, & von Eye, 1993), other types of constraints associated with women's interpersonal relationships may also affect their leisure. Many people have experienced participating in a leisure activity that was not enjoyed just to please someone else. Examples of such situations might include going to a ball game with a boyfriend or girlfriend despite being thoroughly bored by the game; watching children's cartoons on television to please our children/nephews/nieces; taking an elderly relative or parent shopping; or going to an "office party" with a partner or spouse. Little research is available on the frequency or types of situations where leisure participation occurs for others rather than for self. When an individual participates to please others through a sense of obligation, the enjoyment associated with participation is likely to be decreased. A small qualitative study of high school students by Shaw, Caldwell, and Kleiber (1992), showed that females were more likely than males to report participation in activities to please others. These activities related to pleasing parents (e.g., visiting family) and taking part in social activities to please girlfriends or boyfriends. Using leisure activities to please others seems to be more common among women than men since this behavior is associated with the ethic of care and the lack of a sense of entitlement.

Adapting one's leisure behavior to please others can be seen as an example of social control. According to British studies done by Deem (1986), men commonly control their wives' leisure either overtly or covertly. That is, husbands may give "subtle" hints about whether they approve or disapprove of their wives' leisure activities. They may also feel they have the right to allow or not allow their wives to go out in the evenings with friends. This control can happen in the reverse direction as well, with women seeking to control their husbands' leisure time activities.

One type of social control that is almost always in the direction of men controlling women is when an overt or hidden threat of violence exists if the wife or girlfriend does not comply (Green, Hebron, & Woodward, 1987). Because of this type of extreme social control, women who live in abusive relationships probably have no leisure at all in the true sense of the word. The "battered wife syndrome" implies total dependency on the abusive partner. Women in such situations constantly struggle never to upset or displease their abuser and thus, they have very few real choices in their lives.

Women's ethic of care can be seen as an interpersonal constraint as well as an intrapersonal constraint. In fact, the ethic of care is an example of how the three constraints categories can overlap. Caring for others functions as an interpersonal constraint when a woman is aware of her own leisure interests and preferences, but goes along with the wishes of others by putting the needs of friends or family members before her own needs. In a study of women's experiences of Christmas celebrations, Bella (1992) found that women's concerns typically focused on making sure that everyone else was "having a good time" and enjoying Christmas, rather than thinking about their own enjoyment. Similarly, research on women's leisure in an isolated resource town in Northern Canada (Hunter & Whitson, 1992) showed how women put in a considerable amount of effort and energy to ensure that "family leisure" was a positive experience for other family members. In this way the ethic of care can mean that "family leisure" activities are work rather than leisure for some women (Shaw, 1992b).

The earlier discussion of conscious and unconscious intrapersonal constraints is relevant here. The lack of leisure companions is a constraint that will be consciously experienced. Seeking to please others, though, and social control by husbands or boyfriends may not always be overtly recognized. These latter types of interpersonal constraints are more difficult to establish empirically. Control through abuse and the threat of violence is also difficult for people to understand who have not been in an abusive situation themselves.

To find solutions to interpersonal constraints on women, the question of the ethic of care is an interesting one to discuss. The ethic of care also needs to be addressed in leisure education. No clear solution to this constraint exists, because in many ways the ethic of care is a positive aspect of behavior and morality. Moreover, the ethic of care does not only mean caring for others. According to Bialeschki and Michener (1994), women whose children have grown up and left home can apply their ethic of care to caring about themselves and can learn to enjoy leisure of their own. Perhaps the ethic of care is only a problem when a sense of caring is unequally distributed; for example, when one person in a relationship always chooses the leisure activity while the other person always seeks to adapt and fit in. Such a situation not only is a constraint on the leisure of the second person but can also be destructive to the relationship. Thus, an educational solution may be to teach a stronger ethic of care to boys and to teach boys and girls balance between caring for others and entitlement for self, rather than simply reducing girls' caring behaviors.

The social control of women's behavior, including their leisure behavior, is a concern addressed by radical feminists. The proposed solution is not easy, but revolves around changing the fundamental power relations between women and men. Many feminists commonly believe that women will not have equal power in personal relationships until they have equal economic and political power. Statistics in the U.S. and Canada show that women still earn about 71 percent of men's earnings on average, so it is evident that equal economic power has not yet been accomplished. In addition, many women still lack political power as evidenced by a quick count of the number of women in politics. Although the number of female, elected politicians has increased in recent years, women are still a small minority in the U.S. House of Representatives and Senate, in the Canadian federal and provincial parliaments, and in almost every national government worldwide (Seager & Olson, 1986).

Structural Constraints

Most of the empirical research on leisure constraints has focused on structural constraints, or constraints that intervene between the desire to participate and actual participation. The main structural constraints identified by researchers have been a lack of time, money, and facilities or programs (e.g., Jackson, 1988b; Searle & Jackson, 1985). These factors probably represent the majority of structural constraints facing women as well as men. Some differences in the way women tend to experience these constraints relative to men's experiences, however, may exist.

Unlike most men whose time constraints revolve primarily around their paid work obligations, women's lack of time for leisure results from the combination of their paid and unpaid work responsibilities. Lack of time is frequently reported at the highest leisure constraint for both men and women (Searle & Jackson, 1985; Shaw, Bonen & McCabe, 1991), but time problems may be particularly high for women.

Much has been written about the time stress of women who work full time in the labor force because of their "double workday" or "second shift" experience (e.g., Hochschild, 1989; Schor, 1991). Employed women with young children are particularly affected by high demands on their time and a lack of time for leisure (Horna, 1989b; Shank, 1986; Shaw, 1985a). This group is the most severely disadvantaged in today's society in terms of lack of time as a constraint on leisure (Harrington & Dawson, 1995; Witt & Goodale, 1981). Despite some movement towards greater levels of men's participation in housework and childcare, studies continue to document that in most heterosexual relationships, women are responsible for the lioness's share of home and family obligations (e.g., Johnson, in press). Although some attitude changes have occurred with a growing belief that housework and childcare should be more equally divided between partners when both have paid jobs, such a change is not evident in actual behavior.

Responsibility for children and for the household is also a major structural constraint affecting the opportunities for leisure for women who do full-time, unpaid work in the home. Homemakers do not report the same level of time stress as employed mothers (Harrington & Dawson, 1995), but their full-time care of children means they have difficulty finding time for themselves or participating in self-determined leisure. Samuel's (1995) study of married women in France and in other countries showed that mothers do seek opportunities for their own autonomous leisure, and that this is important for them. Finding this time or "just doing it," however, is not always easily accomplished.

Related both to the time stress of employed women and the family responsibilities of women at home is the problem of health status, exhaustion, or lack of energy that many women face. These stresses can be seen as both intrapersonal and structural constraints on some women's leisure. Although leisure participation can reduce stress, lack of energy may make it difficult to initiate participation in the first place. Older women and women with disabilities may also face specific health-related problems that reduce leisure opportunities and/or the quality of leisure experiences (e.g., Henderson, Bedini, Hecht, & Schuler, 1995).

Lack of economic resources is a constraint that has been shown to affect both men and women (e.g., Searle & Jackson, 1985). Its effect, however, generally is stronger on women for various reasons. First, women's incomes on average are substantially lower than men's. Second, women who are homemakers do not have their own independent income and are often reluctant to spend "family money" on their own leisure activities. Third, women are often in a situation of needing money for children's participation in activities as well as their own, so their financial needs are higher than men's. Fourth, one of the most economically deprived groups in North American society today is single parents. The great majority of single parents are women, and the majority of them live below the poverty line. Single parent women along with low-income women, unemployed women, and women of color are more likely to be constrained by economic factors than are white, middle-class women (Shaw, 1994).

Economic constraints also affect transportation to and from leisure areas and facilities. Women who lack economic resources for leisure activities or are physically disabled are also likely to have difficulties with transportation. They are less likely to own a car, and walking or taking public transport can be difficult, inconvenient especially with children, and can be dangerous in certain cities and at particular times of day. Thus, lack of money can have wide ranging negative effects on women's leisure.

Lack of opportunities, facilities, and programs for leisure also constrain leisure. Sometimes traditionally viewed "male activities" (e.g., ice hockey) are not available for girls or women. Another example of a facility-related constraint is when babysitting or childcare is not available during times when women want to participate. The need for childcare provision, fortunately, has received greater recognition by service providers over the last few years. Unfortunately, childcare also costs money to either the individual woman or to the leisure service provider.

Lack of facilities and programs can become perpetuated when women do not express an interest or need for particular opportunities. This problem relates to the issue of intrapersonal constraints that affect women's expressed interest in certain activities. Recreation and leisure service providers will often try to respond to expressed needs, but they are much less likely to try to address lack of interest. Providers may not necessarily feel a responsibility to encourage participation in nontraditional activities and are reluctant to provide programs in which acceptable participation rates are not guaranteed. This reality may be unfortunate but is understandable given that even public recreation agencies are usually required to break even economically, if not to make a profit.

One type of structural constraint on women that has received little attention is lack of safety or fear of violence. A study involving in-depth interviews with undergraduate students (Whyte & Shaw, 1994) showed that these young women were affected by fear of violence in all aspects of their everyday lives, including their leisure. Fear of violence affected where they participated (i.e., they avoided certain areas such as wooded areas which they felt were unsafe), when they participated (i.e., they avoided evenings and nights), and who they participated with (i.e., they avoided participating alone). The study showed that although fear of violence may not necessarily prevent or decrease participation in desired leisure activities, it often affected the quality of such experiences negatively. The women did not like worrying, being constantly on the alert, and having to plan ahead in terms of transportation to activities and finding leisure companions. Fear of violence may be a particularly strong constraint on young women who are single and for those women who do not have their own means of transportation.

Generalized fear of violence as a leisure constraint can also be seen as a form of social control (Green, Hebron, & Woodward, 1987) similar to the social control exerted by an abusive partner. Even women who have never experienced a violent incident themselves or been personally exposed to a threat of violence are still affected by fear in certain situations such as walking alone at night. More research is needed to expand our understanding of the impact of this type of fear on women's leisure participation and quality of experience.

As with the other categories of constraint, different solutions have been proposed to deal with structural constraints. Liberal feminists tend to focus on equality of access to facilities and programs and the need to ensure equal opportunities for women. For example, they have worked hard on trying to obtain equal funding for male and female sports in schools, universities, and municipalities.

Socialist feminists and Marxist feminists typically focus their attention on the economic and work-related constraints affecting women. For them, women's different relationship to paid work is central to understanding inequality in leisure opportunities (Shaw, 1985b). Thus, they stress the need to direct change toward improving women's economic status and bringing about equality in the workplace in order to improve women's leisure lives.

Radical feminists also recognize the importance of the economic and labor market systems. But, for these feminists, social control is also a central concern. Patriarchy is seen to reside in a system of power relations in which men have control (i.e., both individually and collectively) over women's lives. Accordingly, they stress that equal leisure is dependent upon equal power and goes beyond gaining equality in the labor market or on the playing field.

Leisure as Constraining

Almost all the research on leisure constraints has looked at ways in which constraints affect participation and enjoyment of leisure. Shaw (1994), however, has suggested that leisure itself can be seen as constraining. In other words, both constraints to leisure and constraints through leisure exist. According to Shaw, participation in many common recreational activities can function to reinforce traditional gender roles and oppressive gender relations. One example of a constraining leisure-time activity is television watching. As discussed previously, television programs, and the mass media in general, typically depict men and women in stereotypical roles, emphasize the appearance and sexual objectification of women, and rarely show women in positions of power and authority (e.g., Signorielli, 1989). Moreover, heavy television viewing has been associated with sexist, as well as racist and ageist attitudes (Steeves, 1987). To the extent that media activities may be promoting negative attitudes towards women and reinforcing restrictive gender roles, they can be seen to be a constraining influence reducing women's everyday options and choices (Shaw, 1994).

Another example of leisure as constraining is the gendered nature and stereotyping of many sports and physical activities. The so-called "feminine activities," (e.g., dance, gymnastics and synchronized swimming as well as fitness activities such as aerobics), tend to emphasize physical attractiveness and body shape. These activities complement or reinforce traditional ideas about "femininity" (Lenskyj, 1986). Similarly many "masculine" activities that typically emphasize strength, power and physical contact, reinforce traditional ideas about masculinity, and strengthen traditional gender relations in society (Messner & Sabo, 1990). In these ways, leisure activities can be seen to be constraining, either directly or indirectly, on women's and men's lives.

Overcoming Constraints

Constraints, as indicated earlier in this chapter, do not necessarily prevent participation in leisure activities. Recently researchers have been directing attention towards ways in which people negotiate around constraints to continue participation in desired activities (Jackson, Crawford & Godbey, 1993). The negotiation strategies that people use depend on the kinds of constraints they face and on the activities in which they wish to participate (Jackson & Rucks, 1995). For example, evidence shows that people use both cognitive strategies such as ignoring the problems, facing them, or "trying to be positive," and behavioral strategies such as modifying their leisure or nonleisure behavior. Behavioral strategies, though, seem to be considerably more common (Jackson & Rucks, 1995).

Research suggests that negotiation strategies that some women might use to overcome leisure constraints are likely to include: modifying their time spent on other activities such as paid or unpaid work, seeking to improve their financial situation or their health status, and seeking to change their interpersonal relations. They might also change their leisure aspirations and become accepting of a lower level or quality of participation, although this strategy can be seen as constraining leisure rather than overcoming constraints. Nevertheless, many people are creative and successful at negotiating leisure constraints (Henderson & Bialeschki, 1993b; Samdahl & Jekubovich, 1993), and they are probably more likely to be successful when they are highly motivated to continue participation (Allen, 1994).

Despite this evidence of successful negotiation strategies, some people are likely to have more personal resources to enable negotiation, and some types of constraints are probably more easily negotiated than others. For example, modifying time spent in paid work is easier for female professionals with flexible work schedules and for high-income earners who can afford to take a pay cut than it is for low-income blue-collar or pink-collar workers. Modifying the time women spent in unpaid household labor may be easier to manage for women but is likely to be dependent upon changing interpersonal relationships as well, such as persuading a spouse or partner to take on a larger portion of the housework or childcare responsibilities. Evidence suggests that women with higher personal resources such as education, an independent income, self-confidence, and exposure to feminist ideas might be more likely to successfully negotiate for greater equality in their marital relationships (Blaisure & Allen, 1995; Gilbert, 1993).

Clearly more research is needed on women's power to negotiate leisure constraints, and on the differences between women based on their material conditions of life. In a qualitative study of the experience of leisure constraints by women with physical disabilities (Henderson, Bedini, Hecht, & Schuler, 1995), researchers found that these women used a variety of negotiation tactics. The tactics that are available and applicable are likely to vary for low-income versus high-income women, for married versus nonmarried women, for heterosexual versus lesbian women, and for employed women versus full-time homemakers.

The idea of negotiating leisure constraints focuses attention on individual solutions to factors that cause gaps in women's leisure. Sometimes such solutions can be highly successful and women can gain personally from knowledge of possible negotiation strategies. Negotiation strategies are also limited, and should not be thought of as a panacea for dealing with leisure constraints. Some women, as indicated before, are in a more advantageous situation than others to bring about successful strategies to improve the quality of their leisure lives. Other women, caught in extremely difficult financial or interpersonal situations, may not be so fortunate. Mothers of severely disabled children, for example, can face a lack of familial or social support, and their full-time (i.e., sometimes 24 hours per day) responsibility for their child or children leaves them little or no opportunity for leisure. If these mothers are single parents, they are particularly likely to feel lack of support from others, and to face a high financial burden as well. In such situations women's need for leisure can probably only be solved at a community, societal, or structural level through the provision of more, and better, organized social services.

Another example of how individual negotiation strategies may be limited is women's problems with combining paid work and unpaid work, and still finding time for leisure. This problem is difficult for some women to solve on an individual level. Structural changes need to be made to the labor market system for real solutions to be found. For example, paid work is still organized around the idea that the worker who was traditionally a man was free to devote himself to his employment on a full-time basis. He was not expected to be concerned about childrearing, household maintenance, or family problems. Now that both parents in two-parent families are typically employed, changes need to be made both to the family situation (e.g., sharing the housework and childcare/eldercare responsibilities) and to the work situation (e.g., providing work-family policies such as parental leave, daycare, and flexible work schedules). The problem with leisure researchers focusing exclusively on individual negotiation strategies for overcoming leisure constraints is two-fold: first, the individual may blame herself or himself when little success is found; and second, needed broader social structural and institutional changes might get ignored.

Yet another issue for overcoming constraints is the problem faced in dealing with unconscious constraints. Women and girls will not be able to find ways to negotiate self-esteem, body image, the ethic of care, their lack of a sense of entitlement, or even fear of violence unless they recognize such factors as constraints. The purpose of feminist consciousness raising has been to make the problems visible, but some of these constraints are not easy or comfortable to acknowledge. Clearly this possibility of the influence of "hidden" constraints is an important issue for education, and may be particularly crucial for leisure education with adolescent girls. Nevertheless, education alone may not be able to solve such problems; changes are needed to reconstruct traditional gender relations in our society as well.

Strategies to overcome the constraining effects of leisure activities have not been directly addressed by researchers. One way of dealing with constraining activities is to avoid them. For example, a person can avoid watching sexist television shows or movies. Another strategy revolves around the idea of "resistance." This concept has been used by Wearing (1990, 1992) and other researchers to refer to ways in which women can challenge existing gender roles and structures. For example Wearing (1992) found that adolescent women sometimes used leisure activities (e.g., competitive sports) to develop personal identities that challenged traditional ideas of femininity. They gained confidence in themselves as strong, athletic, competitive women who did not have to conform to traditional notions of being feminine. In a similar way, Wearing (1990) and Samuel (1992) found that mothers of young women challenged traditional ideas of mothering and improved the quality of their lives by seeking autonomous and independent leisure for themselves. Independence from the constraining effects of some leisure activities may be possible through participation in a variety of types of self-determined leisure which challenge traditional gender constructions and may lead to individual gains in confidence and empowerment (Freysinger & Flannery, 1992).

Concluding Perspectives

In this chapter we have shown that opportunities for participation in a variety of leisure activities are available for women. The constraints that women face in achieving an enjoyable and satisfying leisure life for themselves, however, are numerous. Individual negotiation strategies can help women to overcome some of these constraints. Nevertheless it should be recognized that not all women have equal access to such negotiation strategies. Thus, structural changes are needed such as changes in the division of responsibilities within families, changes to the organization of paid work, and changes to improve social service benefits for women living under difficult material circumstances. Strategies that challenge existing gender relations both on an individual and societal level are needed, as well as strategies to overcome specific constraints on women's leisure.

Discussion Questions

1. What are some of the problems encountered when viewing women's leisure participation?

2. Discuss how some activities are more feminine or masculine than others.

3. How might a woman's children serve as both an enabler and a constrainer of leisure for a woman?

4. Are minute vacations something important in your life? When are they most likely to occur?

5. What are your favorite leisure activities and how might they differ from the activities of your family members?

6. How might the increase in the numbers of women working be both an asset and a constraint to their leisure?

7. How do you negotiate constraints to leisure in your life?

8. What does entitlement to leisure mean to you?

9. What are the major constraints on your leisure? How do these differ for other women in your family (e.g., your mother, your grandmother)?

10. What is meant by "leisure as constraining?" Why is this an important issue?

Chapter Eight

Making Women's Leisure Visible: "Sniffing Around" and Doing Feminist Research

Now one of the annoying things about scholars is that they are always using Big Words that some of us can't understand... and one sometimes gets the impression that those intimidating words are there to keep us from understanding. That way, the scholars can appear Superior, and will not likely be suspected of Not Knowing Something. After all, from the scholarly point of view, it's practically a crime not to know everything. But sometimes the knowledge of the scholar is a bit hard to understand because it doesn't seem to match up with our own experience of things. In other words, Knowledge and Experience do not necessarily speak the same language....It seems fairly obvious that a lot of scholars need to go outside and sniff around—walk through the grass, talk to animals. That sort of thing.

—The Tao of Pooh, *Hoff, 1982, p. 28-29*

We must be confident in the "ways of knowing" about women's leisure if we are to understand the meanings of both leisure gains and gaps. We learn from research as well as our experiences. Information about women's leisure until the past fifteen years mostly related to intuitive feelings that women had based on their own life experiences. For example "women's leisure, what leisure?" was a common feeling suggested by women who were studied (Green, Hebron, & Woodward, 1990; Henderson, 1991b). Research has helped us better understand women's lives, but research has also shown the gaps that often exist between the findings of feminist scholars and the lives of females. We believe that research done with women as the central focus, the simplest explanation used to describe feminist research, may help us to understand the phenomena of women's leisure and what we currently know from what Pooh suggests about "sniffing around" (Hoff, 1982).

Research about women's leisure may be conducted from positivist or interpretive world views. These world views relate to the utility of the information as well as the methods that are used to collect data. Both world views can help us understand women and leisure. Positivism relates to examining the independent parts that make up a whole, the use of deduction and established theory, rational cause and effect, and objective measurements. Interpretive science makes assumptions about relationships and connectedness, induction and emerging theory, the meanings of phenomena, and subjectivity and perspectivity (Henderson, 1991a). Positivists usually use quantitative methods that focus on statistics whereas interpretive scientists use qualitative methods with words as the building blocks. Feminist researchers may operate from either world view and may use a variety of methods. Feminist research is based on the outcomes of the research and not the methods, as you will see in this chapter.

What Is Feminist Research?

The work of feminist scholars is not only to make women and gender visible in research, but also to uncover hidden dimensions of women's lives and experiences that have been suppressed, distorted, misunderstood, ignored, and trivialized. This work seeks to bring about social change that will improve the life situation of girls and women. Any research that continues to maintain the status quo of women by ignoring the existence of women or focuses only on how women differ from men without concern for social change is not feminist research.

Praxis (i.e., the combining of theory and action), ultimately, is the focus that makes feminist research meaningful (hooks, 1989). The purposes served by praxis, according to Stanley (1990), are to show that no one feminist position exists and that the result is to *change* the world, not just to study it. Feminist scholars also seek to re-create a science that will benefit women as well as other oppressed groups (Bleier, 1988).

Eichler (1980) suggested that feminist research at its best serves as a critique of existing research, a correction of the biases that have existed, and a groundwork for the transformation of social science and society. A feminist critique serves as a means for examining the underlying social structures and practices that have existed in research design and outcomes. These critiques serve several functions: to uncover the roots of discrimination, to illuminate sexist assumptions and biases in research and practice; to identify research concerns and methodologies that are of importance to women; and to promote the consideration of new questions, theoretical formulations, research methods alternatives, and concepts (Harding, 1986; Lott, 1985). Feminism as a world view has been criticized because it sometimes appears to create its own dogma by putting women at the center of the analysis. Putting women at the center is perhaps a necessary "corrective mechanism" particularly when women's lives have been traditionally ignored.

Feminists conducting leisure research often serve as the consciousness of the field by providing more inclusive perspectives on scholarship. A critique of research, however, is not enough; researchers will need to move beyond the critique to corrective action and the transformation of leisure research to help better understand human behavior.

Characteristics of Feminist Research

The perspectives that define feminist research and its application to studying leisure represent particular characteristics of the research process. These characteristics include issues of feminist consciousness, styles or techniques of research, who conducts feminist leisure research, the choice of research participants, and the use of language (Henderson & Bialeschki, 1992).

Feminist research has as its basis a feminist consciousness. This consciousness suggests that women's experiences constitute a different view of reality. The consciousness acknowledges that diversity among women does exist, women have different experiences than men, and that broader gender relations and structures affect the lives of women and men. A feminist researcher must not only have a feminist consciousness, but must also be concerned with changing states of consciousness (Stanley & Wise, 1983) of the women and men being studied. This consciousness involves at the minimum an examination of sexism, and ultimately, a commitment to creating personal and social change as a result of the research.

Feminist researchers sometimes have particular styles that may be evident and should be acknowledged when conducting research. In many ways, these styles or techniques are characteristics of good research. For example, a philosophy such as feminism that has as one of its goals "the right of every woman to equity, dignity, and freedom of choice through the power to control her own life and body within and outside the home" (i.e., the definition from chapter one) would focus on cooperative research efforts that would enhance the personal participation of the researcher; a goal calling for "the removal of all forms of inequality and oppression in society" would suggest a research method that would examine the natural world outside of a laboratory and not devalue individuals by virtue of the methods used. The use of in-depth interviewing, in particular, has been useful in empowering women to speak in their own voices and be heard within the contexts of their lives (Oakley, 1981). On the other hand, feminist leisure researchers should not be overly critical of the contribution to knowledge that can be made using a variety of methods and styles (Peplau & Conrad, 1989; Reinharz, 1992).

Feminist research does not necessarily depend on the sex of the researcher. Both women and men can be involved in feminist research, but women will often ask different questions than men. Since many women researchers experience the "political as personal," they have experienced the world in a different way than most men. Men are not necessarily more sexist than women, but many men have different interests and experiences than women. For leisure research, the addition of more female researchers will not necessarily create more feminist perspectives on research. If feminist researchers continue to pursue their work as business as usual and use only traditional approaches to research, then the status quo will be retained. Both men and women need to be given opportunities to ask new questions from their individual gendered perspectives and from feminist viewpoints. New questions result in conceptualizing problems in different ways, operationalizing measures differently, and scrutinizing sampling procedures. The sex of the researcher has little to do with who should conduct feminist research on leisure behavior if a feminist consciousness predominates and a diversity of ideas and methods are encouraged (Henderson & Bialeschki, 1992).

Feminist research is no more defined by the sex of the researcher than by the sex of the researched (Peplau & Conrad, 1989). Feminist researchers put the experience of women and/or the construction of gender as the focus of analysis, but this focus does not necessarily mean that only women are studied. Feminist research can also focus on the gendered aspects of men's lives (e.g., Messner & Sabo, 1990). Researchers must also concentrate on the external forces that shape women's lives such as social, historical, and political forces (Deem, 1986) as well as changing gender relations. Examples of these issues might include examining the impact on women of the male institution of sport or the nature of institutional discrimination against women as providers of leisure services. A new field of studies is emerging called "men's studies" with a focus on examining how gender structures have limited the choices of males. Although the necessity of this emerging field of study is debated in some circles (e.g., Richardson & Robinson, 1994), feminist research can be embodied within this area. Because males and females share many connections and are defined in relation to one another, a better understanding of one can lead to better understanding the other. Regardless, using only female samples or focusing only on the meaning that women attach to particular situations, may not provide all the data that are necessary to understand leisure.

A final characteristic of feminist research that should be considered is language. Language is a powerful aspect of people's social lives. Feminists seek to be clear about what language connotes and consider the meanings and the impact of language on men and women. For example, some scholars have suggested that leisure is a term that has androcentric (i.e., male-centered) connotations (Bella, 1989; Glancy, 1991), especially when we examine some of the metaphors used such as "scoring," or "taking it to them," or a "mountain assault." In conducting research on women, listening to the definitions of leisure given by women is important. The definitions, when coming from the words of women from a variety of cultural backgrounds, may be quite different than the traditional definitions of leisure (cf., Allison & Duncan, 1987; Fox & Trillo, 1994; Henderson, 1990a, 1990d; Henderson & Bialeschki, 1991a).

Historical Perspectives on Research About Women's Leisure

As evidenced in the previous chapters in this book, issues of gender are beginning to inform the leisure literature, not just as another demographic variable to add to the list to be studied, but as a focus of the impact of structured power relationships on social and economic everyday life (Deem, 1992). Research about women's leisure, however, has not always followed this pattern.

The findings about women's leisure have often been fragmented and sometimes contradictory. Although an integrated understanding seems desirable, the many perspectives that exist and the great diversity that prevails in the situations of different women make a single understanding of women's leisure unrealistic. Moreover few, if any, societies exist where men and women are treated equally, and the specific nature of gender relations varies from culture to culture.

An examination of past research on women and leisure reveals how feminist analysis has evolved over the years. Tetreault's (1985) feminist phase theory provides a useful historical perspective on the evolution of feminist research and writing. In a summary of historical changes in the study of gender, women, and leisure, Henderson (1994b) adapted Tetreault's five phase model for a historical discussion of leisure research. To examine leisure research, five conceptual phases were identified: invisible scholarship (i.e., womanless), compensatory scholarship (i.e., add women and stir), dichotomous differences scholarship (i.e., sex differences), feminist scholarship (i.e., woman-centered), and gender scholarship (Henderson & Shaw, 1994). Gender scholarship is the most recent stage and, as yet, has been least well-defined and applied.

Invisible (Womanless) Scholarship

Little was written about women, let alone gender, in the leisure literature in North America from 1940 until the late 1980s (Henderson, 1993). British leisure researchers wrote about the phenomena of women's leisure about ten years earlier, but during the early stages of the contemporary women's movement, little literature was present. Just as in other disciplines (e.g., Tetreault, 1985), leisure scholars seemed to assume that the male experience was universal, representative of humanity, and constituted a basis for generalizing about all human beings.

Little or no consciousness existed that women required additional study or that any variance existed in the predominant male view. For example, work was conceptualized as paid work or labor market participation, while leisure was conceptualized as time away from paid work including family time and home-based activities. Thus, women's unpaid work in the home, as well as women's experiences of leisure, remained invisible. Not only women were left out of this scholarship, but also people of color, people with disabilities, gay and lesbian people, low income, or any other group who did not fit societal norms.

Compensatory (Add Women and Stir) Scholarship

Related to the invisible scholarship was the emergence of compensatory scholarship in fields such as history and psychology. The add-women-and-stir scholars were conscious that women might be missing from the analyses and that some examples or exceptions to the universal male experience might be needed. Underlying the idea of compensatory research was a notion that women ought to be acknowledged, but such acknowledgment generally meant that women were judged in terms of their contributions based on typical male standards. That is, women were treated as if they represented a "minority" group, different in some ways from the "majority" white-male standard.

In compensatory scholarship, a single chapter or section of a text might be set aside to describe something about women's experiences (Andersen,

1993); these sections give the message that the book is really about men, but women are different so they at least ought to be mentioned. This scholarship may also give the impression that males are the norm and that women ought to fit into that norm somehow.

Dichotomous (Sex Differences) Scholarship

The realization that women existed and were in some way "different" from men resulted in leisure research in the 1970s and 1980s that addressed the dichotomous sex differences between males and females. A critique suggests that although the study of differences can be helpful in understanding behavior, studying differences can also be problematic (Henderson, 1990a). Some say that identifying differences affirms women's value and special nature; others say it reinforces the status quo.

Confirming that a difference exists does little to explain the motivations, satisfactions, and constraints to leisure behavior which may be due to a historical, cultural, and social context. This type of research may polarize males and females and focus on biology, rather than gender, as the "cause" of the differences. Perhaps the main problem with dichotomous scholarship occurs when differences are identified in the absence of any theoretical structure to explain those differences, or in the absence of any cultural or historical context in which to locate such differences. For example, saying that boys play with trucks and girls play with dolls says little about the context in which these activities occur. Further, a question is raised about whether dichotomous research promotes positive social change or simply reinforces what already exists as status quo. This scholarship will be critiqued in more detail later in this chapter.

Feminist (Women-Centered) Scholarship

Some radical and cultural feminists believe that women's qualities and experiences, not men's, should be important in society. Women-centered scholarship examines the experiences of women not in relation to men, necessarily, but in an attempt to understand the importance and meaning of women's lives within their own right. According to Tetreault (1985), in this scholarship the formerly devalued aspects of women's everyday lives assume new value as scholars investigate such areas as work, family and social relationships, and leisure.

A central problem is how leisure should be conceptualized and the inadequacy of traditional definitions for understanding women's leisure.

Finding a definition of leisure more congruent with women's everyday experiences and exploring gender differences in leisure experiences have provided much of the motivation behind feminist empirical research on leisure meanings (e.g., Bialeschki & Henderson, 1986; Samdahl & Kleiber, 1989; Shaw, 1984). Understanding the experiences of different groups of women has created a new world of meanings that has been hidden by androcentric thinking. Such women-centered research serves to counter the devaluation of women and, thus, to empower them. The focus on women has made leisure visible for women and has also opened the door for reinterpreting previous ideas about leisure behavior for both women and men. This research, however, may not focus on gender and gender relations to the extent necessary to understand leisure gains and gaps.

Gender Scholarship

Gender or gender relations refers to cultural meanings and connections associated with one's biological sex. Whether they place a symbolic blue blanket or a pink blanket around a child at birth results in cultural expectations immediately associated with the child (Henderson, 1994b). The meaning of gender is constructed by society and each of us is socialized into that construction. The analysis of gender relations includes, but goes beyond socialization, because an understanding of unequal power relations between men and women on a societal level is the goal. Gender scholarship appears to offer great potential in the 1990s and beyond for understanding leisure for women and men.

Gender interpretations can be applied to different facets of leisure such as constraints, definitions, benefits, participation, and satisfactions. For example, Shaw (1994) has argued that the dominant feminist approach to research on women's leisure has been to understand how women's leisure is constrained as a result of gender relations and gendered life experiences. She also points out some new theoretical directions that are emerging; for example, how leisure activities reinforce or reproduce structured gender relations and, alternatively, how leisure may sometimes be seen as a form of resistance to such power relations. In essence, gender is created, resisted, and transformed in human practices, including leisure. Every time a child plays with a particular type of toy, gender is being learned and practiced in some way.

This historical analysis sets a framework for how all these phases might be used to study women's leisure gains and gaps. The gender analysis phase is most appropriate for many of the issues that present themselves to us today, but all elements offer something to consider and their usefulness will vary based on research issues and gender consciousness.

Feminisms and Leisure Research

Many philosophies and perspectives on feminism exist. As indicated in chapter three, feminism includes philosophies and world views that embody empowerment and social change for women and men. Feminist research seeks primarily to end the invisibility of women and in doing so, inevitably reframes men and redefines them (Baldwin, 1988). Within this inclusive framework of feminist analysis and depending upon the perspectives taken, feminism can mean equality or difference, liberal or radical, personal or political, and other apparent dichotomies (Henderson, 1990a; Henderson & Bialeschki, 1992). Thus, feminist perspectives influence the research questions asked.

Feminists coming from a liberal perspective may be interested in analyzing the gender differences between males and females. Liberal feminists are concerned about the politics of personal experience, how behavior is socially learned, and the effects of socialization. They may ask questions such as "what are the differences in leisure activities between women and men?" and "how do gender-imposed roles detract from women's leisure?" The implications of liberal feminism for policy and for social change include how women can gain leisure and how they can gain access to (equal) power and opportunity within organizations.

Marxist feminist researchers would be interested in institutional structures that affect women's leisure arising specifically from power relationships based on capitalism. This oppression of women would likely be explored from a class perspective that includes the relationship of paid work to leisure. Marxist feminist researchers might be interested in questions such as "how does homelessness affect women's perceptions of leisure?" and "how does women's responsibility for the production of family leisure affect their capacity to address their own leisure needs?" Marxist researchers would suggest that individuals are not responsible for change without addressing greater social issues.

Researchers from a radical feminist perspective ask questions about the androcentrism of leisure. They seek to change the system that defines women in relation to men. Leisure researchers using a radical feminist perspective ask such questions as "is leisure a term to which women can relate?" and "how can sport be reconstructed to reflect women's experiences?" The implications of these questions for social change are fundamental.

Socialist feminists, like Marxists, would be concerned about institutional structures such as gender roles that constrain women's leisure. Leisure researchers using socialist feminism have attempted to explore the meanings of women's leisure in the context of their daily lives and how women address issues of oppression resulting from capitalism and patriarchy. Research questions that might evolve in different socioeconomic settings from a focus on socialist feminism include "what is the meaning of leisure for mothers?" and "how does pornography influence the leisure of women including women in the pornography trade and wives of pornography users?" The implications of socialist feminism research is in how to bring about social change that will help women resist unequal power relationships that result from economic inequalities, as well as value structures that place men's needs before women's.

Feminist Approaches to Leisure Research

No one single feminist approach to gaining knowledge (i.e., epistemology) or doing research (i.e., methodology) is agreed upon by feminists just as no one philosophy of feminism describes the views of all feminists. As science in general undergoes paradigm shifts and leisure scientists begin to examine their roots, feminists are also considering different alternatives in examining conventional views of science. One alternative, the successor perspective, emphasizes the need to create a totally new approach to science that would replace traditional research as we know it today (Harding, 1986). This approach flows from the radical feminism philosophy which suggests that women see the world differently from patriarchy; the previous views about women and their behavior, as compared to men, are completely inadequate. A successor approach suggests that completely new theoretical frameworks and methodologies are needed if women are to be understood.

A second approach to science from a feminist perspective is referred to as feminist empiricism. Feminist empiricist researchers generally believe that focusing only on the nature of the female experience is not responsive to the fundamental aspects of gender and oppressive power. Thus, feminists operating from socialist or Marxist perspectives who question the values and structures of society, would be most likely to support feminist empiricism. Feminist empiricism focuses on reshaping conventional scientific practices, not ignoring or eliminating them, to serve feminist goals (Peplau & Conrad, 1989). Both the successor and the feminist empiricism perspectives on research have advantages and disadvantages. At this point in the study of leisure from feminist perspectives, feminist empiricism appears to offer the most productive way to help interpret the leisure behavior of women and men more fully, to illustrate the impact of gender on leisure and vice versa, and to empower researchers. Proponents of the successor approach, however, would say that much feminist research today is feminist empiricism and it really has not been radical enough to lead to significant social change.

A third approach is feminist standpoint. The feminist standpoint epistemology argues for constructing knowledge from the perspectives of women. The standpoint theory suggests that many perspectives ought to be considered because of the diversity of women; science must be examined with those perspectives in mind. Not only must science include "others" (e.g., women, people of color, people with low incomes, people who are gay or lesbian) but researchers need to "start from where they are" (e.g., as a lesbian, as a woman with a disability) in asking research questions, developing theoretical concepts, designing research, collecting data, interpreting findings, and reflecting needed social change. Harding (1991) suggested that the answer to "Whose science? Whose knowledge?" is up to each researcher. She also suggested that those individuals who are white, middle class, or heterosexual are not condemned to see the world through the distorted lens of privilege, but that research can reflect these "other" views even if the researcher is not of them. In other words, a researcher can see the world through others' eyes and she or he can learn to see the world in new ways if the feminist standpoint epistemology is applied. Other researchers would argue, however, that if you are not female or are not a person of color, you can never adopt that standpoint in doing research.

Each of these approaches has potential for understanding women's lives and their leisure. Each has something special to contribute in terms of understanding equity, dignity, and freedom of choice that can lead to personal and social change: standpoint researchers contribute specific perspectives, empiricists support rigorous research that helps us understand gender in society, and successor research offers the opportunity to move beyond past ways of doing research and thinking about the meanings of leisure.

Feminist Methods of Research

To understand women's leisure, a diversity of approaches may be needed. Some researchers in leisure sciences (e.g., Hemingway, 1990; Henderson, 1990c; Howe, 1993) have expressed concern with how the traditional, normative, positivist research has served our field. In the past ten years, new approaches to data collection and analysis have emerged. Interpretive research and data collection methods using qualitative (i.e., words) data and case studies have been used by many feminists. Critiques of approaches to research and how we create knowledge through methodologies has been linked to the goals of feminism. Thus, the use of methods for obtaining information about women and for examining gender depend upon philosophical feminist views, theories, and approaches to science.

The focus of feminist empiricism is on using the scientific tools that are currently available in new ways. Using the methods that exist does not mean simply using nonsexist research practices, although these practices are a necessary prerequisite for all research, but moving toward new ways of thinking about data and their meaning. Although most feminist leisure researchers (e.g., Deem, 1986; Shaw, 1985b) have questioned core assumptions about traditional science, they have remained committed to systematic empirical inquiry.

An issue that many feminist leisure researchers have addressed relates to research methods. Some feminist researchers have advocated a trend away from the positivism and the use of statistics that generally have been used in examining leisure (e.g., Deem, 1988; Henderson & Rannells, 1988). Feminist research has often been associated with interpretive and qualitative data because they provide the best way to develop new theory and to allow women to "speak in their own voices." Qualitative designs have focused on context and accentuated multiple/interacting influences that have helped us understand the complexity of leisure in women's lives.

Although many feminists have found qualitative data to be useful, all feminist researchers do not have to use methods that yield qualitative data (Reinharz, 1992). Researchers using statistics can be sensitive to feminist concerns depending upon what one counts, aggregates, and analyzes. The debate about methods often relates to one's philosophical feminist position, but most feminist researchers today acknowledge the value of both positivist and interpretive world views and the use of the most appropriate data, whether they are qualitative or quantitative (e.g., Henderson, 1990c, 1991a; Peplau & Conrad, 1989).

Most feminist researchers agree that they may differ from "malestream" (Lenskyj, 1988, p. 233) researchers in the topics studied and the ways that issues are conceptualized, studied, and interpreted, but not necessarily in the research methods (e.g., Deem, 1992; Peplau & Conrad, 1989; Reinharz, 1992). Methods are not the means for defining feminist research nor should they dictate the research questions; using qualitative data may provide better ways to study some research questions, but not others (Jacklin, 1987). Most feminists would encourage a rich variety of methods and challenge the superiority of any one method. They would contend that the method is really not as important as the topic, the way that theory is applied to the problems, and the general beliefs about the knowledge to be constructed. The search for a distinctive research methodology is not fruitful when it obscures more critical issues (Harding, 1987) such as whether understanding women and their leisure gains and gaps and subsequent social change is a result of the research undertaken.

A Critique of Previous Research on Women's Leisure

Most researchers, including feminist researchers, openly dispute the assumption that science is objective and value-free. They acknowledge that all researchers have values and beliefs that affect how they practice science (Bleier, 1988). Dispassionate, disinterested research does not exist. If research is defined as the construction of knowledge from multiple perspectives through cooperative problem solving, research can be used to better understand people and their behavior if it is conducted from a variety of perspectives. The challenge to feminist researchers within a field like leisure studies is to provide a consciousness and a context for understanding how not just women, but black women, lesbians, working mothers, and all groups can be better understood through research that acknowledges value systems that exist. By and large, the faults of past research suggest a problem with the questions asked and the interpretations made, not the fact that research was done.

The research on women's leisure has addressed a variety of concerns. Depending upon one's feminist perspective, one can be more or less critical of research. We must be careful not to be too rigid, but we must be critical if we are to correct and transform research to better inform our understanding of women's experiences. To better understand the value of leisure research, three areas of criticism will be discussed: complexity of behavior, leisure and gender differences research, and the conceptualization of leisure (Henderson, 1990a; Henderson & Bialeschki, 1992).

The Complexity of Behavior

Human behavior is complex and diverse. Since research is not value free and no one method is the best way to examine leisure behavior, the study of leisure must involve a broad examination of behavior from inclusive social, historical, and political perspectives. Gender must be examined in light of the impact of other aspects such as social class, race, age, and sexual orientation. Science, as it currently exists, has far to go before most of these dimensions will be incorporated into the examination of human, including leisure behavior.

Feminist researchers are striving to focus on more than women or gender as a single issue, but are acknowledging the diversity that exists among women and among people in general. For example, if a woman has a disability, her leisure may be affected due to the influence of gender, the stigma of disability, and the interaction of the two (Henderson, Bedini, & Hecht, 1994). Current research designs are focusing more on acknowledging that leisure behaviors and practices, as in other aspects of life, occur within a gendered social context. Understanding gender, however, as we have shown earlier in this book, is a complicated undertaking that involves other identities besides just being female. For example, as evident in chapters five and six, age and development must be taken into account as well.

A Critique of Definitions of Leisure

One of the uses of a feminist critique is to analyze the definitions used in describing women's experiences, including leisure. As most leisure researchers have found, the leisure construct has been highly subjective because individuals construct their own personal definitions. Researchers' attempts to describe this amorphous concept have led to a general agreement that the importance of leisure should relate directly to one's quality of life. Currently, when the concept has been discussed, leisure usually has been categorized as time, activity, or experience related to everyday life.

Wearing and Wearing (1988) have suggested that leisure as time has not been a useful conceptualization for women because many women do not believe they deserve or have the time to engage in leisure. The time dimension of leisure is often based on the duality between paid work and leisure. The dichotomy between work and leisure for women is not as evident since much of women's work also occurs in the sphere of the home. Until women became involved in the paid workforce, compartmentalizing their time into work and leisure was difficult. Time may be a factor in understanding the leisure of some women because of the perception or the reality that it does not exist. The concept of time, however, has limited applicability unless considered within other contexts of women's lives.

Leisure defined as activity has not proved completely adequate in understanding women's leisure as was suggested in chapter seven. As discussed in chapter seven, typical activity checklists that have been used in leisure research have not captured the types of activities that women generally consider leisure such as visiting with friends or taking a quiet bubble bath. No activity can always be leisure because nearly anything may be an obligation under some conditions. Gregory (1982) suggested that women's leisure is unique in that their time and activity are characterized by a high degree of fragmentation, and leisure and work often occur simultaneously. Since home is also a place, if not the primary place, of work for women, no one should be surprised that work and leisure activities are often intertwined and indistinguishable.

When defining leisure as activity, researchers may fail to uncover contextual considerations. For example, women may swim as much as men but when one examines the context in which women are swimming, it may be that they are taking care of children in the process and not just swimming for pleasure as may be more likely the case for men (Henderson, Bialeschki, Shaw, & Freysinger, 1989). Further, as Shaw (1984) found, women are more likely than men to be engaged in more than one activity at a time. Often dual activities such as ironing while watching the television, or talking to a neighbor while looking after children, include both work and leisure elements.

Although choice in an activity may be evident, as stated in chapter four the quality of the experience rather than the activity itself generally makes the activity leisure. With so much contradiction surrounding the meaning and definition of women's leisure activities, the researching of leisure as activity has provided only partial assistance in understanding the role of leisure in women's lives. The conceptualization of leisure as meaningful experience has offered the most useful way to understand women's leisure, but determining the quality of a leisure experience is more difficult than measuring time or activity participation (Shaw, 1986). As Bella (1989) has argued, much of what the observer might label "leisure" is, for many women, demanding, obligatory, and work-related. For example, a traditional family camping trip may be leisure for the family but it generally entails a great deal of work for "mom." This experience may or may not be leisure depending on how it is perceived. Dixey (1987) proposed that to understand women's leisure, we must start with an analysis of women's roles in society. Many women find meanings in a number of aspects of their lives that might be considered leisure.

Within the framework of experience, dimensions of time and activity cannot be overlooked; the focus on the meaning of one's experience of leisure, however, provides a contextual framework for integrating these two dimensions. Further, the discussion of leisure from the framework of experiences and meanings can help to illuminate other contextual dimensions of women's lives.

A Critique of Leisure and Gender Differences

The assumption that no gender differences exist is naive given the gendered context of societies. An assumption of no need to examine sex or gender differences may also suggest that "male" behavior is the norm and that anything that deviates from that behavior may be inferior. To ignore gender differences in leisure research has not been fruitful, but to make gender differences the only or main purpose for research does not help in understanding leisure gaps for women. Williams (1977) told the story of an eighteenth century British writer, Samuel Johnson, who when asked who was smarter, man or woman, replied, "Which man—which woman?" This story illustrates some of the problems with gender difference research that tends to oversimplify complex issues.

Although most feminists would agree that gender differences exist, they have been critical of research on gender differences when these differences sometimes have been used to find a biological basis for inequality between the sexes (Bleier, 1988; Eichler, 1980). Socialist feminists would argue that this research can disguise the underlying power relations and oppression by attributing them to natural biological distinctions. Studies (e.g., McKechnie, 1974; Shamir & Ruskin, 1983; Unkel, 1981) exist in which research on activity participation has been used to rationalize and legitimize the status quo; gender has been treated as a causal factor rather than as one dimension of a social context. Because gender differences research points out those situations or activities where differences occur and tends to downplay those situations when no differences were found, it tends to reinforce the notion of difference. For example, in research on leisure participation, gender difference research might tend to reinforce the idea that "male activities" and "female activities" exist even though activity participation rates are similar. By reinforcing such gender stereotypes, the research may also tend to suggest to the reader, intentionally or not, that differences are to be expected, are appropriate, or are natural (Eagley, 1994; Halpern, 1994).

The question of whether differences are "natural" or not raises the issue of female essentialism. When gender differences are found to exist, such differences may be seen as inevitable or biological; thus, the conclusion might be that changes to improve opportunities for women are fruitless. Again, this argument tends to lead to the view of women as inferior or not needing or wanting improved leisure opportunities. Clearly the problem, as with the issue of seeing men as the "norm," is one of interpretation of research results, rather than a problem with the research itself.

Most feminists are also distressed when gender differences are treated as conclusions rather than as the starting points for scientific inquiry (Grady, 1981) or when gender differences are not based on theory. Most feminists suggest, therefore, that any study that discerns gender differences without a theoretical basis should be viewed cautiously (e.g., Unger, 1979). Theoretical constructs such as gender identity, discrimination theory, and socialization theory can help explain gender differences. One of the risks of atheoretical research is that unexamined assumptions might be made or implications drawn that are irrelevant. For example, because girls may drop out of sports when they reach puberty, it might be assumed that they have no interest in sports. They may, in fact, be interested but do not have the type of opportunities available that they would like or do not receive the same parental encouragement as do boys.

In addition, concern should not be with proof of existence of gender differences, but with the values placed on the differences and the uses made of them (Bernard, 1974). In some research on gender differences the assumption seems to be that the male is the "norm," and that the research is focused on how women are different from this norm. A problem occurs particularly in psychology research when the male psychological configuration is thought to be "normal" suggesting that female psychology may be "abnormal" or "inferior." For example, if women participate in some outdoor activities less than men, does that mean that they are not as environmentally conscious as men or that men are stronger so they participate more? Where this type of interpretation is given to the research, it serves to reinforce the notion of women as inferior. In terms of leisure research this notion might mean that women are seen as less strong, less active and less competitive than men.

Another problem with gender difference research is that it sometimes ignores or masks important differences among women or among men. Unfortunately, dichotomous differences research might be interpreted to mean that all men are the same and all women are the same. As we have tried to show in this book, great diversity exists among women. Age, for example, as shown in chapter six, is an important factor. Age combined with life situation (e.g., marital status, sexual orientation, family situation, work situation), class, and race appear to have a major influence on leisure, although more research needs to be done.

The study of gender differences is obviously susceptible to methodological and conceptual biases. Thus, research on gender differences should be interpreted with caution. For example, how terms are defined may affect results, situational factors affect individual behavior, great overlap may exist in gender differences, frequency distributions relative to differences may be far more useful than arithmetic averages (Bernard, 1974), and the same behavior may be treated and labeled differently for women than for men (i.e., she's aggressive, he's assertive). From a feminist perspective, gender differences found in any research should be examined carefully to make sure they are not inconsequential, accidental, or incidental. To be useful, the focus of gender differences research as it relates to leisure behavior should confront the question of "why" and examine the impact of social and cultural factors.

The key to understanding women's leisure is in determining how much differences matter. Differences can divide people but the diversity created by differences can also enrich life. Differences are not going to go away, but the way differences are addressed in leisure research may change as gender is used as a possible analytic framework for scholarship. Further, in examining differences we must be sure not to assume that gender is the only contributor to difference. Between and within gender differences should be juxtaposed to race, class, ability, ethnicity, and other characteristics. Gender differences alone may not be the explanation of behavior; they do not explain what diversity means when leisure behavior is examined.

Correcting Research on Women's Leisure

For the goals of feminism to be attained, the step in research beyond criticism is to address how research can be corrected to provide more useful interpretations for understanding the experiences of women, their rights, and the inequality and oppression they have faced. New models and approaches to understanding human behavior with women as the focus will help us more fully understand women's leisure.

For feminist research to be corrective in addressing leisure, the research must be reflexive, action-oriented, and reflective of everyday life (Fonow & Cook, 1991). Reflexivity occurs because feminists reflect upon, examine critically, and explore analytically the nature of the research process. The questioning and the consciousness raising that occurs within researchers, the researched, and the readers of research are important components of reflexivity.

The action orientation of the research, as Lather (1991) also suggested, is critical to feminist research. The research ought to be not only about women but *for* women, and the focus on public policy and political action should be described when it is relevant. The emotional or affective aspects of the feminist research should also be acknowledged.

Caring and emotionality as experienced in everyday life cannot be discounted from the perspective of the researcher or the researched. Understanding situational containers and everyday life experiences are necessary to improve our understanding of women's leisure. Leisure does not occur in a vacuum but is continually interacting with family life, work, and home maintenance activities. Further, how an individual defines herself as a female may also relate to her sexuality, marital status, parental status, or other identity factors. Being careful not to exclude women or any disenfranchised group from the research, and ultimately from a discussion of social change, is essential.

Differences must be taken into account if we are to understand power and if we are to correct issues like discrimination and inequalities. We need to expose, claim, and disrupt our previous understanding of women and gender differences so that the quality of life of individual men and women can be enhanced. Our response either professionally or personally can be to deny the extent and nature of differences, to celebrate differences, and/or to challenge the centrality and organizing premises of gender relations, or race relations, or whatever the sources of difference are (Rhode, 1990). Conducting the research is only the first part of this task of addressing the meanings of leisure behavior for males and females and among groups of women.

The Transformative Power of Feminist Scholarship for the Study of Leisure

The transformation of leisure research resulting from feminism includes acknowledging alternative views on questions asked and the research designs and methods used. The transformative process does not advocate a distinctive set of feminist methods for leisure research, but seeks to address the questions that might be important to ask such as: What would our day-to-day world be like if no racism, sexism, and classism existed? What would a leisure research agenda created by women be like? What values would it express and what needs would be met? Do we need a feminist leisure science?

Feminist research applied to the study of leisure is more than just "good" research. The difference between feminist science and "science as usual" is the focus on women and/or gender as the center of the analysis and the ultimate aim of social change. It addresses issues of gender which apply to both males and females, but assures that women are not being ignored or considered as deviant. Female oppression as well as oppression in all forms is taken into account in this research. An additional identifier of a feminist leisure science is the acknowledgment of the cultural diversity among the people who are studied. Transformative research cannot be done without also addressing the ways that women's lives intersect due to race, class, age, and other identities.

The roots of the conceptualizations of leisure may be transformed in the future because of the influence of feminists. The writings of feminists like Bella (1989, 1992) and Lenskyj (1988) cannot be ignored as they question the way that the patriarchy has defined the work/leisure relationship. They also raise problems with the subjective definition of leisure as perceived freedom that is often irrelevant to women whose lives center around family relationships. Liberal feminists, in particular, would suggest that the existing leisure literature must be continually monitored to determine whether the evidence found in an examination of gender differences is relevant to the potential for equal access to leisure. Whether gender differences or gender similarities are found should be irrelevant in light of what these similarities or differences mean within a broader social context.

Acknowledged or not, gender is continually being constructed in our individual worlds and in our society. To construct leisure behavior free of gender-biased views is impossible in a gender-oriented society. When women are studied in relation to men, as occurs in gender differences research, the conclusions may be quite different than when environmental and situational aspects that are more specific to women (i.e., safety, entitlement to leisure) are taken into account (Henderson, Bialeschki, Shaw, & Freysinger, 1989). When leisure is defined and described, the experiences of both men and women as well as the uniqueness to women's or men's lives ought to be acknowledged. If feminist research is successful, then any theory that purports to be general must be able to explain female as well as male behavior (Eichler, 1980).

Cautions in Doing Feminist Leisure Research

In addressing the transformative potential of the feminist study of women's leisure, we must also be careful in the assumptions we make. Although not all feminists would agree, we believe that we must avoid female essentialism or the belief that the feminine nature is ideal and preferable to maleness. We must also avoid essentialist beliefs that suggest that all women are alike. The meaning of being female is a fluctuating, not a fixed state; being female varies historically and contextually.

Assuming that all females experience the world in the same way is risky. One's biological sex alone does not determine behavior, rather it is the way that an individual interprets her or his gender that is important. The female experience cannot be universalized nor can we suggest a "common" world exists for women except, perhaps, within a sense of common oppression. Race, age, education, cultural background, and other characteristics combine to affect each female's leisure experiences. Much of the research on women's leisure experiences has not included research on women of color, or women with diverse life experiences and life situations, although this oversight is beginning to change. The definitions developed so far, therefore, may not be inclusive of all women's experiences, but may be culturally specific. Research from feminist perspectives, however, is providing leisure scholars with new directions to consider in designing and interpreting research in a more inclusive manner.

Concluding Perspectives

Feminist research offers a marker for examining the meanings of gains and gaps in women's leisure. Many gains have been made in studying women's leisure but gaps remain particularly in understanding the diversity of leisure experiences that girls and women may encounter. Gaps also exist in translating the research from theory to practice. The range of methods that may be used to understand the experiences of women in society is extensive. Researching women's leisure allows us to understand more about the broad phenomena of leisure so that our leisure models and theory will include women and other traditionally invisible groups. No one feminist philosophy, theory, or method exists for conducting this research, but many perspectives can aid in the critique, correction, and transformation of society in ways that will result in empowering leisure for both females and males.

Discussion Questions

1. What would leisure research resemble if all of it were based on principles of feminist research?

2. What types of questions about women's leisure require further examination?

3. What is the value of examining gender rather than sex when researching differences?

4. How would you respond to another researcher's challenge that there is no such thing as feminist research, just "good" research?

5. From a feminist perspective, how might you go about researching how women's housework responsibilities relate to leisure?

6. If you were a lesbian, how might your standpoint be different than a heterosexual woman?

7. Based on what you know about feminist philosophy, which approach to research makes the most sense for you personally?

8. Can someone do feminist research without being a feminist?

Chapter Nine

"She Who Continues:" Changing/Enhancing Women's Leisure

She Who continues.
She Who has a being
named She Who is a being
named She Who carries her own name.
She Who turns things over.
She Who marks her own way, gathering.
She Who makes her own difference.
She Who differs, gathering her own events.
She Who gathers, gaining
She Who carries her own ways,
gathering She Who waits,
bearing She Who cares for her
own name, carrying She Who
bears, gathering She Who cares
for She Who gathers her own ways,
carrying
the names of She Who gather and gain,
singing: I am the woman, the woman
*   the woman—I am the first person.*
and the first person is She Who is the first person to
She Who is the first person to no other. There is no
other first person.

She Who floods like a river and
like a river continues
She Who continues

—poem by Judy Grahn, 1978, p. 78

"A man works from dawn to sun, but a woman's work is never done." This old rhyme holds as much truth today as in the past. With the opportunities and technological gains available in the 1990s, many women expect to have more time for themselves and expect not to experience leisure gaps in their lives. They believe their lives ought to be dramatically different from their grand-mothers. In many ways, the lives of most women differ from their ancestors. One of the paradoxes of the lives of many women, particularly in industrial-ized societies, is that their lives are different in terms of opportunities and available resources, yet many women continue to feel stressed, tired, and dissatisfied (Hochschild, 1989; Schor, 1991).

Unfortunately, change regarding women's leisure has been slow. Al-though the lives of women have changed and gains have occurred, many social structures and institutions have not adapted. The responsibilities that women have for childcare, for working in the same way that work has traditionally been done (e.g., full time, 9 a.m. to 5 p.m. with a focus on "moving up"), the devaluation of women and their work, and the division of labor that makes most women responsible for the home and family have resulted in less free time. The lack of institutional change often results in leisure gaps for women and a diminished quality of life.

We contend that change in directions that will add quality to women's lives will not happen without consciously directed effort on the part of individuals as well as institutions within society. The purpose of this chapter is to lay the groundwork for how individuals and institutions might continue to address positive personal and social change regarding women's leisure.

The Complexity of Changing/Enhancing Women's Leisure

Women have been challenged in balancing work, family, and personal interests throughout contemporary history. The need to "juggle" time, however, has become more visible in contemporary society where "equal rights" are expected. The frustration that many women feel because of multiple roles and not having enough time to meet all expectations often results in stress. On the other hand, multiple roles may have positive consequences in entitling women to have many options and opportunities, and thus, to live their lives more fully.

Much has been written about the effects of stress on physical health, not to mention how stress diminishes quality of life and the possibilities for leisure experiences. Many women have numerous roles associated with work and family (i.e., defined in its broadest sense) and each takes time. Not only do balancing paid work, housework, community service, and family care take physical energy, but they also require emotional energy. No wonder many women feel tired and pressed for time (Hochschild, 1989). With the recognition that women have rights related to "life, liberty, and the pursuit of happiness," many women are seeking solutions to find balance in their lives.

Establishing leisure meanings and enhancing how any individual or group finds life satisfaction and quality of life through leisure are dependent on a number of interacting and cumulative factors as we have noted throughout this book. As a summary and a basis for moving on to specifically how women's leisure might be changed, the following formula is offered as a framework for synthesizing how leisure is influenced by a gendered society (Henderson, 1994a):

$$
\begin{aligned}
& \text{Values/Entitlement} \\
+\ & \text{Benefits/Outcomes} \\
+\ & \text{Containers/Opportunities} \\
+\ & \text{Negotiated Constraints} \\
+\ & \underline{\text{Life Situation}} \\
=\ & \textbf{Leisure}
\end{aligned}
$$

The values that one holds dear are essential dimensions to understanding the meanings attached to any phenomenon. The values associated with leisure and the sense that leisure is important are necessary prerequisites for examining meanings. The entitlement or right that an individual has for leisure has been assumed in the study of leisure—if leisure is to have any valence in women's lives, they must first believe that they are entitled to it (Deem, 1986; Henderson & Bialeschki, 1991a; Woodward & Green, 1988). Entitlement to leisure, however, is often highly situational as we have indicated in this book. Even though women often say they want and deserve leisure, they may not see the lack of leisure as a significant problem in their lives. Thus, a sense that a woman can value leisure and have it as an essential part of meaningful interactions and identities (Kelly, 1983a) is an initial dimension for understanding leisure in women's lives.

As we discussed in chapter four, a growing literature has addressed the perceived benefits and outcomes of leisure. Insights about reasons for involvement, motivations, and satisfactions may be better understood within a gendered context. In addressing benefits and outcomes, the central question may be "what do women want?" One of the pervasive outcomes that occurred when middle-class working women described their leisure was their desire to recuperate, recover, or to just "do nothing" (Henderson & Bialeschki, 1991a). This sentiment may reflect women's time, stress, and lack of leisure. Some women may need to recuperate first before they can move to other positive aspects of leisure participation such as leisure affiliation or autonomy. The empowerment that some women may experience through the opportunity to control their bodies through leisure (e.g., sports) can result in a heightened sense of control and positive benefits in other aspects of life (Henderson, Bialeschki, Shaw, & Freysinger, 1989). The outcomes of leisure, however, may not always be positive if women are forced into social leisure settings where they have to assume traditional roles (Shaw, 1994). Those negative outcomes also influence the contributions that leisure makes to the quality of life for individuals and communities.

Types of activities, social settings, and physical locations were described as "containers" for women's leisure. This description may be applicable to males as well as females, but containers seem to be a particularly appropriate word for women because of the notion of "fitting in" leisure. Containers vary greatly from individual to individual. Women in different life situations may have different sized and shaped containers. For example, a working-class single mother with two preadolescent children may find her container different and possibly smaller than a single young professional woman. Additionally, over the life course, containers will change (Henderson, 1990b). Colley (1984) suggested that women choose leisure based on a combination of opportunities available (i.e., containers) and lack of constraints. The fewer constraints to leisure that a woman has, the larger her container and the greater the leisure opportunities are likely to be.

An important variable in the equation is constraints and how they are addressed as we examined in chapter seven. Some feminist researchers have suggested that the study of women's leisure is the study of constraints (e.g., Henderson & Bialeschki, 1991b). Jackson, Crawford, and Godbey (1993) noted that leisure constraints negotiation, or how one decides to experience an activity despite the constraints encountered, is a key to understanding constraints and to finding meanings in leisure. Most women's lives are not devoid of leisure. Despite the personal and social barriers that they may face, most women use a process of negotiation to find some leisure satisfaction in their lives. To change women's leisure in positive ways, macro solutions as well as micro solutions must be found to help women overcome leisure constraints.

If the study of women's leisure has taught us anything in the past fifteen years, we have been shown that leisure is experienced differently by people in diverse life situations. The individual differences that exist among groups of women or among groups of men may be far greater than the differences between men and women. Thus, the understanding of leisure is highly dependent on the social context in which individuals experience leisure, as noted throughout this book. Gender, socioeconomic status, marital status, educational level, race, religion, and a variety of other possible mitigating characteristics cannot be divorced from the study of women's leisure.

The responsibility for responding to women's leisure and addressing the leisure gains and gaps rests with individuals as well as social institutions. This responsibility is tied to perspectives on feminism as well as beliefs about how change occurs. We will discuss four groups that can have an impact on changing women's leisure: society and the institutions within society, individuals, leisure service providers, and researchers.

What Society and Social Institutions Can Do

Most of the feminist literature about women's leisure suggests that even though leisure may be more pronounced among the leisure-rich (e.g., middle-class, young, educated) than the leisure-poor, the leisure of men and women in similar life situations varies considerably (Carrington, Chivers, & Williams, 1987). Women's socialization toward certain activities or away from leisure in general, and the way that women's work has been "hidden" have resulted in many women experiencing gaps in their leisure expression (Green & Hebron, 1988). Wimbush and Talbot (1988) suggested that for women, leisure is a "relative freedom" because so many factors circumscribe the characteristics, lifestyles, and roles that influence leisure.

Unfortunately, when the total picture is examined, leisure is not highly valued in many cultures. The utility and balance that satisfying leisure can provide is not always fully understood. We are not advocating the traditional work ethic be replaced with a leisure ethic, nor should women be encouraged to abandon their labor force involvement and household duties in search of a leisure lifestyle. Women and men should, however, have the right to find a balance in their lives and to have freedom to choose how they will live their lives given the responsibilities and relationships that they have.

Deem (1986) suggested that the social position of women and the environment for women's leisure must change if women are to experience leisure. When people not only believe, but set the political agenda in motion to enable women to gain integrity in all aspects of their lives, then leisure opportunities will naturally follow. For example, issues such as equal pay for equal work not only elevate the social position of women, but also ensure that women will have the spending power necessary for leisure involvement (Henderson & Bialeschki, 1991b). Thus, as women receive more acknowledgment in the society at large, they will also have more opportunities for leisure.

The environment of women's lives also needs to be addressed. Many structural components affect women's leisure. Sharing household duties, reducing crime and violence against women, providing adequate childcare during work as well as free time, and providing safe work and leisure environments in terms of such amenities as lighting, parking, and convenient facilities, are all examples of environmental issues that can enhance women's leisure.

Furthermore, all women just like all men, should have the right to education. Educational systems can provide opportunities for individuals to learn lifetime leisure skills and to critique leisure and work practices that constrain their lives. Education should focus on continuing education for adult men and women as well as on introductory activities for children. In addition, we need to continue to hold meetings and conferences that address the particular concerns and interests of women so the issues are kept in the forefront of reform.

The work environment is a visible institution that needs to be made more user-friendly for women. Changes in work have the potential to affect the leisure lives of women. Certainly a livable minimum wage is not too much to ask. Some women also need better access to vocational counseling so that they can put their skills and abilities to the best use. Although changing somewhat, many women continue to be channeled into traditional female occupations that are low-paying and generally low status. Further, unpaid housework and childcare responsibilities need to be valued in society and acknowledged as being as equally demanding as paid work.

A restructuring of the out-of-home workplace may be necessary. For example, the expectation of the long work week for many professional jobs is a holdover from an earlier time when almost all professional jobs went to men who had wives at home to look after their families. If workplaces were women-friendly they would acknowledge the childcare roles that continue to be the responsibility of women. For example, women and men might be allowed more parental or compassionate leave to take care of children and/or aging relatives. The need for flexible schedules and reduced work schedules that might accommodate other aspects of a woman's life should be acknowledged.

Part-time workers have typically not been given the same status regarding job security as full-time workers. Since more women than men work part-time, improvements in benefits, at least in countries like the United States, would be useful.

Issues that effect women in the workplace such as sexual harassment, sexist language, glass ceilings, and other forms of discrimination should be eliminated not only by legal measures but by a moral conviction from employers of what is right and wrong. Women need to feel safe in the workplace without the potential for violence.

In the workplace and in professions, women should have the opportunity to develop networks, particularly with other women, that will allow them to feel they are "not alone" in their situations. Further, women in organizations ought to have the same opportunities for leadership training and development as do men. They should have guarantees that women will not be overlooked at any part of the organization.

Related to the workplace restructuring is the need to restructure the home as the unpaid workplace of many women. The physical space as well as the family itself are areas in need of change. For example, the expectations around household tasks need to be redefined to include increased responsibilities and greater sharing of tasks with other family members. Affordable quality childcare, usually associated with women who work outside the home, is also needed for women who choose to stay-at-home and who occasionally may need "time off" for personal leisure. Further, the standards of care related to the house may need to be revised. Women have multiple responsibilities other than keeping an immaculate house; if the "spic-and-span" standards were lowered slightly, some women might have more time for other pursuits. Lastly, a redefinition of family roles that would redistribute expectations in a way that reflects the current situations of most women would be helpful. The majority of women are involved in some sort of paid work outside the house; therefore, partners, children, and other "family" members ought to become more equal participants in household and family responsibilities. Family structures are continually evolving as women establish relationships, often have children, separate from relationships, and seek to define their own identities and find leisure.

Additional macro changes that might enhance women's leisure include such aspects as pressuring toy manufacturers and book publishers to develop nonsextyped products. We ought to protest any media representation that reinforces stereotypes of girls and women, including the sexual objectification of females. Textbooks, in particular, must be scrutinized for how they may be unconsciously socializing males and females to particular work and/or leisure behaviors. Conversely, we should support the efforts of media and manufacturers who consciously consider the needs and interests of both males and females. In addition, a major redefinition of the beauty and fashion industry regarding what constitutes "feminine" and "body beautiful" may result in changes in women's leisure.

Many other institutions in society could also be addressed. For example, more females and profeminist males elected to political office and as leaders of large corporations will likely change women's status and ultimately impact their leisure. Schools can do a better job of ensuring that girls and boys get appropriate educational opportunities. Churches can also have a role to play especially in teaching tolerance, respect, and caring for others. Leisure service organizations, as social institutions, will be addressed specifically later in this chapter.

Obviously the need for social change is great in many institutions, and these suggestions barely begin to address all the issues that could be addressed. Individuals who want to change women's leisure must focus on these social institutions since leisure is never divorced from other aspects of people's lives. Changes in institutions such as schools, family, the workplace, media, and government cannot help but have long-term benefits that can result in improved personal leisure for women and men, and girls and boys.

What Individuals Can Do

"Blaming the victim" is sometimes tempting when we begin to examine social change. As shown in the previous section, many changes need to occur in society if we are to have an environment conducive to women's leisure that can also address women's leisure gaps. Although each individual has a role to play in affecting social change, a single individual cannot change things alone. Single individuals can, however, make some personal changes that may enhance their leisure to be more enjoyable or satisfying. For some women, these changes are easier than they are for other women because of life situations. Several suggestions can be offered based on women's leisure research that may provide steps toward improving the quality of an individual's own personal leisure life.

Women's leisure is often associated with social interactions, many that include the family. Many women perceive themselves as family members first and individuals second. For example, Leaman and Carrington (1985) suggested that the culture of femininity channels girls into more concern for others than for their own interests and welfare which sets the stage for familial and other social roles. As indicated in the discussion of constraints in chapter seven, many women are unable to find major blocks of time for leisure in their lives, but tend to "steal" free time as they can. Women often "double up" their activities and may be doing something considered leisure such as watching TV while also doing housework such as ironing. This fragmentation results in women grabbing time whenever they can but often with no set priority in locating leisure within their lives.

One of the most difficult aspects to address about changing women's leisure is that many women do not believe they deserve leisure. This conclusion presents a quandary from a feminist perspective. Many feminists advocate the visibility and rights of women and yet, some of the research findings have suggested that leisure may be antithetical to what women believe they deserve (e.g., Deem, 1986; Wimbush & Talbot, 1988). For example, Shank (1986) concluded that women found that "having it all" was difficult and leisure was often the dimension of their lives that received the least focus. As Hochschild (1989) pointed out, leisure is frequently the first thing to go when a woman feels stressed and tired.

The effect of changing work roles for some women has resulted in contradictory findings about women's leisure. Wimbush and Talbot (1988) suggested that neither women who worked for pay nor worked at home indicated they had the right to take time off from work. Shaw (1988a) found that employment status resulted in a trade-off regarding leisure. Although leisure time was less available, paid work often provided the potential for new leisure partners and broadened leisure options. Harrington and Dawson (1995) found that women who worked part-time felt that they had the most leisure opportunities.

Based on what we know about women's leisure, leisure is often a low priority and frequently becomes the "leftover" time in individuals' lives. One of the problems with changing women's leisure seems to be that many women say that leisure is important in their lives, but their attitudes, the structural constraints of their lives, and their behaviors are not always consistent (Henderson, 1995a). This incongruence can create stress and a less than satisfying life.

Women as individuals are not responsible alone for their lack of leisure. As indicated in the previous chapter and throughout this book, social institutions such as the family and work impact on many women's lives. Evidence, however, does suggest that some women are taking more control over their lives to experience satisfying leisure (Henderson & Bialeschki, 1991a). Women from various cultures who have privilege such as women of the dominant race, with adequate income, and without disabilities or other forms of disadvantagement may be more likely to have access to some types of leisure opportunities, but the potential exists for all women.

Several suggestions, based on research findings, are offered to address the micro changes that can occur in women's leisure:

1. Each woman must examine what provides meaning in her life and what the ideal balance of work, family, and leisure might be. Leisure can be embodied in the form of service to others, religious or spiritual involvement, being with other people, finding something that really impassions a person, or just

relaxing alone. Finding balance involves negotiations with partners, family members, and maybe employers, based on the importance of leisure for everyone.

2. Women need to continue to examine their capabilities and capacity for leisure by developing new areas of competence in leisure. Girls and women need opportunities to learn new recreation skills and to become proficient in these activities.

3. If leisure is a priority in a woman's life, she must plan for it. Just believing leisure is important is not enough unless a woman plans to set aside time for herself to pursue the opportunities. Occasionally, time must be reserved for an activity or just the opportunity to take a few minutes and sit quietly.

4. Women need to determine what spaces they need for leisure whether in the home or in a public facility. Women need to make known their environmental demands for leisure, such as requesting appropriate times to pursue recreation activities and demanding safe opportunities and places for participation in activities.

5. Finding "leisure partners" may be helpful. Researchers suggest that women are more oriented toward relationships, so many women are recognizing the social value of leisure. Women can seek other women as well as men with whom they can find support and with whom they can participate in leisure. Any kind of support that women can give to one another may be helpful.

6. Women may want to acknowledge the value of minute vacations and solitary leisure. Taking a few minutes to read a newspaper, to savor a sunset, or to visit with a friend are examples of minute vacations. Leisure does not have to occur in big blocks of time for it to be refreshing and satisfying.

7. Balance is the essence of a meaningful life for many people. The identification of the constraints to leisure by women and the concomitant attempt to mitigate those constraints through various forms of personal negotiation can result in a broader appreciation of leisure for all individuals.

This discussion has centered on what individual women can do. A role also exists for partners, male or female, who can support individual women in their lives. Spouses and partners can share in child and household work. They can support the ways women may choose to express themselves in their leisure. They can work for some of the social issues described above that will benefit women as well as men. The responsibility is not only for women but can be greatly enhanced by the caring and concern shown by individuals who are significant to women (e.g., fathers, mothers, brothers, children, spouses, partners, friends).

Changing the Provision of Leisure Services

A reason for the prevalence of women's leisure occurring at home or not occurring at all, may be due to the lack of opportunities for recreation outside the home (Deem, 1987). If opportunities for leisure are not available in the community and efforts are not provided to assist women with such services as childcare facilities (Deem, 1986, 1988) or flexible scheduling of activities (Alberta Recreation and Parks Department, 1988), then women have few options for their leisure expression. Another reason why the home, in particular, may be the most common place for leisure is because of safety issues. Thus, leisure service providers also have a potentially important role to play in changing women's leisure if some of these issues are addressed.

This section addresses a particular institution called leisure services. These services refer to parks and recreation, community recreation, voluntary and youth serving organizations, therapeutic recreation, commercial recreation and tourism, and other organizations that address the recreation and leisure needs of a variety of individuals and groups. These leisure service delivery systems are organized differently depending on the community, but all seek to enhance the quality of recreation and leisure for individuals. Since these systems have not been discussed to any extent elsewhere in this text, we will concentrate on identifying how the research on women's leisure might help providers of leisure services facilitate changes in women's leisure.

Not all leisure service providers need to have a specific feminist philosophy to be successful in programming for women, but this philosophy may be useful (Bialeschki & Henderson, 1991). Feminists strive for social change to improve the lives of women while leisure practitioners strive to improve the quality of life of individuals by providing significant and meaningful leisure experiences. The essential component of a feminist approach to leisure programming is the combination of a value orientation with action. The challenge to feminist practitioners within a field like leisure services is to provide a consciousness and a context for understanding not just how women in general, but how women of color, lesbians, working mothers, and all groups of women and men can be addressed through leisure services.

Feminist Ethics Applied to Leisure Services

The personal values that leisure service professionals hold are evidenced in the choices they make about how to do their work. The value of feminist ethics lies in putting women at the center of leisure service planning through critique, resistance, and the explication of morally desirable alternatives.

Underlying all aspects of applied feminist ethics is a *concern for caring*. According to Duquin (1991), any environment that desensitizes us to caring will sabotage ethical practice. An ethic of care may be demonstrated by an interest in the protection, growth, health, and well-being of others whether they are co-workers, participants, clients, or subjects of research. Duquin described, for example, how highly competitive sports can diminish ethical development and ethical relationships by devaluing an ethic of care. Sports programs would look much different for almost all age groups if they were developed around an ethic of care and cooperation rather than always focusing on winning at all costs.

Ecofeminism provides a further extension of an ethic of care; feminist ethics and caring about the environment through environmental ethics are closely tied. Ecofeminists embody their commitment by developing management and programming practices aimed at ending the exploitation of women and of nature in any situation, including leisure pursuits and recreation activities. In essence, the emerging values of ecofeminism suggest that all services (i.e., resource management as well as recreation programming) should focus on respect for, and the diversity of, human beings and the life enhancement of environments. An ecofeminist view of management suggests that one cannot consider the outcome of anything without also examining the process. Applying aspects of ecofeminism can help us consider what we do, why we do it, and how it contributes overall to ending the domination of people and nature.

Feminist ethics applied to leisure services management and programming acknowledges the *power of privilege* and the *diversity* among people. Diversity can be addressed in a variety of situations. Differences between men and women are one aspect as are differences among women. Most women and men do not have comparable life choices to confront. Even if women and men were to obtain "equal rights," the diversity that exists due to race, class, ability/ disability, sexual orientation, age, and other issues of privilege must be addressed from an ethical perspective.

Feminist ethics suggests that "gender inclusivity" not "gender neutrality" ought to be the focus of leisure practice. Marketing efforts aimed at girls and women might be necessary if leisure service providers really want to include them in programs (Henderson, 1995b). Attracting girls and women to programs in which previous participation has been low requires a consistent, concerted assessment, implementation, and evaluation process as experience has shown. The marketing mix with a focus on the product, place, price, and promotion can provide a framework for analyzing how females might be further involved in recreation and physical activity programs. No magic formula exists to attract girls and women into recreation programs. The research and experiences of girls and women, however, may be helpful to professionals trying to create more opportunities for involvement in leisure pursuits. Constraints are not insurmountable if informed marketing plans are developed and implemented, and girls and women are acknowledged as having needs that may not always be the same as those of boys and men.

The Meanings of Feminist Leadership

What leisure services would be provided if only women were administrators, programmers, and leaders? Despite the male managerial structure of many leisure service organizations and the apparent "feminization" of leisure services (Henderson & Bialeschki, 1990, 1993a), both men and women likely will be sharing the leadership of leisure service organizations in the future (Henderson, Bialeschki, & Sessoms, 1990). A lack of research about women in the profession suggests that many unanswered questions exist about the experience of female professionals and what their leadership might have to contribute to changing women's leisure (Frisby, 1992; Henderson, 1992).

Enhancing the career development of female leisure service professionals may help them to work better with providing recreation opportunities for girls and women. Career development is an area that is often different for males than for females because of the traditional family and work expectations of women, the cultural and organizational barriers that may affect women's advancement, and the socialization that women experience (Frisby & Brown, 1991; Henderson, 1992). Further, in studies that have been conducted with successful female professionals, no one single pathway to success existed (Frisby & Brown, 1991).

History has shown that effective female leaders are not "surrogate men" (White, 1988). Based on the goals of feminism such as making women visible and ending the oppression of all people, a feminist administrator, whether male or female, would likely practice a model which would focus on cooperation, team structure, quality output, intuitive/rational problem solving, empathy, and high performance (Loden, 1985). A communal style of leadership that involves cooperation, the personal participation of the leader, an appreciation of the free expression of thought and feeling coupled with an agentic focus on getting the task completed may be an appropriate type of leadership style for a feminist to use. In this type of leadership, staff would be involved at every level of decision making by the guiding direction of the administrator. If this approach to leadership appears to reflect "good leadership" in general, then perhaps feminist leadership with a focus on empowering girls and women through recreation programming would be an important model to implement in the future.

Leisure Programming from Feminist Perspectives

A combination of inclusive programs designed specifically for women and those opportunities that provide equal access by females and males will likely be the best ways to provide recreation opportunities for girls and women (Henderson & Bialeschki, 1995a) and potentially to address leisure gaps. Traditional programs with alternative twists should be encouraged. Feminist recreation professionals would encourage a rich variety and would challenge the assumption that any one program model is superior. These professionals would contend that the program is really not as important as the benefits derived and the ways that the quality of life is improved for girls and women.

In examining the provision of programs for women, it may be necessary to consider how the traditional leisure services foci may not work. For example, the leisure/recreation of many women rarely includes sport (Deem, 1986). Not doing sports, however, may not be a reflection of what women would like but a result of years of socialization, negative experiences, lack of skill, and lack of opportunities that the recreation programmer must address before sports participation will be possible. Further, the times that are typically leisure for most men (i.e., weekends and evenings) are frequently peak obligatory times when many women who are parents or caregivers are involved with childcare and nonpaying work activities (Deem, 1992). Many women suggest that what they want is simply "time for themselves" or a chance to "do nothing;" this need cannot be met by traditional recreation programming. In addition, the home is the most common place where opportunities for leisure, if any, exist because projects done at home can be scheduled at one's convenience and can be easily disrupted if needed. Leisure service professionals may want to consider the implications that these research findings may have for recreation programming.

Not only community recreation providers, but other leisure service professionals such as therapeutic recreation specialists might consider how women's leisure could be changed based on the information we currently have about women's leisure (Henderson, Bedini, & Bialeschki, 1993). Therapeutic recreation specialists, who provide leisure education and opportunities for women with disabilities, specifically can apply feminist principles in some of the following ways: working together with women to help them make decisions about leisure, using values clarification to examine social roles and the meanings of leisure based on the life situation of the woman, paying attention to such issues as safety when facilitating leisure opportunities, helping women with disabilities understand the pressures placed on women in a gendered society and how these gender expectations and responsibilities affect an individual's leisure, and being advocates and helping women become their own advocates for expanded leisure opportunities not only for women with disabilities, but for all individuals.

Professionals within any leisure service delivery system (i.e., community, therapeutic recreation, outdoor recreation, tourism) might want to consider acknowledging the following feminist principles in doing programming:

1. Issues of gender, gender socialization, and the gendered stereotyping of activities should not be ignored.

2. Female oppression and inequality between males and females affect leisure opportunities and accessibility; leisure service providers need to be aware of and seek to overcome such inequalities in their programming.

3. Women as well as other traditional minorities and subordinate groups should be addressed inclusively, not blindly or neutrally, in the provision of services.

4. Women should be asked to express their ideas and should be listened to carefully and seriously. Leisure provision will, thus, become a collaborative experience which will empower all people who are served.

The leisure service provider may also need to include aspects of leisure education along with specific recreation programs that are offered based on these feminist principles and ethics. Leisure education has the potential to encourage the development of leisure lifestyles which are consistent with the interests and resources of the individual woman when such opportunities are available. The mission of leisure education will lie in reshaping the opportunities available for leisure involvements, as well as providing the supportive and skill training services needed to facilitate participation. Women will also be helped to understand the phenomenon of leisure, enlarge independent and social leisure skills, and develop a sense of entitlement to leisure. This leisure education could encourage women and men into activities not traditionally associated with their gender as a way to resist the reproduction of traditional gender roles and relations.

Several summary suggestions might be considered by those practitioners who want to be responsive to the needs of women and provide public opportunities for leisure pursuits. First, examining the perception and reality of the safety of recreation spaces is important along with the times available for women to schedule their leisure. Whyte and Shaw (1994) found that fear and violence constrained leisure enjoyment and opportunities. Glancy (1991) suggested that women are often drawn to recreation programs in semipublic settings when they offer safety, congeniality, and social aspects.

Second, acknowledgment of the great diversity that exists among women based on such constructs as class, age, motherhood, and physical ability must be considered. Some traditional recreation programs are fine for women. Other newer programs may only appeal to women in certain lifestyles. For example, for single parents, an inexpensive "mom's night out" might be offered through the recreation program that would provide childcare as well as a social opportunity for women. Related to the diversity of women is also the possible need for different structures. Some highly skilled, competitive activities may be appropriate as well as other more recreational, social activities. Resources within a leisure service agency should be distributed to address diverse groups of women and a variety of programming forms.

Third, the leisure service provider may want to acknowledge the need for both women-only activities as well as coed and/or family activities. For example, many women feel more comfortable in certain types of physical activities when only women are involved. Other women want to participate in coed and/or family groups. The feminist provider will need to be open to all the possibilities for programming for women that will exist. As noted previously, the focus is on "gender-inclusive," not "gender-neutral" programs.

Fourth, childcare, transportation, and parental support issues will need to be addressed for some girls and women to participate in programs. A variety of solutions may be undertaken, but most will involve getting women involved in designing ways to address their leisure needs.

Fifth, the potential participants in a program must be involved in the decision making. Thus, girls and women must be given opportunities to offer programming suggestions and should be instrumental in any policy or advisory groups that work within a leisure service system. Giving women visible responsible roles in policy and programming decision making is the focus, not just "adding women and stirring."

Finally, issues in programming must be addressed as they pertain to individual female needs and interests. Women who are visible in leadership and supervision of leisure services need to be seen as role models. Marketing techniques should be nonsexist and should avoid perpetuating the idea of women as sex objects (Kemeny & Shaw, 1989; Shaw, 1992b). Activities should be as devoid of attitudinal discrimination as possible. Harassment in sports programs by players, and sometimes coaches, is not uncommon. Further, the sexist language emphasized in sports may also be detrimental to both girls and boys, women and men. The myth that all female athletes are lesbians or that males who do not like sports are faggots must be addressed as must the notion that an individual must have a certain size and weight to participate in particular leisure pursuits. Clothing and image may affect women's enjoyment and comfort level in activities. Further, a tendency still exists among all of us to compare males and females when they participate in activities, particularly sport. Many females, as well as males, do not do certain activities because of the perceived evaluation that occurs about how well or how poorly they are doing or how they perform compared to others.

Leisure service providers cannot address all societal concerns but they can assure that their programs do not contribute further to the leisure gap for females or the leisure gap between males and females. Many of us do not think about the subtle ways that recreation programming may be continuing to reinforce women's lesser status in society.

What Researchers Can Do

The direct link between research and social change is not always evident. We believe, however, that researchers also have an important role to play in changing women's leisure. The studies published about women's leisure and gender issues from feminist perspectives in the last ten years have given visibility to the value of women's leisure. This examination of women's leisure has taken us from a point where women were invisible to a point where we have the potential to better understand women, men, and their relationships to each other because of research. As indicated in this chapter, the research that has been conducted can be applied to social (i.e., institutional) and personal change. In addition, the meaning of gender is beginning to inform the leisure literature as a framework for analyzing the impact of socialization and gender relations in "everyday life" for both women and men (Deem, 1992; Shaw, 1994).

Feminist researchers studying leisure have a number of options available that may result in information that can change and/or improve women's leisure. We will consider two broad options with a number of possible variations that might contribute to enhancing women's leisure: (a) making women and/or other traditionally marginalized groups the focus of leisure research, and (b) developing new approaches to analyzing leisure in the context of gender and diversity. Of course we could continue with the "business as usual" approach to research, but continuing to assume that male norms or the norms of any dominant culture are the standard will not result in change; in the business as usual approach, some people get left out.

Hardly any woman's life is beyond the influence of men in some way. If the proposition is accepted that gender is a central axis around which all social life revolves, then a gender analysis is one way to analyze research concerning leisure behavior. Being female or being male however, is a fluctuating, nonstatic state. One's biological sex alone does not determine behavior, rather it is the way that an individual interprets her or his gender that is important. Our interpretations need to show how some women's experiences and/or men's experiences lead individuals to make choices contingent on contexts and relationships, not just because they are biologically female or male. For example, although both are female, a big difference exists between Mother Theresa and Madonna. In other words, the female experience cannot be universalized nor does a "common" world exist for women except, perhaps, within a sense of common oppression.

Research on, for, about, and by women can provide additional perspectives to consider in designing and interpreting the meanings of leisure gains and gaps in a more inclusive manner. As feminists have espoused in recent years, being female or male is not only an individual experience, but also a cultural experience. Assuming that all females experience the world in the same way is risky and inaccurate. Talking about women globally is impossible without falling into the trap that renders some women invisible, particularly women who are not European American, heterosexual, able-bodied, and middle class (Fox, 1992). Further, acknowledgment does not compensate for exclusion. If feminists are to make gender theory inclusive, women and men who represent a diversity of race, class, and other positions in society must be studied. Radford-Hill (1986) suggested that the political viability of feminism as an agency of change depends on the ability to build a movement that is inclusive rather than exclusive, one that can mobilize from a broad base of support.

We are advocating gender models as the basis for changing women's leisure through future research in the area of leisure studies. Two major drawbacks related to using gender scholarship as a model, however, must be noted. First, the concept of gender is complicated, and thus, the explanations for how socialization and power impact behavior will not be simple explications.

Gender scholarship requires that researchers move beyond observations to analysis and interpretation. A second concern is that the experiences of women must remain visible in the analysis. Although gender and women are not synonymous, women must continue to be salient in the analysis of gender. Further, feminism can continue to provide the ideological lens for studying women with gender providing the theoretical structures. As long as gender impacts behavior, feminists will need to remind us continually of the value of women's experiences (Jaggar, 1991).

Researchers who study women or men from a gender perspective must be careful not to make the mistakes that have been made in the past when studying any one group and assuming the human experience is represented. Inclusive theorizing requires leisure scholars to question who creates knowledge, the universality of theory, the problems with generalizing to all women (or all men), and the impact of diversity on leisure research and leisure behavior. The future of leisure behavior research and the researchers' roles in creating personal and social change will depend upon an ability to build theories that are inclusive and that examine leisure from a broad base of cultural perspectives that address the diverse lived experiences of females and males in a variety of life situations.

If feminist researchers studying women's leisure are to address personal and social change, we must keep in mind who the research is for, who will see it, and who will benefit from it (Pedlar, 1995). Some research might be directed toward other researchers who will build on it. Some research might be directed toward leisure service providers who will use the information to provide better recreation programs for females and males. Some research might be directed toward empowering individual women and men in their own lives. A single research project might address all of these audiences or might target one or two. Researchers who want to address leisure gaps and empowerment must make the research accessible to the audiences they wish to impact. Publishing in journals and magazines, making professional and public presentations, and getting the word out in other ways must also be a part of the research agenda.

This issue of research for social change raises a number of questions. For example, in an ideal world, what would we expect women's leisure to be like? Are there more valuable and less valuable forms of leisure? Should we encourage some forms of recreation/leisure and discourage other forms? To what extent is the role or purpose of research to bring about social change either on the macro or micro level? These questions are not easy to answer, but hopefully this difficulty does not mean that future researchers will shy away from such issues.

Advances in our understanding of women's lives and gender have occurred because of people who have been willing to take a stand on difficult issues. Future progress will also depend on researchers who are willing to question and critique existing ideas, theories, and practices. The challenge for leisure researchers is ongoing. A combination of broad social change and "gender-inclusive" leisure research and practice will be necessary to address leisure gaps.

Finding the Answers to Empower Women

This chapter has presented a summary of some of the ways that society, individuals, leisure service providers, and researchers can contribute to changing/enhancing women's leisure. Much remains to be explored about women and their leisure. Some of the possible questions have been introduced or partially explored in this book, but need more development, especially related to women in a variety of lifestyles and in cultural contexts. Some of the questions that we find particularly interesting are the following:

1. What situational containers offer the best leisure potential for different groups of women?

2. What leisure activities are likely to lead to a sense of empowerment or disempowerment for women in a variety of life situations?

3. What is the impact of types of paid work on women's leisure?

4. How does guilt as a result of role conflict affect women's leisure?

5. How does leisure for women vary cross-culturally?

6. How does the intersection of race, class, and gender affect women's leisure?

7. How do the economics of leisure affect women?

8. What are the impacts on women's leisure as they age?

9. Is family leisure for women a convenience, preference, or an obligation?

10. How are girls being socialized for leisure, aside from sport socialization?

11. What should women's leisure be like?

12. Are there more valuable and less valuable forms of leisure for women?

13. How can intrapersonal constraints best be measured?

14. How do issues such as femininity/body image and violence affect women?

15. How does leisure reproduce gender?

Finding the answers to these questions will not be easy. The invisibility of the female experience in the past emanates from erroneous, stereotypic perceptions. Women's invisibility has hindered the understanding of the reality of the many forms of women's leisure. Empowering ideologies, practical programs, personal strategies, and pluralistic research methods are all needed if we are to change or enhance women's leisure in the future.

Concluding Perspectives

We have provided some perspectives on how women's leisure can be changed through the efforts of society, individual women and men, leisure service providers, and researchers. We are currently in a state of transition with many questions being raised. We need to address change at all levels if women's leisure is to become empowering and gaps are to be overcome. We must reconcile to ourselves that some changes will be slow while others will be quicker. Women alone can do something, but our social institutions will also need to be changed. Ultimately women's leisure will change only when a strong collective of advocates for these changes are successful in convincing societies at-large of the values of inclusive leisure and the moral "rightness" of accepting women as valued participants in all aspects of society.

Discussion Questions

1. Name one thing you could do today to make your leisure more satisfying. What is something your mother could do for herself?

2. Think about a major piece of legislation that is before the National Congress or your state/provincial government. How will that legislation effect women's leisure?

3. What types of research questions do you think need to be answered for us to understand women's leisure better?

4. Talk to a leisure service programmer to find out how decisions are made about programming for females. Are gender issues being taken into account?

5. Examine a research journal that came out in the current year. What does the research tell us about gender-based or feminist issues related to leisure?

6. Examine a newspaper today. How are the issues discussed in the newspaper related to women's leisure?

Chapter Ten

Women and Leisure: The Future Journey

In my first days of activism, I thought I would do this ('this'
being feminism) for a few years and then return to my real life
(what my 'real life' might be, I did not know). Partly, that was
a naive belief that injustice only had to be pointed out in order
to be cured. Partly, it was a simple lack of courage.

But like so many others now and in movements past, I've
learned that this is not just something we care about for a year
or two or three. We are in it for life—and for our lives. Not
even the spiral of history is needed to show the distance
traveled. We have only to look back at the less complete
people we ourselves used to be.

And that is the last Survival Lesson: we look at how far
we've come, and then we know—there can be no turning
back.

—*Steinem, 1983, p. 361-362*

Looking toward the future is not an easy task. People who care about the
future, however, have a stake in creating the future. As we learned from Lerner
(1986, 1993) in chapter three, the fifth step in developing a feminist consciousness is to develop alternative visions for the future. We believe that a
preferable future for women and their leisure can be created through concerted
efforts to visualize what we want and develop steps to achieve our visions.
Depending on what we believe about the leisure gains and gaps in women's
lives, we can take steps to address the inequality, lack of empowerment, or
need for social change that exists.

The purpose of this final chapter is to summarize the current status of
women and leisure, to describe the value of developing alternative futures, to
define general societal trends and their implications for women, and to

describe future conditions for leisure. Several scenarios are provided as a way to illustrate what could occur in the future for women and leisure.

Women Have Come a Long Way—Maybe

To discuss where the issue of women and leisure has been and to look into the future, we must return to our discussion from chapter one of how social change occurs. Is it evolutionary or revolutionary? Does it occur due to changes in attitudes (i.e., idealism) or behaviors (i.e., materialism)? Does the responsibility for change lie within individual women (i.e., micro) or societal institutions (i.e., macro)? Obviously change refers to all these frameworks. We have tried to examine the leisure experiences of women from a variety of perspectives, although our biases as authors cannot help but be reflected in what we have presented.

The preceding chapters have described the status of women and leisure predominantly from the perspective of North American and Western societies. The thesis of this book has been that although gains have been made in most women's lives and leisure, gaps continue to exist. Some women have greater gaps in their leisure than others. Women's entitlement to leisure and the possibilities for their empowerment and free choice through leisure were made exigent. We grounded our discussion in feminisms and tried to show how leisure for women might be studied and understood from a variety of feminist perspectives. Parallels were drawn between feminisms, the conditions that affect most women, and leisure.

By focusing on women's leisure and the scholarship currently available, the invisibility and distortion of the female experience in leisure was highlighted. We proposed that by developing freedom of choice in leisure, the ability to resist societal norms and to negotiate leisure constraints can emerge for women. By addressing leisure we suggested that women's personal power may be advanced in other areas of their lives as well. At the same time as women's status in society is elevated, their leisure potential will also be ameliorated. In other words, leisure was presented as a catalyst for the empowerment of women and a concomitant benefit of increases in women's power.

The leisure gaps we discussed referred to both imbalances within the lives of individual women as well as between and within gender gaps. We also discussed some of the gaps that exist in the provision of leisure services and the information that is obtained and applied in conducting leisure research. The dimensions that comprised the experience of leisure seemed to be shared by both women and men but the allocations of leisure time and some recreation activities may be differentiated by gender. Furthermore, the "containers" of leisure may tend to be different for women compared to men, and different according to women's varied life situations and circumstances.

Women's leisure experiences often are affected by their perceptions of freedom and the concomitant constraints inherent in ascribed gender expectations and relationships. Historically, the oppression of women and the juxtaposition of leisure with work resulted in women's leisure often being primarily relational and role-defined. Although differences prevail between women and men, we emphasized that leisure expression may differ among individual women by age, social class, age and number of children, marital status, employment status, sexual orientation, race, and other individual and social characteristics. The meaning of these differences is yet to be fully understood.

The major constraints to women's leisure include intrapersonal, interpersonal, and structural constraints and constraints that cross or combine these categories. In addition, some leisure activities can be seen as constraining. Women vary in the ways that they define and negotiate these constraints. Some women use the constraints as a means for overcoming or resisting restrictions in their lives. Freedom and constraints within leisure vary over the life course as the roles and events that are part of women's lives change.

For the most part, we suggested that women's leisure is changing in evolutionary ways. When one compares the role and status of women 100 years ago to today, a surface glance indicates that great strides have been made. In some cases, women's leisure is more visible and yet, some of the changes have led to increased stress and decreased leisure time in women's lives. For example, when women are given permission to be "more like men" they sometimes take on those additional stereotyped attributes such as presumed strength and fortitude that may create additional pressures in their lives. Regardless, further social and personal changes are necessary to continue to create better environments for women's leisure and to improve women's status globally.

In the future, improvements in women's lives in general and their leisure lives in particular will require new ways of thinking about the meanings of leisure, as well as new ways of "knowing" about the relationship between women, leisure, and the quality of life. Research grounded in feminist approaches offers many ways of thinking about women and the social change that may occur in the future.

Introduction to the Future

People encounter numerous social upheavals and problems in today's world. The challenge is to be knowledgeable about the future and its possibilities. Incorporating the emerging roles of women is integral to this creative structuring. Speaking about the future is rather nebulous, however. Do we mean the short-range future (i.e., what will occur in the next 10–20 years), a long-range future of the next 20–50 years, or a far-ranging future of 50 years or more? Most of us are concerned about the short-range future although we want to leave a legacy on the earth that will last into the long-range future. Depending upon the range of our future forecasts, we may or may not be able to see the impact of changes in our lifetimes. The time context is important to consider as we discuss the future.

A second dimension to the future is an acknowledgment of whether we are describing preferred or likely futures. The likely future is based upon what researchers and futurists have empirically and systematically determined to be possible. The preferable future is a more ideal future based on what a particular group visualizes should happen. These views are interrelated and often are exemplified by different end results. We need to consider both, but we also must be specific in communicating which one we are describing. The future is more understandable if the likely and the preferable futures are consistent, although this compatibility is often not the case.

Visioning the future is imperative for several reasons. First, systematic reasoning about the long and far-ranging future is often missing in many institutions today. Strategic planning is necessary so organizations can be ready when changes occur, although this planning does not always include the futuristic environmental scanning that sets the stage. Many plans examine only the short-range future which is important but do not necessarily give a broad enough context for understanding social change. Second, all of us ought to be involved in choices and decisions made if we care about social justice for all people, but particularly women. If individuals who care about the goals of feminism are not involved in decisions then the future will be mandated by the existing power structures. Third, examining the future should result in the discovery of both the opportunities offered by the future, as well as the problems that are presented. When women turn away from visioning the future, we abdicate our responsibility for shaping it and changing the aspects that we do not want to have happen.

Futures forecasting is one of the major ways to analyze, envision, and begin to create the preferable future we desire. A forecast rests upon an explicitly stated set of logical assumptions, data, and relationships. In this way forecasting differs from opinions or prophecy. The ultimate goal of futures forecasting is to provide information to assist in planning for the future and to bring about desirable change. To visualize the future of women and their leisure, we must first consider likely directions for the future society and how these aspects may enhance or diminish women's leisure lives. Large-scale thinking must be utilized to avoid getting bogged down in details or becoming single-issue oriented. We must scrutinize the "whole" to understand the parts.

Three major premises underlie the field of futures study and the assumptions that we make in this chapter: (a) the future is not completely predictable, (b) the future is not predetermined, and (c) future outcomes can be influenced by individual choices (Amara, 1981). Further, we must emphasize that the future is being created by people's actions and inactions of today. We must be aware of those actions and how we might influence them in addressing gains and gaps in women's leisure.

General Trends in Society

To forecast the future for women and their leisure, we must examine the trends that are discernible in societies throughout the world today. This view into the crystal ball is extremely complex. For the most part we will examine the short-range future (i.e., 10–20 years into the future) unless otherwise stated. Longer-range futures are harder to predict, although often more fun for speculation. We will examine both likely and preferable futures. Preferable futures are an outgrowth of understanding as much as possible about the likely future.

The short-range future seems to suggest a greater acceleration of the pace of activity in all dimensions of people's lives. In other words, more people are likely to be busier than ever doing a variety of activities. At the same time, people will be questioning the status quo and trying to determine if their frenzied lives are really meaningful. Meaningful activity and the quality of life may take on new dimensions as change accelerates, as time seems to get increasingly short, and as people in diverse situations have an opportunity to deconstruct and reconstruct the "meanings" of their experiences. Although "work and spend" (Schor, 1991) may continue to be the behavior of many Americans, this philosophy may also be questioned.

No simple solutions to economic problems will occur unless our definitions of capitalism are drastically changed. The wage and social gaps between the "haves" and "have nots" will probably increase. Economic issues will continue and the balancing of economic concerns with human and environmental needs will likely be precarious. For example, governments in some countries may need to explore issues such as guaranteed incomes due to the inability to provide jobs for people, health insurance, and environmental protection related to economic necessity.

An acceptance of the diversity in all societies will be necessary, but likely will be slow because both behaviors and attitudes must be addressed. Women of color, lesbians, and other marginalized groups will likely continue to struggle with discrimination and prejudice in the future. The demographics of the population are likely to change in industrialized societies with a continued lower birthrate and an increasing number of older adults. Further, people of color will continue to comprise a greater percentage of people in North America as well as throughout the world. Adults probably will continue to be the focus of society with less emphasis on the youth culture, although concern for children's needs and at-risk youth will grow. Many people, at least in industrialized countries, will continue to marry later, divorce more frequently, and have fewer children. In North America, the trends suggest that the percentage of single persons and single-headed households will also continue to rise in number as will the variety of alternative family situations.

The jobs of the future will likely be service-oriented with education and training required for primarily the higher paying jobs. More diversity will exist among jobs although people may need to have greater specializations to do these jobs. Technology will provide a decrease in the number of jobs and unemployment rates are likely to increase. Some people may opt for sabbaticals or periods of time when they do not work. Fewer people will have "life jobs" and part-time and temporary work may be more easily available than full-time jobs in both industrialized and developing countries. Income will probably remain constant with the cost of living. The increased participation of women in the paid workforce may increase competition for some of the available jobs which may not be the same as the job foci of today.

Future lifestyles are likely to be described as diverse with many options available to people. People will make decisions because of the multiple options that will be available in their lives. The levels of education for individuals in the future will likely make people aware of the options that can be used to create meaning in their lives. Technology also will continue to make life easier for most people but will not negate the need for human interaction. Health issues will be important to people, although a gap between their attitudes and behaviors may continue to exist. While people believe that healthy lifestyles are important, their behavior may not always reflect those attitudes. Technological advances will continue to help people live healthier and happier lives.

Plummer (1989) has suggested that "traditional" values are likely to be replaced with new values in the coming short-term future. He suggested that some of the following changes might be noted: self-denial to self-fulfillment, higher standard of living to a better quality of life, traditional sex roles to blurred sex roles, accepted definition of success to individualized definitions of success, faith in institutions to self-reliance, and a philosophy from "live to work" to "work to live." The concept of self-reliance, for example, suggests that people will be looking for meaning by focusing on networking, citizen involvement, and decentralization in all areas of life. These changes in values reflect the impact of the contemporary women's movement as gains for women have been articulated; these gains will continue to affect men in positive ways as well.

The world is likely to continue to "shrink" in the future. Technology in the form of the electronic highway will literally link every part of the world into one huge communication network, and we will be able to transmit in seconds the images of a global society. Unfortunately, not everyone will have access to that technology. The realization that what is done within one geographical location affects people throughout the world, however, will become even more apparent. A new awareness and concern about environmental issues will become imperative for survival. People will find it difficult to disassociate with dissimilar others when the interconnections become so obvious and easy.

The preceding trends will have direct implications for women's lives and their leisure. As the "traditional" gender expectations and responsibilities of women are enhanced with new options, women's and men's lives will change. The leisure gaps that exist in some women's lives, however, will become neither extinct, nor extant.

Roles of Women in the Future

In considering the leisure and future preferable for women, two predominant views that represent contrasting but eclectic views of feminism will provide the framework for discussion: equality and integrity. The equality perspective suggests that the future will be a linear extension of what exists today; the future will be similar to the present with a focus on the problems women face and how women can "fit into" and find equality in the patriarchal world and thus, modify and reduce the power of the patriarchy.

The integrity view suggests that basic, more radical changes are needed in ways of thinking to improve women's lives in general and their leisure lives in particular. The structure of these frameworks may be evolutionary or revolutionary. A continued movement toward equality might be considered in the likely future, whereas the perspective of integrity will be considered a "revolutionary" or preferable way to bring about social change. On the basis of a preferable future, the possibilities for women seem wide open. In the more likely future, the movement toward equality will likely be *interspersed* with backslides and backlashes regarding traditional forms of gender roles.

The Future of Feminism

Most feminists would agree that the preferred future for women lies in a movement away from sexual polarization and imposed gender roles toward a society where individual roles and personal behavior can be freely chosen. One aspect that is clear today is that many versions of feminism will continue to exist and no one approach will be agreed upon by all in the short-term future. We will likely continue to struggle with the meaning of feminisms. All feminist perspectives, however, will continue to embody the basic goals of correcting the invisibility and distortion of female experience; enabling every woman to have equity, dignity, and freedom of choice; and removing all forms of inequality and oppression in society. The diversity of opinions will be divisive if feminists line up against one another, but these different opinions can also mean that a variety of strategies can be applied to addressing the many issues that face women in the future. Preferably, a more inclusive feminism will exist where opportunities will be created for women to work together for common goals despite differences in approaches and perspectives.

Some individuals would hope that gender does not exist in the future. They would strive for a society where individuals are androgynous (i.e., possessing both male and female characteristics equally) and genderless. This society would also be one that is gender blind or gender neutral. The likelihood, however, is that most of us will continue to live in very gendered cultures. Thus, many feminists would prefer a "gender inclusive" culture that takes into account the needs and interests of women and how women and men can best function together within a variety of options.

Feminism likely will remain a dominant social force in the future, despite the backlash that has occurred in the 1990s. The media is likely to continue to emphasize the *extreme* rhetoric of feminism and not the way it makes life better for all individuals (Faludi, 1991). In a period of social upheaval, this backlash is inevitable as people reevaluate their lives and reflect on the progress that women have made. Some males and females will likely feel threatened or uncomfortable with the changes that have occurred.

Preferably in the future, nonprofessional, poor, and other women who have not been a part of mainstream feminism will become a part of the movement and have opportunities to influence the feminist agenda. Hopefully a place will also be found for those women and men who do not wish to be called feminists (i.e., "I'm not a feminist, but...") but work for many of the goals espoused by politically active feminists. Young people, in particular, have become leery of feminism as representing "victimization" (Wolf, 1994). A greater understanding of feminism will be necessary if young people and other people who have been inadvertently marginalized by the contemporary feminist movement are to subscribe to its tenets in the future. Further debate and educational efforts will continue to define feminism so that the negative implications do not dominate the general public's understanding of its tenets.

Just as the values of society will change slowly, so will some of the perceptions of women. The change in language reflects some of the shifts occurring in feminism that are likely to continue into the future. For example, *Time* magazine (Wallis, 1989) described the changes between the old idea of "having it all" and the new one of "doing it all," fast track to mommy track, consciousness raising to networking, and "room at the top" to the "glass ceiling." These changes in rhetoric represent the issues that feminists will be called upon to address in the short-range future.

Further changes toward equality are likely to occur slowly because of the belief that exists among many women and men that women have already attained equality. The recent battle in the United States, for example, to reverse Affirmative Action is based on some people's beliefs that women now have greater advantage than men. Despite the thrust for greater political control that women have recently asserted, the gains will likely ebb and flow in the coming years. A postfeminist society is not likely in the short-range future, although perhaps someday in a far-ranging future when gender does not make a difference in how people are expected to behave, a need for feminism will not exist. The gains that women have made will continue to be acknowledged, but feminists will not be content with assuming that everything has been "fixed." The media, for example, must be encouraged to continue to address such social issues as rape, teenage pregnancy, and lesbianism not as sensationalized stories but as issues that society must address.

We must be cautious in the future not to overstate the gains that women are making. Many women have been upwardly mobile in their careers, but the number "making it" likely will remain relatively low compared to the general workforce. Further, some women will continue to deny sexual discrimination because they have never experienced discrimination, are unable to recognize it, or believe that sexual discrimination is not a problem because it is no longer legal. Even though attitudes toward women will continue to change, behavior change will also continue at a slow rate (Benokraitis, 1986). In addition, many women and men will remain comfortable with their "traditional" roles, will fear change, and will prefer to maintain the status quo unless they are forced to change.

The patriarchal society will not be replaced with a "gynocentric" society in the short-range or long-range future. Feminists who consider themselves radical will likely continue to seek ways to make women more visible in society beyond addressing equality issues. They will seek a wider separation from male culture and institutions and will advocate for greater recognition of female culture. The belief that feminism can transform the world by focusing on new visions of peace and integrity for all will be an ideal of these feminists. Some feminists may seek to revolutionize ways of thinking about the world while others will seek to remake the world as a matriarchy. Most feminists will find that the agenda for the future will grow longer, rather than shorter, each day.

Future of Women and Work

Women are likely to continue to make gains in the workplace in the short-range future, although these gains may come slowly and in small increments. In most cultures, more women will be employed in the labor force. The U.S. Bureau of Labor (1991) suggested that 60 percent of the labor force will be female by 2000. Optimistically, predictions say that women's earnings in the United States will be 85 percent of men's by 2000, although from the beginning of the contemporary women's movement in the late 1960s until the 1990s, the amount only went from 59 percent to about 71 percent. Importantly, the gains that women make in the workplace have the potential to reflect on all workers which may make work "kinder and gentler" for all individuals.

Women will work for pay both out of necessity and as a way to find meaning in their lives. More women in the full-time and part-time workforce will permit a higher standard of consumption for some two income families. As more women desire entry into the paid workforce, continued structural unemployment, underemployment, and a lack of jobs for women as well as for men, are likely. High competition in some jobs (viz., professional) could even lead to longer working hours and higher stress levels as Schor (1991) has shown. In the preferred future, however, both females and males will have the opportunity to work a shortened workweek and will have the opportunity to pursue other alternative forms of work such as flex-time and sabbatical leaves. These changes will enable more people to have employment as well as allow for more free time for other pursuits throughout people's life spans.

The meaning of work for women will continue to change in the future. Women's work has been typically defined as something that was supposed to be done out of love, instinct, and devotion to some higher cause rather than for the self (Rich, 1977). Many women may still undertake paid and unpaid work for these reasons, but present trends indicate that they will also be seeking additional personal fulfillment and economic rewards in the careers, jobs, service work, and household tasks they pursue. The meanings of work will also probably change as women view work as a more primary life interest than as "something to fall back on" or to provide "extras" in the two income family. A greater continuity of employment, as contrasted to women "dropping in and out" to raise a family, may provide more career mobility for women, particularly in professional jobs. If women's unpaid work at home is shared by other family members, work outside the home likely will take on greater meaning.

In the short-range future, some women will continue to choose to pursue leadership and management positions even though they may continue to face challenges in entering traditionally male-dominated jobs. Some of these problems center on issues of socialization that may make management "foreign" or undesirable to some women (Hennig & Jardim, 1976). For example, women have not typically been socialized to be competitive, yet many management tasks in corporations require high sales productivity. Role conflict may also be created because of the nature of management positions as currently structured and the expected role of the ideal woman as employee, as well as family caregiver. Hopefully, the movement towards more humanistic concerns in management will make professional jobs more attractive and less conflictual for women, as well as men, in the future.

For women to be successful in work environments in the future, two policies must be specifically addressed in the future: gender equity and family policies. Hochschild (1989) has described a "stalled revolution" because the institutions of work, family, and community have not caught up with the present reality of women in the paid workforce. We also might term this occurrence as "structural lag" as institutions in the future will be forced to address value and attitudinal changes that often occur first in society. If the dual responsibilities of work and family are not supported either at home or in the workplace, women will continue to be caught in a double bind. The complex issues of gender equity and family policies likely will receive a great deal of discussion in the future.

Evidence suggests that sex-segregation in jobs will continue. Even though women are more visible in traditionally male-dominated careers (i.e., law, medicine), the percentage of gain will continue to be relatively small (Reskin, 1988). The predominance of women in traditional female occupations, which are largely service oriented, is likely to remain the same in the short-range future, as well. These service jobs will not be the high paying jobs in most cultures. Although women are beginning to enter other areas of work that have been primarily male realms, this change will continue to occur slowly contrary to what the media information might suggest.

Alternative work models for women in the preferred future could enable them to adjust to changing social roles. For example, available and affordable childcare centers would be helpful in allowing women freedom to choose their work opportunities. In addition, alternative work schedules such as flextime, job sharing, and 4-day/36-hour work weeks would be helpful to many women and men who wish to combine family and career. Longer maternity leaves with pay and enforced family leave policies will be preferred ways to improve the work environment for women in the future. Women often "fall into" particular lifestyles for practical or pragmatic reasons rather than from choice. Changes in attitudes toward women working must accompany and perhaps, precede these new models if these models are to be effective.

As women obtain more education, they are likely to have more options open to them in the workplace, although marginalized women likely will experience more restrictions than women from privileged groups. Further, more realistic job counseling for women is preferable with a shift in attitudes, opportunities, and a variety of career choices made possible for women. Regardless of career choices, women as well as men, are likely to change careers every ten years for a variety of reasons.

The personality traits typically thought of as female may be more evident, appreciated, and needed in the workplace of the future. For example, the humanness, sensitivity, and nurturing that are typically thought of as social-ized feminine traits may be important and valued for certain jobs, especially in the service sector. Although increased valuation of these traits may not increase the pay, a combination of characteristic masculine traits (e.g., leadership, assertiveness) and stereotypic feminine traits (e.g., cooperation, gentleness) will be highly desirable in many jobs.

Advanced technology is allowing people in a variety of professional jobs to work at home more easily. As paid work becomes more home-centered, both positive and negative implications will emerge for women. Some women can be a model for these changes since they have had to integrate work and leisure in the home for many years. On the other hand, if housework/family obligations do not change, they may infringe upon paid home-based work. Another disadvantage to home-centered work is that the benefits of working outside the home are eliminated. In the past, one of the values of paid work has been the opportunity to get a person out of the house to meet new people and have social interactions in new environments. Regardless of where work is conducted, individuals will probably have more options within some jobs in the future.

Somewhat higher incomes for women in the future will be symbolic of their increased social status. Direct access to income will continue to be crucial to individual worth, personal and political power, and social prestige. For women to achieve equality in society, they will need to have greater financial means and independence. Clearly, economic independence and equality are inextricably related. Economic independence will progress slowly for women as long as inequality in the workplace exists. From an integrity perspective, a complete restructuring of the capitalist value system needs to be considered and implemented to provide greater opportunities for women and other oppressed groups. A new way of thinking may be necessary if women are to be valued for unpaid work experiences they have in the "second shift" because of the extreme value placed on money in our society (Hochschild, 1989).

In searching for meaning in life, areas of achievement other than formal education and work experiences may become viable options. For example, some people may choose unpaid volunteer work as a primary means of self-expression. This volunteering may be with areas such as church-related or social organizations. Meaning might also be found in avocational pursuits or serious leisure such as amateur sports or a variety of leisure pursuits. Because diversity of lifestyles is likely to occur in the future, paid work may not continue to be the primary definition of success. For older adults in particular who are retired, this redefinition of meaningful activity may be particularly important. Many outlets for meaning, including paid and unpaid work, will hopefully be available for both women and men in the short-range and long-range future.

Future of Women and the Family

The structure and ideology of the family will continue to be central to most women in Western societies even though the reproductive rights of women and the equal division of household labor are likely to become more widely accepted. Preferably, both the expressive role of family caregiving and the instrumental role of "breadwinner" will be valued with a preferable fusion of both in the shared caregiving and provider roles of women and men across the course of their lives. Issues of caregiving may, however, be expanded to include not only dependent children but also aging parents, grandparents parenting grandchildren, adult children caring for aging parents, and family members caring for other family members. Regardless of the family structure chosen in the future, caregiving will hopefully be a shared responsibility of family members as well as society in general. The wider acceptance of daycare services for children and adults and afterschool programs as viable options for working adults will provide new forms of socialization for children and dependent adults. Preferably, women will no longer be solely responsible for raising and caring for others. Not only men's responsibility but the responsibility that communities have for taking care of people is preferable for the future. Feminists must be careful that the definition of family does not expand in ways that could provide additional constraints on the traditional roles of women.

The traditional family structure is likely to continue to reflect the changes already underway. Low birth rates and a higher number of divorces, for example, will result in smaller family sizes (Kelly, 1981). This trend will continue because some women will wait to have children later in life, some will choose a higher standard of living over the expense of supporting children, and others will choose careers that will make child-raising a low priority. In addition, some couples may consciously choose not to have children and some women will consciously choose not to marry. The number of single-female headed households, with and without children, will likely, continue to increase. Many family forms now exist and are likely for the future. Alternatives to the traditional family such as couples living together before marriage, blended families, households of small or large groupings of people living together for an unspecified time and with no specific interpersonal relations, gay and lesbian partnerships and parenting, and transitional periods of living alone and with others in a variety of relationships are more likely in the future.

As these changes in family forms occur, they will likely lead to reduced socialization of women into traditional roles and expectations. For example, when young people see adults sharing work, home, and family tasks, these changed role expectations likely will be adopted by a new generation. Family functions traditionally determined by gender role will gradually change to reflect the broader options that are available. Therefore, other forms of validation and self-definitions outside the family, such as paid work or community service, preferably will become available and accepted for women and men. Already a major attitude change is occurring in that many people believe that work should be distributed equally in the family, although it remains to be seen how this attitude will affect behavior.

Many feminists, especially radical feminists, also believe that women must be liberated from compulsory motherhood (Firestone, 1971). In other words, they believe the role of women in society will change when marriage and reproduction will be strictly a matter of choice and devoid of social pressure to conform. In the preferred future, more women will assert their sexual freedom. Women who choose heterosexual relationships hopefully will do so with issues of equity in the forefront. Some women may choose the lesbian lifestyle that frees them from imposed gender roles even though the stigma attached to gays and lesbians likely will change slowly. Other women will choose to remain single as that lifestyle continues to be more valid and less stigmatized. In general, the lifestyles of women are likely to be diverse and more freely chosen in the future.

Changes in the roles of women in the future will not be without problems. Women will struggle to redefine what it means to be a woman freed from traditional ascribed gender roles and expectations. Women who seek self-esteem, who lead interesting and rewarding lives, and who find their work and leisure contributing to their quality of life are less likely, however, to have negative reactions to the social change that will occur.

Micro Changes in Leisure for Women in the Future

Changes in society's valuation of leisure will affect leisure for everyone, including women. Preferably in the short-range future, leisure will not be defined simply as the antithesis of work but will be prized because of its intrinsic and communal values. If all activity were done for its own sake and not defined as work or leisure, a new definition of life quality would emerge. The adoption of a "worth ethic" (Dustin & Schultz, 1981) would have profound implications for how people might perceive their lives. This focus on worth might be envisioned as self-development and social responsibility as opposed to job status and learning capacity. People would pursue leisure as a respite from the routine of living, as a means for personal identity development, and a way to contribute to their immediate social circle as well as to the larger society.

In the future, individuals are likely to continue to associate a number of outcomes with recreation and leisure. These benefits will include individual growth and self-development; rest and relaxation; social interaction; strengthening of family ties; developing social, physical, and emotional well-being; appreciating the outdoors, and building physical fitness. Leisure will also be seen as an indication of social status through the "display" of leisure possessions. In the preferred future, more emphasis will be put on "quality of being" rather than quantity of activities, quantity of time, or quantity of material possessions. Hopefully, women and men will seek "peak experiences" in their leisure and will look for opportunities for aesthetic response, the achievement of personal goals, the betterment of personal and community environment, and positive feedback from others. In the preferable short-term and long-term leisure world, increasing emphasis will be put upon the concepts of the quality of life, self-actualization, creativity, individualism, and humanism. Moreover, people will view their leisure experiences as individual and self-centered and will expect society to respect the individuality of each person.

Women in the future are likely to continue to avoid leisure gaps just as they will seek to find balance in other aspects of life. Women hopefully will see their lives open to many options that will enable them to be adaptable and flexible in choosing leisure experiences. As women's leisure needs are recognized and valued at a personal as well as a societal level in the preferred future, increased importance will be placed on meeting these leisure needs. Preferably, individual differences among women such as race, class, and marital status will be acknowledged when analyzing leisure needs. The "common world of women" as it relates to the potential for leisure gains and gaps, however, and what women in different lifestyles seek in attaining equal opportunities for leisure will be a focus.

The time available for leisure will vary from woman to woman in the future. For example, with an increased number of women working, especially in professional positions, and with more female-headed households, women may find that their "clock time" will be more constrained than ever (Shaw, 1991). With changes in perceptions of leisure and a belief in entitlement to leisure, women may make leisure a higher priority and may choose to use free time for meaningful leisure pursuits. In addition, with a change in the sharing of household and caregiving responsibilities, new family forms, and creative work structures, some women may find they have more access to discretionary time.

Perceived freedom, intrinsic motivation, and enjoyment will continue to be both the conscious and unconscious motivations for leisure in the future. Women likely will continue to seek affiliative or relational leisure and this interaction will be highly valued, but they will also seek independent, autonomous, and self-determined leisure. Entitlement to leisure will provide a basis for making time and space available for women's leisure, but this right to entitlement will evolve slowly. As gender roles change, new meanings will be associated with affiliative and self-determined leisure for women.

As in the past, women probably will continue to integrate their work and leisure because of their role responsibilities. Some leisure scholars believe that the ideal future is one where the lines between work and leisure will be so blurred that they will no longer be dichotomized; all meaningful activity (i.e., traditional paid and unpaid work as well as leisure) will be valued. Other scholars suggest that work must be evident for leisure to exist and that a defining dimension between leisure and nonleisure is a work component. More research will be conducted to help to solve the controversy, although the problem may be about the definitions of work and leisure more than the reality of the concepts.

The "containers" for leisure will probably expand in both the short-range and long-range futures as women's social status is improved. Although new leisure situations and spaces may unfold for women, the home will likely continue as a primary place where leisure will occur. However, with smaller family sizes, women may not consider family recreation to be synonymous with their personal recreation. Leisure outside the home may be used as a substitute for some of the companionship, personal support, and regular interaction that may be lost in society due to family transitions such as divorce (Kelly, 1981) or less family support as one ages. As traditional family roles and responsibilities consume less of a woman's time and offer less prescribed meaning through the course of life, the role of leisure both inside and outside the broadly defined family will likely assume increased importance and meaning.

Typical and atypical recreation activities will likely be open to women in the future, although some social stigma may continue to be attached to traditional gender-typed leisure pursuits. More opportunities for skill development through women-only organizations and recreational equipment designed specifically for women may encourage participation and enhance the potential for satisfying leisure experiences. Some women will become more highly skilled in typical leisure pursuits such as sports and may become intensely committed to excellence in their leisure activities. Because education is a good predictor of recreation participation, women may take advantage of more opportunities for leisure as their educational level increases. In addition, since recreation is a cumulative experience, participation in one type of activity may encourage participation in others (Zuzanek, 1978).

Income is another factor that has implications for leisure and recreation participation. When survival and subsistence are priorities, little excess income is available for recreation. Because women will make slow progress toward equal pay, most women in the short-range future likely will not have access to large amounts of discretionary income to use for recreation. As sufficient income becomes available to women in cultures throughout the world, more opportunities should theoretically exist for a variety of leisure pursuits.

Feminism, with its focus on choices and the removal of imposed gender roles, will preferably provide a framework for contextualizing women's leisure in the future. When women are no longer oppressed by societal mores, imposed gender roles, and devaluation, their leisure will also become more accepted, available, and meaningful. In the same way, as women take control of their leisure lives, they will be empowered to question traditional gender roles and constraints operant in all aspects of their lives.

Macro Changes in Leisure for Women in the Future

Women's leisure in the future must be addressed from both macro and micro perspectives that affect women's lives as a whole. The macrosphere of change includes shifts in institutional roles provided by governments, leisure service providers, and other organizations. The movements in many countries toward privatization may mean that the government's role will be decreased in women's lives and some forms of change in the future may be more difficult to achieve.

Most governments have done little to directly address women's leisure in the past and this trend is likely to continue. Laws that have been passed to give women access to resources and equal opportunities have affected their leisure, although the purposes of most laws has not been to directly influence leisure.

Almost everything that happens in society has some implications for women's leisure and will continue to do so in the future. The United Nations Declaration of Human Rights will have a more prominent position in many countries and will enable women to make further gains in leisure. Progress likely will be slow. Broad issues such as violence directed toward women will continue to affect women's leisure unless addressed not only nationally, but also internationally. Women in industrialized countries will need to consider the needs of women in developing countries when determining research agendas and future directions if global changes are to occur.

Leisure service providers of the future preferably will move beyond a narrow focus on recreation activities toward enabling and facilitating a variety of leisure experiences for women. In other words, providers will think in terms of human experiences, not just activities. Recreation programming will move from merely responding to what women want to examining how inner needs can be met. Programs for wide variations of family structures, mixed age and sex groups, and older adults will also be encouraged in the future as will programming to promote cultural identities. The employed single parents, often restricted in both time and money, will require special attention and providers will attempt to address their needs and those of their families. Affordable childcare or eldercare may be available to some extent for women in conjunction with recreation programs, although this amenity will likely not be widespread. These leisure and recreation providers, however, probably will struggle with how to move from a "gender-neutral" approach to a "gender-inclusive" one.

Scenarios About Women and Leisure in the Future

Using some of the approaches to feminism along with a conservative backlash view of society, five possible future scenarios are presented based upon information in this book. The scenarios are offered as catalysts to stimulate thinking, not as predictions of the future. To change the role of women and leisure, a vision must be constructed of what the preferable future should hold. Some of the ideas presented are not necessarily desirable but could occur. Readers are encouraged to pick and choose the ideas that will be most useful in visualizing their desired future.

"Handmaid's Tale" Scenario (Backlash View)

The year is 2020. Women's primary role is within the family. Gender-imposed roles are strictly rewarded and the division of labor between men and women is extreme. Women are expected to be gentle, nurturing, and define themselves in relation to men and family obligations. Women are economically dependent upon their husbands who control all the family income, even income made by a woman if she must work outside the home in part-time work. The duty of women is to bear, raise, and socialize children for their future gender-distinct adult roles.

Women who do not conform to these rigid societal expectations (i.e., heterosexual marriage and mothering) are discriminated against by receiving only the most menial low-paying jobs. Men have control over all decision making and women are not allowed to voice their opinions on "anything that matters." Reproductive rights issues have reverted to their pre-1970s standards as have equal rights issues. Older women are particularly vulnerable within this system if they outlast their family usefulness and protection.

The predominant social ethic revolves around status-laden productive work. A person is judged by the type and amount of work completed within the public sphere of the labor market. Women who must work (i.e., due to lack of male sponsorship) hold the lowest status jobs. Distinctions based on life situation such as race, ethnicity, and age are used openly to discriminate among workers. Lesbians have been driven underground because of the extreme pressure of heterosexuality and the punishment for deviancy. Religious organizations are involved in promoting the values defined by the heterosexual white males in society. Women's major contribution is to the invisible economy located within the home. This household and family work is not valued, but can serve as a source of retribution if done poorly (e.g., raising deviant children or nonattendance to spouse needs).

Leisure is viewed as a frivolous pursuit within this society and is practically nonexistent for all but the upper class. The few leisure opportunities that do exist for women are role appropriate in that they focus on family interaction or tangible end products that will serve some useful household purpose. The meaning of leisure is hard to determine for women because the past criteria of freedom to choose, intrinsic motivation and reward are not within women's reality. No resistance to gender roles through leisure is permitted; thus, any sense of entitlement or empowerment is absent. Leisure pursuits cannot interfere with the primary roles of childbearer and childraiser, so physical limitations on activity are adhered to strictly with the few outlets for activity directed toward health improvement for childbearing. Most women do not object to this standard because they accept that they are dependent upon the patriarchal system and find their value and self-worth in their biological destiny that must be fulfilled in order to be a complete woman.

"Wanderground" Scenario (Radical Feminism)

Twenty-five years from now, women have taken control of society and a matriarchy has replaced the patriarchy. In the late-1990s women organized themselves in a global solidarity that allowed their collective power to emerge and predominate. Consensual, nonhierarchical models are the norm for all businesses and governmental structures. Women exercise the "power within," place value on human life, and encourage diversity among individuals. These values provide abundant opportunities for women and men to explore and fulfill their potential without the past restrictions of gender roles, masculinity/femininity, and repressive social structures. The society has moved away from the emphasis on the individual and resulting class structures as exemplified in capitalism, toward a greater sense of community and concern for all members of the society.

Work is shared by women and men, although less time is spent in traditional work with flex time and shortened work weeks as the norm. Most menial work has been alleviated through technological advances and all work is considered a valuable contribution to society. The "worth ethic" is more important than the work or leisure ethic. Housework is communally shared or individuals who enjoy and are "good at" these activities are encouraged to do them. The activities of housework and family caregiving are valued and seem to be just as important as traditional paid work because they contribute to the betterment of all. Volunteerism and community service are common for everyone because a caring, nurturing attitude is valued and a commitment exists to join together to create a superior quality of life for all people.

Families in the "wanderground" society are diverse. Many forms of living arrangements are possible and no judgment is placed on the gender of one's significant other or the number of significant others that one may have. Divorce is no longer existent because all significant relations are discussed and agreements are established to clarify expectations. These agreements are readily amended or dissolved when necessary. Childrearing is the responsibility of both men and women and is considered best done when many adult caregivers can share the experience. Children are socialized to believe that they are capable of pursuing any desired occupations, relationships, and leisure experiences. No gender-imposed roles are evident. The focus is on the individual and what she or he is capable of being, along with a sense of community care for all members.

The matriarchy has solved many of the global problems by transformational thinking. The threat of global destruction no longer exists. Enough food and housing are available worldwide in part due to the value placed on the ethic of care. Health issues are the responsibility of each individual but governments make sure that adequate healthcare is available for all. Environmental problems are being solved as quickly as possible, although severe problems remain because of a lack of environmental concern at the end of the previous century. Everyone has recognized the benefits of voluntary simplicity and have placed less importance on personal material possessions.

The distinctions between work and leisure are minimal. Both women and men are able to engage in "meaningful activity" which may be traditional recreation activities or may be integrated with traditional forms of work. A diversity of activities is available for people. Although activities are sometimes competitive, much activity is cooperative with the focus on relationships. Health and wellness are the central focus of all undertakings. Providers of organized activities offer a diversity of programs at costs that all can afford. Leisure both inside and outside the home is common. Women and men take responsibility for their own leisure lifestyles with guidance available from facilitators, leisure counselors, and leisure enablers.

The "Equal Rights" Scenario (Liberal Feminism)

Total equality has come to most women in the year 2020. Women are receiving equal pay for their work and have equal opportunities in all aspects of life. Essential components of the former patriarchal structure still remain, but women now have equal opportunities within that structure.

The nature of work remains much the same, but a confluence of gender-stereotyped work has occurred. More men are employed in the service sector than in the 1990s, while more women are in professional positions. Housework is equally shared by males and females as are the childrearing activities. Some opportunities exist for outside childcare, but each woman or man has the choice of whether to stay home and care for the child or an elderly parent and receive a subsidy for these efforts, or work for pay. This decision is generally made by both the husband and wife. The traditional family of husband, wife, and children is still the norm, although diversity in family forms is gaining acceptance.

Women are given choices in their lives and can choose traditional roles if they wish. Women have worked for equality, and they are responsible for the way that their lives are lived. Because of the emphasis on equality, women and men do not have as much freedom as in the past. In some situations, free choice has been a trade-off to guarantee equality for all.

Education has been an equalizing factor for women. People felt in the late-1990s that if all women were given educational opportunities, they would be able to succeed in the job market with men and be able to self-actualize. This assumption has proven to be true.

Leisure opportunities for women and men are homogeneous, although leisure is not a high priority for either women or men and, in fact, is considered peripheral. Similar activities and facilities are available for both sexes and many coed activities are encouraged. Women have opportunities to be in women-only situations on a limited basis. Little justification exists for women-only activities now that women have equal opportunity that has been guaranteed through legislative mandates and policy implementation. Women have the same entitlement to leisure as men and are free to express their identities through a variety of possibilities in both the private and public spheres.

The "Social Issue" Scenario (Socialist Feminism)

In the socialist feminist view of the world in 2020, a modified socialist democratic governmental structure exists. This governmental structure has developed in response to the inadequacy of the old patriarchal capitalist structure that was insensitive to oppression based on aspects of race, class, age, and gender and the intersection of these life conditions. Women are not favored more than any other group; however, acknowledgment exists that women have been oppressed in a society that has viewed "different" as deviant. The power of the system rests in the power of the people to make laws for the common good. Women have benefited from all the social reforms that have taken place; their lives are less oppressed and they have gained many opportunities as a result of social change inspired by socialist feminist perspectives.

Work is shared by all. All work has value with household work and family responsibilities recognized as equal in importance to paid employment. The family does not represent the old structure that was oppressive to women; instead a woman is valued beyond her reproductive capabilities. The raising of children is a shared responsibility with much of the work done through cooperative nurseries, daycare centers, schools, and other social programs for childcare and families. The collective efforts are thought to help reduce the last remnants of the class structures inherent to capitalism and patriarchy. Housework is done by whomever has the time to do it but is no longer considered the sole responsibility of women. All people are guaranteed a wage and compensated for the contributions they make to society. Social problems are addressed through programs that give special assistance to individuals needing help in areas such as healthcare, birth control, and housing.

Leisure is considered important for all because of its recuperative value. Many leisure opportunities exist with the focus on the improvement of physical, mental, and emotional health. Access to leisure is equal regardless of gender, race, or class. Leisure is affordable to all and provided for by the government. The government controls leisure policy with input from the people and leisure is considered necessary for the overall health of the nation.

"Productive Work" Scenario (Marxist Feminism)

In the year 2020, the Marxist organizers have finally succeeded in upsetting the bourgeois. The repressed proletariat has become organized and vocal. The workers have rejected the oppression of the class system that was a result of the capitalism of the late twentieth century. As the economic differences among the classes were magnified, a rejection of the capitalist social structures was initiated. The government has been changed from a capitalist democracy to one based on Marxist principles. Everyone is treated the same with the power distributed equally among women and men.

Productive work is the key aspect to the society. Although women have benefited from the social changes, their needs have not been singled out for special attention. Work within the home is necessary to keep the workforce in prime condition, but this responsibility is equally shared by women and men. The household work, however, remains more or less invisible and not as valued as the work done in the public sphere.

Families are considered a useful structure for reproducing the workforce but the expectations that women will be the primary caregivers has changed. Much of the childcare and education of the children occurs in the government-sponsored schools and programs.

Leisure has become valued for its utilitarian value. It helps keep the workforce healthy, relaxed, and socially satisfied. Old forms of leisure experience garnered through church activities are practically nonexistent; however, voluntary community activity is strongly encouraged for all responsible community members.

Writing Our Own Future

Each person must take an active role in forming her or his own future. For women, many choices must be made concerning work and leisure, family and household, gender roles, and the quality of life. Making leisure gains and surmounting gaps require a concerted effort to know the quality of life that one prefers. People can create the desired future with efforts directed at both the macro and micro levels. On the micro level, women can take control of their own lives and make choices that will lead to a meaningful and satisfying lifestyle. On the macro level, work for social change through legal mandates, attitude adjustments, and social reforms is necessary. Changes in the status of women will come with equal rights, reproductive rights, and higher education. Such change will effect the leisure experiences and leisure opportunities of women. Reciprocally, by taking control of their lives and bodies through leisure, women may also redefine their status and create social change. The interrelationship between leisure and social change cannot be explicated at this time; further efforts are needed to understand the meaning and significance of leisure for all people, but especially for women.

By visioning the future we can gain some control over the future. If we see something in the future that does not seem appropriate, we can work to change it. On the other hand, if we have a preferable vision of the future we can move toward that direction. Visioning the future is a bit like going to school: when we know why we are doing it (e.g., because it will lead to a chosen career), a commitment to the effort is easier. The same is true with the future. If we see something is important about our own personal leisure or the leisure of women in general in the future, then we can work toward attaining that future.

Every individual has the right to leisure. The challenge for the future may be in getting individuals, as well as society, to recognize the importance of this right, not only for the well-being of individual females and males, but for the overall quality of life that each of us deserves on this earth. Entitlement to leisure as well as the empowerment of women through leisure is critical to the social changes that are necessary as we move toward a global society in the twenty-first century. In the future, removing leisure gaps and finding empowerment through leisure for all people is imperative.

Concluding Perspectives

In this chapter we have gazed into our crystal ball and tried to offer some ideas about the likely short-range future journey for women and leisure. Our crystal ball is no better than yours. None of us knows the future, but we do know that each of us can be active in creating the future. We can be both optimistic and pessimistic about the future. The concerted effort of feminists committed to empowering women and other disadvantaged groups is needed to work toward the social change that is desirable. We will need to use all the tools for social change to achieve more gains and reduce the gaps. The future for women and their leisure is waiting to be created by us.

Discussion Questions

1. Is leisure possible when there is no work? When there is nothing to compare work to?

2. What is it about the homemaker role that makes it a "deadening" experience for some women? How might it be restructured to make it more meaningful and rewarding?

3. What sociostructural changes need to occur before a satisfying leisure life can be had? What personal changes?

4. What will be the likely future relationship between women's work and leisure?

5. Write your own preferred personal and social scenario for the future. What societal changes will need to occur for these scenarios to become a reality?

6. Select one aspect of women's leisure that is a concern for you. From a feminist perspective, describe how this concern could be addressed in the future.

7. What gains are women likely to make regarding their leisure in the next 25 years? What gaps will continue to remain after the next 25 years?

8. What will the future be like based on personal identities and social situations? For example, if you are a person of color, how might your future be different from a person of white heritage? A person who is lesbian or gay? A person with a disability? A working-class woman?

References

Alberta Recreation and Parks Department. (1988, January). Women and leisure. *A Look at Leisure, 21*, pp. 1-12.

Alcoff, L. (1995). Cultural feminism versus post-structuralism: The identity crisis in feminist theory. In N. Tuana and R. Tong (Eds.), *Feminism and philosophy: Essential readings in theory, reinterpretation, and application* (pp. 434-456). Boulder, CO: Westview Press, Inc.

Allen, J. (1994). *Constraints negotiation strategies in the corporate wellness setting.* Unpublished master's thesis, University of Waterloo, Waterloo, ON.

Allen, K. R. and Chin-Sang, V. (1990). A lifetime of work: The context and meanings of leisure for aging black women. *The Gerontologist, 30*, 734-740.

Allen, L. R. (1991). Benefits of leisure services to community satisfaction. In B. L. Driver, P. J. Brown, and G. L. Peterson (Eds.), *Benefits of leisure* (pp. 331-350). State College, PA: Venture Publishing, Inc.

Allison, M. and Duncan, M. (1987). Woman, work, and leisure: The days of our lives. *Leisure Sciences, 9*, 143-162.

Altergott, K. and McCreedy, C. C. (1993). Gender and family status across the life course: Constraints of five types of leisure. *Loisir et Société/Society and Leisure, 16*(1), 151-180.

Amara, R. (1981, April). The future field: How to tell good work from bad. *The Futurist*, pp. 61-71.

American Association of University Women (AAUW). (1991). *Shortchanging girls, shortchanging America: A call to action.* Washington, DC: AAUW.

An identity crisis of ice and snow. (1992, March 2). *U.S. News and World Report, 112*, p. 62.

Andersen, M. (1993). *Thinking about women: Sociological perspectives on sex and gender.* New York, NY: Macmillan Publishing, Co.

Anderson, D. F., Lorenz, F. O., and Pease, D. G. (1986). Prediction of present participation from children's gender, past participation, and attitudes: A longitudinal analysis. *Sociology of Sport Journal, 3*, 101-111.

Angrist, S. (1967). Role constellation as a variable in women's leisure activities. *Social Forces, 45*(3), 423-431.

Anthony, S. B. and Harper, J. H. (Eds.). (1981). *History of woman suffrage* (Vol. 4). Rochester, NY: Susan B. Anthony. Cited in P. Welch and H. Lerch, *History of American physical education and sport* (p. 86). Springfield, IL: Charles C. Thomas Publisher.

Archer, J. and McDonald, M. (1990). Gender roles and sports in adolescent girls. *Leisure Studies, 9*, 225-240.

Astin, H. S. (1976). Continuing education and the development of adult women. *The Counseling Psychologist, 6*(1), 55-60.

Atchley, R. C. (1993). Continuity theory and the evolution of activity in later life. Older women's leisure activity and quality of life. In J. R. Kelly (Ed.), *Activity and aging* (pp. 5-16). Newbury Park, CA: Sage Publications, Inc.

Atchley, R. C. (1994, November). *Is there life between life course transitions? Applying life-stage concepts in gerontological research.* Paper presented at the Gerontological Society of America's Annual Scientific Meeting, Atlanta, GA.

Baber, K. and Allen, K. (1992). *Women and families: Feminist reconstructions.* New York, NY: The Guilford Press.

Baber, K. M., and Monaghan, P. (1988). College women's career and motherhood expectations: New options, old dilemmas. *Sex Roles, 19*, 189-203.

Backus, J. L. (1982). *Letters from Amelia, 1901-1937.* Boston, MA: Beacon Press.

Bailey, N. (1993). Women's sport and feminist movement: Building bridges. In G. Cohen (Ed.), *Women in sport: Issues and controversies*, (pp. 297-304). Newbury Park, CA: Sage Publications, Inc.

Baldwin, J. (1988). A talk to teachers. In R. Simonson and S. Walker (Eds.), *The Graywolf annual five: Multicultural literacy* (pp. 3-12). St. Paul, MN: Graywolf Press.

Bandura, A. (1973). *Aggression: A social learning analysis.* Englewood Cliffs, NJ: Prentice-Hall Press.

Bardige, B., Ward, J. V., Gilligan, C., Taylor, J. M., and Cohen, G. (1988). Moral concerns and consideration of urban youth. In C. Gilligan, J. V. Ward, and J. M. Taylor (Eds.), *Mapping the moral domain* (pp. 159-174). Cambridge, MA: Harvard University Press.

Barnett, L. A. and Chick, G. E. (1986). Chips off the ol' block: Parents' leisure and their children's play. *Journal of Leisure Research, 18*, 266-283.

Barnett, L. A. and Kleiber, D. A. (1982). Concomitants of playfulness in early childhood: Cognitive abilities and gender. *The Journal of Genetic Psychology, 141*, 115-127.

Barnett, R. C. and Baruch, G. K. (1978). Women in the mid-years: A critique of research and theory. *Psychology of Women Quarterly, 3*, 187-197.

Barnett, R. C. and Baruch, G. K. (1983). *Women's involvement in multiple roles, role strain, and psychological distress.* Unpublished paper. Wellesley, MA: Wellesley College Center for Research on Women.

Barrett, M. (1980). *Women's oppression today.* London, UK: Verso.

Barrett, M. and McIntosh, M. (1991). *The antisocial family* (2nd ed.). London, UK: Verso.

Baruch, G. (1967). The achievement motivation in women: Implications for career development. *Journal of Personality and Social Psychology, 5*, 260-267.

Baruch, G., Barnett, R., and Rivers, C. (1983). *Lifeprints.* New York, NY: McGraw-Hill, Inc.

Bateson, M. C. (1989). *Composing a life.* New York, NY: Penguin.

Bax, E. B. (1913). *The fraud of feminism.* London, UK: Grant Richards, Ltd.

Belenky, M. F., Clinchy, B. M., Goldberger, N. R., and Tarule, P. K. (1986). *Women's ways of knowing.* New York, NY: Basic Books, Inc.

Bella, L. (1989). Women and leisure: Beyond androcentrism. In E. Jackson and T. Burton (Eds.), *Understanding leisure and recreation: Mapping the past, charting the future,* (p. 151-180). State College, PA: Venture Publishing, Inc.

Bella, L. (1992). *The Christmas imperative.* Halifax, NS: Fernwood Publishing.

Benhabib, S. (1987). The generalized and the concrete other: The Kohlberg-Gilligan controversy and feminist theory. In S. Benhabib and D. Cornell (Eds.), *Feminism as critique: On the politics of Gender* (p. 87). Minneapolis, MN: University of Minnesota Press.

Benokraitis, N. (1986). *Modern sexism.* Englewood Cliffs, NJ: Prentice-Hall Press

Bernard, J. (1974). *Sex differences: An overview.* New York, NY: MSS Modular Publications, Inc.

Bernard, M. (1984). Leisure rich and leisure poor: The leisure patterns of young adults. *Leisure Studies, 3*, 343-361.

Bialeschki, M. D. (1984). *An analysis of leisure attitudes and activity patterns of women related to locus of control and perceived choice.* Unpublished doctoral dissertation, University of Wisconsin, Madison, WI.

Bialeschki, M. D. and Henderson, K. A. (1986). Leisure in the common world of women. *Leisure Studies, 5*, 299-308.

Bialeschki, M. D. and Henderson, K. A. (1991). The provision of leisure services and feminism. *World Leisure and Recreation Journal, 33*(3), 30-33.

Bialeschki, M. D. and Michener, S. (1994). Re-entering leisure: Transition within the role of motherhood. *Journal of Leisure Research, 26*, 57-74.

Bialeschki, M. D., Pearce, K., and Elloit, L. (1994, October). *'I don't want a lifestyle—I want a life:' The effect of role negotiation on the leisure of lesbian mothers.* Paper presented at the Leisure Research Symposium of National Recreation and Park Association, Minneapolis, MN.

Bibby, R. W. and Posterski, D. C. (1992). *Teen trends: A nation in motion.* Toronto, ON: Stoddart Publishing Co. Ltd.

Birrell, S. (1990). Women of color, critical autobiography, and sport. In M. Messner and D. Sabo (Eds.), *Sport, men, and the gender order* (pp. 185-200). Champaign, IL: Human Kinetics.

Blackwell, A. B. (1875, October). *On marriage and work.* Paper presented at the Third Women's Congress of the Association for the Advancement of Women, Syracuse, NY. In N. F. Cott (Ed.), *Root of bitterness* (pp. 351-355), 1972. New York, NY: E. P. Dutton.

Blair, S. L. and Lichter, D. T. (1991). Measuring the division of household labor: Gender segregation of housework among American couples. *Journal of Family Issues, 12*, 91-113.

Blaisure, K. R. and Allen, K. R. (1995, February). Feminists and the ideology and practice of marital equality. *Journal of Marriage and the Family, 57*, 5-19.

Bleier, R. (1988). Introduction. In R. Bleier (Ed.), *Feminist approaches to science* (pp. 1-18). New York, NY: Pergamon Press, Inc.

Bloch, P. H. (1993). Involvement with adornments as leisure behavior: An exploratory study. *Journal of Leisure Research, 25*, 245-262.

Blyth, D. A., Simmons, R. G., and Carlton-Ford, S. (1983). The adjustment of early adolescents to school transitions. *Journal of Early Adolescence, 3*, 105-120.

Bolla, P. and Pageot, J. (1987, May). *Sex differences in sports activity among university students.* Paper presented at The Fifth Canadian Congress on Leisure Research, Halifax, NS.

Bonen, A. and Shaw, S. M. (1995). Recreational exercise participation and aerobic fitness in men and women: Analysis of data from a national survey. *Journal of Sports Medicine, 13,* 297-303.

Bordo, S. (1995). Reading the slender body. In N. Tuana and R. Tong (Eds.), *Feminism and philosophy: Essential readings in theory, reinterpretation, and application,* (pp. 467-489). Boulder, CO: Westview Press, Inc.

Boutilier, M. A. and SanGiovanni, L. F. (1994). Politics, public policy, and Title IX: Some limitations of liberal feminism. In S. Birrell and C. L. Cole (Eds.), *Women, sport, and culture,* (pp. 97-109). Champaign, IL: Human Kinetics.

Bowers, E. (1934). *Recreation for girls and women.* New York, NY: A. S. Barnes & Co.

Bowman, P., and Howard, C. (1985). Race-related socialization, motivation and academic achievement: A study of black youths in three generation families. *Journal of the American Academy of Child Psychology, 24,* 134-141.

Brenner, J. and Ramas, M. (1984). Rethinking women's oppression. *New Left Review, 144,* 33-71.

Brock-Ute, B. (1985). *Educating for peace.* New York, NY: Pergamon Press.

Brooks-Gunn, J. and Kirsch, B. (1984). Life events and the boundaries of mid-life for women. In G. Baruch and J. Brooks-Gunn (Eds.), *Women in mid-life* (pp. 11-30). New York, NY: Plenum Press.

Brown, E. B. (1991). Polyrhythms and improvisation: Lessons for women's history. *History Workshop Journal, 31,* 85-90.

Bryson, L. (1987). Sport and the maintenance of masculine hegemony. *Women's Studies International Forum, 10,* 349-360.

Bunch, C. (1985). *Bringing the global home.* Denver, CO: Antelope Publications.

Butcher, J. (1985). Longitudinal analysis of adolescent girls' participation in physical activity. *Sociology of Sport Journal, 2,* 130-143.

Cahn, S. K. (1994). *Coming on strong: Gender and sexuality in twentieth-century women's sport.* New York, NY: The Free Press.

Caldwell, L. L. and Smith, E. A. (1988). Leisure: An overlooked component of health promotion. *Canadian Journal of Public Health, 79* , S44-S48.

Calisthenics. (1831). *The Journal of Health, 2*, 191.

Canada Fitness Survey. (1985). *Changing times: Women and physical activity.* Ottawa, ON: Author.

Card, C. (1991). The feistiness of feminism. In C. Card (Ed.), *Feminist Ethics,* (pp. 3-34). Lawrence, KS: University Press of Kansas.

Carnegie Council on Adolescent Development. (1992). *A matter of time: Risk and opportunity in the nonschool hours.* New York, NY: Carnegie Corporation.

Carpenter, G. (1985). The leisure feminist link. *Leisure Information Quarterly, 12*(3), 5-6.

Carrington, B., Chivers, T., and Williams, T. (1987). Gender, leisure, and sport: A case study of young people of South Asian descent. *Leisure Studies, 6,* 265-279.

Cheek, N. H. and Burch, W. R. (1976). *The social organization of leisure in human society.* New York, NY: Harper & Row.

Chiriboga, D. A. (1981). The developmental psychology of middle-age. In J. G. T. Howells (Ed.), *Modern perspectives in the psychiatry of middle age* (pp. 3-25). New York, NY: Brunner/Mazel, Inc.

Chodorow, N. (1978). *The reproduction of mothering: A psychoanalysis and the sociology of gender.* Berkeley, CA: University of California Press.

Coakley, J. (1980). Play, games, and sport: Developmental implications for young people. *Journal of Sport Behavior, 3,* 99-118.

Coakley, J. and White, A. (1992). Making decisions: Gender and sport participation among British adolescents. *Sociology of Sport Journal, 9,* 20-35.

Cole, C. L. (1994). Resisting the canon: Feminist cultural studies, sport, and technologies of the body. In S. Birrell and C. L. Cole (Eds.), *Women, sport, and culture* (pp. 5-29). Champaign, IL: Human Kinetics.

Coleman, D. and Iso-Ahola, S. E. (1993). Leisure and health: The role of social support and self-determination. *Journal of Leisure Research, 25,* 111-128.

Coleman, J. S. (1961). *The adolescent society.* New York, NY: The Free Press.

Colley, A. (1984). Sex role and exploration of leisure behavior. *Leisure Studies, 3,* 335-341.

Colley, A., Nash, J., O'Donnell, J., and Restorick, L. (1987). Attitudes to the female sex role and sex-typing of physical activities. *International Journal of Sport Psychology, 18*, 19-29.

Collins, P. H. (1993). The social construction of black feminist thought. In L. Richardson and V. Taylor (Eds.), *Feminist frontiers III* (pp. 20-30). New York, NY: McGraw-Hill, Inc.

Comfort, A. (1976). *A good age*. New York, NY: Crown Publishers.

Cookson, P. S. (1986). A framework for theory and research on adult education participation. *Adult Education Quarterly, 36*(3), 130-141.

Coontz, S. (1988). *The social origins of private life: A history of American families, 1600-1900*. New York, NY: Verso.

Coontz, S. (1992). *The way we never were: American families and the nostalgia trap*. New York, NY: Basic Books, Inc.

Cooper, K. L. and Gutmann, D. L. (1987). Gender identity and ego mastery style in middle-aged, pre- and post-empty nest women. *Gerontologist, 27*(3), 347-352.

Covey, L. A. and Feltz, D. L. (1991). Physical activity and adolescent female psychological development. *Journal of Youth and Adolescence, 20*, 463-474.

Cozens, F. and Stumpf, F. (1974). The role of the school in the sports life of America. In G. Sage (Ed.), *Sport and American society* (2nd ed.) (pp. 104-131). Reading, MA: Addison-Wesley Publishing Co., Inc.

Crawford, D. W., Godbey, G., and Crouter, A. C. (1986). The stability of leisure preferences. *Journal of Leisure Research, 18*, 96-115.

Crawford, D., Jackson, E., and Godbey, G. (1991). A hierarchical model of leisure constraints. *Leisure Sciences, 9*, 119-127.

Cross, K. P. (1981). *Adults as learners*. San Francisco, CA: Jossey-Bass, Inc.

Csikszentmihalyi, M. (1975). *Beyond boredom and anxiety*. San Francisco, CA: Jossey-Bass, Inc.

Csikszentmihalyi, M. (1981). Leisure and socialization. *Social Forces, 60*(2), 332-340.

Csikszentmihalyi, M. and Larson, R. (1978). Intrinsic rewards in school crime. *Crime and Delinquency*, 322-335.

Csikszentmihalyi, M. and Larson, R. (1984). *Being adolescent: Conflict and growth in the teenage years*. New York, NY: Basic Books, Inc.

Csikszentmihalyi, M., Rathunde, K., and Whalen, S. (1993). *Talented teenagers: The roots of success and failure*. Cambridge, UK: Cambridge University Press.

Daly, M. (1978). *Gynecology: The metaethics of radical feminism*. Boston, MA: Beacon Press.

Darkenwald, G. G. and Merriam, S. (1982). *Adult education: Foundations of practice*. New York, NY: Harper & Row.

Darlison, E. (1984). The politics of women's sport and recreation: A need to link theory and practice. *Women and Recreation Conference*. Wellington, New Zealand: Council for Recreation and Sport.

Darlison, E. (1985). Women and leisure—Barriers to participation. *Proceedings of workshop conducted by the Department of Sport, Recreation, and Tourism* (pp. 16-17), Sydney, Australia: Department of Sport, Recreation and Tourism.

Dattilo, J., Dattilo, A. M., Samdahl, D. M., and Kleiber, D. A. (1994). Leisure orientations and self-esteem in women with low incomes who are overweight. *Journal of Leisure Research, 26*, 23-38.

Davis, J. (1990). *Youth and the condition of Britain: Images of adolescent conflict*. London, UK: Althlone Press.

Dawson, D. (1986). Leisure and social class: Some neglected theoretical considerations. *Leisure Studies, 8*(1), 47-61.

Deaux, K. and Major, B. (1990). The social-psychological model of gender. In D. L. Rhode (Ed.), *Theoretical perspectives on sexual difference*, (pp. 89-99). New Haven, CT: Yale University Press.

de Castillejo, I. (1973). *Knowing woman: A feminist psychology*. New York, NY: Harper Colophon Books.

Deegan, M. J. and Brooks, N. A. (1985). Introduction—Women and disability: The double handicap. In M. J. Deegan and N. A. Brooks (Eds.), *Women and disability: The double handicap* (pp. 6-22). New Brunswick, NJ: Transaction Publishers.

Deem, R. (1982). Women, leisure and inequality. *Leisure Studies, 1*, 29-46.

Deem, R. (1986). *All work and no play? The sociology of women and leisure*. Milton Keynes, UK: Open University Press.

Deem, R. (1987). Unleisured lives: Sport in the context of women's leisure. *Women's Studies International Forum, 10*, 423-432.

Deem, R. (1988). Feminism and leisure studies: Opening up new directions. In E. Wimbush and M. Talbot (Eds.), *Relative freedoms* (pp. 1-17). Milton Keynes, UK: Open University Press.

Deem, R. (1992). The sociology of gender and leisure in Britain—Past progress and future prospects. *Loisir et Société/Society and Leisure, 15*(1), 21-37.

Degler, C. (1981). Can we reconcile the demand of family and women's individuality. *Phi Kappa Phi Journal, 61*(4), 22-23.

de Grazia, S. (1964). *Of time, work, and leisure.* Garden City, NY: Anchor Books.

Deisher, R. (1989). Adolescent homosexuality: Preface. *Journal of Homosexuality, 17*(1/2), xiii-xv.

Dickinson, R. L. (1887). The corset. *New York Medical Journal, 11*(5), 14-28.

Dinnerstein, D. (1977). *The mermaid and the minotaur.* New York, NY: Plenum Press.

Dittmar, M. L. (1994). Relations among depression, gender, and television viewing of college students. *Journal of Social Behavior and Personality, 9*, 317-328.

Dixey, R. (1987). It's a great feeling when you win: Women and bingo. *Leisure Studies, 6*, 199-214.

Donovan, J. (1993). *Feminist theory: The intellectual traditions of American feminism.* New York, NY: Continuum.

Douvan, E. (1979). Sex role learning. In J. C. Coleman (Ed.), *The school years* (pp. 79-94). London, UK: Methuen.

DuBois, E., Buhle, M. J., Kaplan, T., Lerner, G., and Smith-Rosenberg, C. (1980). Politics and culture in women's history: A symposium. *Feminist Studies, 6*(1), 29.

Dulles, R. F. (1965). *A history of recreation.* New York, NY: Appleton-Century-Crofts.

Duquin, M. E. (1991). Sport, women, and the ethic of care. *Journal of Applied Recreation Research, 16*, 262-280.

Duret, P. (1994). Leisure, physical activities and sense of justice in children. *World Leisure and Recreation, 36*(1), 16-18.

Dustin, D. L. and Schultz, J. H. (1981). The worth ethic as our credo: Yea or Nay? *Parks and Recreation, 16*(9), 61-63.

Eagley, A. H. (1994). On comparing women and men. *Feminism and Psychology, 4,* 513-522.

Eastwood, D. and Carter, R. (1981). The Irish dune consumer. *Journal of Leisure Research, 13*(4), 273-281.

Eckert, S. and Cannon, J. (1981). Through the eyes of women in the wilderness. *The Creative Women, 4*(4), 4-7.

Ehrenreich, B. (1995). Life without father: Reconsidering socialist-feminist theory. In N. Tuana and R. Tong (Eds.), *Feminism and philosophy: Essential readings in theory, reinterpretation, and application* (pp. 265-271). Boulder, CO: Westview Press, Inc.

Ehrenreich, B. and English, B. (1973). *Complaints and disorders: The sexual politics of sickness.* New York, NY: The Feminist Press.

Eichler, M. (1980). *The double standard.* New York, NY: St. Martin's Press, Inc.

Eisenstein, Z. R. (1981). *The radical future of liberal feminism.* New York, NY: Longman.

Eisenstein, Z. R. (1995). The sexual politics of the New Right: Understanding the "Crisis of liberalism" for the 1980s. In N. Tuana and R. Tong (Eds.), *Feminism and philosophy: Essential readings in theory, reinterpretation, and application* (pp. 10-26). Boulder, CO: Westview Press., Inc.

Elkind, D. (1967). Egocentrism in adolescence. *Child Development, 38,* 1025-1034.

Erikson, E. H. (1950). *Childhood and society.* New York, NY: W. W. Norton & Co., Inc.

Erikson, E. H. (1968). *Identity: Youth and crisis.* New York, NY: W. W. Norton & Co., Inc.

Faludi, S. (1991). *Backlash: The undeclared war against American women.* New York, NY: Doubleday.

Faludi, S. (1995). I'm not a feminist but I play one on TV. *Ms., 5*(5), 30-39.

Farina, J. (1973). Towards a philosophy of leisure. In *Leisure in Canada,* (pp. 6-16). Ottawa, ON: Department of National Health and Welfare.

Farrell, M. P. and Rosenberg, S. D. (1981). *Men at midlife.* Dover, MA: Auburn House Publishing Co.

Ferree, M. M. (1990). Beyond separate spheres: Feminism and family research. *Journal of Marriage and the Family, 52,* 866-884.

Festinger, L. (1954). A theory of social comparison process. *Human Relations, 7,* 117-140.

Finnan, C. R. (1982). The ethnography of children's spontaneous play. In G. Spindler (Ed.), *Doing the ethnography of schooling* (pp. 356-381). New York, NY: Holt, Rinehart & Winston.

Firestone, J. and Shelton, B. A. (1988). An estimation of the effects of women's work on available leisure time. *Journal of Family Issues, 9,* 478-495.

Firestone, S. (1971). *The dialectic of sex.* New York, NY: Bantam Books.

Fischer, R. B., Blazey, M. L., and Lipman, H. R. (Eds.). (1992). *Students of the third age.* New York, NY: Macmillan Publishing Co.

Fonow, M. M. and Cook, J. A. (Eds.). (1991). *Beyond methodology: Feminist scholarship as lived research.* Bloomington and Indianapolis, IN: Indiana University Press.

Fox, K. (1992). Choreographing differences in the dance of leisure: The potential of feminist thought. *Journal of Leisure Research, 24,* 333-347.

Fox, K. M. (1993, May). *Fortalecendo la red del la vida: Las mujeres, communidad y el tiempo libre [Strengthening the web of life: Women, community and "leisure"].* Paper presented at the Canadian Congress on Leisure Research, Winnipeg, MB.

Fox, K. M. (1994). Negotiating in a world of change: Ecofeminist guideposts for leisure scholarship. *Journal of Leisure Research, 26,* 39-56.

Fox, K. M. and McAvoy, L. H. (1991). Environmental ethics: Strengths and dualism of six dominant themes. In G. Fain (Ed.), *Leisure and ethics* (pp. 185-201). Reston, VA: American Association of Leisure and Recreation.

Fox, K. M. and Trillo, M. (1994, October). *The role of leisure in the cultural transition process for Central American women.* Paper presented at the Leisure Research Symposium, Minneapolis, MN.

Fox-Genovese, E. (1990). Socialist-feminist American women's history. *Journal of Women's History, 1*(3), 181-210.

Fraser, N. and Nicholson, L. J. (1990). Social criticism without philosophy: An encounter between feminism and postmodernism. In L. Nicholson (Ed.), *Feminism/postmodernism* (pp. 19-38). New York, NY: Routledge.

Frederick, C. J., Havitz, M. E., and Shaw, S. M. (1994). Social comparison in aerobics exercise classes: Propositions for analyzing motives and participation. *Leisure Sciences, 16,* 161-176.

Frederick, C. J. and Shaw, S. M. (1995). Body image as a leisure constraint: Examining the experience of aerobic exercise classes for young women. *Leisure Sciences, 17,* 57-73.

Freedman, R. J. (1986). *Beauty bound.* Lexington, MA: Lexington Books.

Freeman, J. (Ed.). (1979). *Women: A feminist perspective.* Palo Alto, CA: Mayfield Publishing Co.

French, M. (1985). *Beyond power.* New York, NY: Ballantine Books.

Freysinger, V. J. (1988). *The meaning of leisure in middle adulthood: Gender differences and changes since young adulthood.* Unpublished doctoral dissertation, University of Wisconsin—Madison, Madison, WI.

Freysinger, V. J. (1990). Successful aging for women. *Proceedings of the Sixth Canadian Congress on Leisure Research* (pp. 330-340). Waterloo, ON: Ontario Research Council on Leisure.

Freysinger, V. J. (1993). The community, programs, and opportunities: Population diversity. In J. R. Kelly (Ed.), *Activity and Aging* (pp. 211-230). Newbury Park, CA: Sage Publications, Inc.

Freysinger, V. J. (1994). Leisure with children and parental satisfaction: Further evidence of a sex difference in the experience of adult roles and leisure. *Journal of Leisure Research, 26,* 212-226.

Freysinger, V. J. (1995). The dialectics of leisure and development for women and men in mid-life: An interpretive study. *Journal of Leisure Research, 27,* 61-84.

Freysinger, V. J. and Chen, T. (1993). Leisure and family in China: The impact of culture. *World Leisure and Recreation, 35*(3), 22-24.

Freysinger, V. J. and Flannery, D. (1992). Women's leisure: Affiliation, self-determination, empowerment and resistance? *Loisir et Société/Society and Leisure, 15*(1), 303-322.

Freysinger, V. J. and Ray, R. O. (1987, September). *Activity involvement of middle-aged women and men: A developmental study.* Paper presented at the National Recreation and Park Association Leisure Research Symposium, New Orleans, LA.

Freysinger, V. J. and Ray, R. O. (1994). The activity involvement of women and men in young and middle adulthood: A panel study. *Leisure Sciences, 16,* 193-217.

Friedan, B. (1993). *The fountain of age.* New York, NY: Simon & Schuster, Inc.

Frisby, W. (1992). Women in leisure service management: Alternative definitions of career success. *Loisir et Société/Society and Leisure, 15*(1), 155-174.

Frisby, W. and Brown, B. (1991). The balancing act: Women leisure service managers. *Journal of Applied Recreation Research, 16*(4), 297-321.

Froelicher, V. F. and Froelicher, E. S. (1991). Cardiovascular benefits of physical activity. In B. L. Driver, P. J. Brown, and G. L. Peterson (Eds.), *Benefits of leisure* (pp. 59-72). State College, PA: Venture Publishing, Inc.

Frye, M. (1995). To be and be seen: The politics of reality. In N. Tuana and R. Tong (Eds.), *Feminism and philosophy: Essential readings in theory, reinterpretation, and application* (pp. 162-174). Boulder, CO: Westview Press, Inc.

Gagnier, R. (1990). Feminist postmodernism: The end of feminism or the end of theory. In D. L. Rhode (Ed.), *Theoretical perspectives on sexual difference*, (pp. 21-30). New Haven, CT: Yale University Press.

Gaines, D. (1990). *Teenage wasteland: Suburbia's dead-end kids*. New York, NY: Pantheon Books, Inc.

Gerber, E., Felshin, J., Berline, P., and Wyrick, W. (1974). *The American woman in sport*. Reading, PA: Addison-Wesley Publishing Co., Inc.

Germain, C. B. (1994). Emerging conceptions of family development over the life course. *Families in Society: The Journal of Contemporary Human Services, 75*, 259-267.

Giele, J. Z. (1982). Adulthood as transcendence of age and sex. In J. Smelser and E. H. Erikson (Eds.), *Themes of work and love in adulthood* (pp. 151-173). Cambridge, MA: Harvard University Press.

Gilbert, L. A. (1993). *Two careers/one family*. Newbury Park, CA: Sage Publications, Inc.

Gilligan, C. (1982a). *In a different voice*. Cambridge, MA: Harvard University Press.

Gilligan, C. (1982b). Why should a woman be more like a man? *Psychology Today, 16*(6), 68-77.

Gilligan, C. (1982c). Adult development and women's development: Arrangements for a marriage. In J. Z. Giele (Ed.), *Women in the middle years* (pp. 89-114). New York, NY: John Wiley & Sons, Inc.

Gilligan, C., Lyons, N. P., and Hanmer, T. J. (Eds.). (1990). *Making connections: The relational worlds of adolescent girls at Emma Willard School*. Cambridge, MA: Harvard University Press.

Gilman, C. P. (1972). On women's evolution from economic dependence. In N. F. Cott (Ed.), *Root of bitterness* (pp. 366-370). New York, NY: E. P. Dutton.

Gissendanner, C. H. (1994). African-American women and competitive sport, 1920-1960. In S. Birrell and C. Cole (Eds.), *Sportswomen and culture*, (pp. 81-92). Champaign, IL: Human Kinetics.

Glancy, M. (1991). The androcentricism complex. In T. Goodale and P. Witt (Eds.), *Recreation and leisure: Issues in a era of change* (3rd ed.), (pp. 413-428). State College, PA: Venture Publishing, Inc.

Gloor, D. (1992). Women verses men? The hidden differences in leisure activities. *Loisir et Société/Society and Leisure, 15*(1), 39-62.

Glyptis, S. and Chambers, D. (1982). No place like home. *Leisure Studies, 1*, 247-262.

Godbey, G. (1985). *Leisure in your life: An exploration.* State College, PA: Venture Publishing, Inc.

Goodale, T. L. and Witt, P. A. (1989). Recreation nonparticipation and barriers to leisure. In E. L. Jackson and T. L. Burton (Eds.), *Understanding leisure and recreation: Mapping the past, charting the future* (pp. 421-449). State College, PA: Venture Publishing, Inc.

Goodsell, W. (1923). *The education of women: Its social background and its problems.* New York, NY: Macmillian Publishing Co.

Gordon, C. (1971). Role and value development across the life cycle. In J. W. Jackson (Ed.), *Role: Sociological studies IV* (pp. 65-105). London, UK: Cambridge University Press.

Gordon, C., Gaitz, C. M., and Scott, J. (1976). Leisure and lives: Personal expressivity across the lifespan. In R. H. Binstock and E. Shanas (Eds.), *Handbook of aging and the social sciences* (pp. 310-341). New York, NY: Van Nostrand Reinhold.

Grady, K. E. (1981). Sex bias in research design. *Psychology of Women Quarterly, 5*, 628-636.

Grahn, J. (1978). *The work of a common woman.* New York, NY: St. Martin's Press, Inc.

Gratton, C. and Holliday, S. (1995). Time limits. *Leisure Management, 15*(5), 30-35.

Green, E. and Hebron, S. (1988). Leisure and male partners. In E. Wimbush and M. Talbot (Eds.), *Relative Freedoms* (pp. 37-47). Milton Keynes, UK: Open University Press.

Green, E., Hebron, S., and Woodward, D. (1987). *Leisure and gender: A study of Sheffield women's leisure experience.* London, UK: The Sports Council and Economic and Social Research Council.

Green, E., Hebron, S., and Woodward, D. (1990). *Women's leisure, what leisure?* London, UK: Macmillan Education Ltd.

Gregory, S. (1982). Women among others: Another view. *Leisure Studies, 1,* 47-52.

Griffin, C. (1981). Young women and leisure: The transition from school to work. In A. Tomlinson (Ed.), *Leisure and social control* (pp. 113-122). Brighton, UK: Brighton Polytechnic.

Griffin, C. (1985). *Typical girls?* London, UK: Routledge.

Griffin, P. (1993). Homophobia in women's sports—The fear that divides us. In G. Cohen (Ed.), *Women in sport: Issues and controversies* (pp 193-203). Newbury Park, CA: Sage Publications, Inc.

Griffiths, V. (1988). From 'playing out' to 'dossing out:' Young women and leisure. In E. Wimbush and M. Talbot (Eds.), *Relative Freedoms* (pp. 48-59). Milton Keynes, UK: Open University Press.

Grossman, A. (1992). Inclusion not exclusion: Recreation service delivery to lesbian, gay and bisexual youth. *Journal of Physical Education, Recreation, and Dance, 63*(4), 45-47.

Gunter, B. and Gunter, N. (1980). Leisure styles: A conceptual framework for modern leisure. *The Sociological Quarterly, 21,* 361-374.

Gutmann, D. L. (1964). An exploration of ego configurations in middle and later life. In B. L. Neugarten and associates (Eds.), *Personality in middle and later life* (pp. 114-148). New York, NY: Atherton Press.

Guttmann, A. (1991). *Women's sport: A history.* New York, NY: Columbia University Press.

Haan, N. (1977). *Coping and defending: Processes of self-environment organization.* New York, NY: Academic Press.

Haggard, L. M. and Williams, D. R. (1991). Self-identity benefits of leisure activities. In B. L. Driver, P. J. Brown, and G. L. Peterson (Eds.), *Benefits of leisure* (pp. 103-120). State College, PA: Venture Publishing, Inc.

Haggard, L. M. and Williams, D. R. (1992). Identity affirmation through leisure activities: Leisure symbols of the self. *Journal of Leisure Research, 24,* 1-18

Hall, E. G., Durburow, B., and Progen, J. (1986). Self-esteem of female athletes and nonathletes relative to sex role type and sport type. *Sex Roles, 15*, 379-390.

Hall, M. A. and Richardson, D. A. (1982). *Fair ball: Toward sex equality in Canadian sport*. Ottawa, ON: Canadian Advisory Council on the Status of Women.

Halpern, D. F. (1994). Stereotypes, science, censorship, and the study of sex differences. *Feminism and Psychology, 4*, 523-540.

Harding, S. (1986). *The science question in feminism*. Ithaca, NY: Cornell University Press.

Harding, S. (1987). The instability of analytical categories of feminist theory. In S. Harding and J. F. Barr (Eds.), *Sex and scientific inquiry* (pp. 283-302). Chicago, IL: University of Chicago Press.

Harding, S. (1991). *Whose science? Whose knowledge?* Ithaca, NY: Cornell University Press.

Harrington, M. and Dawson, D. (1995). Who has it best? Women's labor force participation, perceptions of leisure, and constraints to enjoyment of leisure. *Journal of Leisure Research, 27*, 4-24.

Harrington, M., Dawson, D., and Bolla, P. (1992). Objective and subjective constraints on women's enjoyment of leisure. *Loisir et Société/Society and Leisure, 15*(1), 203-222.

Harris, A. T. (1994). *Children's perceptions of fun in organized youth sport settings*. Unpublished Master's Thesis, Miami University, Oxford, OH.

Harrison, J., Chin, J., and Ficarrotto, T. (1995). Warning: Masculinity may be dangerous to your health. In M. S. Kinnel and M. A. Messner (Eds.), *Men's lives* (pp. 237-249). Boston, MA: Allyn & Bacon, Inc.

Hartsock, N. C. M. (1995). The feminist standpoint: Developing the ground for a specifically feminist historical materialism. In N. Tuana and R. Tong (Eds.), *Feminism and philosophy: Essential readings in theory, reinterpretation, and application* (pp. 69-90). Boulder, CO: Westview Press, Inc.

Havinghurst, R. J. (1957-58). The leisure activities of the middle-aged. *American Journal of Sociology, 63*, 152-162.

Havighurst, R. J. (1961). The nature and value of meaningful free-time activity. In R. W. Kleemeier (Ed.), *Aging and leisure: A research perspective into the meaningful use of free-time* (pp. 309-344). New York, NY: Oxford University Press.

Havighurst, R. J. (1972). Life style and leisure patterns: Their evolution through the life cycle. *Proceedings of the International Course in Social Gerontology, 3,* 35-48.

Havitz, M. E. and Dimanche, F. (1990). Propositions for testing the involvement construct in recreational and tourism contexts. *Leisure Sciences, 12,* 179-195.

Hemingway, J. L. (1990). Opening windows on an interpretive leisure studies. *Journal of Leisure Research, 22*(4), 303-308.

Henderson, K. A. (1982). Jane Addams: Pioneer in leisure services. *Journal of Physical Education, Recreation, and Dance, 53*(2), 42-46.

Henderson, K. A. (1983). The motivation of men and women in volunteering. *Journal of Volunteer Administration, 1*(2), 20-24.

Henderson, K. A. (1984, October). *An analysis of sexism in leisure research.* Paper presented to the National Recreation and Park Association Leisure Research Symposium, Orlando, FL.

Henderson, K. A. (1986). Global feminism and leisure. *World Leisure and Recreation Association, 28*(4), 20-24.

Henderson, K. A. (1990a). Anatomy is not destiny: A feminist analysis of the scholarship on women's leisure. *Leisure Sciences, 12,* 229-239.

Henderson, K. A. (1990b). An oral history perspective on the containers in which American farm women experienced leisure. *Leisure Studies, 9,* 121-133.

Henderson, K. A. (1990c). Reality comes through a prism: Method choices in leisure research. *Loisir et Société/Society and Leisure, 13*(1), 169-188.

Henderson, K. A. (1990d). The meaning of leisure for women: An integrative review of the research. *Journal of Leisure Research ,22*(3), 228-243.

Henderson, K. A. (1991a). *Dimensions of choice: A qualitative approach to recreation, parks, and leisure research.* State College, PA: Venture Publishing, Inc.

Henderson, K. A. (1991b). The contributions of feminism to an understanding of leisure constraints. *Journal of Leisure Research, 23*(4), 363-377.

Henderson, K. A. (1992). Being female in the park and recreation profession in the 1990s: Issues and challenges. *Journal of Park and Recreation Administration, 10*(2), 15-30.

Henderson, K. A. (1993). A feminist analysis of selected professional literature about girls/women from 1907–1990. *Journal of Leisure Research, 25,* 165-181.

Henderson, K. A. (1994a). Broadening an understanding of women, gender, and leisure. *Journal of Leisure Research, 26,* 1-7.

Henderson, K. A. (1994b). Perspectives on analyzing gender, women, and leisure. *Journal of Leisure Research, 26,* 119-137.

Henderson, K. A. (1995a). Women's leisure: More truth than facts. *World Leisure and Recreation Association Journal, 37*(1), 9-13.

Henderson, K. A. (1995b). Marketing recreation and physical activity programs to females. *Journal of Physical Education, Recreation, and Dance 66*(6), 53-57.

Henderson, K. A. and Allen, K. R. (1991). The ethic of care: Leisure possibilities and constraints for women. *Loisir et Société/Society and Leisure, 14,* 97-113.

Henderson, K. A., Bedini, L. A., and Bialeschki, M. D. (1993). Feminism and the client-therapist relationship: Implications for therapeutic recreation. *Therapeutic Recreation Journal, 27*(1), 33-43.

Henderson, K. A., Bedini, L. A., and Hecht, L. (1994). "Not just a wheelchair, not just a woman:" Self-identity and leisure. *Therapeutic Recreation Journal, 28*(2), 73-86.

Henderson, K. A., Bedini, L. A., Hecht, L., and Shuler, R. (1995). Women with physical disabilities and the negotiation of leisure constraints. *Leisure Studies, 14,* 17-31.

Henderson, K. A. and Bialeschki, M. D. (1986). Outdoor experiential education (for women only). In M. Gass and L. Buell (Eds.), *Proceedings Journal* (pp. 35-41). Moodus, CT: Association of Experiential Education 14th Annual Conference.

Henderson, K. A. and Bialeschki, M. D. (1987). Qualitative evaluation of a women's week experience. *Journal of Experiential Education, 10*(6), 25-29.

Henderson, K. A. and Bialeschki, M. D. (1990). The feminization of leisure services. *Journal of Park and Recreation Administration, 8*(3), 1-12.

Henderson, K. A. and Bialeschki, M. D. (1990-91). Ecofeminism: Recreation as if nature and woman mattered. *Leisure Information Quarterly, 17*(1), 1-5.

Henderson, K. A. and Bialeschki, M. D. (1991a). A sense of entitlement to leisure as constraint and empowerment for women. *Leisure Sciences, 12,* 51-65.

Henderson, K. A. and Bialeschki, M. D. (1991b). Girls' and women's recreation programming—Constraints and opportunities. *Journal of Physical Education, Recreation, and Dance, 62*(1), 55-58.

Henderson, K. A. and Bialeschki, M.D. (1992). Leisure research and the social structure of feminism. *Loisir et Société/Society and Leisure, 15*(1), 63-75.

Henderson, K. A. and Bialeschki, M. D. (1993a). Professional women and equity issues in the 1990s. *Parks and Recreation, 28*(3), 54-59.

Henderson, K. A. and Bialeschki, M. D. (1993b). Negotiating constraints to women's physical recreation. *Loisir et Société/Society and Leisure, 16*(2), 389-412.

Henderson, K. A. and Bialeschki, M. D. (1993c). Exploring an expanded model of women's leisure. *Journal of Applied Recreation Research, 18*(4), 229-252.

Henderson, K. A. and Bialeschki, M. D. (1994). The meanings of physical recreation for women. *Women in Sport and Physical Activity Journal, 3*(2), 22-38.

Henderson, K. A. and Bialeschki, M. D. (1995a). Inclusive physical activity programming for girls and women. *Parks and Recreation, 30*(3), 70-78.

Henderson, K. A. and Bialeschki, M. D. (1995b). The status and career development of women in leisure services. *Journal of Park and Recreation Administration, 13*(1), 27-43.

Henderson, K. A., Bialeschki, M. D., and Sessoms, H. D. (1990). Occupational segregation? Women and leisure services. *Leisure Today in Journal of Physical Education, Recreation, and Dance, 60*(10), 49-52.

Henderson, K. A., Bialeschki, M. D., Shaw, S. M., and Freysinger, V. J. (1989). *A leisure of one's own: A feminist perspective on women's leisure.* State College, PA: Venture Publishing, Inc.

Henderson, K. A. and Rannells, J. S. (1988). Farm women and the meaning of work and leisure: An oral history perspective. *Leisure Sciences, 10,* 41-50.

Henderson, K. A. and Shaw, S. M. (1994). Research on women, and leisure: Past, present, and future. In L. Barnett (Ed.), *Research about leisure: Past, present, and future* (pp. 121-139). Champaign, IL: Sagamore Publishing.

Henderson, K. A., Stalnaker, D., and Taylor, G. (1988). The relationship between barriers to recreation and gender-role personality traits for women. *Journal of Leisure Research, 20*(1), 69-80.

Hendry, L. B., Shucksmith, J., Love, J. G., and Glendinning, A. (1993). *Young people's leisure and lifestyles*. New York, NY: Routledge.

Hennig, M. and Jardim, A. (1976). *The managerial woman*. New York, NY: Pocket Books.

Henry A. Murray Research Center. (1995, Spring). Women, work and family. *Murray Research Center News*. Cambridge, MA: Radcliffe College.

Higginbotham, E. B. (1993). *Righteous discontent: The women's movement in the Black Baptist Church 1880-1929*. Cambridge, MA: Harvard University Press.

Hoagland, S. L. (1988). *Lesbian ethics*. Palo Alto, CA: Institute of Lesbian Studies.

Hochschild, A. with Machung, A. (1989). *The second shift*. New York, NY: Viking.

Hoff, B. (1982). *The Tao of Pooh*. New York, NY: E. P. Dutton.

Holahan, C. K. (1994). Women's goal orientations across the life cycle: Findings from the Terman Study of the Gifted. In B. F. Turner and L. E. Troll (Eds.), *Women growing older* (pp. 35-67). Newbury Park, CA: Sage Publications, Inc.

Holman, T., and Epperson, A. (1984). Family and leisure: A review of the literature with research recommendations. *Journal of Leisure Research, 16*(4), 277-294.

Holman, T. B. and Jacquart, M. (1988). Leisure activity patterns and marital satisfaction: A further test. *Journal of Marriage and the Family, 50*, 69-78.

Holmes, P. (1994, October). *Essential dimensions of the play experience for 3 year olds and 9 year olds*. Paper presented at the Leisure Research Symposium, Minneapolis, MN.

hooks, b. (1984). *Feminist theory from margin to center*. Boston, MA: South End Press.

hooks, b. (1989). *Talking back: Thinking feminist, thinking black*. Boston, MA: South End Press.

hooks, b. (1994a). *Outlaw culture: Resisting representations*. New York, NY: Routledge.

hooks, b. (1994b). *Teaching to transgress: Education as the practice of freedom*. New York, NY: Routledge.

Horna, J. (1985). The social dialectic of life career and leisure: A probe into the preoccupations model. *Loisir et Société/Society and Leisure, 8*(2), 615-630.

Horna, J. (1987). *The leisure component of the parental role.* Paper presented at the Fifth Canadian Congress in Leisure Research, Halifax, Nova Scotia.

Horna, J. (1989a). The dual asymmetry in the married couple's life: The gender differentiated work, family, and leisure domains. *International Journal of Sociology of the Family, 19*, 113-130.

Horna, J. L. (1989b). The leisure component of the parental role. *Journal of Leisure Research, 21*, 228-241.

Horna, J. (1993). Married life and leisure: A multidimensional study of couples. *World Leisure and Recreation, 35*(3), 17-21.

How a girl beat Leander at the hero game. (1926). *The Literary Digest, 90*, 67.

Howard, D. R. and Madrigal, R. (1990). Who makes the decision: The parent or the child? The perceived influence of parents and children on the purchase of recreation services. *Journal of Leisure Research, 22*, 244-258.

Howe, C. Z. (1993). Naturalistic research design: An interrelated approach to data collection and analysis. In M. J. Malkin and C. Z. Howe (Eds.), *Research in therapeutic recreation: Concepts and methods,* (pp. 235-254). State College, PA: Venture Publishing, Inc.

Huesmann, L. R. and Eron, L. D. (1983). Factors influencing the effect of television violence on children. In M. M. A. Howe (Ed.), *Learning from television: Psychological and education research* (pp. 153-174). London, UK: Academic Press.

Hultsman, W. (1991, October). *Barriers to participation among youth: An extension.* Presented at the Leisure Research Symposium, Baltimore, MD.

Hultsman, W. (1993). The influence of others as a barrier to recreation participation among early adolescents. *Journal of Leisure Research, 25*, 150-164.

Hunt, J. G. (1980). Sex stratification and male biography: From deprivation to ascendancy. *Sociological Quarterly, 21*, 143-156.

Hunter, P. L. and Whitson, D. J. (1992). Women's leisure in a resource industry town: Problems and issues. *Loisir et Société/Society and Leisure, 15*(1), 223-244.

Huyck, M. H. (1994). The relevance of psychodynamic theories for understanding gender among older women. In B. F. Turner and L. E. Troll (Eds.),

Women growing older (pp. 202-237). Newbury Park, CA: Sage Publications, Inc.

Iso-Ahola, S. (1979a). Basic dimensions of definition of leisure. *Journal of Leisure Research, 11*(1), 28-39.

Iso-Ahola, S. (1979b). Some social psychological determinants of perceptions of leisure: Preliminary evidence. *Leisure Sciences, 2*(3-4), 305-314.

Iso-Ahola, S. (1980a). *The social psychology of leisure and recreation.* Dubuque, IA: William C. Brown Co.

Iso-Ahola, S. E. (1980b). Toward a dialectical social psychology of leisure and recreation. In S. E. Iso-Ahola (Ed.), *Social psychological perspectives on leisure and recreation* (pp. 19-37). Springfield, IL: Charles C. Thomas Publisher.

Iso-Ahola, S. and Weissinger, E. (1984). Leisure and well-being: Is there a connection? *Parks and Recreation, 19,* 40-45.

Iso-Ahola, S. E. and Crowley, E. D. (1991). Adolescent substance abuse and leisure boredom. *Journal of Leisure Research, 23,* 260-271.

Iso-Ahola, S. E. and Weissinger, E. (1990). Perceptions of boredom in leisure: Conceptualization, reliability, and validity of the leisure boredom scale. *Journal of Leisure Research, 22,* 1-17.

Iso-Ahola, S. E., Jackson, E. L., and Dunn, E. (1994). Starting, ceasing, replacing leisure activities over the human lifespan. *Journal of Leisure Research, 26,* 227-249.

Jacklin, C. N. (1987). Feminist research and psychology. In C. Farnham (Ed.), *The impact of feminist research in the academy* (pp. 95-107). Bloomington, IN: Indiana University Press.

Jackson, E. (1988a). Integrating ceasing participation with other aspects of leisure behavior. *Journal of Leisure Research, 20*(1), 31-45.

Jackson, E. L. (1988b). Leisure constraints: A survey of past research. *Leisure Sciences, 10,* 203-215.

Jackson, E. L., Crawford, D. and Godbey, G. (1993). Negotiation of leisure constraints. *Leisure Sciences, 15*(1), 1-11.

Jackson, E. L. and Rucks, V. C. (1995). Negotiation of constraints by junior-high and high-school students: An exploratory study. *Journal of Leisure Research, 27,* 85-105.

Jackson, E. L. and Witt, P. A. (1994). Change and stability in leisure constraints: A comparison of two surveys conducted four years apart. *Journal of Leisure Research, 26*, 322-336.

Jaggar, A. M. (1983). *Feminist politics and human nature.* Totowa, NJ: Rowman & Allanheld.

Jaggar, A. M. (1991). Feminist ethics: Projects, problems, prospects. In C. Card (Ed.), *Feminist ethics,* (pp. 78-104). Lawrence, KS: University Press of Kansas.

Jaggar, A. M. (1995). The politics of socialist feminism. In N. Tuana and R. Tong (Eds.), *Feminism and philosophy: Essential readings in theory, reinterpretation, and application* (pp. 299-324). Boulder, CO: Westview Press, Inc.

Jansen-Verbeke, M. (1987). Women, shopping and leisure. *Leisure Studies, 6,* 71-86.

Johnson, L. C. (Ed.). (in press). *Canadian families.* Toronto, ON: Thompson Educational Publishing, Inc.

Johnstone, J. W. and Rivera, R. J. (1965). *Volunteers for learning.* Chicago, IL: Aldine Press.

Josephs, R. A., Markus, H. R., and Tafarodi, R. W. (1992). Gender and self-esteem. *Journal of Personality and Social Psychology, 63,* 391-402.

Jung, C. J. (1933). *Modern man in search of a soul.* New York, NY: Harcourt, Brace, and World.

Kane, M. A. (1987, October). *The relationship between sex-role stereotyped leisure behavior and social assessments of physical attractiveness.* Paper presented at the Leisure Research Symposium, New Orleans, LA.

Kane, M. J. (1988). The female athletic role as a status determinant within the social systems of high school adolescents. *Adolescence, 23,* 253-264.

Kane, M. J. (1990). Female involvement in physical recreation—Gender role as a constraint. *Journal of Physical Education, Recreation and Dance, 61*(1), 52-56.

Kaplan, J. (1979). *Women and sports.* New York, NY: Viking Press.

Kaplan, M. (1975). *Leisure: Theory and policy.* Springfield, IL: Charles C. Thomas Publisher.

Kaufman, S. R. (1987). *The ageless self: Sources of meaning in later life.* Madison, WI: University of Wisconsin Press.

Kaufman, S. R. (1993). Values as sources of the ageless self. In J. R. Kelly (Ed.), *Activity and Aging* (pp. 17-24). Newbury Park, CA: Sage Publications, Inc.

Kelly, J. (1984). *Women, history, and theory: The essays of Joan Kelly.* Chicago, IL: University of Chicago Press.

Kelly, J. R. (1974). Socialization toward leisure: A developmental approach. *Journal of Leisure Research, 6*(3), 181-193.

Kelly, J. R. (1981). Leisure and family change: 1960-1990. *Journal of Physical Education, Recreation, and Dance, 52*(8), 47-50.

Kelly, J. R. (1982). *Leisure.* Englewood Cliffs, NJ: Prentice-Hall Press.

Kelly, J. R. (1983a). *Leisure identities and interactions.* London, UK: George Allen & Unwin.

Kelly, J. R. (1983b). Leisure styles: A hidden core. *Leisure Sciences, 5*(4), 321-338.

Kelly, J. R. (1987). *Freedom to be: A new sociology of leisure.* New York, NY: Macmillan Publishing Co.

Kelly, J. R. (1990). *Leisure* (2nd ed.). Englewood Cliffs, NJ: Prentice-Hall Press.

Kelly, J. R. (1991). Commodification and consciousness: An initial study. *Leisure Studies, 10*, 7-18.

Kelly, J. R. and Kelly, J. R. (1994). Multiple dimensions of meaning in the domains of work, family, and leisure. *Journal of Leisure Research, 26*, 250-274.

Kelly, J. R., Steinkamp, M. W., and Kelly, J. R. (1986). Later life leisure: How they play in Peoria. *The Gerontologist, 26*(5), 531-537.

Kemeny, L. and Shaw, S. M. (1989). Fitness promotion for adolescent girls: The impact and effectiveness of promotional material which emphasizes the slim ideal. *Adolescence, 24*, 677-687.

King, Y. (1995). Healing the wounds: Feminism, ecology, and nature/culture dualism. In N. Tuana and R. Tong (Eds.), *Feminism and philosophy: Essential readings in theory, reinterpretation, and application* (pp. 353-373). Boulder, CO: Westview Press, Inc.

Kinsley, B. and Graves, F. (1983). *The time of our lives. Explorations in time use, Vol. 2.* Ottawa, ON: Canada Employment and Immigration Commission.

Kivel, B. (1994). *The paradox of coming out: Lesbian and gay youth and leisure.* Paper presented at the Leisure Research Symposium, Minneapolis, MN.

Kivel, B., Pearce, K., and Lyons, K. (1995, May). *Where does feminism fit in post (fill in the blank) world?* Paper presented at the International Conference on Women and Leisure: Toward a New Understanding, Athens, GA.

Kleiber, D. A. (1980). Free time activity and psycho-social adjustment in college students: A preliminary analysis. *Journal of Leisure Research, 12*(3), 205-212.

Kleiber, D. A. (1985). Motivational reorientation in adulthood and the resource of leisure. In D. Kleiber and M. Maehr (Eds.), *Advances in motivation and achievement.* Greenwich, CT: JAI Press, Inc.

Kleiber, D. A., Caldwell, L., and Shaw, S. M. (1993). Leisure meanings in adolescence. *Loisir et Société/Society and Leisure, 6*, 99-114.

Kleiber, D. A., Larson, R., and Csikszentmihalyi, M. (1986). The experience of leisure in adolescence. *Journal of Leisure Research, 18*, 169-176.

Kleiber, D. A. and Kane, M. J. (1984). Sex differences and the use of leisure as adaptive potentiation. *Loisir et Société/Society and Leisure, 7*, 165-173.

Kleiber, D. A. and Kelly, J. R. (1980). Leisure, socialization, and the life cycle. In S. E. Iso-Ahola (Ed.), *Social psychological perspectives on leisure and recreation* (pp. 91-137). Springfield, IL: Charles C. Thomas Publisher.

Kleiber, D. A. and Rickards, W. H. (1985). Leisure and recreation in adolescence. In G. Wade (Ed.), *Constraints on leisure* (pp. 289-317). Springfield, IL: Charles C. Thomas Publisher.

Knobe, B. D. (1905). Chicago Women's Athletic Club. *Harper's Bazaar, 39*, 539-546.

Knox, A. B. (1977). *Adult development and learning.* San Francisco, CA: Jossey-Bass, Inc.

Kohlberg, L. (1976). Moral stages and moralization: The cognitive-developmental approach. In T. Lickona (Ed.), *Moral development and behavior: Theory, research and social issues* (pp. 31-53). New York, NY: Holt, Rinehart & Winston.

Koopman-Boyden, P. and Abbott, M. (1985). Expectations for household task allocation and actual task allocation: A New Zealand Study. *Journal of Marriage and the Family, 47*, 211-219.

Kramarae, C. and Spender, D. (1992). Exploding knowledge. In C. Kramarae and D. Spender (Eds.), *The knowledge explosion: Generations of feminist scholarship* (pp. 1-24). New York, NY: Teachers College Press.

Kraus, R. (1978). *Recreation and leisure in modern society* (2nd ed.). Santa Monica, CA: Goodyear.

Kubey, R. and Csikszentmihalyi, M. (1990). *Television and the quality of life.* Hillsdale, NJ: Lawrence Erlbaum Associates, Inc.

La Fountaine, E. (1982, September). *Forum of false consciousness among professional women.* Paper presented at Feminist Research in the '80s, DeKalb, IL.

Lamond, C. C. (1992). *Constrained by an ethic of care? An exploration of the interactions between work, family, and leisure in the everyday lives of female staff registered nurses.* Unpublished masters thesis, University of Waterloo, Waterloo, ON.

Larson, R. W. and Kleiber, D. A. (1993). Structured leisure as a context for the development of attention during adolescence. *Loisir et Société/Society and Leisure, 16*(1), 77-98.

Lather, P. (1991). *Getting smart: Feminist research and pedagogy with/in the postmodern.* New York, NY: Routledge.

Laws, G. (1995). Understanding ageism: Lessons from feminism and post-modernism. *The Gerontologist, 35,* 112-118.

Leaman, O. and Carrington, B. (1985). Athleticism and the reproduction of gender and ethnic marginality. *Leisure Studies, 4,* 205-217.

Lenskyj, H. (1986). *Out of bounds: Women, sport, and sexuality.* Toronto, ON: The Women's Press.

Lenskyj, H. (1988). Measured time: Women, sport, and leisure. *Leisure Studies, 7,* 233-240.

Lenz, E. and Myerhoff, B. (1985). *The feminization of America.* Los Angeles, CA: Jeremy P. Tarcher, Inc.

Lerner, G. (1975). Placing women in history: Definitions and challenges. *Feminist Studies, 3,* 5-14.

Lerner, G. (1977). *The female experience: An American documentary.* Indianapolis, IN: Bobbs-Merrill.

Lerner, G. (1979). *The majority finds its past: Placing women in history.* New York, NY: Oxford University Press.

Lerner, G. (1986). *The creation of patriarchy.* New York, NY: Oxford University Press.

Lerner, G. (1993). *The creation of feminist consciousness.* New York, NY: Oxford University Press.

Lever, J. (1976). Sex differences in games children play. *Social Problems, 23,* 478-487.

Levinson, D. J. (1974). The psychosocial development of men in early adulthood and mid-life transition. In D. Ricks, A. Thomas, and M. Roff (Eds.), *Life history research in psychopathology* (pp. 243-258). Minneapolis, MN: University of Minnesota Press.

Livson, F. B. (1981). Paths to psychological health in the middle years: Sex differences. In D. H. Eichorn (Ed.), *Past and present in middle life* (pp. 195-221). New York, NY: Academic Press.

Loden, M. (1985). *Feminine leadership or how to succeed in business without being one of the boys.* New York, NY: Times Books.

Loevinger, J. (1976). *Ego development: Conceptions and theories.* San Francisco, CA: Jossey-Bass, Inc.

Lopata, H. A. and Barnewolt, D. (1984). The middle years: Changes and variations in social role commitments. In G. Baruch and J. Brooks-Gunn (Eds.), *Women in midlife* (pp. 83-108). New York, NY: Plenum Press.

Lott, B. (1985). The potential enrichment of social/personality psychology through feminist research and vice versa. *American Psychologist, 40,* 155-164.

Loy, J. W. and Ingham, A. G. (1973). Play, games, and sport in the psychosocial development of children and youth. In G. L. Rarick (Ed.), *Physical activity: Human growth and development.* New York, NY: Academic Press.

Luschen, G. (1974). The interdependence of sport and culture. In G. Sage (Ed.), *Sport and American society,* (2nd ed.) (pp. 46-60). Reading, PA: Addison-Wesley Publishing Co., Inc.

Lynch, R. (1991, July). *The cultural repositioning of Rugby League Football in Australia.* Paper presented to the World Leisure and Recreation Association Congress, Sydney, Australia.

Maas, H. S. and Kuypers, J. A. (1975). *From thirty to seventy.* San Francisco, CA: Jossey-Bass, Inc.

MacKinnon, K. (1995). Sexuality, pornography, and method: "Pleasure under patriarchy." In N. Tuana and R. Tong (Eds.), *Feminism and philosophy:*

Essential readings in theory, reinterpretation, and application (pp. 134-161). Boulder, CO: Westview Press, Inc.

MacPherson, B. D. (1984). Sport participation across the life cycle: A review of the literature and suggestions for future research. *Sociology of Sport Journal, 1*, 213-230.

Maddox, G. L. (1987). Aging differently. *The Gerontologist, 27*, 557-564.

Malamuth, N. M. and Donnerstein, E. (1984). *Pornography and sexual aggression.* Orlando, FL: Academic Press, Inc.

Mandle, J. (1979). *Women and social change in America.* Princeton, NJ: Princeton Book Co.

Mannell, R. C. and Bradley, W. (1986). Does greater freedom always lead to greater leisure? Testing a person x environment model of freedom and leisure. *Journal of Leisure Research, 18*, 215-230.

Joseph, J. (1987). "Warning." In Martz, S. (Ed.), *When I am an old woman I shall wear purple* (p. 1). Watsonville, CA: Papier-Mache Press.

Maslow, A. (1954). *Motivation and personality.* New York, NY: Harper.

Mauldin, T. and Meeks, C. B. (1990). Time allocation of one- and two-parent mothers. *Lifestyles: Family and Economic Issues, 11*, 53-69.

Maxwell, F. S. (1979). *The measure of my days.* New York, NY: Penguin Books.

May, E. T. (1988). *Homeward bound: American families in the cold war era.* New York, NY: Basic Books, Inc.

McKechnie, G. (1974). The psychological structure of leisure: Past behavior. *Journal of Leisure Research, 6*, 27-45.

McRobbie, A. (1991). *Feminism and youth culture.* London, UK: Macmillan Education Ltd.

Melnick, M. J., Vanfossen, B. E., and Sabo, D. F. (1988). Developmental effects of athletic participation among high school girls. *Sociology of Sport Journal, 5*, 22-36.

Merriam, S. and Mullins, L. (1981). Havighurst's adult developmental tasks: A study of their importance relative to income, age, and sex. *Adult Education, 31*(3), 123-141.

Messner, M. A. and Sabo, D. F. (Eds.). (1990). *Sport, men, and the gender order: Critical feminist perspectives.* Champaign, IL: Human Kinetics.

Metheny, E. (1970). Symbolic forms of movement: The feminine image in sports. In G. H. Sage (Ed.), *Sport in American society* (pp. 291-303). Reading, MA: Addison-Wesley Publishing Co., Inc.

Metheny, E. (1973). Symbolic forms of movement: The feminine image in sports. In M. Hart (Ed.), *Sport in the socio-cultural process* (pp. 277-290). Dubuque, IA: William C. Brown.

Miedzien, M. (1991). *Boys will be boys: Breaking the link between masculinity and violence.* New York, NY: Doubleday.

Mitten, D. (1992). Empowering girls and women in the outdoors. *Journal of Physical Education, Recreation, and Dance, 63*(2), 56-60.

Mitten, D. (1995, May). *Women choosing to spend outdoor pursuit leisure time with other women—Why do some women choose all-women groups and some women avoid all-women groups?* Paper presented at the International Conference on Women and Leisure: Toward a New Understanding, Athens, Georgia.

Mobily, K. E., Lemki, J. H., Ostiguy, L. J., Woodard, R. J., Griffee, T. J., and Pickens, C. C. (1993). Leisure repertoire in a sample of midwestern elderly: The case for exercise. *Journal of Leisure Research, 25,* 84-99.

Montemayor, R. and Eisen, M. (1977). The development of self-conceptions from childhood to adolescence. *Developmental Psychology, 4,* 314-319.

Morgan, R. (1982). *The anatomy of freedom.* New York, NY: Anchor Press/ Doubleday.

Morgan, R. (Ed.). (1984). *Sisterhood is global.* New York, NY: Anchor Press/ Doubleday.

Murphy, J. F. (1974). *Concepts of leisure.* Englewood Cliffs, NJ: Prentice-Hall Press

Nelson, M. B. (1995). *The stronger women get, the more men love football: Sexism and the American culture of sports.* New York, NY: Harcourt Brace & Company.

Neugarten, B. L. (1968a). Adult personality: Toward a psychology of the life cycle. In B. L. Neugarten (Ed.), *Middle age and aging* (pp. 137-147). Chicago, IL: University of Chicago Press.

Neugarten, B. L. (1968b). The awareness of middle age. In B. L. Neugarten (Ed.), *Middle age and aging* (pp. 93-98). Chicago, IL: University of Chicago Press.

Neugarten, B. L. (1977). Personality and aging. In J. E. Birren and K. W. Schaie (Eds.), *Handbook of the psychology of aging* (pp. 626-649). New York, NY: Academic Press.

Neulinger, J. (1974). *The psychology of leisure.* Springfield, IL: Charles C. Thomas Publisher.

Neulinger, J. (1981). *The psychology of leisure* (2nd ed.). Springfield, IL: Charles C. Thomas Publisher.

Neulinger, J. (1982). Leisure lack and the quality of life: The broadening scope of the leisure professional. *Leisure Studies, 1,* 53-63.

Nock, S. L. and Kingston, P. W. (1988). Time with children: The impact of couples' work-time commitments. *Social Forces, 67,* 59-85.

Noe, F. and Elifson, K. (1976). The pleasures of youth: Parent and peer compliance toward discretionary time. *Journal of Youth and Adolescence, 5,* 37-58.

Norton, M. (1979). Eighteenth-century American women in peace and war. In N. Cott and E. Pleck (Eds.), *A heritage of her own* (pp. 136-161). New York, NY: Simon & Schuster, Inc.

Oakley, A. (1981). Interviewing women: A contradiction in terms. In H. Roberts (Ed.), *Doing feminist research* (pp. 30-59). London, UK: Routledge & Kegan Paul.

O'Brien, M. (1995). Reproducing Marxist man. In N. Tuana and R. Tong (Eds.), *Feminism and philosophy: Essential readings in theory, reinterpretation, and application* (pp. 91-103). Boulder, CO: Westview Press, Inc.

Offer, D., Rostov, E., and Howard, K. I. (1984). *Patterns of adolescent self-image.* San Francisco, CA: Jossey-Bass, Inc.

Olds, E. (1986). *Women of the four winds.* Boston, MA: Houghton Mifflin Company.

Orenstein, P. (1994). *Schoolgirls: Young women, self-esteem, and the confidence gap.* New York, NY: Doubleday.

Orthner, D. K. (1975). Leisure activity patterns and marital satisfaction over the marital career. *Journal of Marriage and the Family, 37,* 91-102.

Orthner, D. K. and Mancini, J. (1978). Parental family sociability and marital leisure patterns. *Leisure Sciences, 1*(4), 365-372.

Orthner, D. K. and Mancini, J. A. (1991). Benefits of leisure for family bonding. In B. L. Driver, P. J. Brown, and G. L. Peterson (Eds.), *Benefits of leisure* (pp. 289-302). State College, PA: Venture Publishing, Inc.

Osgood, N. and Howe, C. Z. (1984). Psychological aspects of leisure: A life cycle developmental perspective. *Loisir et Société/Society and Leisure, 7*(1), 175-195.

Paffenbarger, R. S., Hyde, R. T., and Dow, A. (1991). Health benefits of physical activity. In B. L. Driver, P. J. Brown, and G. L. Peterson (Eds.), *Benefits of leisure* (pp. 49-58). State College, PA: Venture Publishing, Inc.

Paglia, C. (1990). *Sexual personae: Art and decadence from Nefertiti to Emily Dickinson.* New Haven, CT: Yale University Press.

Paxson, F. (1974). The rise of sport. In G. Sage (Ed.), *Sport and American society* (2nd ed.). Reading, PA: Addison-Wesley Publishing Co., Inc.

Pedlar, A. (1995). Relevance and action research in leisure. *Leisure Sciences, 17*(2), 133-140.

Peiss, K. (1986). *Cheap amusements: Working women and leisure in turn-of-the-century New York.* Philadelphia, PA: Temple University Press.

Peper, K. (1994). Female athlete=lesbian: A myth constructed from gender role expectations and lesbiphobia. In R. J. Ringer (Ed.), *Queer words, queer images: Communication and the construction of homosexuality* (pp. 193-208). New York, NY: New York University Press.

Peplau, L. A. and Conrad, A. (1989). Beyond nonsexist research. *Psychology of Women Quarterly, 13,* 379-400.

Peterson-Lewis, S. (1993). Aesthetic practices among African-American women. In K. Welsh-Asante (Ed.), *The African aesthetic: Keeper of the traditions* (pp. 103-142). Westport, CT: Greenwood Press.

Piaget, J. (1954). *The construction of reality in the child.* New York, NY: Basic Books, Inc.

Pieper, J. (1952). *Leisure: The basis for culture.* New York, NY: Random House, Inc.

Pietromonaco, K., Manis, J., and Frohardt-Lane, K. (1986). Psychological consequences of multiple roles. *Psychology of Women Quarterly, 10,* 373-382.

Plummer, J. T. (1989). Changing values. *The Futurist, 23*(1), 8-13.

Radford-Hill, S. (1986). Considering feminism as a model for social change. In T. DeLauretis (Ed.), *Feminist studies/Critical studies* (pp. 157-172). Bloomington, IN: Indiana University Press.

Rapoport, R. and Rapoport, R.N. (1975). *Leisure and the family life cycle.* London, UK: Routledge and Kegan Paul.

Raymore, L. A., Godbey, G. C., and Crawford, D. W. (1994). Self-esteem, gender, and socioeconomic status: Their relation to perceptions of constraint among adolescents. *Journal of Leisure Research, 26,* 99-118.

Raymore, L., Godbey, G., Crawford, D., and von Eye, A. (1993). The nature and process of leisure constraints: An empirical test. *Leisure Sciences, 15,* 99-114.

Reinharz, S. (1992). *Feminist methods in social research.* New York, NY: Oxford University Press.

Reskin, B. (1988, March). *Women and work.* Paper presented to the University of North Carolina Department of Sociology, Chapel Hill, NC.

Rhode, D. L. (Ed). (1990). *Theoretical perspectives on sexual difference.* New Haven: Yale University Press.

Rich, A. (1977). Conditions for work: The common world of women. *Heresies, 3.*

Rich, A. (1986a). Resisting amnesia: History and personal life (1983). In *Blood, bread, and poetry: Selected prose 1979-1985.* New York, NY: W. W. Norton & Co. Inc.

Rich, A. (1986b). Compulsory heterosexuality and lesbian existence. In *Blood, bread, and poetry: Selected prose, 1979-1985.* New York, NY: W. W. Norton & Co. Inc.

Richardson, D. and Robinson, V. (1994). Theorizing women's studies, gender studies, and masculinity: The politics of naming. *The European Journal of Women's Studies, 1,* 11-27.

Riddick, C. C. (1993). Older women's leisure activity and quality of life. In J. R. Kelly (Ed.), *Activity and aging* (pp. 86-98). Newbury Park, CA: Sage Publications, Inc.

Riddick, C. and Daniels, S. (1984). The relative contribution of leisure activities and other factors to the mental health of older women. *Journal of Leisure Research, 16,* 136-148.

Riddick, C. C. and Stewart, D. G. (1994). An examination of the life satisfaction and importance of leisure in the lives of older female retirees: A comparison of Blacks to Whites. *Journal of Leisure Research, 26,* 75-87.

Riegel, K. (1976, October). The dialectics of human development. *American Psychologist,* pp. 689-700.

Riley, M. W., Johnson, M., and Foner, A. (Eds.). (1972). *Aging and society: A sociology of age stratification.* New York, NY: Russell Sage Foundation.

Riley, M. W., Kahn, R. L., and Foner, A. (1994). *Age and structural lag.* New York, NY: John Wiley & Sons, Inc.

Roberts, K. and Parsell, G. (1994). Youth cultures in Britain: The middle class take-over. *Leisure Studies, 13,* 33-48.

Roberts, N. (1995, May). *Women of color in outdoor recreation: The role of culture and ethnicity.* Paper presented at the International Conference on Women and Leisure: Toward a New Understanding, Athens, GA.

Roberts, P. and Newton, P. M. (1987). Levinsonian studies of women's adult development. *Psychology and Aging, 2,* 154-163.

Robertson, B. (1994, October). *Leisure of male adolescents who engage in delinquent behaviour: Role of family.* Paper presented at the Leisure Research Symposium, Minneapolis, MN.

Rodeheaver, D. (1987). When old age became a social problem, women were left behind. *The Gerontologist, 27,* 741-746.

Rodeheaver, D. and Datan, N. (1985). Gender and the vicissitudes of motivation in adult life. In D. A. Kleiber and M. Maehr (Eds.), *Advances in motivation and achievement* (pp. 169-187). Greenwich, CN: JAI Press, Inc.

Rosaldo, M. Z. (1974). Women, culture and society. In M. Z. Rosaldo and L. Lamphere (Eds.), *Women, culture, and society* (pp. 17-42). Stanford, CA: Stanford University Press.

Rosenau, P. M. (1992). *Postmodernism and the social sciences: Insights, inroads, and intrusions.* Princeton, NJ: Princeton University Press.

Rossi, A. (1980). Lifespan theories in women's lives. *Signs, 6,* 4-32.

Russell, J. C. (1990). The evolution of an ecofeminist. In I. Diamond and G. F. Orenstein (Eds.), *Reweaving the World* (pp. 223-230). San Francisco, CA: Sierra Club Books.

Ryff, C. D. (1985). The subjective experience of life-span transitions. In A. S. Rossi (Ed.), *Gender and the life course* (pp. 97-113). Hawthorne, NY: Aldine Publishing.

Sabo, D. F. (1988). Title IX and athletics: Sex equity in schools. *Updating School Board Policies, 19*(10), 14.

Sadker, M. and Sadker, D. (1986). Sexism in the classroom: From grade school to graduate school. *Phi Delta Kappan, 67*(7), 512-515.

Sage, G. H. (1990). *Power and ideology in American sport.* Champaign, IL: Human Kinetics.

Sales, E. (1977). Women's adult development. In I. Frieze (Ed.), *Women and sex roles: A social psychological perspective* (pp 157-190). New York, NY: W. W. Norton & Co. Inc.

Samdahl, D. (1988). A symbolic interactionist model of leisure: Theory and empirical support. *Leisure Sciences, 10*(1), 27-39.

Samdahl, D. M. (1992a). Leisure in our lives: Exploring the common leisure occasion. *Journal of Leisure Research, 24*(1), 19-32.

Samdahl, D. (1992b, October). *The effect of gender socialization on labeling experience as "leisure."* Paper presented to the National Recreation and Park Association Leisure Research Symposium, Cincinnati, OH.

Samdahl, D. M. and Jekubovich, N. (1993). *Constraints and constraint negotiation in common daily living.* Paper presented at the Canadian Congress on Leisure Research 7, Winnipeg, MB.

Samdahl, D. M. and Kleiber, D. A. (1989). Self-awareness and leisure experience. *Leisure Sciences, 1*, 1-10.

Samuel, N. (1992). L'aspiration des femmes a l'autonomie: Loisir familial et loisir personnel. *Loisir et Société/Society and Leisure, 15*(1),343-354.

Samuel, N. (1995). *Some leisure of their own: One of the keys towards women's autonomy.* Paper presented at the International Conference on Women and Leisure: Toward a New Understanding, Athens, GA.

Sanchez, L. (1994). Gender, labor allocations, and the psychology of entitlement within the home. *Social Forces, 73*(2), 533-553.

Sapiro, V. (1994). *Women in American society*. Mountain View, CA: Mayfield Publishing Co.

Sargeant, D. A. (1909). What athletic games, if any, are injurious for women in the form in which they are played by men? *American Physical Education Review, 11*, 176, 179, 181.

Schaef, A. (1981). *Women's reality*. Minneapolis, MN: Winston Press.

Schaffer, M. T. S. (1911). *Old Indian trails of the Canadian Rockies*. New York, NY: The Knickerbocker Press.

Schooler, C. and Schaie, K. W. (Eds.). (1987). *Cognitive functioning and social structure over the life course*. Norwood, NJ: Ablex Publishing Co.

Schor, J. (1991). *The overworked American: The unexpected decline of leisure*. New York, NY: Basic Books, Inc.

Schor, J. (1995, May). *Consumerism, time and gender: Toward a reconstruction of social space*. Paper presented at the International Conference on Women and Leisure: Toward a New Understanding, Athens, GA.

Schwartz, J. (1982). *Radical feminists of heterodoxy*. Lebanon, NH: New Victoria Publishers, Inc.

Scott, D. and Willits, F. K. (1989). Adolescent leisure and adult leisure patterns: A 37-year follow-up study. *Leisure Sciences, 11*, 323-335.

Scott, J. W. (1986). Gender: A useful category of historical analysis. *American Historical Review, 91*, 1053-1075.

Scott, J. W. (1988). *Gender and the politics of history*. New York, NY: Columbia University Press.

Seager, J. and Olson, A. (1986). *Women in the world: An international atlas*. New York, NY: Simon & Shuster, Inc.

Searle, M. S. and Jackson, E. L. (1985). Socioeconomic variations in perceived barriers to recreation participation among would-be participants. *Leisure Sciences, 7*, 227-249.

Searle, M. S., Mactavish, J. B., and Brayley, R. E. (1993). Integrating ceasing participation with other aspects of leisure behavior: A replication and extension. *Journal of Leisure Research, 25*, 389-404.

Searle, M. S., Mahon, M. J., Iso-Ahola, S. E., Sdrolias, H. A., and van Dyck, J. (1995). Enhancing a sense of independence and psychological well-being among the elderly: A field experiment. *Journal of Leisure Research, 27*, 107-124.

Sedgwick, E. K. (1990). *Epistomology of the closet*. Berkeley, CA: University of California Press.

Shamir, B. and Ruskin, H. (1983). Sex differences in recreational sport behavior and attitudes: A study of married couples in Israel. *Leisure Studies, 2*, 253-268.

Shank, J. (1986). An exploration of leisure in the lives of dual career women. *Journal of Leisure Research, 18*, 300-319.

Shapiro, L. (1990, May 28). Guns and dolls. *Newsweek*, pp. 56-65.

Shaw, S. J. (1991). Black club women and the creation of the National Association of Colored Women. *Journal of Women's History, 3*(2), 10-25.

Shaw, S. M. (1982). *The sexual division of leisure: Meanings, perceptions and the distribution of time*. Unpublished doctoral dissertation, Department of Sociology and Anthropology, Carleton University, Ottawa, ON.

Shaw, S. M. (1984). The measurement of leisure: A quality of life issue. *Loisir et Société/Society and Leisure, 7*(1), 91-107.

Shaw, S. M. (1985a). Gender and leisure: Inequality in the distribution of leisure time. *Journal of Leisure Research, 17*(4), 266-282.

Shaw, S. M. (1985b). The meaning of leisure in everyday life. *Leisure Sciences, 7*, 1-24.

Shaw, S. M. (1986). Leisure, recreation, or free time? Measuring time usage. *Journal of Leisure Research, 18*, 177-189.

Shaw, S. M. (1987, September). *Employment, non-employment, and leisure.* Paper presented at the National Recreation and Park Association Leisure Research Symposium, New Orleans, LA.

Shaw, S. M. (1988a). Gender differences in the definition and perception of household labor. *Family Relations, 37*, 333-337.

Shaw, S. M. (1988b). Leisure in the contemporary family: The effect of female employment on the leisure of Canadian wives and husbands. *International Review of Modern Sociology, 18*(1), 1-15.

Shaw, S. M. (1989). Fitness and wellness for young women: The image paradox. *Recreation Canada, 47*(2), 33-38.

Shaw, S. M. (1990a, May). *Where has all the leisure gone? The distribution and redistribution of time.* Paper presented at the Sixth Canadian Congress on Leisure Research, Waterloo, ON.

Shaw, S. M. (1990b, October). *Integration versus segmentation: An analysis of women's everyday experiences of work and leisure.* Paper presented at the National Recreation and Park Association Leisure Research Symposium, Baltimore, MD.

Shaw, S. M. (1991). Women's leisure time—Using time budget data to examine current trends and future predictions. *Leisure Studies, 10*, 171-181.

Shaw, S. M. (1992a). Dereifying family leisure: An examination of women's and men's everyday experiences and perceptions of family time. *Leisure Sciences, 14*, 271-286.

Shaw, S. M. (1992b). Body image among adolescent women: The role of sports and physically active leisure. *Journal of Applied Recreation Research, 16*, 349-357.

Shaw, S. M. (1994). Gender, leisure, and constraint: Towards a framework for the analysis of women's leisure, *Journal of Leisure Research, 26*, 8-22.

Shaw, S. M. (in press). Family activities and family leisure. In L. C. Johnson (Ed.), *Canadian families*. Toronto, ON: Thompson Educational Publishing.

Shaw, S. M., Bonen, A., and McCabe, J. F. (1991). Do more constraints mean less leisure? Examining the relationship between constraints and participation. *Journal of Leisure Research, 23*(4), 286-300.

Shaw, S. M., Caldwell, L. L., and Kleiber, D. A. (1992). *Time use and discretionary activities among adolescents: Boredom, stress, and social control*. Paper presented at the Canadian Sociology and Anthropology Meetings, Charlottetown, PEI.

Shaw, S. M., Kleiber, D. A., and Caldwell, L. L. (1995). Leisure and adolescent development: An examination of the relationship between leisure and identity formation for male and female adolescents. *Journal of Leisure Research, 27*(3), 245-263.

Shaw, S. M. and Smale, B. J. A. (1994, October). *Adolescent development and the psycho-social benefits of physically active leisure*. Presented at the Leisure Research Symposium, Minneapolis, MN.

Signorielli, N. (1989, December). Children, television, and gender roles. *Journal of Adolescent Health Care*, 1-9.

Simmons, R., Blyth, D. A., Vancleave, F. F., and Bush, D. M. (1979). Entry into adolescence: The impact of school structure, puberty, and early dating on self-esteem. *American Sociological Review, 44*, 948-967.

Skinner, B. F. (1971). *Beyond freedom and dignity*. New York, NY: Alfred A. Knopf, Inc.

Smale, B. J. A. and Dupuis, S. L. (1993). The relationship between leisure activity participation and psychological well-being across the lifespan. *Journal of Applied Recreation Research, 18*, 281-300.

Smale, B. J. A. and Shaw, S. M. (1994). *Teenage drop-outs: Explaining the decline in physical activity and participation during adolescence*. Paper presented at the Tenth Commonwealth and International Scientific Congress, Victoria, BC.

Smelser, N. J. (1980). The vicissitudes of work and love in Anglo-American society. In N. J. Smelser and E. H. Erikson (Eds.), *Themes of work and love in adulthood* (pp. 105-119). Cambridge, MA: Harvard University Press.

Smith, E. A. and Caldwell, L. L. (1994). Participation in high school sports and adolescent sexual activity. *Pediatric Exercise Science, 6*, 69-74.

Smith, E. A., Caldwell, L. L., Shaw, S. M., and Kleiber, D. A. (1994, October). *Development as action in context: Active and reactive leisure orientations among adolescents.* Paper presented at the Leisure Research Symposium, Minneapolis, MN.

Smith, S., Stewart, T., and Brown, B. (1980). Open-ended participation question in sport and physical recreation survey: A possible sex bias. *Research Quarterly for Exercise and Sport, 51,* 732.

Spretnak, C. (1982). *The politics of women's spirituality.* Garden City, NY: Anchor Press.

Stanley, L. (Ed.). (1990). *Feminist praxis: Research, theory, and epistemology in feminist sociology.* London, UK: Routledge.

Stanley, L. and Wise, S. (1983). *Breaking out: Feminist consciousness and feminist research.* London, UK: Routledge and Kegan Paul.

Stanton, E. C., Anthony, S. and Gage, M. (Eds.). (1889). *History of woman suffrage, Vol 1.* Rochester, New York, NY: Charles Mann. In P. Welch and H. Lerch, (1981), *History of American physical education and sport* (pp. 50, 60-62). Springfield, IL: Charles C. Thomas Publisher.

Stanworth, M. (1981). *Gender and schooling.* London, UK: Hutchinson.

Starhawk. (1982). *Dreaming the dark.* Boston, MA: Beacon Press.

Stebbins, R. A. (1982). Serious leisure: A conceptual statement. *Pacific Sociological Review, 25*(2), 251-272.

Stebbins, R. A. (1992). *Amateurs, professionals and serious leisure.* Kingston, ON: McGill-Queen's University Press.

Stebbins, R. A. (1994). The liberal arts hobbies: A neglected subtype of serious leisure. *Loisir et Société/Society and Leisure, 17*(1),173-186.

Steeves, H. L. (1987). Feminist theories and media studies. *Critical Studies in Mass Communication, 4*(2), 95-135.

Steinem, G. (1983). *Outrageous acts and everyday rebellions.* New York, NY: New American Library.

Steiner-Adair, C. (1990). The body politic. In C. Gilligan, N. P. Lyons, and T. J. Hanmer (Eds.), *Making connections* (pp. 162-182). Cambridge, MA: Harvard University Press.

Stephens, A. (1992). *Wild women: Crusaders, curmudgeons, and completely corsetless ladies in the otherwise virtuous Victorian era.* Berkeley, CA: Conari Press.

Stewart, W. A. (1976). *A psycho-social study of the formation of early adult life structure in women.* Unpublished doctoral dissertation, Columbia University, New York, NY.

Stimpson, C. (1988). *Where the meanings are.* New York, NY: Methuen.

Stoller, E. P. and Gibson, R. C. (1994). *Worlds of difference: Inequality in the aging experience.* Newbury Park, CA: Sage Publications, Inc.

Stratta, T. M. (1993). *An ethnography of the sport experience of the African-American female athlete.* Unpublished doctoral dissertation, Southern Illinois University at Carbondale, Carbondale, IL.

Streather, J. (1989). One-parent families and leisure. In F. Coalter (Ed.), *Freedom and constraint: The paradoxes of leisure* (pp. 175-186). London, UK: Routledge.

Sugar, M. (1979). *Female adolescent development.* New York, NY: Brunner/Mazel, Inc.

Szinovacz, M. (1992). Leisure in retirement: Gender differences in limitations and opportunities. *World Leisure and Recreation, 35*(3), 14-17.

Talbot, M. (1979). *Women and leisure.* A review for the Sports Council/Sport and Social Research Council. Joint Panel on Recreation and Leisure Research. London, UK: Sport and Social Research Council.

Taylor, V. and Whittier, N. (1993). The new feminist movement. In L. Richardson and V. Taylor (Eds.), *Feminist frontiers III* (pp. 533-545). New York, NY: McGraw-Hill, Inc.

Teish, L. (1985). *Jamalaya: The natural woman's book of personal charms and practical rituals.* San Francisco, CA: Harper & Row.

Tesch, S. (1983). Review of friendship development across the life span. *Human development, 26*(5), 266-276.

Tetreault, M. L. (1985). Feminist phase theory: An experience-derived evaluation model. *Journal of Higher Education, 56,* 364-384.

Theberge, N. (1991). A content analysis of print media coverage of gender, women and physical activity. *Journal of Applied Sport Psychology, 3,* 36-48.

Thompson, E. H. (Ed). (1994). *Older men's lives.* Newbury Park, CA: Sage Publications, Inc.

Thorne, B. (1992). Feminism and the family: Two decades of thought. In B. Thorne and M. Yalom (Eds.), *Rethinking the family* (pp. 3-30). Boston, MA: Northeastern University Press.

Tilly, L. A. (1989). Gender, women's history, and social history. *Social Science History, 13*, 439-462.

Tinning, R. and FitzClarence, L. (1992). Postmodern youth culture and the crisis in Australian secondary school physical education. *Quest, 44*, 287-303.

Tirone, S. C. and Shaw, S. M. (1995, May). *The meaning of leisure for new Canadians: Perceptions of immigrant women from India.* Paper presented at the Qualitative and Ethnographic Research, Hamilton, ON.

Tober, P. (1988). Historical perspective: Evolution of employee services and recreation. *Employee Services Management, 31*(1), 11-16.

Tong, R. (1989). *Feminist thought.* Boulder, CO: Westview Press, Inc.

Tuana, N. and Tong, R. (1995). Preface. In N. Tuana and R. Tong (Eds.), *Feminism and philosophy: Essential readings in theory, reinterpretation, and application* (pp. xi-xii). Boulder, CO: Westview Press, Inc.

Turner, B. F. (1994). Introduction. In B. F. Turner and L. E. Troll (Eds.), *Women growing older* (pp. 1-34). Newbury Park, CA: Sage Publications, Inc.

Turner, B. F. and Troll L. E. (Eds.). (1994). *Women growing older.* Newbury Park, CA: Sage Publications, Inc.

Ulrich, L. T. (1979). Virtuous women found. In N. Cott and E. Plack (Eds.), *A heritage of her own* (pp. 58-80). New York, NY: Simon & Schuster, Inc.

Ulrich, R. S., Dimberg, U., and Driver, B. L. (1991). Psychophysiological indicators of leisure benefits. In B. L. Driver, P. J. Brown, and G. L. Peterson (Eds.), *Benefits of leisure* (pp. 73-89). State College, PA: Venture Publishing, Inc.

Unger, R. K. (1979). *Female and male.* New York, NY: Harper & Row.

Unkel, M. (1981). Physical recreation participation of females and males during the adult life cycle. *Leisure Sciences, 4*(1), 1-27.

U.S. Bureau of Labor. (1991). *Statistics.* Washington, DC: Department of Labor.

Vaz, K. M. (1995). Introduction. In K. M. Vaz (Ed.), *Black women in America* (pp. 1-15). Newbury Park, CA: Sage Publications, Inc.

Veblen, T. (1899). *The theory of the leisure class.* New York, NY: Viking Press.

Veroff, J. and Smith, D. A. (1985). Motives and values over the adult years. In D. A. Kleiber and M. Maehr (Eds.), *Advances in motivation and achievement* (pp. 1-53). Greenwich, CT: JAI Press, Inc.

Vinick, B. H. and Ekerdt, D. J. (1991). The transition to retirement: Responses of husbands and wives. In B. B. Hess and E. W. Markson (Eds.), *Growing old in America* (pp. 305-317). New Brunswick, NJ: Transaction Publishers.

Wallis, C. (1989, December 4). Onward, women! *Time*, 80-89.

Ward, V. J. (1990). Racial identity formation and transformation. In C. Gilligan, N. P. Lyons, and T. J. Hanmer (Eds.), *Making connections* (pp. 215-232). Cambridge, MA: Harvard University Press.

Warhol, R. (1995). Feminism. In C. N. Davidson and L. Wagner-Martin (Eds.), *The Oxford companion to women's writing in the United States* (pp. 307-314). New York, NY: Oxford University Press.

Warren, M. A. (1995). The moral significance of birth. In N. Tuana and R. Tong (Eds.), *Feminism and philosophy: Essential readings in theory, reinterpretation, and application* (pp. 48-64). Boulder, CO: Westview Press, Inc.

Waterloo for Berkeley girls. (1896, April 5) *The San Francisco Examiner*, p. 1. In P. Welch and H. Lerch (1981), *History of American physical education and sport* (p. 11). Springfield, IL: Charles C. Thomas Publishers.

Wearing, B. (1990). Beyond the ideology of motherhood: Leisure as resistance. *Australian and New Zealand Journal of Sociology, 26*, 36-58.

Wearing, B. (1991). Leisure and women's identity: Conformity or individuality? *Loisir et Société/Society and Leisure, 14*(2), 575-586.

Wearing, B. (1992). Leisure and women's identity in late adolescence: Constraints and opportunities. *Loisir et Société/Society and Leisure, 15*(1), 323-342.

Wearing, B. (1994). The pain and pleasure of gendered leisure. *World Leisure and Recreation, 36*(3), 4-10.

Wearing, B. and McArthur, M. (1988). The family that plays together stays together: Or does it? *Australian and New Zealand Journal of Sex, Marriage, and Family, 9*, 150-158.

Wearing, B. M. and Wearing, S. L. (1988). All in a day's leisure: Gender and the concept of leisure. *Leisure Studies, 7*, 111-123.

Webster, K. (1995, June 3). Woman arrested for using men's weight room. *The Herald-Sun*, Durham, NC, p. A4.

Weiss, M. R. and Bredemeier, B. J. (1990). Moral development in sport. In K. B. Pandolf and J. O. Holloszy (Eds.), *Exercise and sport sciences review, 18*, 331-378. Baltimore, MD: Williams and Wilkins.

Weissinger, E. and Iso-Ahola, S. E. (1984). Intrinsic leisure motivation, personality and physical health. *Loisir et Société/Society and Leisure, 7,* 217-228.

Welch, P. and Lerch, H. (1981). *History of American physical education and sport.* Springfield, IL: Charles C. Thomas Publisher.

Welsh-Asante, K. (Ed.). (1993). *The African aesthetic: Keeper of the traditions.* New York, NY: Greenwood Press.

Welsh-Asante, K. (1994). Images of women in African dance. *Sage: A Scholarly Journal on Black Women, 8*(2), 16-19.

West, C. (1993). *Race matters.* New York, NY: Vintage Books.

White, J. (1988) Women in leisure service management. In E. Wimbush and M. Talbot (Eds.), *Relative freedoms* (pp. 149-160). Milton Keynes, UK: Open University Press.

Whitson, D. and Macintosh, D. (1989). Gender and power: Explanations of gender inequalities in Canadian national sport organizations. *International Review of Sociology of Sport, 24*(2), 137-150.

Whyte, L. B. and Shaw, S. M. (1994). Women's leisure: An exploratory study of fear of violence as a leisure constraint. *Journal of Applied Recreation Research, 19*(1), 5-21.

Willard, F. E. (1979). How I learned to ride the bicycle. In S. Twin (Ed.), *Out of the bleachers: Writings on women and sport,* (pp. 103-114). Old Westbury, NY: Feminist Press.

Williams, F. B. (1900). The club movement among colored women of America. In B. T. Washington, N. B. Wood and F. B. Williams (Eds.), *A new Negro for a new century,* (p. 383), Chicago, IL: American Publishing House.

Williams, J. (1977). *Psychology of women.* New York, NY: W. W. Norton & Co., Inc.

Wimbush, E. and Talbot, M. (Eds.). (1988). *Relative freedoms.* Milton Keynes, UK: Open University Press.

Winkler, K. J. (1990, May 23). Scholar whose ideas of female psychology stir debate, modifies theories, extends studies to young girls. *The Chronicle of Higher Education,* pp. A6, A8.

Witt, P. and Goodale, T. (1981). The relationship between barriers to leisure enjoyment and family stages. *Leisure Sciences, 4,* 29-49.

Wolf, N. (1991). *The beauty myth: How images of beauty are used against women.* New York, NY: William Morrow & Co. Inc.

Wolf, N. (1994). *Fire with fire: The new female power and how to use it.* New York, NY: Fawcett Columbine.

Women on bicycles. (1889, Feb. 12 and Feb 17). *The New York Times*, 2.

Women's Sports Foundation. (1989). *Minorities in sport: The effects of varsity sports participation on the social, educational, and career mobility of minority students.* New York: Women's Sports Foundation.

Wood, J. T. (1994). *Gendered lives: Communication, gender and culture.* Belmont, CA: Wadsworth Publishing Co.

Woodward, D. and Green, E. (1988). 'Not tonight, dear!' The social control of women's leisure. In E. Wimbush and M. Talbot (Eds.), *Relative freedoms* (pp. 131-146). Milton Keynes, UK: Open University Press.

Yoesting, D. and Burkhead, D. (1973). Significance of childhood recreation experience on adult leisure behavior: An exploratory analysis. *Journal of Leisure Research, 5,* 25-36.

Yoesting, D. R. and Christensen, J. E. (1978). Re-examining the significance of childhood recreation patterns on adult leisure behavior. *Leisure Sciences, 1,* 219-229.

Zuzanek, J. (1978). Social differences in leisure behavior: Measurement and interpretation. *Leisure Sciences, 1,* 271-293.

Zuzanek, J. and Smale, B. J. (1993). Life-cycle variations in across-the-week allocation of time to selected daily activities. *Loisir et Société/Society and Leisure, 15*(2), 559-586.

Index

Other Books From Venture Publishing, Inc.

Other Books From Venture Publishing, Inc.

The Leisure Diagnostic Battery: Users Manual and Sample Forms
    by Peter A. Witt and Gary Ellis
Leisure Diagnostic Battery Computer Software
    by Gary Ellis and Peter A. Witt
Leisure Education: A Manual of Activities and Resources
    by Norma J. Stumbo and Steven R. Thompson
Leisure Education II: More Activities and Resources
    by Norma J. Stumbo
Leisure Education Program Planning: A Systematic Approach
    by John Dattilo and William D. Murphy
Leisure in Your Life: An Exploration, Fourth Edition
    by Geoffrey Godbey
A Leisure of One's Own: A Feminist Perspective on Women's Leisure
    by Karla Henderson, M. Deborah Bialeschki, Susan M. Shaw and
        Valeria J. Freysinger
Leisure Services in Canada: An Introduction
    by Mark S. Searle and Russell E. Brayley
Marketing for Parks, Recreation, and Leisure
    by Ellen L. O'Sullivan
Models of Change in Municipal Parks and Recreation: A Book of Innovative Case Studies
    edited by Mark E. Havitz
Outdoor Recreation Management: Theory and Application, Third Edition
    by Alan Jubenville and Ben Twight
Planning Parks for People
    by John Hultsman, Richard L. Cottrell and Wendy Zales Hultsman
Private and Commercial Recreation
    edited by Arlin Epperson
The Process of Recreation Programming Theory and Technique, Third Edition
    by Patricia Farrell and Herberta M. Lundegren
Protocols for Recreation Therapy Programs
    edited by Jill Kelland, along with the Recreation Therapy Staff Alberta
        Hospital Edmonton
Quality Management: Applications for Therapeutic Recreation
    edited by Bob Riley
Recreation and Leisure: Issues in an Era of Change, Third Edition
    edited by Thomas Goodale and Peter A. Witt
Recreation Programming and Activities for Older Adults
    by Jerold E. Elliott and Judith A. Sorg-Elliott
Reference Manual for Writing Rehabilitation Therapy Treatment Plans
    by Penny Hogberg and Mary Johnson
Research in Therapeutic Recreation: Concepts and Methods
    edited by Marjorie J. Malkin and Christine Z. Howe
Risk Management in Therapeutic Recreation: A Component of Quality Assurance
    by Judith Voelkl
A Social History of Leisure Since 1600
    by Gary Cross
The Sociology of Leisure
    by John R. Kelly and Geoffrey Godbey

-------------------*Other Books From Venture Publishing, Inc.*

A Study Guide for National Certification in Therapeutic Recreation
        by Gerald O'Morrow and Ron Reynolds
Therapeutic Recreation: Cases and Exercises
        by Barbara C. Wilhite and M. Jean Keller
Therapeutic Recreation in the Nursing Home
        by Linda Buettner and Shelley L. Martin
Therapeutic Recreation Protocol for Treatment of Substance Addictions
        by Rozanne W. Faulkner
A Training Manual for Americans With Disabilities Act Compliance in Parks and Recreation
    Settings
        by Carol Stensrud
Understanding Leisure and Recreation: Mapping the Past, Charting the Future
        edited by Edgar L. Jackson and Thomas L. Burton

  Venture Publishing, Inc.
1999 Cato Avenue
State College, PA 16801

Phone: (814) 234-4561; FAX: (814) 234-1651